THE ZEN MONASTIC EXPERIENCE

THE ZEN MONASTIC EXPERIENCE

BUDDHIST PRACTICE IN
CONTEMPORARY KOREA

Robert E. Buswell, Jr.

PRINCETON UNIVERSITY PRESS   PRINCETON, NEW JERSEY

Library of Congress Cataloging-in-Publication Data
Buswell, Robert E.
The Zen monastic experience : Buddhist practice in contemporary
Korea / Robert E. Buswell, Jr.
p. cm.
Includes bibliographical references and index.
ISBN 0-691-07407-0
1. Monastic and religious life (Zen Buddhism)—Korea (South)
2. Songgwangsa (Sŭngju-gun, Korea). I. Title.
BQ9294.4.K6B87   1992
294.3'657'095195—dc20   91-40118   CIP

This book has been composed in Linotron Sabon

Princeton University Press books are printed
on acid-free paper, and meet the guidelines
for permanence and durability of the Committee
on Production Guidelines for Book Longevity
of the Council on Library Resources

Printed in the United States of America

5   7   9   10   8   6

To Kusan *Sŭnim* and the Monks of Songgwang-sa

Contents

List of Plates

Following p. 106

Preface

THIS BOOK has grown out of five years I was privileged to spend as a Buddhist monk in Korean monasteries between 1974 and 1979, primarily at Songgwang-sa. When I returned to the United States in 1979, Lewis Lancaster of the University of California, Berkeley, proposed that we coauthor a book on Buddhist monastic life and architecture in contemporary Korea. I began to draft several proposed sections of that book, but the pressures of other obligations left neither of us with time to pursue the project. Reluctantly, I put it aside. Finally, after a decade-long hiatus, I was able to return my attentions to the book in 1989 and have supplemented my previous work with material gleaned from two additional trips to Songgwang-sa in November 1987 and July 1988.

This book is an account of how Zen was practiced in Songgwang-sa, a representative large Korean Buddhist monastery, primarily during the 1970s. There are slight differences in the daily schedule, the interpretation of official duties, and so forth, from one monastery to the next, but substantially all of the largest monasteries followed similar regimens. But this is also a way of life that is undergoing profound change. Korea in the early and mid-1970s, when most of this fieldwork was conducted, was already well into its period of rapid industrialization, with all the accompanying social changes. Still, relatively little of that progress had then reached the isolated Chŏlla region, where Songgwang-sa was located, and the monastic life there was hardly affected by these encroachments. That is no longer the case some two decades later.

The way of life presented here is also one to which few Koreans, let alone Westerners, have had access. Even in Korea, little has been written on contemporary monastic lifestyle or institutions, or even on the recent history of the order. This account will therefore offer only a tentative first look at this fascinating period in the religious history of Korean Buddhism.

While much of this book derives from the personal testimony of contemporary monks I knew in Korea, I have sought as much as possible to avoid compromising the identity of my sources. Only those monks who have become public figures because of the highly visible positions they occupy in the major monasteries—such as Sŏn master or abbot—will be cited by name.

I consider it my distinct privilege to have had close associations with many Koreans throughout my life. I am especially grateful to the monks of Songgwang-sa, who continue to be one of my principal sources of inspiration. There are too many friends in Korea to acknowledge individually here, but they all should know that I remain deeply affected by my contacts with them throughout the years. I should at least thank personally Hyŏnho, Pŏpchŏng, and Posŏng sŭnims, monastic officials at Songgwang-sa who always gave me much valuable aid and advice; Hyŏn'go sŭnim, who nursed me back to health during a nasty bout of hepatitis; Hyŏnŭm sŭnim, who was a great confidant to all the foreign monks; and Kwanghun sŭnim, who answered patiently my many requests for information as I was writing the book. The list could go on and on, and I apologize for not mentioning everyone by name. I have also benefited from several visits with Ilt'a sŭnim at Haein-sa, and from contacts with his many disciples, with whom I practiced at Songgwang-sa, particularly Hyeguk sŭnim. The Kim family, and especially Porisim, were fervent supporters of the foreign saṃgha during my years in Korea, despite our many foibles, and I remember with much fondness their visits to Songgwang-sa.

This book is respectfully dedicated to Kusan sŭnim, the Sŏn master at Songgwang-sa during my years there. There is no one besides my parents who has had as profound and sustained an impact on my life as Kusan did. Westerners seeking to study Buddhism in Korea had no stronger proponent than Kusan, and I personally would never have been able to practice for so many years with the Korean monks in the main meditation hall at Songgwang-sa without his constant backing. Korean monks from other monasteries who came to practice at Songgwang-sa were often suspicious of a foreigner's motivations in meditating; Kusan did everything possible to assuage their concerns about my presence among them. He has my deepest gratitude, and that of all the other foreigners who have trained at Songgwang-sa.

This book would never have been conceived without the encouragement of Lewis Lancaster. I first met Professor Lancaster when he led a research trip to Korean monasteries in the spring of 1978. When I eventually returned to the United States in 1979, still wearing my Korean monk's robes, Professor Lancaster took me under his wing and made arrangements for me to return to school at the University of California, Berkeley, and later to enter the Buddhist Studies program there. While we were unable to pursue the collaborative project we had planned, this book reflects his own profound interest and concern with the contemporary traditions of Buddhism throughout Asia. I should add that I might never have made it to Asia in the first place without the contacts graciously arranged by Gerald Larson, whose classes first inspired me to contemplate a monastic vocation, and later a scholarly career, in the study of Buddhism.

Several people offered much advice and encouragement throughout the writing of this book. The two readers for the press, T. Griffith Foulk of the University of Michigan and Laurel Kendall of the American Museum of Natural History, gave detailed and trenchant reviews, which were extremely valuable to me in revising the manuscript for publication. The book improved markedly from their careful and insightful readings. Without the enthusiasm and interest of my editor at Princeton University Press, Margaret Case, the book would have languished on my hard disk for several more years. She challenged me constantly to put more of myself into the book, and her advice was crucial in developing a wider framework for my material. Michael Wenger, president of the San Francisco Zen Center, was a sensitive and concerned reader of a very early draft of the manuscript. He prodded me to address issues about monastic life with which committed Western practitioners were concerned, hopefully broadening the potential appeal of the book. Others who were sources of inspiration and encouragement include Michel Strickmann, who constantly challenged me to find ways to draw on my field experience in my scholarship; my close colleagues and friends Sung Bae Park, Robert Gimello, Peter Gregory, Bernard Faure, and Luis Gómez; my UCLA colleagues Peter Lee, John Duncan, and Jacques Maquet; Martine Batchelor, whom I still remember fondly as Songil; and Chi Kwang *sŭnim*, who has always been so generous with her time and assistance during my recent visits to Korea.

Portions of this book were first related as lectures at a number of institutions, including Stanford University; University of Arizona; University of Chicago; University of Wisconsin, Madison; the San Francisco Zen Center; and the Zen Center of Los Angeles. I would also like to thank the following agencies for permission to reprint materials first published elsewhere: the Korean Cultural Center, Los Angeles, for permission to reprint sections of my article on Songgwang-sa, which appeared in its journal, *Korean Culture*, along with some photos from its archives; Hyŏnho *sŭnim*, abbot of Songgwang-sa, for permission to publish sections of Kusan's *Nine Mountains*; and the Institute of East Asian Studies of the University of California, Berkeley, for permission to include material from an article on Buddhist lay associations, which appears in Chapter Six. The photographs in the book were taken by the official Songgwang-sa photographer, Mr. Kim Taebyŏk, and appear with the permission of the abbot, Hyŏnho *sŭnim*. The black-and-white reproductions appearing herein do not do justice to the spectacular color of Mr. Kim's original prints.

Finally, I extend my appreciation to Jong Myung Kim, Susan Sugar (who later prepared the index), Dan Altschuler, and Judy Koeppel, who served as my research assistants, and Roger Hart, who helped with word processing. Funds for graduate student research assistantships were provided by the Committee on Research of the UCLA Academic Senate, whose assistance is gratefully acknowledged.

Conventions Used

TEXTS FROM the Sinitic Buddhist canon are cited according to standard numbers in the *Taishō* printed edition (abbreviated as *T*): *Taishō shinshū daizōkyō*, edited by Takakusu Junjirō and Watanabe Kaikyoku (Tokyo: Daizōkyōkai, 1924–1935). Full citations from the *Taishō* canon are given in the following fashion: title and fascicle number (where relevant); *T[aishō]*; *Taishō* serial number; *Taishō* volume number; page, register (a, b, or c), line number(s)—for example, *Ta-fang-kuang fo hua-yen ching* 23, *T* 278.9.542c27–543a1. Scriptures appearing in the Pali canon are cited according to their standard Pali Text Society editions. Buddhist terminology that appears in *Webster's Third New International Dictionary* I consider to have entered the English language and leave unitalicized (except in interpolated translations), but I have retained the original diacritics: for example, sūtra, śāstra, nirvāṇa. For a convenient listing of a hundred such words, see Roger Jackson, "Terms of Sanskrit and Pāli Origin Acceptable as English Words," *Journal of the International Association of Buddhist Studies* 5 (1982): 142. Other foreign words are italicized only at their first appearance in the book, in interpolated translations, and when used as honorifics (for example, Kusan *sŭnim*).

THE ZEN MONASTIC EXPERIENCE

Zen Monasticism and the Context of Belief

The problem of meaning resides in practice,
not theory.
Renato Rosaldo

THOSE OF US in the West who have first been exposed to Zen Buddhism through English-language materials will have been enchanted—or perhaps appalled—by the colorful stories of the school's ancient patriarchs and masters. Whatever one's reaction, it is hard to remain neutral toward a religious tradition that purportedly depicts its most revered of teachers as torching their sacred religious icons, bullying their students into enlightenment, rejecting the value of all the scriptures of Buddhism, even denying the worth of Zen itself. The thematic elements in this literary picture of Zen are now so well known among Westerners as to invite caricature: the spontaneity and iconoclasm of the enlightened masters, the radical discourse and rhetoric, the brash challenge to religious ritual and systematization, the zealous esteem of practice over doctrine. Even drinking and sex can be "good Zen," to quote the Zen Buddhist protagonist of a recent American spy novel.[1]

Three representative examples, all well known in Western literature on Zen, should suffice to illustrate the sort of characterization to which I am referring.

> Once the monks of the Eastern Hall and the Western Hall were disputing about a cat. Nan-ch'üan, holding up the cat, said, "Monks, if you can say a word of Zen, I will spare the cat. If you cannot, I will kill it!" No monk could answer. Nan-ch'üan finally killed the cat. In the evening, when Chao-chou came back, Nan-ch'üan told him of the incident. Chao-chou took off his sandal, put it on his head, and walked off. Nan-ch'üan said, "If you had been there, I could have saved the cat!"[2]

[1] Russell Warren Howe, *Flight of the Cormorants* (San Diego: Harcourt Brace Jovanovich, 1989), see esp. pp. 208, 349.

[2] The fourteenth case of the *Mu-men kuan* (The Gateless Checkpoint), T 2005.48.294c; quoted from Zenkei Shibayama, *Zen Comments on the Mumonkan*, trans. by Sumiko Kudo (New York: Harper and Row, 1974), p. 107, though I give the Chinese forms of the Zen masters' names. The story is also told in the biography of Nan-ch'üan P'u-yüan (748–835), in the *Ching-teh ch'uan-teng lu* (Record of the Transmission of the Lamp, Compiled during

While they were out gathering rattan, Master Shui-liao asked Ma-tsu, "What is the real meaning of Bodhidharma's coming from the west?" Ma-tsu replied, "Come closer and I'll tell you." When Shui-liao was quite close, Ma-tsu kicked him in the chest, knocking him to the ground. In a daze, Shui-liao got up, clapping his hands and laughing loudly. Ma-tsu asked, "What insight did you have that has made you laugh?" Shui-liao said, "Hundreds of thousands of approaches to dharma and immeasurable sublime meanings are on the tip of one hair; today I have completely understood their source." Ma-tsu then ignored him.[3]

Lin-chi went to see Master Ta-yü, who asked him: "Where do you come from?" "From Huang-po." "What instruction did Huang-po give you?" "When I asked him for the real meaning of Buddhism, he immediately struck me. Three times I put this question to him, and three times I received blows. I don't know where I was at fault." Thereupon Master Ta-yü exclaimed, "Your master treated you entirely with motherly kindness, and yet you say you do not know your fault." Hearing this, Lin-chi was suddenly awakened and said, "After all, there isn't much in Huang-po's Buddhism!" Master Ta-yü took hold of him and exclaimed, "You young devil! A moment ago you complained that you did not understand your master's teaching, and now you say that there is not much in Huang-po's Buddhism. What have you seen after all? Speak out! Speak out!" Three times Lin-chi poked Ta-yü in the ribs with his fist. Ta-yü pushed him away and said, "Your teacher is Huang-po. There is nothing here that is of any concern to me."[4]

Much of this picture of Zen derives from portrayals found in such normative texts of the tradition as the lamp anthologies (Ch. *teng-lu*), huge collections of the hagiographies and basic instructions of hundreds of masters in the various lineages of Zen.[5] But such texts were never intended to serve as guides to religious practice or as records of daily practice; they were instead mythology and hagiography, which offered the

---

the Ching-teh Era) 8, *T* 2076.51.258a3–7; see the translation in Chung-yuan Chang, *Original Teachings of Ch'an Buddhism: Selected from* The Transmission of the Lamp (New York: Pantheon, 1969), p. 156. Chao-chou is Chao-chou Ts'ung-shen (778–897).

[3] The dialogue appears in the *Ching-teh ch'uan-teng lu* 8, *T* 2076.51.262c; quoted in Robert E. Buswell, Jr., *The Korean Approach to Zen: The Collected Works of Chinul* (Honolulu: University of Hawaii Press, 1983), p. 247. Ma-tsu is Ma-tsu Tao-i (709–788); Shui-liao is Hung-chou Shui-liao (d.u.), a disciple of Ma-tsu.

[4] *Ching-teh ch'uan-teng lu* 12, *T* 2076.51.299b20–c4; quoted from Chung-yuan Chang, *Original Teachings of Ch'an Buddhism*, p. 117. Lin-chi is Lin-chi I-hsüan (d. 866); Ta-yü is Kao-an Ta-yü (d.u.), a disciple of Kuei-tsung Chih-ch'ang (d.u.), in the Nan-yüeh line.

[5] Specifically, texts such as the definitive *Ching-teh ch'uan-teng lu* (Record of the Transmission of the Lamp, Compiled during the Ching-teh Era), *T* 2076.51.196a–467a. Representative selections from this important anthology are translated in Chung-yuan Chang, *Original Teachings of Ch'an Buddhism*.

student an idealized paradigm of the Zen spiritual experience. Many scholars of Zen have mistakenly taken these lamp anthologies at face value as historical documents and presumed that they provide an accurate account of how Zen monks of the premodern era pursued their religious vocations. They do not. There are sources available on Zen monastic practice, deriving from epigraphy, local and monastery gazetteers, Buddhist traditional encyclopedias, pilgrims' accounts, monk's diaries, and the "jottings" of the literati, but these have been only rarely assayed by scholars of Zen.[6] The damage has been done, however, and I suspect it will take many more years of corrective scholarship before ingrained Western notions of the nature of Zen practice will begin to change.

Other scholars have sought to circumvent the interpretive difficulties intrinsic to these hagiographical anthologies by pursuing instead theoretical studies in Zen philosophy and thought. But without access to Zen's monastic life—the context within which that thought evolved—much of the import of Zen beliefs and training may never be known, or at least may be prone to misinterpretation. As I. M. Lewis has convincingly argued, religious beliefs are "functions of situations and circumstances," and describing those beliefs is "meaningless unless accompanied by a minutely detailed exposition of their deployment in actual situations. . . . The detachment of beliefs from their ambient circumstances produces gross distortion and misunderstanding."[7]

But there is one accessible source that may help us answer the question of how Zen beliefs are "deploy[ed] in actual situations": the Zen monasteries of contemporary East Asia, and especially Korea. Korea's Buddhist monasteries maintain institutional structures and follow schedules of training that have significant continuities with those of their counterparts in China and Japan.[8] Modern Zen training offers a matrix within which to evaluate the way one tradition of Zen understands—and puts into practice—the doctrines and teachings of its religion. While Zen training in Korea will differ in certain respects from that followed by the patriarchs and ancient masters of classical Ch'an in China or by Zen monks in Japan, it is an authentic model of how the monks of one national tra-

[6] One Western scholar who promises to make a major contribution to our understanding of Zen by culling these sources is Professor T. Griffith Foulk of the University of Michigan, from whom I received many valuable comments on an earlier draft of this book.

[7] I. M. Lewis, *Religion in Context: Cults and Charisma* (Cambridge: Cambridge University Press, 1986), pp. 20–21. The title of my introduction is adapted from the first chapter of Lewis's book.

[8] For the institutions and practices of the classical Zen schools, see Satō Tatsugen, *Chūgoku Bukkyō ni okeru kairitsu no kenkyū* (Studies on the Precepts of Chinese Buddhism) (Tokyo: Mokujisha, 1986), pp. 479–554; and Nishimura Eshin, *Zenrin shugyōron* (Praxis in Zen Monasteries) (Kyoto: Hōzōkan, 1987).

dition of Zen have tackled "the practical matter of how to live with [their] belief."[9]

Korean Zen—known as Sŏn—is also a tradition worthy of far more attention than it has gleaned to date in Western scholarship. Indeed, given the pervasive emphasis on Japanese forms of Zen found in Western literature on the tradition (as indicated by our common English usage of the Japanese pronunciation "Zen" to represent all the national branches of the school), we may forget that there are other, equally compelling and authentic approaches to Zen thought and practice found elsewhere in Asia.

In this book I seek to treat the Zen tradition of Korea as a living system of practices and institutions. My focus will be on the details of Korean monastic training, a Buddhist tradition where Zen thought and practice dominate, but I believe this data will be relevant to understanding the monastic traditions of Zen in Japan, China, and Vietnam as well. In order to ensure that I am allowing the contemporary tradition to represent itself directly, I will leave aside the anecdotes about the ancient Zen masters that punctuate most treatments of Zen practice and will provide only enough historical background to anchor the present-day tradition.[10] My

---

[9] Renato Rosaldo, *Culture and Truth: The Remaking of Social Analysis* (Boston: Beacon Press, 1989), pp. 6–7.

[10] There are few models to follow in undertaking such a study of contemporary Zen monasticism. One of the first such attempts was Daisetz Teitaro Suzuki's *The Training of the Zen Buddhist Monk* (1934; reprint, New York: University Books, 1965). This is an exciting and accessible work, which has done as much as any single book to inspire Western interest in Zen. But Suzuki's book, like much of the rest of his oeuvre, is really more concerned with relating anecdotes about the ancient Zen teachers found in the classical *kung-an* collections than with the actual practice of the Zen monk in Japan. A stimulating and, from a scholarly standpoint, more successful account of modern East Asian Buddhist monasticism is Holmes Welch's *The Practice of Chinese Buddhism: 1900–1950*, Harvard East Asian Studies 26 (Cambridge: Harvard University Press, 1967). Welch's book is deservedly one of the classics of Western Buddhist studies and provides a valuable, realistic depiction of Buddhist monastic training in China during the early decades of the twentieth century. In a scholarly tour de force, Welch has organized a massive amount of personal testimony from refugee Chinese monks into a coherent and compelling tale of monastic culture. But because China was closed to the West at the time Welch was writing (in the 1960s), he was never able to spend time himself in Chinese monasteries on the mainland and had no choice but to rely almost entirely on secondhand accounts. Because he was writing about a way of life that had all but vanished in pre–Cultural Revolution China, Welch was also compelled to take a pronounced historical perspective on his material. Koji Sato's *The Zen Life*, with photographs by Sosei Kuzunishi, trans. by Ryojun Victoria (New York: Weatherhill, 1972), is an admittedly apologistic tract, almost a call to Zen practice, but it does contain some striking photographs of Japanese Zen monks in training. But by far the best photo essay on Zen monastic life is Kwan-jo Lee's *Search for Nirvana: Korean Monks' Life* (Seoul: Seoul International Publishing House, 1984). A very different type of book, and one of my favorites on Japanese Zen, is Giei Satō's *Unsui: A Diary of Zen Monastic Life*, text by Eshin Nishimura, ed. by Bardwell L. Smith (Honolulu: University Press of Hawaii, an East-West Center Book, 1973).

modest goal is to convey in as straightforward a manner as I can an accurate sense of what Zen monks actually do each day and how they live out their religion in practice.[11]

Complementing this goal of adding to Western knowledge of Zen in practice, I hope also that this book will make some contribution to the study of contemporary Korean religion. Despite the fact that Korea is a society in which Buddhists still constitute the religious majority, Buddhism has been almost totally neglected in fieldwork on contemporary religion on the peninsula. In the last decade, several valuable studies have appeared exploring the relationships between personal experience and ritual practice in the Korean shamanic tradition as well as the interfaces between Confucian doctrine and lived social practice, but next to nothing with regard to Buddhism. This book will be a first step at redressing some of this imbalance in coverage.

Satō's thoroughly charming drawings of Zen monks in training are each accompanied by brief descriptions by Eshin Nishimura. Janwillem van de Wetering has given more novelistic accounts of his encounters with Zen monastic training in his books *The Empty Mirror: Experiences in a Japanese Zen Monastery* (Boston: Houghton Mifflin, 1974) and *A Glimpse of Nothingness: Experiences in an American Zen Community* (Boston: Houghton Mifflin, 1975). More recently, David L. Preston has applied modern sociological theory to the study of a group of American converts to Zen in his book *The Social Organization of Zen Practice: Constructing Transcultural Reality* (Cambridge: Cambridge University Press, 1988). While Preston's is a provocative and at times insightful study, these American Zen groups are such an unusual hybrid—almost a secularized monasticism—that I did not always find his material relevant to understanding traditional monastic training. A useful study of Chinese Ch'an monastic institutions and training appears in Nishimura Eshin, *Zenrin shugyō-ron*. Chinese traditional monastic structures and regulations are surveyed in Satō Tatsugen, *Chūgoku Bukkyō ni okeru kairitsu no kenkyū*, pp. 479–554. There are no comparable studies in Korean for either the premodern or contemporary periods of Korean Buddhist monasticism.

For general background on Indian Buddhist monasticism, see Mohan Wijayaratna, *Buddhist Monastic Life: According to the Texts of the Theravāda Tradition*, trans. by Claude Grangier and Steven Collins (Cambridge: Cambridge University Press, 1990); Sukumar Dutt, *Buddhist Monks and Monasteries of India: Their History and Their Contribution to Indian Culture* (1962; reprint, Delhi: Motilal Banarsidass, 1988); and his pioneering *Early Buddhist Monachism: 600 B.C.–100 B.C.* (London: Kegan Paul, Trench, Trubner and Co., 1924); Nathmal Tatia, *Studies in Buddhist and Jaina Monachism* (Bihar: Research Institute of Prakrit, Jainology and Ahimsa, 1972).

For an interesting comparative study of the ideals, history, and regulations of the monastic institutions of Christianity and Buddhism, see Patrick G. Henry and Donald K. Swearer, *For the Sake of the World: The Spirit of Buddhist and Christian Monasticism* (Minneapolis: Fortress Press, 1989). Perhaps the most disarmingly charming treatment of the joys forthcoming from monastic life (joys that are transportable across traditions) is Patrick Leigh Fermor's *A Time to Keep Silence* (London: John Murray, 1957). As a layman who is intensely attracted to the monastic alternative, Fermor has sufficient distance to convey accurately and accessibly the humaneness and subtle pleasures of the contemplative life.

[11] Pace Richard F. Gombrich, *Precept and Practice: Traditional Buddhism in the Rural Highlands of Ceylon* (Oxford: Clarendon Press, 1971), pp. 4–5, 320.

PERSONAL CONSIDERATIONS BEHIND THIS BOOK

These discrepancies I am positing between Western portrayals of Zen and the testimony of its living tradition were first brought home to me during five years I spent at a Buddhist monastery in Korea. Unlike most Western scholars and practitioners of Zen, I first learned about the tradition through living the life of a Zen monk, not through reading English-language books about Zen. Only well after starting monastic training in Korea did I begin to read any of the Western scholarship about Zen. But something seemed askew. Zen as I was experiencing it as a monk living in a monastic community just did not quite mesh with Zen as I found it described in this literature. This disparity puzzled me and prompted me to examine more carefully the foundations of Zen thought and meditation practice.

Part of the problem, I presumed, was that Zen seemed so different from Buddhism as I had experienced it earlier as a monk in Southeast Asia. My own monastic study of Zen thought started as a result of trying to understand how Zen—which claimed to be Buddhist, but which seemed in so many ways to be almost diametrically opposed to the tenets and practices of much of the rest of the Buddhist religion—could be reconciled with the mainstream of the Sino-Indian tradition. Could "Zen," in other words, still be "Buddhism"?

When I broached this question with Korean monks, they found it ludicrous.[12] Of course we are Buddhists, they would reply, and could readily point to the Buddha images in their shrine halls to verify this fact, if not the protracted succession of Zen masters they recognized, going back to Śākyamuni Buddha himself. But the monks' attempts to assuage my concerns were never completely satisfying. Since leaving the monastery in 1979 to return to the academy, I have built my scholarly career upon the problem of placing Zen within the wider context of pan-Asiatic Buddhist thought. This has led to two books that explore the development of Zen thought and meditative techniques and their affinities with other strands of Buddhist doctrine and practice.[13] As I look back on my career now, however, this quandary I faced in understanding Zen's connections with the rest of Buddhism might not have occurred had I been

---

[12] This question is not as absurd as it might at first seem. A recent popular encyclopedia, for example, explicitly distinguishes the two: Harvey Cox, ed., *The Encyclopedia of Eastern Philosophy and Religion: Buddhism, Hinduism, Taoism, and Zen* (Boulder, Colo.: Shambhala, 1988).

[13] Robert E. Buswell, Jr., *The Korean Approach to Zen: The Collected Works of Chinul* (Honolulu: University of Hawaii Press, 1983); and *The Formation of Ch'an Ideology in China and Korea: The Vajrasamādhi-Sūtra, a Buddhist Apocryphon* (Princeton: Princeton University Press, 1989).

content to let monastic practice itself represent the experience of Zen Buddhism and not attempt to unravel its theory, as Renato Rosaldo encourages in the epigraph that opens this introduction.[14]

MONASTICISM AND THE CONTEXT OF ENLIGHTENMENT

I expect some readers will presume that, in my concern with what might be considered the "external trappings" of the Zen tradition, I am neglecting the internal religious training that is thought to be the lifeblood of the religion. Who really cares, some might ask, about the minutiae of monastic training, about what time the monks get up in the morning, or what duties they perform in the monastery? All that really matters in Buddhism—and especially in Zen—is enlightenment; and that enlightenment has little to do with monastic organization, daily routines, and other cultural artifacts of the religion. I have often heard such arguments, especially it seems from Western Zen practitioners, but I reject them out of hand. I have come to believe that Buddhism weaves doctrine, praxis, and lifeway together into an intricate tapestry. In this tapestry, the daily rituals of Buddhism reticulate with its teachings and its practices, each aspect intimately interconnected with the other. The regimens of monastic life—indeed, the entire cultural context of Buddhist training—therefore interface directly with doctrine and practice.[15] The monks, after all, come to realize their enlightenment through the daily routine of the monastery. To understand the significance to Buddhist adepts of the religion's teachings and meditative techniques, therefore, we must view them within the context of monasticism.

But even if, for the sake of argument, we were to concede that enlightenment is the summum bonum of Zen, monastic life provides one of the few contexts available (apart from doing the training oneself) through which to comprehend what that experience might mean. Enlightenment, after all, is but a phase in a regimen of training that pervades all aspects of Buddhism's monastic institutions. That regimen functions like the rules of the game of baseball: unless we know those rules and understand the meaning of a single, a double, or a triple, the full significance of a home run will not be clear.[16] So, too, without understanding the regimen of

[14] Rosaldo, *Culture and Truth*, p. 6.

[15] See the introduction by Robert M. Gimello and myself to our coedited volume, Robert E. Buswell, Jr., and Robert M. Gimello, eds., *Paths to Liberation: The Mārga and Its Transformations of Buddhist Thought*, Studies in East Asian Buddhism, no. 7 (Honolulu: University of Hawaii Press, a Kuroda Institute Book, 1992).

[16] My baseball analogy here is inspired by Ninian Smart, *Reasons and Faiths: An Investigation of Religious Discourse, Christian and Non-Christian* (London: Routledge and Ke-

monastic life, we have little basis upon which to comprehend the meaning of enlightenment—Zen's home run, as it were. By divorcing the experience of enlightenment from its soteriological context, a context that to a great extent involves monastic training, would we not then be guilty of marginalizing the significance of this religious goal?

There is still another reason why the regimen of the monastery might offer one of the few available entrées to the religious experiences of Buddhist monks. Buddhist monks typically treat their spiritual training as an intensely personal enterprise, one that should not be discussed with anyone who is not a member of the order. In fact, one of the 250 precepts that monks accept upon their full ordination forbids them from discussing with anyone other than their fellow monks the experiences achieved through their meditation; violation of this precept is an offense demanding expiation.[17] And if a monk should falsely claim to have achieved spiritual powers through his practice when he has not, he would be subject to permanent expulsion from the order.[18] Erring on the side of discretion, most Korean monks refuse to talk about their own meditative development with anyone other than the Zen master, or perhaps a handful of their closest colleagues. But by observing the way such monks live, we may glean some sense of the ways in which they have been affected by Zen beliefs and the results that are forthcoming from undertaking Zen training.[19]

---

gan Paul, 1958); see also Robert Gimello's and my use of this metaphor to describe the Buddhist path of practice in the introduction to our coedited volume, Buswell and Gimello, *Paths to Liberation.*

[17] *Pācittika* no. 7; *pāyantika* no. 8; see the translation of this rule in Charles S. Prebish, *Buddhist Monastic Discipline: The Sanskrit Prātimokṣa Sūtras of the Mahāsāṃghikas and Mulasarvāstivādins* (University Park: Pennsylvania State University Press, 1975), pp. 74–75.

[18] *Pārājika* no. 4; see Prebish, *Buddhist Monastic Discipline*, pp. 52–53.

[19] My focus on monks in this book should not be taken to imply that women are not following such regimens. There are many nuns in Korea, and even the monks recognize that the asceticism of their female counterparts is often more severe than that found in the monasteries. As a monk, however, I obviously had no access to the nunneries and know nothing firsthand about their way of life. Hopefully, a nun will one day offer a similar treatment of life in Korean Buddhist nunneries. From what nuns I know have told me, in large measure the regimens at the large monasteries and nunneries are substantially the same, so my account should be broadly representative of the life followed by both sections of the order. A brief account of the daily life of Korean nuns appears in Martine Batchelor's "Buddhist Nuns in Korea," *Karuna*, Winter 1990–1991, pp. 16–18. Two interesting articles by Samu Sunim tell the life stories of two important Korean nuns: "Eunyeong Sunim and the Founding of Pomun-jong, the First Independent Bhikshuni Order," *Spring Wind—Buddhist Cultural Forum* (special issue on Women and Buddhism) 6 (1986): 129–62; and "Manseong Sunim, A Woman Zen Master of Modern Korea," ibid., pp. 188–93.

THE VALUE OF THE MODERN TRADITIONS IN
UNDERSTANDING ZEN

In the preceding discussion, I have made much of the difficulties of comprehending Zen beliefs through interpretations of written documents divorced from their historical and cultural contexts. What I am also suggesting by such comments is that data drawn from direct observation of the living tradition of Buddhism can offer students and scholars of Buddhism new and innovative ways of understanding the religion. The text-based approach to Buddhist Studies, to use historian Hayden White's term, "prefigures" scholarly discourse on the tradition and discourages scholars of the religion from pursuing other approaches.[20] Even though many of us Buddhist specialists spend much time overseas studying Buddhist texts with our Asian counterparts in universities and research centers, rarely has any of our work reflected the Buddhism that then surrounds us. As Michel Strickmann remarks, in a harsh, but not altogether undeserved, criticism of contemporary Buddhist Studies: "Although many North American 'Buddhologists' (as they barbarically term themselves) enjoy long periods of publicly subsidized residence in Japan, most seem to prefer the atmosphere of libraries and language schools to that of the society in which they temporarily dwell. Nor do American university programs in Buddhist Studies appear to encourage research and fieldwork in the living Buddhist tradition; their neo-scholasticism excludes the phenomenal world."[21] By ignoring Buddhism's living tradition, scholars of the religion risk succumbing to the Orientalist dogma described by Edward Said, in which "abstractions about the Orient, particularly those based on texts representing a 'classical' Oriental civilization, are always preferable to direct evidence drawn from modern Oriental realities."[22]

---

[20] "I have been forced to postulate a deep level of consciousness on which a historical thinker chooses conceptual strategies by which to explain or represent his data. On this level, I believe, the historian performs an essentially *poetic* act, in which he *pre*figures the historical field and constitutes it as a domain upon which to bring to bear the specific theories he will use to explain 'what was *really* happening' in it" (emphasis in original). Hayden White, *Metahistory: The Historical Imagination in Nineteenth-Century Europe* (Baltimore: Johns Hopkins University Press, 1973), p. x; see also the more detailed account of the self-reflexive nature of this prefiguring ibid., pp. 30–31.

[21] Michel Strickmann, "The Consecration Sūtra: A Buddhist Book of Spells," in *Chinese Buddhist Apocrypha*, ed. by Robert E. Buswell, Jr. (Honolulu: University of Hawaii Press, 1990), p. 108 n.3.

[22] Edward W. Said, *Orientalism* (New York: Random House, Vintage Books, 1978), p. 300.

MARGINALIZATIONS OF THE BUDDHIST MONASTIC TRADITION

But previous accounts of Buddhist monasticism in Western scholarship are not as helpful as they might have been in correcting these distortions about the religion. This inadequacy results, I believe, from two extreme views, which have led to some serious misunderstandings about the nature of the monastic life. First, monks have been viewed as otherworldly adepts, enthralled in matters so profound that they hardly deign to interact with mere mortals—or perhaps are no longer even capable of such interactions. This negative view of Buddhist practice has a long history in Western scholarly writing. For example, Max Weber in his *The Religion of India* draws on descriptions of the arhat in Pali scriptures to portray the Buddhist saint as apathetic, cool, and aloof. But even he has trouble reconciling this portrayal with the pervasive ecstasy appearing in the poems these enlightened men and women wrote in the Pali *Verses of the Elders* (*Theragāthā* and *Therīgāthā*).[23] I suspect, too, that some of this attitude derives from the Orientalist stereotype of the mystical religiosity of the monolithic East.[24]

A second stereotype is that monks are maladjusted sociopaths who are withdrawing from a world in which they are unable to function. This is the underlying message of Melford Spiro's devastating—and controversial—critique of the sociological and psychological forces driving the Buddhist monastic impulse. Spiro classifies the unconscious motivational bases for recruitment into the Buddhist monkhood in Burma into three categories, which he terms the need for dependency, narcissism, and emotional timidity. As an example of Spiro's approach, let me summarize his treatment of the first category. Burmese monks are, Spiro claims, "characterized by strong dependency needs [and are] symbolically the structural equivalent of a child. . . . In exchange for this renunciation [viz. ordination as a monk] he can even as an adult continue to enjoy the dependency of early childhood." Of course, the celibacy that is expected of such a renunciatory lifestyle may seem to be challenging, but Spiro suggests that monks "are willing to pay this price because, at least for many of them, celibacy is really not a price. . . . Monks are characterized by (among other things) latent homosexuality and an above-average fear

---

[23] As Max Weber notes in his *The Religion of India*, trans. by Hans H. Gerth and Don Martindale (trans., New York: Free Press, 1958): "The tone to which the hymns of ancient Buddhism are attuned is triumphant joy" (p. 212). Weber's account of the aloof Buddhist arhat appears ibid., p. 208. This point is lucidly made by Gombrich in his *Precept and Practice*, p. 319, following the analysis of Gananath Obeyesekere.

[24] Said, *Orientalism*, esp. chap. 3; note also the treatment of Said's positions in James Clifford, *The Predicament of Culture: Twentieth-Century Ethnography, Literature, and Art* (Cambridge: Harvard University Press, 1988), p. 259.

of female- and mother-figures. . . . The monastic role permits a person characterized by fear of women to lead a life of female-avoidance, and the all-male monastery permits the sublimated expression of latent homosexuality."[25]

Given the penchant of academics to qualify their every statement, one has to appreciate any scholar who speaks his mind as bluntly as does Spiro here. Still, his analysis is, I fear, a classic illustration of the problems of emotional distancing, cultural marginalization, and usurpation of authority that contemporary processual anthropologists have found in traditional objectivist ethnography. Such objectivist treatments, one critic says, "have failed to grasp significant variations in the tone of cultural events" and seriously distort the character of indigenous cultures.[26]

In the same vein, I would suggest that where Spiro attempts to describe the psyche of Buddhist monks in Western psychoanalytic terms, Buddhist monasticism could also be treated on its own terms, as presenting an alternative worldview that has as much claim to authenticity as anything offered by the West. Where Spiro's observations may have suggested to him that the monastic impulse is "a means of avoiding responsibility and satisfying the need for dependency,"[27] I believe I could make an equally strong case that monasticism provides a valid means of avoiding the sensual attachments that can be a very real distraction to meditation. Monks are acutely aware that family ties are an intensely emotional attachment—and therefore distraction—and intentionally limit, if not cut off completely, their contacts with their families. Spiro, however, would reduce this same motivation to "emotional timidity."

The normalizing idiom of such objectivist descriptions of Buddhist practice trivializes monastic experiences and forces them to fit "our" Western patterns of secular culture, patterns that may be utterly alien to the Asian monastic culture in which those experiences take place. At times, even Spiro seems ready to admit as much, as for example when he remarks that "the entire ideology of Buddhism and its outlook of worldly abnegation support the attitude of noninvolvement. For Buddhism, to be detached is not a vice but a virtue. It is only through detachment that nirvana can be achieved. Hence, detachment (*upekkhā*) is a quality to be cultivated, a goal to be attained; the entire monastic discipline, especially the contemplative life, is a means to that end."[28] Why, then, must we

---

[25] Melford E. Spiro, *Buddhism and Society: A Great Tradition and Its Burmese Vicissitudes*, 2d expanded ed. (Berkeley and Los Angeles: University of California Press, 1982), pp. 342–43.

[26] Rosaldo, *Culture and Truth*, p. 50; for a trenchant summary of this critique, see ibid., pp. 46–67.

[27] Spiro, *Buddhism and Society*, p. 339.

[28] Ibid., p. 349.

revert to Western modes of analysis when those of the indigenous culture are just as (if not more) appropriate and effective?[29]

To help alleviate the problems of marginalization and authority that occur in objectivist ethnography, some anthropologists and literary critics have urged experimentation with new styles of ethnographic writing.[30] James Clifford has been the principal exponent of the movement away from experiential and interpretive modes of ethnographic writing, in which the anthropologist maintains complete power over the portrayal of his or her subjects. He has advocated instead experimentation with what he terms "dialogical" and "polyphonic" forms of writing, which would allow the informants to appear as full collaborators cum writers themselves in the ethnography.[31]

While I am sensitive to the concerns raised by such commentators, I remain unconvinced that such a dialogic form (whatever exactly that might be) would be most appropriate for the monastic communities that are my subject here. There are several reasons for this doubt, some personal, some methodological. Part of my reticence stems from the fact that this book has not evolved out of the usual fieldwork setting from which most ethnography derives. I went to Korea not to study monks, but to live as a monk. During those five years, I absorbed most of my knowledge about monastic life and monastic residents simply by living the life. I chose to be not an outside observer, gazing down upon the monastery as if from on high, but someone committed to the tradition.[32] This choice freed me from many of the concerns anthropologists are presently raising about the techniques of traditional fieldwork. I did not have to pay in-

[29] A similar criticism could be made of the analyses of other cultures found in Géza Róheim, *Psychoanalysis and Anthropology: Culture, Personality and the Unconscious* (New York: International Universities Press, 1950).

[30] Much of the impetus for this reappraisal of traditional ethnographical writing stems from the groundbreaking article by my colleague Jacques Maquet, "Objectivity in Anthropology," *Current Anthropology* 5 (1964): 47–55.

[31] James Clifford, "On Ethnographic Authority," *Representations* 1, no. 2 (1983): 118–46; and see the insightful discussion of Clifford's positions in Paul Rabinow, "Representations Are Social Facts: Modernity and Post-Modernity in Anthropology," in *Writing Culture: The Poetics and Politics of Ethnography*, ed. by James Clifford and George E. Marcus (Berkeley and Los Angeles: University of California Press, 1986), pp. 243–47.

[32] Renato Rosaldo remarks that "the fieldworker's mode of surveillance uncomfortably resembles Michel Foucault's Panopticon, the site from which the (disciplining) disciplines enjoy gazing upon (and subjecting) their subjects." "From the Door of His Tent: The Fieldworker and the Inquisitor," in Clifford and Marcus, *Writing Culture*, p. 92. Mary Louise Pratt also notes that traditional ethnographies are written as if by "an observer fixed on the edge of a space, looking in and/or down upon what is other." "Fieldwork in Common Places," ibid., p. 32. Note also Rosaldo's description of the objectivist ethnographer as an analyst who "positions himself as a spectator who looks on from the outside," in his *Culture and Truth*, p. 56.

formants, for example, in order to get private interviews, nor did I seek to analyze quantitatively how the monks spend their time, as might anthropologists trained in the academy. (None of these objections has, so far as I am aware, been made regarding the work of Korean anthropologists.) I was more like a captive or castaway, whom Mary Louise Pratt suggests would actually be a better "participant-observer" than an ethnographer.[33] Even though I did not conceive of myself as a participant-observer in the technical sense of the term, I had to be constantly observing in order to be able to participate effectively and with a minimum of disruption to the community. Since I also did not begin this project as an entrée into the profession of anthropology, I have also not had to suffer through the process of "disciplining" that comes about as field notes are written up into a dissertation and the prospective initiate into the community of anthropologists made to show his or her virtuosity in manipulating the methodologies and techniques of the discipline.[34] By seeking to write what I may term scholarly reportage, not anthropology, perhaps I will be able to avoid some of these pitfalls noted in ethnographical writing.

Another reason that reportage about the monastic life may be more effective than ethnography is that the typical tools of anthropology and sociology are not always effective when dealing with ordained religious, as others before me have discovered to their chagrin. One scholar who tried to use such tools, my own mentor, Lewis Lancaster (whom I first met while I was still a monk in Korea), remarked that the Korean monks he interviewed were often reluctant to say much about themselves in person. Questionnaires administered in private were little better, since the monks often simply refused to answer questions they deemed inappropriate, or would respond in ways they presumed were expected of someone living a cloistered life. From my own career in the monastery, I know that many monks dislike discussing with outsiders issues they consider irrelevant to their "homeless" (ch'ulga) life, since an interest in such matters would suggest an attachment to the world outside the monastery—anathema to a Buddhist monk. Lancaster notes from his own field experience that "it was only possible to secure what appears to be reliable information from interviews that lasted in some cases for several days and involved time spent in discussing Buddhist doctrine."[35] I would even go so

[33] Mary Louise Pratt, "Fieldwork in Common Places," p. 38.

[34] See George E. Marcus, "Ethnographic Writing and Anthropological Careers," in Clifford and Marcus, *Writing Culture*, pp. 262–66. See also I. M. Lewis's perceptive comments about the "metaphysical significance" of fieldwork in the profession of anthropology in his *Religion in Context*, pp. 1–18.

[35] See Lewis R. Lancaster, "Buddhism and Family in East Asia," in *Religion and The Family in East Asia*, ed. by George A. De Vos and Takao Sofue (1984; reprint, Berkeley and

far as to say that only by living together with the monks *as a monk* does the researcher have much hope of gaining an accurate picture of the monks' lives and the motivations that underlie it.

After some experimentation, I have also come to feel that the dialogic style seems contrived and forced in describing a monastic environment, where monks are encouraged to remain detached and aloof—and often silent. In some crucial ways, the self-effacing tone of "experiential" modes of writing seems rather more appropriate for describing a religious tradition like Buddhism, whose fundamental doctrine of "nonself" (*mua*; Skt. *anātman*) offers such a radical critique of individuality. Indeed, the monastery may be one community where the detached tone of objectivist ethnography may be strangely more effective and accurate than personal narrative. The dialogic mode could, to the contrary, create an artificial sense of individuation, which much of monastic training is designed to subvert. And after creating such individuation, such a style might then in turn produce the same sense of separation between the monk cum writer and his subjects (who are, after all, his fellow residents) that the dialogic style is intended to avoid. Because of this concern, I have opted instead to use the third person throughout; still, even when I use such seemingly distancing modes of discourse as "the monks," I am including myself. But I have taken to heart one of the more compelling criticisms of traditional anthropological writing: that ethnographers seem to vanish from their books after their introductions.[36] While I do not intend this book to become a self-reflexive meditation on my own personal experiences, I will punctuate my account of monastic life with relevant personal accounts, where those may help clarify my own background and agenda.

MONKISH STEREOTYPES

Despite attempts made in the scholarly literature to characterize and/or categorize Buddhist monks, most are doomed because of the failure to recognize the simple fact that most monks are no different from anyone else one meets in everyday life. They run the gamut of human characters,

---

Los Angeles: University of California Press, 1986), p. 149. Another scholar, working with contemporary shamans in Korea, notes a similar tendency on the part of her informants to try to dictate the angle her study should take; Chungmoo Choi, "The Competence of Korean Shamans as Performers of Folklore" (Ph.D. diss., Indiana University, 1987), pp. 14–15.

[36] Both Mary Louise Pratt ("Fieldwork in Common Places," pp. 31–32) and Renato Rosaldo ("From the Door of His Tent," p. 93) remark on the curious fact that ethnographers tend to vanish from their books after the incumbent introduction describing their arrival in the field.

from the introspective and sober to the intellectual and urbane to the playful and mischievous. There are the careful detail men, who prefer to work alone on the monastery's financial ledgers. There are the gregarious socializers, who take charge of entertaining the lay visitors to the monastery. There are the dedicated contemplatives, who spend months isolated from their fellow monks, intent on their meditation. There are the devoted scholars, who gladly spend an entire day tracing a single scriptural allusion. And there are the vigorous manual laborers, who are most content working alongside the hired hands tilling the fields or hauling logs down from the mountains.

Monks are, in short, perfectly ordinary people. If they are extraordinary at all, it is only because of the way of life they have chosen to pursue. They have their virtues and their vices, their preferences and aversions, their strengths and weaknesses of character, just as we all do. The monastery, like any large social organization, attracts a whole range of individuals, with varying interests and skills, all of whom have to be put to use in the service of the religion. The Buddhist monastic life must be wide enough in scope to be able to accommodate these various types and make them productive members of a religious community. Anyone who has had more than a passing acquaintance with monks would know that this is obvious. That I feel compelled to state the obvious shows how ingrained I have found the above two profiles of monks to be.

Thomas Merton went a long way toward dispelling many of the lugubrious Western stereotypes about Catholic monks in his autobiography, *The Seven Storey Mountain*,[37] and his many subsequent books, all so deservedly well known as not to need introduction here. While I have never spent any time in Christian monasteries and cannot speak for their religious specialists, I was privileged to meet several Catholic monks during my career in Buddhist monasteries and felt remarkable affinities with their vocations.[38] Buddhism needs its own Thomas Merton, its own fervent internal advocate, to dispel the myths about Asian Buddhist monks. That is not, however, my intent here. I returned to lay life about one year after coming back to the United States and have since pursued a career in academe. While I retain a healthy respect and admiration for Buddhist cenobites, and still count several of them as friends, it would be presumptuous in the extreme for me to speak on their behalf. I will be satisfied if I am able to create some sensitivity toward the calling of Zen monks and an appreciation for the way of life they have chosen to pursue.

[37] Thomas Merton, *The Seven Storey Mountain* (New York: Harcourt, Brace and World, 1948).

[38] Peter Levi, a former Jesuit, notes the same impression in his meeting with Buddhist monks. *The Frontiers of Paradise. A Study of Monks and Monasteries* (New York: Paragon House, 1987).

THE ORIGINS OF THIS BOOK

This book describes the life followed by Korean Buddhist monks at Songgwang-sa (Piney Expanse Monastery), one of the four largest monasteries of the modern Korean Buddhist tradition, where I spent five years in training between 1974 and 1979. In many ways, this book is a product of my own process of learning about Zen Buddhism and its monastic institutions. In 1972, after a year of college, I left school to ordain as a Buddhist novice (*sami*; Skt. *śramaṇera*) in Thailand in the strict Thammayut (Dhammayuttika) Order of Theravāda Buddhism; once I turned twenty years old, I took the precepts of a fully ordained monk (*pigu*; Skt. *bhikṣu*). After enduring a year of ill health brought on by the tropical climate, I finally left Thailand for a tiny hermitage on Landau Island in Hong Kong, where I spent another year studying Hua-yen and Ch'an texts with a Chinese Buddhist monk. After a year in virtual isolation, however, I longed once again to live among a saṃgha of monks, as I had in Thailand, and to put more time into my meditation practice.

During my year in Thailand, I had met a couple of Korean monks who had come there on pilgrimage and had ended up staying for several years. They told me and a couple of other Western monks about the Buddhist monasteries of Korea. It was my first contact with anyone Korean, and my first inkling that Korea even had a Buddhist tradition. One of my fellow Western monks from Thailand ended up going to Korea while I was in Hong Kong, and in several letters to me told how strong the practice tradition was there. One evening, I resolved to move on to Korea and begin Sŏn practice. This decision seems incredibly impulsive to me now, since I knew absolutely nothing about Korea, let alone any of the language, and had read only one book on Zen in my life (the *Platform Sūtra of the Sixth Patriarch*).[39] I somehow had passed over the works of D. T. Suzuki, Alan Watts, and Paul Reps, and so was little affected by typical Western views of Zen. From what little reading I had done, I was not much impressed with Zen, and in fact even today, after practicing Sŏn for some fifteen years, I still see myself as something of a closet Hīnayānist. But from one standpoint, this utter ignorance of the culture, the language, and the tradition was a blessing in disguise: I had no choice but to become an involved observer in order just to get through the daily regimen and clarify in my own mind why I was doing this form of practice. While I did not go to Korea to study monastic institutions and lifestyles, that is effectively what I was compelled to do.

I took leave of my Chinese abbot (who a few years later came to see me

[39] Philip Yampolsky, trans., *The Platform Sutra of the Sixth Patriarch* (New York: Columbia University Press, 1967).

in Korea and tour the monasteries there) and left for Korea, where I arrived in September 1974, still wearing the saffron robes of a Thai monk. The first order of business when I arrived at Pŏmnyŏn-sa, the Seoul branch temple of Songgwang-sa, was to exchange my tropical robes for a hand-me-down set of warmer Korean robes. The next order of business was to take care of a badly ingrown toenail, which had been infected for several months. The abbot of Pŏmnyŏn-sa graciously made all the arrangements for the operation and escorted me down to Songgwang-sa a week later. I hobbled into Songgwang-sa on crutches, my left foot swathed in bandages. Many of the Korean monks had fought in the Vietnam War, and several of them went out of their way to let me know that Korean soldiers badly wounded in the war refused to use crutches. Needless to say, it was not an auspicious beginning to my sojourn in Korea.

The Koreans accepted both of my Thai ordinations and I joined the community at Songgwang-sa as a fully ordained monk, or bhikṣu. Perhaps sensing my scholarly bent even then, the master gave me the Buddhist name Hyemyŏng (Brightness of Wisdom).

Until I could learn something of the language, I communicated with the Koreans by writing classical Chinese, which all the monks could read and write. When that did not work, another Westerner who had arrived at Songgwang-sa a few months before me helped with translation. About a month or so later, I entered my first three-month winter retreat, still hardly able to communicate and barely understanding what Sŏn practice entailed. More on that experience later.

With the end of the retreat in the spring of 1975, I was invited to the Peace Corps language school in Chŏnju, which used me as a willing guinea pig for a couple of weeks to train their teachers in a new language-teaching technique that they wanted to try on the next group of American volunteers. With that solid grounding in the language and my background in Chinese to help me along, I felt comfortable conversing in Korean by the time the summer meditation retreat began. Finally, I could begin to study seriously the Korean monastic tradition and especially its unique style of Zen training.

Kusan (1908–1983), the teacher at Songgwang-sa during my years there, was the only Sŏn master of a major Korean monastery who had any real interest in disseminating Korean Buddhist practice in foreign countries. During his career, Kusan took three separate teaching tours to Western cities and established branch temples of Songgwang-sa in Los Angeles, Carmel, and Geneva. More important for this book, however, his monastery was at the time the only one in Korea that allowed foreigners to participate in the traditional Buddhist training. While I could travel freely among Korean monasteries during the vacation seasons of spring and autumn, I was never able to spend a retreat season elsewhere. During Kusan's fourteen-year tenure at Songgwang-sa, some fifty foreigners of several different nationalities came to practice under his direction at Songgwang-sa. Because of language and cultural problems, most of these foreigners were eventually segregated in a separate compound at Songgwang-sa, where a Puril International Meditation Center was established in 1976. I was one of the first foreigners to come to Songgwang-sa well before there was a separate foreign enclave. Because my background in Chinese helped me to learn Korean fairly quickly, I was fortunate to be one of the handful of Western monks allowed to continue practicing together with the Koreans in the main meditation hall at Songgwang-sa. The account of monastic culture I will present in this book will therefore reflect life as it was lived by Korean monks in one of the major practice centers of their religion.

CHAPTER ONE.

Buddhism in Contemporary Korea

IN ORDER to make my point about the discrepancy between the depictions of Zen in Western works on the school and the living system of Zen practice, I have described the religion in the introduction as if it were a single, monolithic tradition. This description, of course, oversimplifies what is actually a much more complex historical situation. Zen is not coextensive with any one school, whether that be Korean Sŏn or Japanese Rinzai Zen. There have actually been many independent strands of what has come to be called Zen, the sorting out of which has occupied scholars of Buddhism for the last few decades. These sectarian divisions are further complicated by the fact that there are Zen traditions in all four East Asian countries—China, Korea, Japan, and Vietnam—each of which has its own independent history, doctrine, and mode of practice. While each of these traditions has developed independently, all have been heavily influenced by the Chinese schools of Ch'an (Kor. Sŏn; Jpn. Zen; Viet. Thiền). We are therefore left with an intricate picture of several independent national traditions of Zen, but traditions that do have considerable synergy between them. To ignore these national differences would be to oversimplify the complicated sectarian scene that is East Asian Zen; but to overemphasize them would be to ignore the multiple layers of symbiosis between Zen's various national branches.[1] These continuities and transformations[2] between the different strands must both be kept in mind in order to understand the character of the "Zen tradition."

This book will focus on the monastic practice of Zen in one of these national traditions, one that has many levels of symbiosis with both China and Japan. This is the Zen tradition of Korea, where it is known as Sŏn. While Korean Buddhism did not begin as an exclusively Sŏn tradition, Sŏn was introduced into Korea perhaps as early as the late seventh century during Ch'an's incipiency on the Chinese mainland. By the thir-

---

[1] I have tried elsewhere to demonstrate this symbiosis between the national traditions of Zen. See Robert E. Buswell, Jr., *The Formation of Ch'an Ideology in China and Korea: The Vajrasamādhi-Sūtra, A Buddhist Apocryphon*, Princeton Library of Asian Translations (Princeton: Princeton University Press, 1989).

[2] I am adapting here concepts S. J. Tambiah proposed to understand the relation between historical religion and contemporary practice in Thai Theravāda Buddhism. See Tambiah, *Buddhism and the Spirit Cults in North-east Thailand*, Cambridge Studies in Social Anthropology, no. 2 (Cambridge: Cambridge University Press, 1970), pp. 374–76.

teenth century, Sŏn came to dominate Buddhist doctrine and praxis, virtually eclipsing all other branches of Korean Buddhism after the fifteenth century. It was able to assert this dominance by absorbing many of the distinctive insights of its rival Korean schools, eventually subsuming those other branches into what came to be known as the indigenous Chogye school of Korean Buddhism. ("Chogye" is the Korean pronunciation of "Ts'ao-ch'i," the name of the mountain of residence of the sixth patriarch of Chinese Ch'an, Hui-neng, adumbrating the fundamental Zen stance of Korean Buddhism.) Because of its assimilative character, Sŏn Buddhism in Korea may be rather more tolerant and accommodating of the approaches of other schools of Buddhism than might other East Asian traditions of Zen. Despite this caveat, there are enough continuities between the various Zen schools that much of Korean Sŏn practice has its analogues in the other national traditions of East Asian Zen as well. So I believe a close examination of the monastic practices of Korean Sŏn will provide insights relevant to the Zen tradition throughout the region.

Let me begin this look at contemporary Sŏn practice by providing some general background on the development of Buddhism in Korea; material on the history of the Korean Sŏn tradition will be found in Chapter Seven.

EARLY BUDDHISM IN KOREA

Buddhism first came to Korea during the fourth century A.D. Virtually from its inception on the peninsula, the religion was a principal force behind social and technological change in Korea. Along with their religion, Buddhist missionaries introduced to Korea a wide cross-section of Sinitic culture and thought, including the Chinese writing system, calendrics, and architecture. Buddhist spiritual technologies were also considered to offer powers far superior to those of the indigenous religion of Shamanism.[3] For all these reasons, Buddhism became an integral part of the religio-political nexus of Korea during the Unified Silla (668–935) and Koryŏ (937–1392) dynasties. Buddhism therefore provided the foundation for Korean national ideology for over a millennium.

During those two periods, Buddhism functioned as a virtual state religion. Buddhism received munificent material and political support from the royal court and in exchange interceded with the buddhas and bodhisattvas on behalf of the nation's welfare. The Buddhist presence was ubiq-

---

[3] For background on this period, see Inoue Hideo's important article "Chōsen ni okeru Bukkyō juyō to shinkan'nen," which I have translated as "The Reception of Buddhism in Korea and Its Impact on Indigenous Culture," in *Introduction of Buddhism to Korea: New Cultural Patterns*, Studies in Korean Religion and Culture, vol. 3, ed. by Lewis Lancaster and Chai-shin Yu (Berkeley: Asian Humanities Press, 1989), pp. 29–78.

uitous throughout the country, exerting its hold over the nation with an extensive network of both mountain monasteries and city temples. During the Koryŏ dynasty, for example, the head monasteries of both of the two major branches of the tradition—Kyo, or doctrinal study, and Sŏn, or Zen meditation training—were based in the capital of Kaesŏng, and thousands of monks pursued their vocations in urban enclaves. Monasteries were awarded vast tracts of paddy and forest lands, which were worked by armies of serfs awarded to the temples by the secular authorities. Monasteries also pursued such commercial enterprises as noodle making, tea production, and distillation of spirits. The financial power of the monasteries was so immense that it severely strained the fabric of the Koryŏ economy, contributing to the demise of that kingdom and the rise of the Chosŏn dynasty.[4]

The foundation of the Chosŏn dynasty (1392–1910), with its pronounced Neo-Confucian sympathies, brought an end to Buddhism's hegemony in Korean religion and upset this ideological status quo. Buddhism's close affiliation with the vanquished Koryŏ rulers led to centuries of persecution during this Confucian dynasty. While controls over monastic vocations and conduct had already been instituted during the Koryŏ period, these pale next to the severe restrictions promulgated during the Chosŏn dynasty. The number of monks was severely restricted—and at times a complete ban on ordination instituted—and monks were prohibited from entering the metropolitan areas. Hundreds of monasteries were disestablished (the number of temples dropping to 242 during the reign of T'aejong [r. 1401–1418]), and new construction was forbidden in the cities and villages of Korea. Monastic land holdings and temple slaves were confiscated by the government in 1406, undermining the economic viability of many monasteries. The vast power that Buddhists had wielded during the Silla and Koryŏ dynasties was now exerted by Confucians. Buddhism was kept virtually quarantined in the countryside, isolated from the intellectual debates of the times. Its lay adherents were more commonly the illiterate peasants of the countryside and women, rather than the educated male elite of the cities, as had been the case in ages past. Buddhism had become insular, and ineffective in generating creative responses to this Confucian challenge.[5]

[4] For background on the socioeconomic role of Buddhism in traditional Korea, see An Kyehyŏn, Han'guk Pulgyo-sa yŏn'gu (Researches on Korean Buddhist History) (Seoul: Tonghwa Ch'ulp'ansa, 1986), esp. pp. 289–94. I have surveyed briefly the place of Buddhist monasteries in Korean society; see Robert E. Buswell, Jr., The Korean Approach to Zen: The Collected Works of Chinul (Honolulu: University of Hawaii Press, 1983), pp. 17–21.

[5] For accounts of these periodic restrictions placed on Buddhism during the Chosŏn period, see An Kyehyŏn, Han'guk Pulgyo-sa yŏn'gu, pp. 288–89; U Chŏngsang and Kim Yŏngt'ae, Han'guk Pulgyo-sa (A History of Korean Buddhism) (Seoul: Sinhŭng

Foreign pressures on the late Chosŏn court brought the first real break in this state of affairs. Japanese suzerainty over Korea began in 1905 with the appointment of a Japanese adviser to the Chosŏn dynasty throne and was formalized in 1910 with the official annexation of Korea. Ironically, perhaps, the Japanese colonial presence was initially of some advantage to Buddhism. Japan was itself a Buddhist country and its envoys empathized with the pitiable plight of Korean monks under the Chosŏn administration. It was Japanese lobbying at the turn of the century, for example, that forced the Kojong (r. 1864–1907) government to remove restrictions on Buddhist activities in the capital and allowed Buddhist monks to enter the cities for the first time in some three hundred years.

But Japanese support for Buddhism was hardly benign. Missionaries from such Japanese Buddhist sects as the Nichiren Shōshū and Jōdo Shinshū lobbied to be allowed to proselytize in Korea. While such missionary activities began in the Japanese expatriate enclaves, the Japanese colonial administration subsequently encouraged missionaries to extend their activities into Korean communities as well, as a means of exerting ideological control over the native populace.

Periodic attempts were even made to force Korean Buddhism to merge with one or another Japanese sect, moves that would have obliterated the independent identity of the indigenous church. To the Koreans, the most notorious of these attempts was an agreement reached in October 1910 by Yi Hoegwang (1840–after 1925) of the new Wŏnjong (Consummate school) to merge Korean Buddhism into the Japanese Sōtō school, the Zen school whose "gradualist" ideology, the Koreans protested, had the least affinities with the putative "subitism" of traditional Korean Buddhism. While this merger was soon scuttled, it nevertheless attests to the seriousness of these new political pressures the Japanese exerted on Korean Buddhism.[6]

Ch'ulp'ansa, 1976), pp. 134–38; Yi Kiyŏng, *Han'guk ŭi Pulgyo* (Korean Buddhism) (Seoul: Sejong Taewang Kinyŏm Saŏphoe, 1974), pp. 159–62; and Kamata Shigeo, *Chōsen Bukkyoshi* (History of Korean Buddhism) (Tokyo: Tokyo University Press, 1987), pp. 202–13. The most thorough, if at times supercilious, coverage of Chosŏn Buddhism remains Takahashi Tōru's *Richō Bukkyo* (Yi Dynasty Buddhism) (1929; reprint, Tokyo: Kokusho Kankōkai, 1973).

[6] Korean scholarship on Buddhism during the Japanese colonial period is often nativistic and must be used with caution. Useful surveys of this period include Sŏ Kyŏngju, "Han'guk Pulgyo paengnyŏnsa" (A Hundred-Year History of Korean Buddhism), *Sŏnggok nonch'ong* 4 (August 1973): 37–78; Kang Sŏkchu and Pak Kyŏnggŭn, *Pulgyo kŭnse paengnyŏn* (The Most Recent Hundred Years of Buddhism) (Seoul: Chungang Ilbo, 1980); and Yu Pyŏngdŏk, "Ilche sidae ŭi Pulgyo" (Buddhism during the Japanese Colonial Period), in *Han'guk Pulgyo sasangsa*, Sungsan Pak Kilchin paksa hwagap kinyŏm (History of Korean Buddhist Thought, Pak Kilchin Festschrift), ed. by Sungsan Pak Kilchin paksa hwagap kinyŏm saŏphoe (Iri, Chŏlla Pukto, Korea: Wŏn'gwang University Press, 1975), pp. 1159–87. In English, see the survey in Wi Jo Kang, *Religion and Politics in Korea under the Japanese Rule,*

SCHISM BETWEEN CELIBATE AND MARRIED CLERGY

But perhaps the most severe threat to traditional Korean Buddhism was the Japanese support for a married clergy. Since Korean Buddhists had traditionally observed celibacy, this step threatened the ethical basis of the religion and led to serious upheavals within the church. As had happened earlier in Meiji Japan, the Japanese imperial government eventually required that monks marry in order to hold important ecclesiastical or monastic positions.[7]

Throughout most of the Chosŏn dynasty, celibacy remained institutionalized within the Buddhist church. But during the declining years of the dynasty, adherence to the precepts had become increasingly lax among the ecclesia, a problem exacerbated by decreased governmental supervision of internal monastic conduct. As contact with incoming Japanese missionary monks brought the news that even that most prosperous of Asian Buddhist nations permitted monks to take wives, some of the first documented instances of marriage among Korean monks are noted. By the turn of the century, it had become common knowledge among Koreans that many monks were secretly marrying, regardless of the restrictions still in place. The *Chosŏn Pulgyo wŏlbo* (Korean Buddhism Monthly) of November 1912, for example, reported that many monks neither wore monk's clothing nor kept the precepts—both discreet codes for marriage.[8]

But what Korean scholarship sometimes ignores is that calls for a married clergy did not come initially from Japanese colonial forces, but instead from Korean Buddhist intellectuals. Perhaps the most influential of these native reformers was Han Yongun (1879–1944; sobriquet Manhae). Monk, social and religious reformer, renowned poet (he authored *Nim ŭi chimmuk*, "Silence of the Beloved," one of the first modern poems in vernacular Korean), influential magazine editor, and translator, Yongun is perhaps best remembered in Korea as one of the thirty-three leaders of the March First Movement (Samil Undong), the independence movement from Japanese rule that was initiated in 1919.[9]

Studies in Asian Thought and Religion, vol. 5 (Lewiston, N.Y., and Queenston, Ontario: Edwin Mellen Press, 1987).

[7] For a recent treatment of the Meiji persecution of Buddhism, see James Edward Ketelaar, *Of Heretics and Martyrs in Meiji Japan: Buddhism and Its Persecution* (Princeton: Princeton University Press, 1990).

[8] The testimony of this journal may be somewhat suspect, since it is considered to have been the organ of pro-Japanese factions within the Korean Buddhist order. See Henrik H. Sørensen, "Korean Buddhist Journals during Early Japanese Colonial Rule," *Korea Journal* 30, no. 1 (January 1990): 19.

[9] Korean studies on Han Yongun are voluminous. Among the more accessible treatments

While still in his teens, Yongun had participated in the Tonghak (Eastern Learning) Rebellion during the last decade of the nineteenth century, which sought to purge Western influences from Korean society and restore native Korean values. Looking back into his country's own traditions led Yongun to Buddhism, and in 1905, at the age of twenty-seven, he ordained as a monk at Paektam-sa on Sŏrak Mountain. Profoundly influenced by the important Chinese reformer Liang Ch'i-ch'ao's (d. 1929) writings on the West, he went to Vladivostok in 1905–1906 in an unsuccessful attempt to travel to the United States via Siberia and Europe. In 1908, Yongun was, however, able to travel to Japan, where he was amazed by the conciliation he found there between traditional forms of Buddhism and modern technological culture. Profoundly affected by his overseas experiences and distressed at what he considered the degenerate state of his own tradition of Buddhism—poor learning, little meditation training, and lax observance of precepts—Yongun called on Korean Buddhism to evolve along what he termed modern, scientific lines, while still drawing from its wellspring in Asian spiritual culture.

To express his vision of such a contemporary form of Buddhism, Yongun wrote in 1910 a treatise calling for what were at the time radical changes in the Korean tradition. This tract is his seminal *Chosŏn Pulgyo yusillon* (Treatise on the Reformation of Korean Buddhism),[10] one of the first attempts by a Korean to explore ways in which Western liberalism might be applied in a Korean context.

Yongun saw the world in melioristic terms, as in a continual state of evolution that would culminate ultimately in an ideal civilization. He considered that the tide of reform then sweeping the world in science, politics, and religion would leave Korea, and specifically Korean Buddhism, behind if they did not learn to respond to these changes. To survive, Koreans must transform their nation from a static, tradition-bound country into a dynamic society at the forefront of this tide.

Yongun lamented Buddhism's unfortunate decrepitude during the Chosŏn dynasty and attributed much of this fate to its isolation from the rest of society; if Buddhism was to regain its past prestige, he advocated, it must secularize. In March and September of 1910, Han Yongun sent

is Han Chongman, "Pulgyo yusin sasang," in Sungsan Pak Kilchin paksa hwagap kinyŏm wiwŏnhoe, *Han'guk Pulgyo sasangsa*, pp. 1121–58, and esp. 1140–54. In English, see Mok Chong-bae, "Han Yong-un and Buddhism," *Korea Journal* 19, no. 12 (December 1979): 19–27; and An Pyong-jik, "Han Yong-un's Liberalism: An Analysis of the 'Reformation of Korean Buddhism,' " ibid., 13–18.

[10] Han Yongun, *Chosŏn Pulgyo yusillon* (Treatise on the Reformation of Korean Buddhism), trans. by Yi Wŏnsŏp (Seoul: Manhae Sasang Yŏn'guhoe, 1983). In these notes, I will cite the photolithographic reprint of Yongun's original Sino-Korean text, included as the appendix to this edition.

separate petitions to the Japanese cabinet (*chungch'u-wŏn*) and then the monastery supervisory board (*t'onggam-pu*), asking that they lift restrictions on monks and nuns taking a spouse and allow both the freedom (but not the obligation) to marry.[11]

Yongun's arguments in favor of married clergy appealed to common sense, Buddhist doctrinal teachings, and potential benefits to the society, religion, and the colonial government. Social stratification within Buddhism between the celibate clergy and the married laity, Yongun explained, inhibited the religion's ability to adapt to the changing circumstances of modern life. In an argument remarkably similar to those proposed by reformists within the Catholic church of our own age, celibacy, Yongun suggested, was no longer relevant in the present secular climate. Because this precept remained in place, many monks who would otherwise remain in the order if allowed to marry were instead seceding. Monks numbered only five to six thousand during Yongun's time, and their numbers would continue to remain small as long as this outdated restriction remained in place, he claimed. And privately, many monks were ignoring the rule on celibacy and marrying anyway, causing unnecessary scruples of conscience. If monks were allowed to marry and produce offspring who would be Buddhist by birth, Buddhism would be better able to compete with other religions and widen its own sphere of influence in society, thereby protecting its viability.

In addition to these practical benefits accruing from allowing monks to marry, doctrines fundamental to the Korean Buddhist tradition, such as the seminal notion of "the unimpeded interpenetration of all phenomena" (*sasa muae*), left no valid grounds for claiming that such a natural human affair was unwholesome and thus deserving of being prohibited. The main reason monks were practicing celibacy, Yongun argued, was because of the *Vinaya* prohibition against sexual intercourse. But this quintessential doctrine of interfusion offered an elegant solution to this restriction: since truth and falsity have no real essence, nor merit and demerit any fixed nature of their own, all such extremes are actually interfused. Thus celibacy and marriage are really no different, and neither should be demanded in monastic practice. True, marriage might make it rather more difficult to maintain monastic discipline and decorum. Nevertheless, Han argued, the potential benefits accruing to the religion from having monks who understood secular life were so great that marriage ought to be allowed.[12] The Buddha originally abolished marriage only as an expedient means of practice for those of lesser capacity—presumably

---

[11] Both memorials are appended to the section on marriage in Han Yongun, *Chosŏn Pulgyo yusillon*, pp. 63–64, 64–65.

[12] See discussion in Han Chŏngman, "Pulgyo yusin sasang," p. 1153, citing Han Yongun *chŏnjip* (The Collected Works of Han Yongun), p. 119.

meaning those monks still attached to sexual desire, or those too dull to understand this doctrine of interfusion, though Yongun does not clarify precisely what he means here. While this prohibition had not been an inviolate feature of Buddhism since the inception of the religion, it nevertheless was an ancient ecclesiastical law. Therefore the monks could not individually decide to ignore it and start marrying on their own. A government proclamation was necessary to allow marriage. Neither agency, however, responded to Yongun's petition.[13]

Rebuffed by the government, Han Yongun instead tried to lobby the ecclesiastical leaders of Korean Buddhism to accept such a move. In his "Essay on the Future of Buddhism and the Question of Whether Monks and Nuns Should Be Allowed to Marry" in his *Chosŏn Pulgyo yusillon* (On the Reformation of Korean Buddhism),[14] Yongun reiterated his arguments in systematic fashion, exploring the rationale behind the prohibition against clergy marriage and justifying why it was no longer applicable in contemporary society. Han lists the four major arguments for prohibiting marriage and repudiates each, as follows.

1. Clergy marriage controverts ethical norms (*hae ŏ yulli*). Yongun replies that most people consider the greatest ethical sin to be not marriage, but a lack of filial piety. By not carrying on the lineage of the family, the celibate monk is offending the hundreds of thousands of generations of both ancestors and potential successors. Yongun here has simply revived a perennial argument, used often against Buddhism throughout its history in East Asia, that celibates were unfilial; but it is a startling twist that a progressive Buddhist is now using it against more conservative factions within the order.

2. Clergy marriage injures the nation (*hae ŏ kukka*). Han replies that in civilized countries (meaning the West), where people are free to choose their own marriage partners, the population has expanded rapidly, allowing rapid economic and social progress as well. This may seem to us today to be a rather naive position for Yongun to adopt, but it is drawn from wider arguments of an emerging Korean nationalism. Yongun's position resonates in particular with those of progressive intellectuals after the 1880s, who felt that fundamental changes were necessary in traditional Korean society in order to support the establishment of a modern nation-state along Western lines.[15]

---

[13] For insightful discussion of Yongun's rationale for allowing monks to marry, see Yi Nŭnghwa, *Chosŏn Pulgyo t'ongsa* (A Comprehensive History of Korean Buddhism) (1918; reprint, Seoul: Ŭryu Munhwasa, 1959), vol. 1, pp. 617–20.

[14] Han Yongun, *Chosŏn Pulgyo yusillon*, pp. 58–63.

[15] See Michael Edson Robinson, *Cultural Nationalism in Colonial Korea, 1920–1925*, Korean Studies of the Henry M. Jackson School of International Studies (Seattle: University of Washington Press, 1988), esp. chap. 1.

3. Clergy marriage impedes proselytization (*hae ŏ p'ogyo*). Although Buddhists are trying to disseminate their religion throughout the world, if they restrict marriage and do not allow potential adherents to have a family, Yongun explains, who would have any interest in converting to Buddhism? And even if they were successful in convincing some people to ordain, they would finally only revert to lay life anyway.

4. Clergy marriage inhibits reform (*hae ŏ p'unghwa*). Humans have strong desires for food and sex; indeed, persons who have physical bodies but say they have no such desires are braggarts and liars. But if people forcibly try to repress their desires by clinging to the precepts, the stronger those desires will become, bringing immense grief on them and rendering any happiness impossible. "If we reflect upon Buddhist history after the end of the Koryŏ dynasty," Yongun tells us, "we see that the attempt to maintain the monkish purity ruined Buddhism as a whole." Yongun suggests here that the outmoded, conservative response of Buddhism to the challenge of the Neo-Confucian persecution—holding fast to the precepts—led to its present dire straits. Moral reforms stood a better chance of succeeding if marriage were allowed than if Buddhism demanded that monks force themselves to maintain an outmoded, irrelevant precept.

Han's petitions and lobbying to allow marriage initially gained little support within the Buddhist order. In March 1913, for example, at a meeting of the abbots of the (then) thirty head monasteries, an agreement was reached prohibiting wives from living in the temples, as well as forbidding women from lodging overnight.[16] But these restrictions were difficult to maintain, given the calls for secularization occurring among some of the reformers within the order and the support the Japanese governor-general later offered for a married clergy. Eventually, monks maintaining celibacy were in the minority. Finally, in October 1926, the prohibition against marriage was repealed by the head abbots, who were the representatives to the centralized ecclesiastical council controlled by the Japanese. From that point on, monks were officially allowed to marry (*taech'ŏ*) and eat meat (*sigyuk*). Within three years, some 80 percent of monasteries formally eliminated the restriction on having wives in residence, marking the end of an era for traditional Korean Buddhism and the beginnings of a full-fledged schism in the order between married monks (*taech'ŏsŭng*) and celibate monks (*pigusŭng*).[17]

The married clergy instituted during the Japanese colonial period forced profound changes in Korean monastic life, changes that continue

---

[16] *Taemaesin*, 16 March 1913; excerpted in *Han'guk kŭnse Pulgyo paengnyŏnsa* (The Last Century of Buddhism in Korea) (Seoul: Minjoksa, n.d.), vol. 1, *kwŏn* 1, *Sŭngdan p'yŏnnyŏn*, p. 43.

[17] Takahashi, *Richō Bukkyo*, p. 953; Kang Sŏkchu and Pak Kyŏnggŭu, *Pulgyo kŭnse paengnyŏn*, pp. 70–73.

to have an impact on the contemporary tradition. Monks with families needed guaranteed sources of income, prompting monks to accumulate private property and often take gainful employment. Such moves not only reduced the amount of property held in common by the monasteries, thus creating economic hardship for the bhikṣus who refused to take secular jobs, but also limited the amount of time spent in such traditional monastic vocations as doctrinal study, meditation practice, and proselytization. Conveniently for the Japanese colonial administration as well, married monks were more sedentary, tied as they were to their families and jobs, and thus less able than celibate monks to travel freely about the country, fomenting demonstrations or possibly spying.

POSTLIBERATION REFORMS

The conflict between married and celibate factions intensified with liberation from Japan after World War II and, especially, after the Korean War ended in 1953. The celibate monks sought to reassert what they perceived to be the indigenous lifeways of Korean Buddhism and to remove all traces of Japanese influence—what they termed a "purification movement" (chŏnghwa undong). As part of this movement, the celibates launched a vigorous campaign against the married monks who had dominated the ecclesiastical hierarchy during the Japanese colonial period.

On 5 August 1955, President Syngman Rhee (Yi Sŭngman) issued an order calling for the resignation of all "Japanized" monks (Waesaek sŭngnyŏ) from monastic positions, an order that was to herald the eventual restoration of the celibate bhikṣus to hegemony within Korean Buddhism.[18] But the married monks refused to cede control of the monasteries without a fight. With continued, and increasingly violent, confrontations occurring over title to the monasteries, the Ministry of Education proposed a compromise plan, which would have yielded to the celibate bhikṣus title to thirty major monasteries. While the married monks did

[18] Rhee's sympathy for the celibate monks stemmed from a visit to one of the monasteries controlled by the married monks. Rhee is said to have been appalled to find women's clothes hanging from clotheslines around the temple compound and decided then to help restore the celibates to control of Korean Buddhism. For discussion of this event and its impact on Rhee's subsequent policies, see Kang Sŏkchu and Pak Kyŏnggŭn, Pulgyo kŭnse paengnyŏn, pp. 241–44; Yi Kiyŏng, "Pulgyo sasang" (Korean Thought), in Han'guk hyŏndae munhwasa taegye (Outline of Contemporary Cultural History in Korea) (Seoul: Koryŏ University, Minjok Munhwa Yŏn'guso, 1985), vol. 2, pp. 749–50; Yi Hŭisu, T'och'akhwa kwajŏng-esŏ pon Han'guk Pulgyo (Korean Buddhism as a Process of Indigenization) (Seoul: Pulsŏ Pogŭpsa, 1971), pp. 189–91.

finally turn over two monasteries (Pongŭn-sa and Kaeun-sa) to the bhikṣus, they refused to award them any of their other property.[19]

Despite widespread nativistic contempt for the married monks, the bhikṣus were also not immune from criticism. One of the charges commonly made against them was their poor observance of the Buddhist precepts. During a debate in the National Assembly on 13 June 1955 concerning the dispute between the married and celibate monks, a representative noted, "Nowadays, one cannot find a single monk who is keeping all of the 250 precepts of the Buddhist *Vinaya*; hence, in this country there are no real bhikṣus."[20] Such stinging criticism may be one reason why there has been such a resurgence of interest in the *Vinaya* among contemporary Korean monks and the establishment of *Vinaya* study centers at several monasteries. The bhikṣus seem to recognize that to legitimate their claim to being the true representatives of the Korean Buddhist tradition, they would have to show themselves to be the transmitters of an orthodox Korean Buddhist practice and way of life.

The married monks, by contrast, presented themselves as devoted to teaching, proselytizing, and eleemosynary activities among the masses. Bhikṣus, they claimed, were but ignorant meditators, unable to teach because they did not have the requisite knowledge of Buddhist doctrine. Simply because the bhikṣus were celibate did not mean they were superior to the married monks, whose religious work spoke more eloquently than some vague, poorly practiced ideal such as *Vinaya* observance.

Throughout the rest of the 1950s, the schismatic battle for control of the monasteries was fought by lawyers in the courts and by the monks themselves on the monastic campuses. Most litigation was resolved in favor of the celibate monks, but these court victories were often hollow. In many cases, the married monks refused to abandon the monasteries that had long been their homes, and the bhikṣus were compelled to live together awkwardly with the married monks and their families. In the face of such intransigence, bhikṣus sometimes resorted to physical force to remove the married monks from the monasteries; indeed, older bhikṣus with whom I have spoken told many stories of celibates ordaining young thugs off the streets to bring muscle to their movement. (One of

[19] See Chŏng Pyŏngjo, "Han'guk Pulgyo ŭi hyŏnhyang kwa munjejŏm" (The Present Condition of Korean Buddhism and Problematic Points), in *Pulgyo yŏn'gu* (Buddhist Studies) 2 (1986), p. 196. This is one of the few scholarly articles written concerning the post-Liberation period of Korean Buddhism. There is, however, an invaluable collection of primary materials (newspaper reports, excerpts from magazine articles, excerpts from government documents, etc.) gathered from these fractious decades included in *Han'guk kŭnse Pulgyo paengnyŏnsa*, 2 vols. Although the printing is maddeningly illegible, any historian who has the patience to work his or her way carefully through this collection will glean important insights about this period.

[20] *Tonga Ilbo* (East Asian Daily News), 16 June 1955.

the biggest problems they said this policy created was how to handle these thugs once the battles over the control of the monasteries were won.) But both sides in the conflict were truculent and refused to compromise. Married monks rioted in monasteries and demonstrated in Seoul when they were defeated in litigation.[21] But bhikṣus too were equally unruly, as when several were arrested in 1960 for disorderly conduct in the Supreme Court Building.[22] Finally, in March 1962, the government was forced to step in to mediate the conflict and ordered an extraordinary assembly convened of both celibate and married monks. That convocation was told to organize a unified Buddhist administrative organ, and the government made it clear that it would manage the monasteries directly if cooperation failed.[23] In January 1962, a Buddhist Reconstruction Committee was finally organized, with fifty members drawn from both factions to bring about the reconciliation and centralized ecclesiastical control of monasteries held by the two groups.[24] But such joint control remained an elusive goal, given the intractableness of the two sides. Ultimately, two separate orders were established. On 12 April 1962, the celibate bhikṣus formally organized themselves into the Chogye-chong,[25] the traditional name of the predominant Buddhist order during the Koryŏ and Chosŏn dynasties. The married monks established the T'aego-chong, taking their name from the late Koryŏ period monk T'aego Pou (1301–1382), who was presumed to have brought the Chinese Lin-chi (Kor. Imje) lineage to Korea at the end of the Koryŏ period, and to whom most subsequent Korean Buddhists traced their transmission line. There is now little official communication between the T'aego and Chogye orders, let alone any form of centralized Buddhist administrative organ for all the sects of contemporary Buddhism.

Government support for the celibate monks ultimately culminated in a series of litigation successes. In 1961, after nearly a decade of court victories, the Supreme Court finally ruled in favor of the bhikṣus and formally awarded the celibates title to virtually all of the major monasteries of the nation. The married monks were understandably bitter about the ruling and tried various subterfuges to subvert it. According to the main news organ of the celibates, Tae-Han Pulgyo (Korean Buddhism), the

[21] As but one of many examples, on 14 March 1961, fifty-three married monks invaded Pulguk-sa and fought against the celibate monks who had assumed control of that monastery; see the report in Tonga Ilbo, 15 March 1961.

[22] The arrests were finally stayed on 7 January 1961, after the Supreme Court ruled in favor of the Chogye Order in the dispute. See Tae-Han Pulgyo (Korean Buddhism), 25 February 1961.

[23] See the reports in Tonga Ilbo, 18 March 1962 and 24 March 1962.

[24] Tae-Han Pulgyo, 1 September 1962.

[25] More precisely the Taehan Pulgyo Chogye-chong (The Chogye Order of Korean Buddhism).

married monks submitted false evidence in favor of their claims and illegally invaded temples that bhikṣus had occupied, trying to retake them. They attempted, the newspaper claimed, to subvert the installation of Tongsan sŭnim (1890–1965) as supreme patriarch (chongjŏng) of the Chogye Order by submitting to the Ministry of Culture and Information, which was supervising the elections, false evidence that he was unworthy of the appointment.[26] The loss of most of its major monasteries was a major blow to the T'aego Order. That sect now retains only a few of the small urban temples that were built during the Japanese occupation. The T'aego Order continues to decline, barely able to ordain sufficient numbers of new monks to staff even the few temples that remain in its control. Its survival beyond the present generation is very much in doubt.

Two decades of internecine strife had so preoccupied the Buddhists that they neglected to create much of a presence for themselves within wider Korean society. As the litigation came to an end, the Chogye Order finally began to give serious consideration to measures that would help to make Buddhism more relevant to contemporary lay Koreans. Filling the vacuum partially created by the Buddhist neglect of proselytization, Christian missionaries had made immense inroads in Korea, especially after the Korean War. The reasons for Christianity's spectacular successes in Korea are varied and complex, and beyond the scope of this short survey.[27] But what can hardly be questioned is that Koreans came to associate Christianity with modernization, democratization, and social and economic progress. Buddhism, by contrast, was often viewed as part of the insular worldview and backward society that had brought so much suffering to Korea over the last century. Even though the Buddhist purification movement had received much coverage in the press, Buddhist monks still had minimal contacts with ordinary Koreans and so were unable to counter this pervasive impression.

Publication of the Pulgyo sŏngjŏn (Buddhist Bible) on 7 December 1972,[28] a one-volume anthology of major Buddhist scriptures in vernacular Korean, was one of the first public attempts made by the Chogye Order to make Buddhism accessible and relevant to contemporary lay people. Since virtually all the basic texts of Korean Buddhism are composed in Sino-Korean (literary Chinese), few Koreans could read them without special training. Such vernacular translations were crucial if Buddhism was to have any hope of success in proselytization. But the fact

---

[26] Tae-Han Pulgyo, April 1961.

[27] For an accessible survey, see Donald S. Clark, Christianity in Modern Korea, Asian Agenda Report, no. 5 (Lanham, Md.: University Press of America, 1986).

[28] Pulgyo sŏngjŏn (Buddhist Bible), ed. by Tae-Han Pulgyo Chogye chong Pulgyo sŏngjŏn p'yŏnch'anhoe (Seoul: Tae-Han Pulgyo Chogye-chong Pulgyo Sŏngjŏn P'yŏnch'anhoe, 1972; frequent reprints).

that Buddhists adopted the term "bible" (sŏngjŏn) for their own collection of sacred scriptures shows the impact Christian missionaries were having in Korean religious life. Christians were setting the agenda, and Buddhists were scrambling to react.

Because all the major religious centers of Korean Buddhism were located deep in the mountains (after the disestablishment of city monasteries during the Chosŏn persecutions), the monks remained isolated from the increasingly urbanized population of Korea. Even though some city monasteries were founded to provide centers for urban Buddhist activities, their numbers were hardly sufficient to be a major force in Korean religious life. This paucity of monasteries is especially striking when contrasted with the ubiquity of Christian churches in Korea. When you drive through the Korean countryside, you will see Christian churches in almost every village and town. These churches are often prominently located on a high knoll, dominating the landscape as they would in New England, and provide a potent Western symbol to inspire and galvanize the population. Buddhism has no such presence among the population.

But the increasingly powerful Christian church was not the only threat to Buddhist institutions. The social agenda of the newly independent Korean government also had a serious impact on Buddhism. Since at least the Koryŏ dynasty, monasteries had been deeded vast tracts of paddy and forest land, which they could then lease out for income. But the continued disputes after liberation caused both confiscation of and damage to monastic properties and prompted a series of land reforms that drastically reduced the monasteries' land holdings, and in turn their annual income. Holdings of paddy land by Korean monasteries dropped from sixteen million p'yŏng (one pyŏng is approximately 3.952 square yards) in 1945 to only three million p'yŏng in 1965.[29] Though the government offered financial incentives if monasteries would develop their grounds as national parklands, these government subventions hardly made up for the economic shortfall. The financial plight was especially severe for monasteries that required extensive rebuilding after the destruction wrought by the Korean War.

Despite all these various threats to its continued existence, however, the monastic tradition of Buddhism in Korea remains remarkably resilient. While certainly affected by the world around them, Buddhist monks have been reluctant to make radical changes in their institutions and way of life. The monasteries remain bastions of elite culture, which as yet brook few challenges from the increasingly Westernized culture of secular Korea. As of 1986, a Chogye Order census claimed that it controlled 1,628 monasteries and has ordained some 7,708 monks and 4,153 nuns. The

[29] *Tae-Han Pulgyo,* 24 October 1965.

order claims the adherence of over fourteen million laypersons, though this number is certainly inflated, given the perennial fluidity of religious affiliations in East Asia. The Chogye Order also supports one major Buddhist university, Tongguk Taehakkyo, which has about fifteen thousand students enrolled in its nine colleges and four graduate schools. The university also includes special seminaries for training monks and nuns. Finally, the order administers another eight Buddhist high schools, one elementary school, and two other academic institutes.[30] These numbers attest to the continued impact Buddhism has in contemporary Korea.[31]

The Chogye Order is administered from a national office (*chongmuwön*), headquartered at Chogye-sa in Seoul.[32] Chogye-sa was first built in 1929 and reconstructed and expanded in 1955 to serve as the headquarters of the celibate monks. The Chogye Order adopted much of the administrative structure put in place under the Japanese occupation, including the head monastery (*ponsan*) system.[33] The Chogye head office

Census of Korean Buddhism (1972–1983)

Date of Census	Temples (total) Registered	Unregistered	Religious Monks	Nuns	Lay Adherents Male	Female
12/20/1972	1,915		18,599		8,095,381	
	na	na	12,254	6,345	2,131,927	5,963,454
10/31/1979	8,032		23,480		13,390,975	
	2,610	5,422	15,389	8,091	4,364,600	9,026,375
10/31/1980	7,244		22,260		12,329,720	
	3,068	4,176	13,978	8,282	3,872,293	8,457,427
12/31/1983	7,253		20,755		11,130,288	
	3,163	4,090	14,206	6,549	3,969,584	7,160,704

Source: This chart appears in Chŏng Pyŏngjo (1986, p. 198), and is based on census information published by the Korean Ministry of Culture and Information. These figures may differ from those claimed by the various orders of Korean Buddhism.

[30] These figures are taken from *Korean Buddhism* (Seoul: Chogye Order, 1986), chap. 5.

[31] After expanding through the 1970s, Buddhist institutions seem to have been on the decline during the 1980s, both in total number of temples and ordained religious, as the accompanying chart suggests. Chŏng Pyŏngjo ("Han'guk Pulgyo ŭi hyŏnhyang kwa munjejŏm," p. 199) attributes this decline to the continued instability in Buddhist religious orders, the backwardness of Buddhist missionary activities, the small numbers of younger Buddhists, and the shortage of meeting halls and proselytizing materials. The apparent increase in monasteries from the early 1970s to the early 1980s is not relevant, since the earlier figures did not count unregistered temples, which are small private temples, often housed in a private home and staffed by the lay owner of the house, not a monk or nun.

[32] Chogye-sa is located in Susong-tong in the Chongno district of Seoul.

[33] During the Japanese occupation period, there were 31 head monasteries, which administered a network of 1384 smaller branch monasteries.

loosely supervises a national network of twenty-five head monasteries, each in charge of its own religious parish (*kyogu ponsa*), which in turn control between them a total of 1,550 branch monasteries.[34] Of these twenty-five head monasteries, four have been designated *ch'ongnim* (lit. "grove of trees"; the Sinitic translation for Skt. *vana* or *vindhyavana*), where separate compounds for Sŏn meditation, doctrinal study, *Vinaya* studies, and Pure Land recitation have been established: Haein-sa, Songgwang-sa, T'ongdo-sa, and most recently Sudŏk-sa. My account will focus on the life led at these largest centers of the Korean monastic tradition, and especially that at Songgwang-sa.

After this brief survey of contemporary Buddhism in Korea, let me explore the daily and annual schedules followed by all Korean monasteries, before turning to a short history of Songgwang-sa, the monastery that will be the focus of this book.

[34] The twenty-five head monasteries of the Chogye Order (with number of branch monasteries in parentheses) are as follows: Chogye-sa (187); Yongju-sa (66); Sinhŭng-sa (35); Wŏlchŏng-sa (68); Pŏpchu-sa (59); Magok-sa (78); Sudŏk-sa (37); Chikchi-sa (58); Tonghwa-sa (72); Ŭnhae-sa (52); Pulguk-sa (61); Haein-sa (82); Ssanggye-sa (51); Pŏmŏ-sa (114); T'ongdo-sa (92); Koun-sa (57); Kŭmsan-sa (87); Paengyang-sa (30); Hwaŏm-sa (23); Sŏnam-sa (1); Songgwang-sa (41); Taehŭng-sa (48); Kwanŭm-sa (38); Sŏnun-sa (36); and Pongsŏn-sa (77). Chŏng Pyŏngjo, "Han'guk Pulgyo ŭi hyŏnhyang kwa munjejŏm," p. 200.

CHAPTER TWO

Daily and Annual Schedules

"SURI, SURI, MAHASURI," the chief verger intones from the center of the courtyard, the predawn stillness abruptly shattered by the rhythmic beats of his wooden clacker (*mokt'ak*) resounding among the wooden buildings of the monastery campus. It is three in the morning and another day has begun at the Korean Buddhist monastery of Songgwang-sa.

As the verger slowly wends his way among the different compounds of the monastery, chanting the incantation from the *Thousand Hands Sūtra* (*Ch'ŏnsu-kyŏng*) and striking his clacker, the monks quickly rise.[1] At the first sharp crack of the clacker, the monks practicing in the meditation hall are up; they have only ten minutes to put away their bedding and wash up before the morning sitting period begins. The young monks on the support staff of the monastery rise and pull their floor desks away from the wall of the large hall that does triple duty as the monastery's main dormitory and refectory; they will spend these few precious minutes of free time before the start of morning service to study their primer of monastic discipline. In the postulants' room, the prospective ordinands force themselves to wake, still not used to the six hours of sleep and many exhausted from the long hours of work the previous day. Once they have roused themselves, they try to memorize a bit more of the chants they are learning before also attending the service. In the small individual rooms that ring the office compound, the treasurer has yet to retire; he has been up all night processing the entrance fees paid by the busloads of tourists who flocked to sightsee at the monastery the day before. It will be five in the morning before he will finally be able to get some rest, and he will be up again in a couple of hours to make a trip to the bank to deposit the proceeds. The elderly monks staying in private rooms in compounds around the monastery rise to quaff cups of tea brought to them by their attendants. After attending the service, they may write a few letters to the laypersons who offer support to them and their disciples. The vocations of these various groups of monks may each be different, but all are essential to the running of a large training center such as Songgwang-sa.

[1] The monk is free to recite almost any chant, though the *Thousand Hands Sūtra* is most common. For the full text of a standardized early morning wakeup chant (*chojo yegyŏng*), see Pulgyo sŏjŏk sent'ŏ, eds., *Pulgyo pŏbyo kŭgŭm* (Primer of the Essentials of the Buddhist Teachings) (Seoul: Hongbŏbwŏn, 1970), pp. 1–20.

Throughout the Korean peninsula, other monks are starting their day in much the same fashion, at monasteries that follow nearly identical schedules.

DAILY SERVICES

As the chief verger finishes his wakeup chant, a series of gongs, wooden fish, drums, and bells from the Bell and Drum Tower (Chonggo-ru) signal the impending start of the morning service at 3:45 A.M. This service takes place in the main buddha hall (*Taeung-chŏn*), the focus of the monastery's layout and the hub of ceremonial activities in the monastery.

As the large temple bell strikes twenty-eight times, the monastery residents make their way to the main buddha hall. The monks are arrayed inside the hall by their compound of residence (meditation hall, support division, etc.) and seniority (years as a novice or as a fully ordained monk). Monks always enter the buddha hall in their stocking feet through the same door, leaving their shoes outside on the concrete step. The support monks from the kitchen and office compounds enter through the left door and occupy that side of the hall. While the meditation monks do not attend regular morning or evening services, when they do join the assembly for the predinner ceremony at midday, they will occupy the right side of the hall. In a custom that differs from that followed in most Buddhist countries, in Korea the farther away a monk is from the image, the more senior he is. The seniormost monks occupy cushions at the very back of the hall, with the Sŏn master in the center, flanked on the left by the abbot (head of the support division of the monastery) and on the right by the rector (head of the practice division). The remaining senior monks and officeholders fan out towards the side walls in seniority order. At the very front of the hall are laypeople and postulants. They are often so far forward that the altar may actually be in back of them. Directly behind them in order are any nuns who may be visiting the monastery, novices, and newly ordained bhikṣus. Everyone at the temple except the meditation monks is expected to attend the service, though the proctor and others with pressing office duties are given much leeway about participating.

Once the large temple bell has finished tolling, all the monks in the monastery should have assumed their spots in the hall. At that point someone in the congregation, usually one of the senior postulants, strikes three rounds on the large gong inside the hall to start the service. The verger strikes the mokt'ak once to have all the monks rise from their seated positions and then leads them in three full prostrations. There follows a devotional service honoring the buddhas, the bodhisattvas, and a few of the monks who played crucial roles in the development of Korean

Buddhism (for this chant, see the appendix). The only instrument used to mark the beat of the chant is the mokt'ak, the stylized Korean version of the hollow wooden fish (Ch. *mu-yü*) so popular in Chinese monasteries. The Sŏn master then recites alone a short prayer for the protection of the monastery and the nation, after which all the participants turn toward the painting of the dharma-general Wit'a (Wei-t'o) on the left wall and recite the *Heart Sūtra*. The participants bow together toward the altar, wheel around and bow to the Sŏn master and senior monks, and then file out of the hall in order of seniority. The whole ceremony has taken only about fifteen minutes.[2]

ANNUAL SCHEDULE

In addition to this daily schedule, which is about the same across the peninsula, Korean monasteries follow an annual schedule that is virtually identical as well. Korean monasteries divide their year into four three-month periods. Summer (the middle of the fourth through the middle of the seventh lunar months, usually May through August) and winter (the middle of the tenth through the middle of the first lunar months, usually November through February) are reserved for formal religious retreats (*kyŏlche*, lit. binding rule),[3] while spring and autumn are free seasons (*haeje*, lit. slackened rule).[4] During the retreat seasons, no monks in any of the monastic units are permitted to leave the monastery on anything other than temple business or the most urgent of personal matters, such as a death in the family. In the meditation hall, the monks are following a rigorous schedule of upwards of fourteen hours or more of sitting meditation practice daily. With the large number of residents at Songgwang-sa during the retreat period (well over a hundred monks, postulants, and lay workers), the monks in the various support positions (kitchen, office, attendants, etc.) will be kept busy all day long performing their incumbent duties. The postulants know they will have no free time at all once the morning service is over, and try to learn a few more verses of the required chants all monks must know, verses they will recite over and over throughout their workday until they are memorized.

Songgwang-sa is not nearly so hectic during the free seasons. The num-

---

[2] The procedure for evening service is virtually the same, omitting only the protection prayer. Other minor differences at night are that the sequence of instruments used in the Bell and Drum Tower is inverted, the large bell is tolled thirty-three times, and the gong inside the hall is struck only one round.

[3] For this term, see *Pai-chang ch'ing-kuei* 7, T 2025.48.1150a20–b4, and esp. 1153a26–c11.

[4] For this term, see ibid., 1155a14.

ber of resident monks will fall to twenty or so. In some free seasons the monastery seems utterly deserted during the first few weeks after the retreat is over—one monk staying by himself in the meditation hall, for example, or six monks plus the postulants attending morning services. Most of the monks in meditation hall will go off on "pilgrimage" (really more of a vacation) for the three months of the haeje break, not committing themselves to reside at another monastery until the week or so before the next retreat begins. Some of the younger support monks at Songgwang-sa—who during their first few years of working for their home monastery may never have had a chance to visit other temples— may finally get permission from their vocation master (ŭnsa) to travel to, say, T'ongdo-sa and pay their respects to the Sŏn master there. If they are determined to practice meditation or study in the seminary—and are willing to brave later the wrath of their vocation master back at Songgwang-sa—they may decide not to return to their home monastery (where they would be saddled again with duties) but to remain elsewhere for the next retreat. The postulants may finally find a few minutes after the noon meal to study the novice precepts, before going off to work in the fields in the afternoon. For everyone in the monastery, the free season provides a minor, but welcome, slackening of the rigid retreat schedule.

CEREMONIES AND COMMEMORATIVE SERVICES

The annual schedule followed in Korean monasteries, as in Zen monasteries elsewhere in East Asia, is punctuated by regular rituals and ceremonies, ranging from the New Year's celebration, to the Buddha's Birthday, to monthly commemorations of the monastery's past teachers. In China, documents detailing Ch'an monastic regulations, such as the *Pure Rules of Pai-chang* (*Pai-chang ch'ing-kuei*), suggest that ritual occupied a crucial spot in the religious life of Ch'an monasteries,[5] and Griffith Foulk's recent work on contemporary Japanese Zen monasticism details a busy schedule of ritual observances that continue throughout the year.[6] This seeming ubiquity of ritual is a bit deceptive, however. During my years as a monk in Korean Sŏn monasteries, such ceremonial events were actually a minor part of our life, more often viewed by the monks as oc-

[5] For these Ch'an monastic codes, see Martin Collcutt, *Five Mountains: The Rinzai Zen Monastic Institution in Medieval Japan*, Harvard East Asian Monographs, no. 85 (Cambridge: Harvard University Press, 1981), pp. 133–45.

[6] The annual observances held at Myōshin-ji, a head monastery of the Japanese Rinzai sect, are described in T. Griffith Foulk, "The Zen Institution in Modern Japan," in *Zen: Tradition and Transition*, ed. by Kenneth Kraft (New York: Grove Press, 1988), tab. 2, pp. 160–61.

casional nuisances than as events of real moment in our training. Only a few monks are directly involved in the majority of ceremonies: one or two monks who are ritual specialists perform the whole ceremony entirely on their own, without any audience at all. Only for the more important rituals does the rest of the congregation even attend, and usually as nothing more than silent witnesses. The entire assembly joins as active participants only for the most expensive of rituals: the large death ceremonies sponsored by the wealthiest of patrons. Even then, however, virtually all of the ritual is performed by the two official vergers, the rest of the monks joining only in a brief sūtra recitation.[7]

Why then do such ceremonies seem to be such a relatively insignificant part of the life of Sŏn practitioners in Korea? I suspect that, from a historical standpoint, some of this deemphasis derives from the difficult conditions Buddhism faced during the Chosŏn dynasty. During the Koryŏ period, when Buddhism occupied a central place in the national ideology, documents suggest that monasteries were heavily involved in ritual observances on behalf of Buddhist patrons, the monastery itself, and even the royal court.[8] The centuries of persecution during the Chosŏn dynasty, however, eradicated many of the associations among the monasteries, the state, and the wider Korean populace. The ceremonial role of Buddhist monasteries may have been severely impaired during this period, compelling the monks to turn to the more introspective vocations of meditation and scholarly exegesis, or simply to play the vital role of caretakers of the temples. Even though attempts are being made today to restore these connections between the laity and the monks, as I will explore in Chapter Six, Buddhist monks continue to place pride of place on meditation, followed well behind by scholarship. Ritual is commonly perceived as lower on the hierarchy of religious vocations than either meditation or doctrinal study, ranking about on a par with administration.

But the apparent emphasis on ceremonies and rituals that we find in the normative texts of the Zen tradition may again be deceptive. Rituals are clearly demarcated events, which are simply easier to study and keep track of than is the complex, "open-ended human process" (Rosaldo 1989) that is daily life. This bounded quality of rituals accounts for the

---

[7] During elaborate death ceremonies, the entire congregation of monks, meditation monks included, will read aloud the "P'u-yen; Poan" (Universal Eye Bodhisattva) chapter of the *Yüan-chüeh ching* (Book of Consummate Enlightenment), which describes a meditation on the parts of the body as a way of generating an understanding of impermanence; see *Yüan-chüeh ching*, T 842.17.914b–915b.

[8] Hung Yunsik, "Koryŏ Pulgyo ŭi sinang ŭirye" (Religious Rituals in Koryŏ Buddhism), in *Han'guk Pulgyo sasangsa* (History of Korean Buddhist Thought), Sungsan Pak Kilchin paksa hwagap kinyŏm, ed. by Sungsan Pak Kilchin paksa hwagap kinyŏm wiwŏnhoe (Pak Kilchin Festschrift Committee) (Iri, Chŏlla Pukto, Korea: Wŏn'gwang University Press, 1975), pp. 674–77.

preference ethnographers have always had for framing their descriptions of other cultures in terms of such rituals—puberty rites, marriage ceremonies, funerals, and so forth. Ethnographies tend to "focus on visibly bounded arenas where one can observe formal and repetitive events, such as ceremonies, rituals, and games. . . . Most ethnographers prefer to study events that have definite locations in space with marked centers and outer edges. Temporally, they have middles and endings. Historically, they appear to repeat identical structures by seemingly doing things today as they were done yesterday. Their qualities of fixed definition liberate such events from the untidiness of everyday life so that they can be 'read' like articles, books, or as we now say, *texts*."[9] The seeming importance of ritual in Zen texts may derive from a similar sort of tendency to describe the tradition in terms of events that have such definite locations in space and time. But when we look instead at monastic life as it is actually practiced—as involving complex, drawn-out processes of meditation, study, and work—such clearly demarcated rituals pale by comparison. Except for the handful of monks who become ritual specialists, the rest of the congregation remains almost completely unaffected by the ritual calendar.

Of the ceremonies that are regularly scheduled, among the more important are the commemorative services for the previous meditation masters of the monastery (sŏnsa-che), which occur the first day of each lunar month. Offerings are made at every shrine hall in the monastery, the only time that services are held in the many smaller shrines scattered around the complex. While there might be a more elaborate ceremony in larger shrines, these services are generally quite simple. After cleaning the hall, filling the water vessel on the altar, and placing a rice offering next to it, the verger of the shrine performs a brief ceremony, often consisting of nothing more than making three full prostrations while striking his bamboo clacker (chukpi). But even for these regular ceremonies, only about ten monks will be involved, expending about ten minutes of time apiece.

The largest commemorative service at Songgwang-sa is the annual observance for the founder of the monastery, Chinul (1158–1210), which is celebrated on full-moon day of the third lunar month, usually in mid-April. This ceremony is the biggest public event sponsored by the monastery, lasting for three full days and attracting several hundred laypeople for the duration. In addition to a public ceremony in remembrance of Chinul, which includes several lectures outlining his contributions to the Korean Buddhist tradition, Songgwang-sa also sponsors novice and full ordinations; a bodhisattva-precepts' ceremony is also held for the assembled laity. These ordinations will be discussed in subsequent chapters.

[9] Renato Rosaldo, *Culture and Truth: The Remaking of Social Analysis* (Boston: Beacon Press, 1989), p. 12.

Buddha's Birthday

The Buddha's Birthday (*Puch'ŏnim osin-nal*) is the highlight of the Buddhist ceremonial year in Korea, and is celebrated with opulent festivals at all temples throughout the country. In Korea, the Buddha's Birthday is considered to fall on the eighth day of the fourth lunar month, usually early in May, about two weeks prior to the beginning of the summer retreat. This holiday is noted for the large displays of paper lanterns lit by candles, which are strung from shrine to shrine throughout the monastery, and hung row upon row inside the central courtyard.

For a week prior to the ceremony, all the monks gather throughout the entire day to make the lanterns. As the Buddha's Birthday ceremony occurs during the free season, the monastery is usually well below full strength, leaving a lot of work for the few who remain in residence. Leftover lanterns from the previous year's celebration are taken out of storage, the faded paper removed, and the wire frames reused to make new lanterns. Strips of rice paper swabbed with wheat starch are pasted to the wire frame; once these have dried, decorations cut from colored tissue paper are pasted to the sides to create the finished lamp. The most ornate style is that of the lotus lantern (*yŏndŭng*), in which paper petals are cut and folded, and then pasted one by one over the entire surface of the lantern until it resembles a large lotus flower. While most of the monks could handle rolling and pinching the small pieces of paper that would be used for the petals, few of us showed much talent for pasting them aesthetically into recognizable lotus shapes. After a few pathetic attempts, we usually turned this job over to the laywomen who worked in the monastery or to nuns from one of Songgwang-sa's branch temples. As the lamps are finished, they are stored in an enclosed veranda to the side of the dining room until the big day.

All the lanterns must be finished the day before the ceremony. The lay workers have already strung rope between all the small shrines and halls throughout the monastery. The next morning, after sweeping the grounds, the lanterns are taken out of storage by the monks and strung from the wire. (If rain is expected, the lanterns will instead be hung in bunches under the eaves of the shrines.) The monks man a booth at the main gate of the monastery where lanterns are offered for "sale." The custom is that Buddhists who wish to make merit for their families buy a lantern and have the monks write a merit certificate for it, which includes all of their immediate family and perhaps deceased relatives. Pŏpchŏng *sŭnim*, an eminent scholar-monk resident at Songgwang-sa, traced this custom to the *Jātaka* tales of the Buddha's previous lives. He told the story of a poor woman who sold her hair in order to buy some oil, which she then used to light a small lantern on behalf of the Buddha. Many rich people had already offered huge lamps to the Buddha; though embarrassed by her small lantern, she made the offering anyway. Later, a strong wind blew out all the lanterns except that of the poor woman, showing thereby the strength of her devotion to the Buddha. It is with such devotion in mind that Pŏpchŏng said lanterns should be offered on the Buddha's Birthday.[10] When I resided at Songgwang-sa, the largest lamps inside the main shrine hall itself were always dedicated to President Park Chung-hee and his wife (who was considered to be a strong supporter of Buddhism, at a time when many government officials were adherents of Protestant Christian sects), the governor of the province, the county chief, and other important political figures.

The regular midday dinner service is greatly extended on this day. Many congratulatory speeches are made by local government figures, representatives of Buddhist lay organizations, and monastery officials. Finally, the Sŏn master gives a dharma lecture, and the regular dinner service is then held. Afterwards, the monks carry all the offering dishes back into the refectory, where a regular offering ceremony takes place at a makeshift altar. Finally, everyone feasts on the huge amount of delicacies.

The monks are then supposedly free until later in the afternoon. But because at Songgwang-sa the Buddha's Birthday is the one time of year when the entire monastery is open to the public, most monks are charged with guarding the various shrines and halls. Private compounds where the monks actually live and practice are always off limits during the regular year so that tourists will not disturb the monks. On this day, however, everyone is free to roam at will, the only restriction being that laypeople are not allowed to open the doors to the meditation hall or private rooms—a restriction that is, nevertheless, frequently disregarded. Imagine the surprise of an elderly "grandmother" (halmŏni) when she slid open the paper-covered door to peek inside and found an American monk—and one who could reprimand her in Korean, besides!

At around four in the afternoon, any remaining lamps are hung around

---

[10] The locus classicus for this lamplighting custom appears in the *Fo-shuo shih-teng kung-teh ching* (Sūtra Spoken by the Buddha on the Merit Deriving from Offering Lamps), T 702.16.804a–b. It describes the merit forthcoming from offering lamps as follows: "If someone, wanting to make merit, respectfully offers a bright lamp or even a small candle before the images enshrined inside a stupa or shrine . . . , that merit cannot be comprehended by any of the śrāvakas or pratyekabuddhas; only the buddhas, the tathāgatas, can comprehend it" (p. 804a20–24). The custom of offering lamps is also mentioned in *P'u-hsien p'u-sa hsing-yüan tsan* (Eulogy to the Vows Practiced by the Bodhisattva Samantabhadra), T 297.10.880a18, 25. For the Lamplighting Ceremony (Yŏndŭng-hoe) during the Koryŏ period, see Hung Yunsik, "Koryŏ Pulgyo ŭi sinang ŭirye," pp. 674–77. For the origins of the Yŏndŭng-hoe, see Yi Pyŏngdo, *Han'guksa: Chungse p'yŏn* (Korean History: Medieval Period) (Seoul: Ŭryu Munhwasa, 1976), pp. 292–94.

the monastery in preparation for the evening lighting ceremony. If there are extra lanterns that were not sold to lay adherents, the monks wrote the names of their own families and relatives on a merit certificate and pasted it to a leftover lantern, so that they too could earn merit for their families. Despite "leaving home" (ch'ulga), the monks still feel the need to express their filial piety in this subtle way.[11]

That evening, the laypeople who have "bought" a lantern come to the monastery and search for their lamp. Once they have found it, they place a candle inside the lantern and light it. At around 7:30 P.M., after the evening service, the monks go out and light any lanterns that the purchasers have not lit themselves. The monks must maintain constant vigilance while the candles are burning; if any lantern should catch fire, they either knock it to the ground or blow out the flames, so that adjoining lanterns are not ignited. For the rest of the evening, the invocation "Sŏk-kamoni-pul" (Śākyamuni Buddha) will be chanted in the main buddha hall over the public address system, with monks taking half-hour shifts leading the chanting. Everyone, both laypeople and monks, will walk around the monastery viewing the lanterns from different angles. The monks always take a short hike up into the hills surrounding the monastery to get a sweeping view of the whole panorama. Finally, in late evening, the candles are blown out and the ceremony comes to an end. The next morning all the paper is cleaned up from the monastery and the lanterns are taken as is to the storage area to be saved for use next year.

At many temples, and especially the smaller missionary centers in the cities, the temple will hold a "Bathing the Buddha" ceremony (yokpul-sik) in the morning before the Buddha's Birthday ceremony proper.[12] A small image of Śākyamuni Buddha immediately after birth—hand held high over his head, taking his first seven steps, and proclaiming, "In heaven and on earth, I alone am foremost (Pali: aggo'ham asmi lokassa jeṭṭho'ham asmi lokassa)"[13]—is placed in a miniature building rather like a manger and draped with flowers. Laypeople line up and, after placing an offering before the Buddha, receive a cup of "holy water," which they pour over the Buddha's head to "bathe" him. They are then given a cup of pure medicinal water from a large tub to drink. Throughout the long queue for their turn to bathe the Buddha, the laity chant together the name of Śākyamuni Buddha. In addition, if the temple has any relics (sari;

[11] For the persistence of observances of filial piety among monks throughout the Asian traditions of Buddhism, see Gregory Schopen, "Filial Piety and the Monk in the Practice of Indian Buddhism: A Question of 'Sinicization' Viewed from the Other Side," T'oung Pao 70 (1984): 110–26.

[12] For an account of how this ceremony was celebrated in Chinese Ch'an monasteries, see Pai-chang ch'ing-kuei 2, T 2025.48.1116a.

[13] Ch'ang A-han ching, T 1.1.4c1–2; Mahāpadāna Suttanta, Dīgha-nikāya ii.15.

Skt. *śarīra*) in its possession, these are displayed on this day, to be viewed and honored by the lay people. Although this ceremony is one of the simplest performed in the monastery, it is one of the largest income-producing events of the year, especially for smaller temples in the cities. For financial as well as pious reasons, the monasteries go all out to ensure the success of these ceremonies.

New Year's Celebration

One of the few official respites from the daily monastic routine occurs during the celebration of the lunar New Year (*sŏllal*), which usually occurs in late January or early February of the solar calendar.[14] This celebration begins on New Year's Eve and continues for the next three days. Except for morning and evening services, the monks have virtually the whole period off to socialize, play games, and of course to feast.

On New Year's Eve, the entire monastery is cleaned in preparation for the events to come. Every monk in the monastery will be busy with assigned tasks that will occupy them throughout most of the day. Incense holders, candle holders, and other ritual utensils, all of which are made of stainless steel or bronze, are washed and polished. Even the installed buddha and bodhisattva images will be wiped off with a wet cloth and polished, if necessary. After the monastery is clean, a large bath is prepared for all the monks.

Early in the morning on New Year's Day, the monks gather for morning chanting. But on this day even the meditation monks join, the only time during the entire year that they attend regular services. The kitchen staff will have prepared a massive offering in front of the altar in the main buddha hall. After the usual morning prayer in the middle of the service, the Sŏn master chants alone a long supplication (*ch'ugwŏn*), calling upon a lengthy list of buddhas and bodhisattvas to intercede on the monastery's behalf during the upcoming year. As each of the names of the buddhas and bodhisattvas is mentioned in the course of the prayer, all the monks bow in unison. Once the regular service is finished, the monks return to their compounds and the verger of the main buddha hall continues the ceremony on his own. About an hour later, at around 5:30 in the morning, the temple gong sounds to summon the monks back to the main buddha hall, again dressed in full ceremonial regalia. At that time the regular dinner offering, which otherwise occurs before noon, is performed. During that ceremony, which takes another twenty minutes, the Sŏn master

[14] For secular New Year's celebrations, see Griffin Dix, "The New Year's Ritual and Village Social Structure," in *Religion and Ritual in Korean Society*, ed. by Laurel Kendall and Griffin Dix (Berkeley: Institute of East Asian Studies, 1987), pp. 93–117.

recites a special prayer asking that everyone connected with the monastery have a happy new year and make great strides in his practice. Afterwards, each monk takes part of the huge offering down from the altar and carries it back to the refectory. There, the head verger and one assistant continue with another offering service. The makeshift altar there is taken down, the food whisked back to the kitchen, and breakfast finally served. New Year's breakfast is the biggest meal of the day, if not the entire year, and is usually far too much for even the monks to finish. Afterwards the monks retire to their various compounds, where they eat special candies and fruit and down cup after cup of warm milk.

Later in the morning, the monks go off in groups of three to five to pay respects to the elder monks and senior officials around the monastery. As they enter a senior monk's room, they prostrate themselves three times and wish their senior success in his practice and good health during the year to come. The senior monk often tells a story about his own career to encourage his juniors in their own practice, or simply exhorts his visitors to strive harder this year. After this brief exchange, the monks prostrate themselves again, and then withdraw to visit another monk on their rounds. After the postulants have finished cleaning up after the huge breakfast, they, too, will go off in groups to offer their own New Year's greetings.

Once the salutations are finished, the monks again return to their compounds to relax and chat. A small midday lunch is served, and the afternoon is again free. Since New Year comes about two weeks before the end of the winter retreat period, the Sŏn master usually delivers to the meditation monks the mail he has been holding for them over the previous ten weeks. The master's attendant also supplies everyone with writing materials, and the meditation monks pass their free time composing replies. The New Year's celebration often marks the effective end of the winter meditation retreat. After hearing from their friends, many of the monks are already thinking of where they will be going after the retreat is over and it is often difficult to regain any practice momentum in the hall after the break from routine.

After evening service, which the meditation monks need not attend, the proctor will throw a big party for all the monks in the refectory. The senior monks meet in the Sŏn master's room for their own private gathering, which is much more staid than the sometimes raucous horseplay that goes on at the main party. The proctor brings out still more food for the monks attending, but the highlights of the evening are various games, which are only played during the New Year's break. One of the most popular is yut nori, a traditional Korean board game, rather like Chinese checkers. Two teams each have four markers (yut mal) apiece, which they must move around the board (yut p'an). Four wooden sticks flattened on one side (*yut karak*) are thrown up in the air. If one flat side lands up, the team can move one of its markers forward one space; if two flat sides are up, two spaces, and so forth. The first team to get all four of its markers around the board wins.[15] The monastery divides into competing teams, often the meditation monks versus the support staff, and the losers are forced to carry the winners piggyback around the room. Later in the evening, as usually happens at Korean parties, everyone eventually takes turns singing songs for the group. Americans, very much unlike Koreans, seem to have lost their appreciation for traditional folk songs. It was enough for me to belt out one verse of "I've Been Workin' on the Railroad" during these inevitable songfests.

Another game known only in the monasteries that is also played on New Year's Day is *Sŏngbul-to* (Achieving Buddhahood), a board game rather like a spiritual form of Monopoly. A makeshift board is laid out on the floor and the players move tokens around the board, seeking to avoid falling into hell and trying eventually to pass beyond all the six realms of existence—denizens of hell, hungry ghosts, animals, humans, aśuras, and gods—until they have achieved buddhahood. In a more complicated version of the game that has recently been published, the board takes the player through all the six realms of existence and eventually leads to the fifty-two stages of the Buddhist path. The player finally arrives at the five houses of Ch'an, culminating in the Imje (Ch. Lin-chi; Jpn. Rinzai) school. From there the player jumps to the three bodies of the buddha until he ultimately reaches "great enlightenment" (*taegak*) at the top of the board.[16]

The day after New Year's is again free. Noon may find a special offering by one of the monastery's lay supporters and, indeed for the next week, there will be frequent offerings by the laity. After perhaps a smaller party that evening, the monastery will return to its regular routine the next morning, and the winter retreat will continue.

Now that we know a bit about the daily and annual schedules of Korean temples, let me look more closely at the monastery that will be the venue of this book: Songgwang-sa.

[15] See, among many possible references to *yut nori*, Ch'oe Sangsu, *Han'guk minsok nori ŭi yŏn'gu* (Studies in Korean Folk Games) (Seoul: Sŏngmun'gak, 1985), pp. 11–52; *Han'guk minsok taegwan: Susi p'ungsok, chŏnsŭng nori* (A Survey of Korean Folk Customs) (Seoul: Koryŏ Taehakkyo Minsok Munhwa Yŏn'guso, 1982), pp. 476–92.

[16] The game of *Sŏngbul-to*, with board, dice, and directions was published by the Puril Ch'ulp'ansa in 1986. A reference book and explanation to the game was published by P'yŏnjippu (Compilation Committee), ed., *Sŏngbul hapsida: Sŏngbul-to-rŭl t'onghan Pulgyo immun* (Let's Achieve Buddhahood: A Primer of Buddhism through the Game of *Sŏngbul-to*) (Seoul: Puril Ch'ulp'ansa, 1984).

CHAPTER THREE.

Songgwang-Sa and Master Kusan

MOST BUDDHIST monasteries in Korea are nestled deep in mountain valleys, where they will be partially sheltered from the severe winter storms roaring down into the Korean peninsula from Siberia. Songgwang-sa is typical in this regard, protected on three sides by a tall mountain ridge with another mountain peak far in the distance guarding the site from the north. Not only does such a location provide shelter, but it also satisfies many of the requirements of Sinitic geomancy (*p'ungsu*; Ch. *feng-shui*, lit. wind and water) for a site protected from baleful influences.[1] Songgwang-sa is located next to a stream, where the monks clean vegetables and do their laundry, and is in close proximity to fresh spring water for drinking and cooking. The site also has enough space for paddy land and vegetable fields, where much of the food eaten in the temple can be grown, and adequate forests to provide sufficient kindling for cooking and heating.

THE LAYOUT OF KOREAN MONASTERIES

When I first came to Songgwang-sa in 1974, I was immediately struck by the deep sense of calm surrounding the site. From the small village below the temple, pilgrims to Songgwang-sa start a gentle, half-mile climb up to the monastery. The trail winds through pine forest, following the stream that runs alongside the monastery. Just below the main temple complex there is a field of large stone stelae, each about eight feet in height, on which are inscribed records of the monastery's history. In the same area

---

[1] For the Korean variety of Sinitic geomancy, see Hong-key Yoon's valuable study, *Geomantic Relationship between Culture and Nature in Korea*, Asian Folklore and Social Life Monographs, vol. 88 (Taipei: Chinese Association for Folklore, 1976). See also the comments of the Danish architect Johannes Prip-Møller about the importance of feng-shui in the siting of Chinese monasteries in his *Chinese Buddhist Monasteries: Their Plan and Its Function as a Setting for Buddhist Monastic Life* (1937; reprint, Hong Kong: Hong Kong University Press, 1982), pp. 3–4. For a general description of a protected site, see Holmes Welch, *Taoism: The Parting of the Way* (1957; revised ed., Beacon Press, 1966), p. 133: an ideal site was guarded on the north, sloped to the south, and had hills to both west and east, with the eastern hill slightly larger; there should also be a river nearby that would purify the site. Songgwang-sa comes close to being such a site.

is an old stone hitching post, where government officials would have dismounted in the past before entering the temple.

Pilgrims enter the main monastery complex via the *ilchu-mun* (single-beam gate), which resembles a stylized version of the Japanese *torii*, the gate to a Shintō shrine. They must then immediately pass through a short entry hall, right between statues of the four heavenly kings (*sach'ŏn-wang*), supernal dharma-protectors who are charged with guarding the monastery against intrusions by malignant spirits. These kings are larger-than-life statues carved in the most grotesque of caricatures, who look perfectly suited for their appointed task.[2] Next pilgrims pass beneath the Drum and Bell Tower (Chonggo-ru), which houses the implements used to sound the time of daily events in the monastic life.[3]

Supplicants have now passed beyond the more mundane levels of the Songgwang-sa and have reached the monastery's central campus. They are facing the main buddha hall, the Taeung-chŏn (Basilica of the Great Hero). The Taeung-chŏn is the architectural and ideological center of the monastery. In most monasteries, the main hall enshrines an image of Vairocana, the law-body (*dharmakāya*) buddha, the principal divinity of the Flower Garland (Kor. Hwaŏm; Hua-yen) school of Buddhism. The Hwaŏm school, which teaches the multivalent levels of relationship among all phenomena in the universe, has provided the principal doctrinal foundation to the Korean Buddhist tradition since the eighth century. This ubiquity of Vairocana images in Korean monasteries testifies to the continued importance of Hwaŏm philosophy in Korean Buddhist thought, despite the present domination of Korean Buddhist religious practice by Sŏn meditation. This main image is enshrined on a huge wooden altar, which extends from the floor all the way to the ceiling, some twenty-five feet up. The altar is built away from the front wall of the Taeŭng-chŏn so that devotees can circumambulate the image, though this is rarely done nowadays. Behind the image and its accompanying statues is a huge, multicolored *t'aenghwa* (scroll painting) of a Buddhist pantheon.[4] A portrait of Wit'a (Ch. Wei-t'o), the guardian general of Buddhism, is located on one of the side walls of the Taeung-chŏn, the same arrangement found in China after the sixteenth century.[5] Cushions for the

[2] Johannes Prip-Møller notes that halls for the four heavenly kings did not appear in China until after 742; *Chinese Buddhist Monasteries*, pp. 20–24.

[3] In China the drum and bell towers were often separate towers located at either side of the monastery's front entrance; see ibid., pp. 7–9. In Korea, these are usually combined as one tower, which is almost always located inside the temple compound, usually directly in front of the main shrine hall.

[4] See Henrik H. Sørensen, "The *T'aenghwa* Tradition in Korean Buddhism," *Korean Culture* 8, no. 4 (Winter 1987): 13–25.

[5] In Korea, there is no separate Wei-t'o tien (Wit'a-chŏn), as in Chinese monasteries; see Prip-Møller, *Chinese Buddhist Monasteries*, p. 206.

most senior monks are placed along the back of the hall, farthest from the image.

The Taeung-chŏn, like all monastery buildings, is crafted from wood in the traditional post-and-beam style of construction, with multiple brackets (tap'o) supporting the eaves. Because the wood decays, such buildings must be periodically refurbished to maintain their integrity. Even the most ancient of monasteries, therefore, will rarely have any buildings older than a couple of centuries, although, of course, those may be exact copies of structures raised long before. Buildings are constructed without nails, each wooden piece carefully hewn to fit perfectly with the others, like a giant Tinkertoy set. Walls of dried mud and straw fill in the spaces between the supporting columns. The main supporting columns are painted burgundy and the walls yellow, often with folk art paintings on the panels. The eaves of the buildings are painted in the bright "cinnabar and blue-green" (tanch'ŏng) style—intricate patterns of red, green, blue, and yellow, which can sometimes border on the garish. The structures are finally topped with roofs of dark grey tiles.

The Taeung-chŏn's central position in the monastic compound often highlights a distinctive quality of the monastery. This is especially obvious in the case of the sambo chongch'al, the "three-jewel monasteries" of T'ongdo-sa, Haein-sa, and Songgwang-sa. These are three of the largest monasteries in Korea, all ch'ongnims, each of which is considered to represent one of the "three jewels" (sambo; Skt. triratna) of Buddhism: the Buddha, the founder of the religion; his dharma, or teachings; and the saṃgha, or congregation of monks. At the Buddha-jewel monastery of T'ongdo-sa, for example, relics said to be of the Buddha Śākyamuni himself are enshrined in a reliquary, or stūpa (Kor. t'ap), directly behind the main buddha hall. Rather than installing a buddha image on the altar of the main hall, as would any other temple, T'ongdo-sa has instead left the back wall of the hall open so that the relics themselves, rather than a graven image, represent the buddha. At Haein-sa, the dharma-jewel monastery, the two huge halls storing the woodblocks of the Korean Buddhist canon are located high on a hill directly behind and overlooking the main buddha hall. This subordination of the main buddha hall serves to accentuate the superiority of the dharma, represented by the canon, at Haein-sa. At Songgwang-sa, the saṃgha-jewel monastery, the meditation hall is located one level above and in back of the main buddha hall, again as a way of emphasizing the importance of the meditation hall and its monk practitioners.

Songgwang-sa, like many large monasteries, is laid out to resemble vaguely an ocean-seal chart (haein-to; Skt. sāgaramudrā-maṇḍala) or dharma-realm chart (pŏpkye to; Skt. dharmadhātu-maṇḍala), a diagram used in Korean Hwaŏm doctrine to indicate the complex web of interrelationships governing everything in existence.[6] The many residences and shrines are sited so as to curve sinuously around the monastic complex, along a path leading back to the central Taeung-chŏn. On the small hill overlooking the Taeung-chŏn are the meditation and lecture halls and the Sŏn master's residence, both isolated from the main temple complex for solitude and privacy. Off to the sides of the monastery are separate compounds for the support divisions of the monastery: the office and kitchen. Scattered throughout the complex are smaller shrine halls for important bodhisattvas, the patriarchs of Sŏn, the past Sŏn masters of Songgwang-sa, and various divinities. Most Korean monasteries contain a large central courtyard, giving them a sense of openness that one does not find in their Chinese counterparts. Songgwang-sa's campus is perhaps the most exaggerated example of this, since the entire central portion of the monastery was burned to the ground during the Korean War and much of it has been left vacant.

Under the monastery campus is an intricate system of waterworks and drainage canals. Rather than having gutters on each building, water drains off the roof around the perimeter of each building, and canals lead the runoff away from the buildings. A separate water system also carries water from mountain springs to the various living quarters around the monastery.

In the mountains surrounding Songgwang-sa are smaller hermitages, where elderly monks and retired abbots live. Although physically separate from the rest of the monastery, these hermitages function as if they were actually compounds within the main monastic complex. Near the monastery is a large field of stūpas, which contains some thirty reliquaries of past Sŏn masters and eminent monks who resided at Songgwang-sa. At viewpoints scattered around the monastery are stūpas of many of the national masters who presided over Songgwang-sa during the Koryŏ dynasty.

The most obvious feature of large training monasteries such as Songgwang-sa is the separate compounds into which the monastic campus is divided. These compounds are independent living and working units. A high wall constructed of rock and mud entirely surrounds each compound, isolating it from the public portions of the monastery and accentuating this sense of separateness. Each compound will have its own

---

[6] This diagram has been derived from the *svastika* form of the magic square, or *nandyā-varta*, the "abode of happiness" figure; see E. B. Havell, *The Ancient and Medieval Architecture of India* (1915; reprint, New Delhi: S. Chaud, 1972), pp. 15–18. The diagram was introduced into Korea by the founder of the Hwaŏm school, Ŭisang (625–702), in his *Hwaŏm ilsŭng pŏpkye-to*; the chart appears in *T* 1887A.45.711a and is reproduced in Steve Odin, *Process Metaphysics and Hua-yen Buddhism: A Critical Study of Cumulative Penetration vs. Interpenetration* (Albany: State University of New York Press, 1982), p. xxi.

central plaza as well, as if it were the monastery in microcosm. A complete compound would include a large room with a heated *ondol* floor (described below)—what the Koreans call simply a *kŭnbang* (great room)—where upwards of thirty monks could live and practice full time. Double sliding paper doors are placed regularly along the walls of the room, the monks entering the room always through the door closest to their assigned spot inside. A small shrine is placed midway along one of the longer walls of the great room, but otherwise the interior is unadorned. At one end of the great room there will be a small outside hearth, where the monks stoke the fire that heats the ondol floor and boils water in a large iron cauldron. In more complex compounds, there might also be a block of individual ondol rooms just off the main hall for senior monks or monastery officials. Compounds also include a large granite water reservoir, into which is channeled fresh water from the monastery's mountain springs.

The largest of these compounds was intended originally to function independently, its monks living and practicing together separately from the rest of the monastery. Food would have been cooked in the cauldron over the hearth and served inside the compound's great room. Nowadays, except on a few special occasions when extra hearths are needed, food is cooked only in the kitchen compound and most of the monks take their meals in its great room, which serves as the monastery's refectory. The only exceptions would be monks in official support positions, who are often too busy to eat at the regular times; they eat when they have time on long tables in the kitchen, together with the lay workers and postulants.

The great rooms of Korean monasteries are extremely adaptable precisely because of their simplicity. If the temple needs room for monks to study, it can bring in small floor desks, and the great room becomes a seminary. At mealtimes, the monks take their wrapped set of bowls off the shelf along the outer perimeter of the room, and the great room becomes a refectory. When the monks sleep, they simply pull quilts and wooden pillows from a side room or built-in cabinets, and the great room turns into a dormitory. Place one or two rows of cushions along the middle of the hall, and the great room is transformed into a meditation hall. As a monastery's needs change, such compounds can be converted wholesale to fulfill completely different functions. Pŏmŏ-sa, near Pusan, is an interesting example of such a transformation. The monastery had been a major meditation center, and the monastery created large guest quarters to accommodate the itinerant monks who flocked to the temple during the free season. But after the Sŏn master's death, few meditation monks visited the monastery any longer, and those guest quarters were converted into a separate lecture hall. Pŏmŏ-sa has become identified more recently as a center of Buddhist doctrinal study, rather than a meditation monastery. This adaptability of Korean architecture makes the monastery's vocational specialty (something akin to its sectarian identity) much more fluid than one would find in China.

Such adaptability is crucial at the largest monasteries, especially at the four ch'ongnims of Haein-sa, Songgwang-sa, T'ongdo-sa, and Sudŏk-sa. The ch'ongnims are meant to operate as major monastic centers, where the distinctive practices and doctrines of each of the main strands of the Korean Buddhist tradition are to be maintained: Sŏn meditation, Kyo (especially Hwaŏm) doctrine, Pure Land recitation of the Buddha Amitābha's name, and *Vinaya* (monastic discipline) observance. Whereas most monasteries are primarily devoted to one or another of these various strands of Korean Buddhist training, the ch'ongnims offer a place where all can be practiced in harmony with one another, following the ecumenical vision of Buddhism that has been such an integral component of the Korean tradition since the time of Wŏnhyo (617–686) and Chinul (1158–1210).

Haein-sa is one of the best examples of how a ch'ongnim combines practice in all these different areas of Buddhism through the creative use of its compounds. Haein-sa has three meditation halls, all located within one large, separate compound. The younger novices in the seminary live in their own compound and do everything in that great room, from studying to eating to sleeping. In the same compound, right behind the refectory, is the library, which the study monks may enter directly without having to pass through another compound. There is also a small *Vinaya* compound, which formed in the mid-1970s, when the celibate order began to place more emphasis on training in monastic discipline. While it has only a small number of monks in residence, about ten when I visited in 1978, it was still essential that it be represented in the ecumenical mélange of the ch'ongnim. There is no specific Pure Land compound at Haein-sa, but each of the vergers (*chijŏn*) of the various shrines in the monastery—the head verger (*nojŏn*) of the Taeung-chŏn, and the vergers of the shrines devoted to the bodhisattvas Avalokiteśvara (Kwanŭm or Kwanseŭm) and Kṣitigarbha (Chijang), the sixteen arhat-protectors, and so on—performs his own independent devotional service, which often includes a pronounced Pure Land component. These services are usually performed alone, for about an hour at a stretch, some four times daily: following the early morning service in the main shrine hall, before dinner, before supper, and after evening service. These devotions include a standard worship service, followed by recitation of a buddha's or bodhisattva's name; often the name of Kwanseŭm *posal* (Avalokiteśvara Bodhisattva), the bodhisattva of compassion, will be recited in all the shrines. The vergers often live together with the younger monks in the kitchen compound, though a few will have private rooms elsewhere in the monastery. The independent shrines where they perform these daily devotions are located throughout the public areas of the main monastery compound. This makes the central campus of many older monasteries quite dense with small shrine halls, some no more than one *kan* (approximately six square feet) in size.

The ondol floor is a novel Korean way of heating the monks' residences in the monastery. The severe climate of the Korean peninsula, buffeted as it is by continental cold waves from Siberia, demands some sort of heating system. Rather than the raised brick bed (*k'ang*) that the northern Chinese warmed for sleeping, the Koreans have gone one step further: they heat the entire room. To construct the ondol floor, a foundation of rocks about three and a half feet high is raised around the perimeter of the room. Circling the interior of this perimeter is a one-foot-wide open channel, where the fire circulates, eventually exiting from a tile or rock chimney placed at the far end. A large raised foundation made of rocks and mud is created in the middle of the floor, which will help support the massive weight of the rock floor. On top of this platform are placed rows of large rocks, which mark the separate channels for the fire. These rocks are about one foot square, and are set in rows so that eight-inch channels are made between them. Large flagstones are then placed over all these foundation stones. These flagstones range from three inches in thickness, at the end nearest the fire box, where the fire is hottest, to one inch at the far end of the floor. The floor is then sealed with two inches of mud over the flagstone, followed by one inch of cement. Finally the entire floor is carefully sealed with thick oiled paper, so that no smoke can escape. As the floor ages and the inevitable cracks appear as the mud and cement dries, oiled-paper patches will be pasted over these cracks. A fire box is placed at the far end of the floor, dug into the ground beneath where the floor will be, so that the smoke and flames will rise directly into the surrounding open channel above. As the fire roars down the channels under the ondol floor, it rapidly heats the flagstones, warming the mud and cement and heating the entire room. The floor is toasty even on the coldest winter evenings, and the rocks will continue to heat the floor all through the night. Only occasionally in the winter will an extra fire have to be made in the morning to remove the chill. Monastery etiquette demands that a visitor always be ushered to the warmest spot in the room, easily found from the quilt that is left spread over the floor there to retain warmth.

The office is located in a separate compound near the main gate, also with a great ondol room and smaller individual rooms for the various monastic officers. The abbot may have his own room off these offices. Larger monasteries like Songgwang-sa will also have a library, with old xylographic books in literary Chinese, modern secondary studies on Buddhism in vernacular Korean, and typically the printed Japanese Taishō edition of the Sinitic Buddhist canon. Songgwang-sa used to have a large library, which unfortunately was burned during the Korean War. Collecting has begun anew over the last several years, and the library is now stored temporarily in a large open attic over a wing of individual rooms until a new building is built.[7]

Most monasteries will also have two small shrines to the Seven Stars (*ch'ilsŏng*; of the Big Dipper asterism) and to the Mountain God (*sansin*), two important deities of Korean shamanism. Koreans consider the Seven Stars to be the protectors of children (especially younger children),[8] while the Mountain God is a powerful local spirit who guards a family's ancestral home.[9] The presence of such shrines in Buddhist monasteries is evidence often used to support claims that Korean Buddhism is an amalgamation of imported Buddhism with indigenous religious traditions. But this putative symbiosis is, in my experience, very much overstated. True, Songgwang-sa did have a Seven Stars shrine, but its presence seemed rather more of an afterthought than a serious attempt to accommodate shamanistic practices. The shrine was located on the steep side of a hill at the back of the meditation compound, in an area that laypeople were forbidden to enter; the laity were therefore unable to supplicate the stars directly, as they would in shamanistic shrines. Unlike the Buddhist shrines scattered around the monastic campus, the Seven Stars shrine also did not enjoy a daily worship service and had no verger assigned to it specifically. The shrine to the Mountain God fared a bit better. At Songgwang-sa, that shrine was located next to the Hwaŏm-chŏn, the Flower Garland Basilica, where xylographs of Buddhist scriptures were stored, and it received a daily worship service, performed by the Hwaŏm-chŏn's verger. Perhaps the Mountain God's shrine was located at that strategic spot precisely to help guard the woodblocks of the canon. But the near-total absence of shamanistic elements in Korean Buddhist beliefs, practices, or ritual observances is eloquent testimony ex silentio to the negligible effect shamanism has had on the elite monastic culture of Buddhism.[10]

---

[7] For the ground plans of Zen monasteries in China and Japan, see Martin Collcutt, *Five Mountains: The Rinzai Zen Monastic Institution in Medieval Japan*, Harvard East Asian Monographs, no. 85 (Cambridge: Harvard University Press, 1981), pp. 171–220. For a typical plan of a Chinese Buddhist monastery, see Prip-Møller, *Chinese Buddhist Monasteries*, pp. 1–195.

[8] The Seven Stars are protectors of children, especially those under the age of seven, and guardians of the safety and careers of grown sons; see Laurel Kendall, *Shamans, Housewives, and Other Restless Spirits: Women in Korean Ritual Life* (Honolulu: University of Hawaii Press, 1985), p. 127.

[9] Ibid., pp. 130–31.

[10] It would be interesting to explore whether the impact of shamanism is more pronounced in the practice of lay Buddhists. Fieldwork is needed.

It is Buddhism's influence on shamanism that is much more obvious and profound. Shamanism has appropriated such Buddhist buddhas and bodhisattvas as Avalokiteśvara, the bodhisattva of compassion, and Bhaiṣajaguru, the buddha of healing, as its own tutelary spirits.[11] The Buddhist king of the gods, Śakraḥ (devānām Indraḥ), has become the principal shamanic deity protecting the fortunes of the family.[12] A shaman's shrine is called a "dharma hall" (pŏptang), the generic Buddhist term for any Buddhist religious shrine, and a shaman's religious activities are termed "buddhist services" (pulgong).[13] Such Buddhistic influences on shamanism are much deserving of further research; very little has been done so far but to note their presence. But the symbiosis is decidedly one-sided, and contemporary practice in Korean Buddhist monasteries betrays little impact from the indigenous traditions.

THE HISTORY OF SONGGWANG-SA

Songgwang-sa (Piney Expanse Monastery), the monastery that will be the focus of much of this book, has a long and illustrious history. The monastery is located on Chogye Mountain in the far southwest of the peninsula, some eighteen miles from the sea.[14] Since the Chosŏn dynasty, its long tradition of practice has led to its being considered the Sŭngbo sach'al: the monastery representative of the jewel of the monastic community (saṃgharatna) in Buddhism. Although Songgwang-sa is slightly

[11] See Kendall, Shamans, Housewives, p. 84.

[12] Chang, Yun-shik, "Heavenly Beings, Men and the Shaman: Interplay between High and Low Culture in Korean History," in Che-irhoe Han'guk-hak Kukche haksul hoeŭi nonmunjip/Papers of the First International Conference on Korean Studies (Sŏngnam: Academy of Korean Studies, 1979), p. 1067.

[13] Kendall, Shamans, Housewives, pp. 55, 83.

[14] Much of this section is adapted with permission from my article "Songgwang-sa: The Monastery of the Sangha Jewel," Korean Culture 10, no. 3 (Autumn 1989), pp. 14–22. A massive sourcebook of all extant materials pertaining to the history of Songgwang-sa was completed in 1932 by its former abbot, Im Sŏkchin; see his Chogye-san Songgwang-sa sago (Repository of the History of Songgwang-sa on Chogye Mountain), Han'guk saji ch'ongsŏ (Anthology of Korean Monastic Records), no. 2 (Seoul: Asea Munhwa-sa, 1977), reprinted in 1987 by the Puril Ch'ulp'an-sa as Taesŭng Sŏn-chong Chogye-san Songgwang-sa sago. Im Sŏkchin also wrote a more popular history of the monastery, rich in documentation and wide in scope; see his Taesŭng Sŏnjong Chogye-san Songgwang-sa chi (The Story of Songgwang-sa, of the Mahāyāna school of Sŏn, on Chogye Mountain) (Chŏlla namdo: Songgwang-sa, 1965). The most accessible survey of the history and architecture of the monastery is found in Songgwang-sa, Han'guk ŭi sach'al (Korean Monasteries), no. 9, ed. by Han'guk Pulgyo yŏn'gu-wŏn, gen. eds. Yi Kiyŏng and Hwang Suyŏng (Seoul: Ilchi-sa, 1975). See also Robert E. Buswell, Jr., The Korean Approach to Zen: The Collected Works of Chinul (Honolulu: University of Hawaii Press, 1983), pp. 27, 29–36 for additional material on the history of Songgwang-sa.

smaller in scale than either T'ongdo-sa or Haein-sa, the monasteries representative, respectively, of the jewels of the Buddha and the Dharma, its role in the development of the Korean Buddhist tradition is perhaps the greatest of the three. Even though relatively isolated in South Chŏlla province, one of the main bastions of Christianity in contemporary Korea, the monastery remains one of the major centers of Buddhist practice and is frequented by monks from around the country. Since its near-total destruction during the Korean War, Songgwang-sa has been rebuilt to its original scale over the last two decades. The temple was also restored in 1969 to the status of a ch'ongnim, the first monastery after Haein-sa to be so honored. This fact testifies to the esteem in which Songgwang-sa continues to be held in Korea.

Songgwang-sa is one of the twenty-five head monasteries (*ponsa*) of the present-day Chogye Order, administering a religious parish that takes in much of the southwestern portion of South Chŏlla province. Although nominally under the control of the main headquarters of the Chogye Order in Seoul, Songgwang-sa, like most monasteries, functions with almost complete autonomy. While its personnel decisions (such as appointments to high monastic office), for example, are submitted to Seoul for approval, a monastery's decisions are invariably rubber-stamped. Only in the most dire of circumstances—such as an irreconcilable schism among the residents—would the ecclesiastical headquarters deign to interfere in a monastery's internal affairs. This ecclesiastical bureaucracy serves a tenuous oversight function, enough to placate the concerns of the government's Division of Religious Affairs (a subdivision of the old Ministry of Culture and Information) that there be a centralized source of information on Buddhist religious affairs. Under Songgwang-sa's control are a network of forty-one branch temples, most of them small sites with only a couple of monks in residence. To ensure loyalty, the abbots of such branch temples are generally chosen from among the monks belonging to the head monastery's vocation families. As long as the branch temple runs smoothly and remains economically viable, the head monastery will leave the abbot to his own devices in developing his network of support.

Very little is known about the early history of Songgwang-sa. According to records dating from the middle of the Koryŏ dynasty, the temple was first constructed in the latter part of the Silla dynasty (ca. early tenth century) by a certain Hyerin, who is variously referred to as either a Sŏn or Hwaŏm master. The temple, then called Kilsang-sa, was of relatively small size: The reports call it variously a hermitage or a small temple, some one hundred kan in size, or about six hundred square feet.[15] No

---

[15] See *Taesŭng Sŏnjong Chogye-san Susŏn-sa chungch'ang-ki* (Record of the Reconstruction of Susŏn-sa [Songgwang-sa]), in Yi Nŭnghwa, *Chosŏn Pulgyo t'ongsa* (A Comprehen-

further information is available on either Hyerin or this early period of Songgwang-sa's history, lacunae that have led some scholars to doubt the whole story of this initial foundation.

Over the centuries after Hyerin's founding, time is supposed to have taken its toll on the monastery, and by the Koryŏ dynasty, all of its buildings had fallen into ruins. Sometime during the reign of the Koryŏ king Injong (r. 1123–1146), the mountain monk Sŏkcho, another empty cipher in the early history of Songgwang-sa, is said to have decided to rebuild the temple on a much larger scale. He supposedly gathered an army of workers and had arranged the construction materials, but unfortunately died before the work could be completed. For lack of a contractor, the reconstruction ground to a halt and the temple returned to obscurity.

The founding of the Songgwang-sa we know today was accomplished by Chinul (1158–1210), the national master Puril Pojo, who developed a distinctively Korean style of Sŏn practice. Catalyzed by his own personal insight into the fundamental complementarity of Buddhist meditation and doctrine, Chinul sought to develop a comprehensive system of Buddhism in which Sŏn meditation would be practiced in tandem with training in the Hwaŏm scholastic teachings. Students were expected to generate through their doctrinal understanding a sudden awareness that their minds were inherently enlightened. Based on that understanding, they then would continue on to investigate the enigmatic remarks of previous Sŏn masters concerning the nature of enlightenment, remarks collected in the quintessentially Sŏn "cases" (kongan), which we in the West usually know as kōans, following the Japanese pronunciation. By focusing intently on a kongan's "critical phrase" (hwadu; Ch. hua-t'ou), the crucial point or underlying theme of such a Sŏn case, eventually those students would experience directly the truth that they had initially understood only intellectually—the truth that they were themselves buddhas. At that point they would be able to act enlightened, not merely be enlightened. Chinul therefore advocated what he termed a "sudden awakening/gradual cultivation" (tono chŏmsu) approach to practice, in which the initial awakening engendered by Hwaŏm doctrinal understanding was bolstered through gradual cultivation of Sŏn meditation and finally verified through direct realization.[16]

---

sive History of Korean Buddhism) (1918; reprint, Seoul: Poryŏn'gak, 1979), vol. 3, p. 347; see also additional sources on the history of Kilsang-sa in Korean Approach, pp. 85–86 n. 134.

[16] For Chinul's life and thought, see Buswell, Korean Approach, and the paperback abridgment Tracing Back the Radiance: Chinul's Korean Way of Zen, Classics in East Asian Buddhism, no. 2 (Honolulu: University of Hawaii Press, a Kuroda Institute Book, 1991); id., "Chinul's Systematization of Chinese Meditative Techniques in Korean Sŏn Buddhism," in Traditions of Meditation in Chinese Buddhism, Studies in East Asian Buddhism, no. 4,

In 1190, Chinul formed a retreat group at Kŏjo-sa in North Kyŏngsang province to put into practice his approach to Buddhism. By 1197, seven years after the formation of this Samādhi and Prajñā Community, the group had achieved widespread fame and was attracting people from all strata of society until "those who were studying under him had become like a city."[17] Kŏjo-sa's small site made expansion impossible there and Chinul finally sent his disciple Suu (d.u.) on a scouting mission to the Kangnam region, which includes most of present-day Chŏlla province, to look for a site suitable for a major meditation center. After visiting a number of mountain areas, Suu arrived at Songgwang Mountain, where he found the dilapidated remains of a small temple, the old Kilsang-sa. Although the temple was much too small for the requirements of Chinul's retreat group, the location was ideal: "The site was outstanding, the land was very fertile, the springs were sweet, and the forests were abundant. It could truly be called a place appropriate for cultivation of the mind, nourishment of the nature, the gathering of an assembly, and the making of merit."[18]

In 1197, together with his dharma brothers Ch'ŏnjin and Kwakcho, Suu began to remodel and to expand the monastery. After the completion of the project in 1207, King Hŭijong (r. 1204–1211), an ardent supporter of Chinul's, changed the temple's name to Susŏn-sa (Cultivation of Ch'an Community), the name that is still used today for the meditation hall at Songgwang-sa. Finally, by the early part of the Chosŏn dynasty, the monastery came to be known as Songgwang-sa, after the original name of the mountain on which it was located. Around the same time, the mountain's name changed to Chogye Mountain, the Korean pronunciation of "Ts'ao-ch'i," the name of the mountain where the sixth patriarch of Ch'an, Hui-neng (638–713), had lived. The Korean monks attribute this name change to the fact that the terrain is so similar in the two places, but it was more probably another show of respect for the special tradition of Sŏn that Chinul founded.

Under the direction of Chinul and his immediate successor, Hyesim (1178–1234), the national master Chin'gak, Songgwang-sa became the center of Korean Buddhism for the remainder of the Koryŏ dynasty and

---

ed. by Peter N. Gregory (Honolulu: University of Hawaii Press, a Kuroda Institute Book, 1986), pp. 199–242; id., "Chinul's Ambivalent Critique of Radical Subitism in Korean Sŏn Buddhism," *Journal of the International Association of Buddhist Studies* 12, no. 2 (1989): 20–44; and id., "Chinul," in the *Encyclopedia of Religion*, ed. by Mircea Eliade et al., s.v. See also the valuable monograph by Hee-Sung Keel, *Chinul: The Founder of Korean Sŏn Buddhism*, Berkeley Buddhist Studies Series, vol. 6 (Berkeley: Institute of South and Southeast Asian Studies, 1984).

[17] *Susŏn-sa chungch'ang-ki*. Yi Nŭnghwa, *Chosŏn Pulgyo t'ongsa*, vol. 3, p. 347.

[18] Ibid.

a leading monastery of the Korean tradition up through the present time.[19] Both Chinul and Hyesim were awarded the title of national master (*kuksa*), the highest rank in the Buddhist ecclesiastical hierarchy during the Koryŏ, and their fourteen putative successors at the monastery were similarly honored.[20] Their portraits are all displayed today in the National Master's Hall (Kuksa-chŏn) in the upper compound of the monastery beside the meditation hall. Through the efforts of these eminent monks, the community at Songgwang-sa became the major center in Korea for both meditation practice and doctrinal study. Masters from the five traditional schools of scholastic Buddhism and the Nine Mountains schools of the indigenous Sŏn tradition gathered together at Songgwang-sa, propelling the monastery to the vanguard of the ecumenical movement that dominated Korean Buddhism from the mid-Koryŏ period onwards.[21] Because of the strong practice traditions of the monastery and the fact that it was the home of the sixteen national masters of the Koryŏ, Songgwang-sa is considered the saṃgha-jewel temple of Korean Buddhism.

Already in Chinul's time, the community is said to have numbered over five hundred people, housed in over 180 kan of new structures. To accommodate the continued influx of people, expansions of the monastery started during Hyesim's tenure. By the time of the sixth national master, Wŏn'gam Ch'ungji (1226–1292), there are records of a few thousand people practicing in the main monastery campus as well as in hermitages and smaller temples scattered around Chogye Mountain. Indeed, by the later years of the Koryŏ dynasty, the monastic tradition established at Songgwang-sa was held in such wide esteem that the court of King Kongmin (r. 1351–1374) issued a proclamation declaring Songgwang-sa to be "the finest monastery in the East."[22]

Songgwang-sa's campus seems to have degenerated toward the end of the Koryŏ dynasty, probably because the financial decrepitude of the kingdom dried up a major source of the monastery's support. When Kobong Pŏpchang (1350–1428), the sixteenth and last of the national mas-

---

[19] Detailed eyewitness reports of Songgwang-sa during Hyesim's tenure are found in the record of an inspection of the monastery performed by astronomical and calendrical officials from the Bureau of Astronomy and Meteorology during the Koryŏ dynasty. Their report provides a census of the monastic inmates and a detailed listing of all monastery structures, with location and size indicated. See the summary of this report in Buswell, *Korean Approach*, p. 88 n.166.

[20] For a roster of these sixteen national masters of Koryŏ-period Songgwang-sa, see Buswell, *Korean Approach*, p. 35.

[21] The five scholastic schools are traditionally listed as the Vinaya, Nirvāṇa, Dharma Nature, Avataṃsaka, and Yogācāra; see Buswell, *Korean Approach*, p. 8, for a chart. The Nine Mountains schools are listed in Buswell, *Korean Approach*, pp. 10–11.

[22] Quoted in Im Sŏkchin, *Chogye-san Songgwang-sa chi*, p. 161.

ters, arrived at Songgwang-sa in 1395, he found the monastery in a poor state of repair and began a major reconstruction job, which was completed by his immediate disciples in 1427, during the first decades of the Chosŏn dynasty. The widespread destruction wrought throughout the Chŏlla area in 1592 and 1597 by the invasions of the Japanese general Toyotomi Hideyoshi (1536–1598) took its toll on Songgwang-sa as well. Although only four compounds of the monastery were burned, the Japanese incursions forced most of the monks to depart for other temples or to return to lay life. The monastery was virtually deserted.

A few years later, reconstruction of these destroyed sections commenced under the leadership of the monk Ŭngsŏn (d.u.). But what really brought the monastery back to life was the interest Puhyu Sŏnsu (1543–1615), a renowned monk of the period, took in reviving the monastery. Arriving at Songgwang-sa in 1614 with over four hundred disciples, he repaired a number of the monastery's halls and shrines and offered a sū-tra-lecture series during the winter retreat, which was attended by over six hundred people. Although Sŏnsu left for Ch'ilbul-am (Seven Buddhas Hermitage) on Chiri Mountain the following spring, his presence had attracted an eminent clientele of monks to Songgwang-sa, who were then able to sustain the monastery's traditions throughout the remainder of the Chosŏn period.

The next major disaster to strike the monastery was the great fire of 1842, which began on the evening of 2 March in the Nakha-tang (the present Tosŏng-tang) and burned for two days straight, effectively destroying all of the buildings and all but a few of the images and religious items. The monks managed to save the Buddhist trinity in the main shrine hall, the statue of Kṣitigarbha (Chijang) bodhisattva in the Myŏngbu-chŏn, the large bell in the bell tower, and the woodblocks of the *Flower Garland Sūtra* (*Hwaŏm-kyŏng*; Skt. *Avataṃsaka-sūtra*), but everything else was lost. Five shrines, eight dormitories, and twelve lesser halls were burned, a total of 2,152 kan of buildings in all.

Monks and laypeople immediately began reconstructing the monastery to its previous scale, an enterprise that finally required fourteen years and 11,290 taels of gold. The reconstruction, supervised by the monks Kibong and Yongun, restored the monastery to its former glory, and subsequent repairs by later abbots transformed the monastery into a gem of Chosŏn dynasty architecture. From 1924–1928 alone, nineteen halls and shrines were built or repaired by the monk Yuram.

Its beauty was not to last long, however. The communist-inspired Yŏsu/Sunch'ŏn rebellion of January 1948 initiated a series of attacks that were to plague the monastery through the Korean War. Continued assaults led the UN forces to cut down the thick forest surrounding the monastery to remove any hidden guerilla enclaves. Continued communist intrusions onto the monastery grounds eventually compelled all of the younger monks to abandon the temple, to avoid forced conscription. The elderly monks, who did not have to worry about being drafted by the communists, voluntarily stayed behind to guard the temple and maintain the daily devotions. In February 1951, the ultimate atrocity took place. Communist guerrillas took the monastery, brutally butchering all of the old monks who remained in residence. In May, when an Allied counter-attack forced the guerrillas to abandon their position, the entire central portion of the monastery, including the main shrine hall, the library, and the majority of the monks' quarters, went up in flames. Again Song-gwang-sa was reduced to ashes.

After the end of the war, Ch'wibong, a monk who had spent virtually all of his seventy years at the temple, began yet another reconstruction. He and the abbot, Kŭmdang, initiated a thousand-day chanting retreat (ch'ŏnil kido-hoe) to raise money for the project. Between 1955 and 1961 a new bell tower and museum were erected, the main buddha hall was rebuilt, and four other shrines were reconstructed. But a crisis not atypi-cal of the period then faced the monastery: The Chogye Order had won a judgment in district court against the married monks who continued to occupy Songgwang-sa, but the residents refused to hand over the mon-astery to the celibates. Suryŏn (later Kusan) *sŭnim* (1908–1983) led into Songgwang-sa a small group of Chogye monks belonging to the dharma lineage of Hyobong (1888–1966), who had been the Sŏn master at Songgwang-sa between 1937 and 1946.[23] Kusan and his small band of bhikṣus challenged the married monks in a series of confrontations start-ing in 1965. An uneasy truce was eventually reached, with married and celibate monks living side by side for two years in the main compound. Finally an accommodation was reached on 2 September 1967, whereby the monastery itself would be occupied only by Chogye monks and the remaining married monks would be removed to a small hermitage behind the monastery. Two elderly married monks (by then widowers) still lived at that hermitage during my years at Songgwang-sa. Two years later, on 15 April 1969, Songgwang-sa was designated a ch'ongnim and Suryŏn was appointed its *pangjang*, or Sŏn master, taking for himself the new dharma-name of Kusan.

Kusan immediately began large-scale reconstruction of Songgwang-sa. He built a new meditation hall, the largest in Korea, and a massive lecture

---

[23] Hyobong was one of the most eminent bhikṣus of the Japanese occupation period. A disciple of Sŏktu *sŭnim* (d. 1954), he served as the Sŏn master at both Songgwang-sa (1937–1946) and Haein-sa (1946–1947), and was head of the Chogye Order headquarters (ch'ongmu wŏnjang) in Seoul between 1957 and 1958. His sermons and letters are collected in *Hyobong ŏrok* (The Discourse Records of Hyobong), ed. by Hyobong mundo-hoe (Seoul: Puril Ch'ulp'ansa, 1975).

hall, constructed a main buddha hall in the central courtyard, and repaired most of the minor shrines around the monastery. Kusan's strong leadership and his concern to revive the Sŏn tradition of the temple's founder, Chinul, returned Songgwang-sa to the forefront of the Korean Buddhist tradition.

THE LIFE OF KUSAN

Kusan *sŭnim* (1908–1983) was the Sŏn master at Songgwang-sa between 1969 and 1983, and the teacher under whom I trained during my years in Korean monasteries.[24] Since he will be such a central figure in my treatment of contemporary Sŏn training in Korea, I will relate his career briefly here.

Kusan was born in Namwŏn, a small city in North Chŏlla province, in 1909. His family worked a farm in the area and he spent much of his childhood until the age of fifteen studying the Chinese Classics at the local Confucian academy (*sŏdang*). After finishing his studies, he worked as a barber for the next fourteen years, helping the family out from time to time with the farm work.

When he was twenty-six, he came down with a serious illness, which no doctor could cure. As a last resort, Kusan decided to travel to nearby Chiri Mountain and start a hundred-day chanting retreat, reciting Avalokiteśvara's mantra, "Om maṇi padme hum," in the hopes that the Bodhisattva of Compassion would come to his aid. At the end of his retreat, he said, his health was fully restored.

Now fully committed to Buddhism, Kusan journeyed three years later to Songgwang-sa, where he received novice (*śramaṇera*) ordination under Hyobong *sŭnim* (1888–1966), one of the preeminent Sŏn masters of the first half of the twentieth century. After another year of service at his home monastery, he received his bhikṣu (monk) ordination at T'ongdo-sa, the Buddha-jewel monastery and the traditional site of ordination platforms in Korea.

Although he had studied in a Confucian academy, Kusan was not really

[24] Several accounts of Kusan's career have appeared in Korean and English. One of the first was the appendix to Ku San, *Nine Mountains* (Songgwang-sa: International Meditation Center, 1976). This annotated translation and explanation of Kusan's teachings was made by Hyehaeng (Renaud Neubauer), Hamwŏl (Stacey Krause), and myself (Hyemyŏng), in 1976, and privately published by Songgwang-sa; copies are still available in Korea. Some of this material has been retold more recently in Kusan Sunim, *The Way of Korean Zen*, trans. by Martine Fages, ed. with an introduction by Stephen Batchelor (New York: Weatherhill, 1985), pp. 41–51. See also Kusan's collected sermons, *Sŏk saja: Kusan Sŏnsa pŏbŏ chip* (Stone Lion: The Dharma Talks of Sŏn Master Kusan) (Cholla Namdo: Chogye Ch'ongnim Songgwang-sa, 1982).

of scholarly bent and had little interest in the academic study of Buddhist texts. He instead devoted most of his time to meditation training, focussing on the hwadu, or meditative topic, of Chao-chou's "no" (*mu*). Although he spent several years in retreat in meditation halls around the country, Kusan eventually became estranged from the frivolous practitioners whom he thought frequented the halls and decided to return to solitary practice in an isolated hermitage. Kusan often said that his concentration on the hwadu had become so intense by that time that he could no longer fall asleep; whenever he lay down to rest, his hwadu continued to shine brightly in his mind.

In 1943, after several years of continued investigation on the hwadu "no," Kusan had his first, partial breakthrough. He describes this experience in a lecture he delivered during the winter retreat of 1976–1977. I will excerpt this entire description, which is interesting as well for illuminating the ascetic lifestyle of meditation monks who practice in mountain hermitages:

> In the past I was staying at a hermitage named Sudo-am (Cultivating the Path Hermitage) near Ch'ŏngam-sa (Blue Grotto Monastery), altogether for about five years. I was entrusted with responsibility for looking after that small hermitage, which was as destitute as an egg shell. During those five years it was mainly through alms gathering that I was able to obtain provisions for the small community of about seven or eight monks.
>
> Among the monks there was a certain Pŏpch'un *sŭnim*, who practiced hard both day and night. One morning Pŏpch'un accompanied me to a small town in the locality, named Sangju, where we had some business to take care of. We were invited to have lunch at the house of a lay adherent in the town. Unfortunately, after the meal my companion had completely "ruined his stomach" in a way that was beyond cure. Now in those days in that town there were no hospital facilities available where this monk could undergo an operation. We went to different physicians specialized in Eastern and Western medicine trying to arrange for treatment. Finally we found a doctor who examined him and, discreetly taking me aside, asked, "Hasn't this venerable been suffering for a while from some kind of stomach disorder?"
>
> Actually there had been a time when this monk was living on Chiri Mountain, observing the ascetic practice of abstaining from eating grains and cooked foods, subsisting mainly on powdered pine needles and wild plants. After following this regimen for some two or three years, he happened to be in Chinju one day, where a laywoman, knowing of the hardships he had been enduring in the mountains, prepared some fancy glutinous rice especially for him. After such a long period of abstinence, you can imagine his delight during that meal. But having long been accustomed to raw food, his stomach could not bear such a heavy meal and was damaged permanently. This was

the cause of his illness, which had now become so acute. If he were not taken to T'aegu, the nearest city, for an operation before the next morning, he had little chance of surviving. This doctor urged me to take good care of him in the meanwhile. By the time we had consulted the doctor and received his diagnosis, we both knew that it would be quite impossible to get him to T'aegu in time to save him.

While helping him back to the layperson's home, Pŏpch'un rested his head on my shoulder and sighed in distress, "Please practice earnestly and endeavor to ferry me across to nirvāṇa." This was his last request. I knew then that my companion had given up all hope of survival. I replied, "It is the monk's way of life to be aware of the impermanence of life. We must be prepared for our departure at any moment. Friends on the path should assist one another from one life to the next. So if I get enlightened first, I will help liberate you, and vice versa. So you don't need to worry."

Finally the next morning, at about 6 A.M., he "yielded up his spirit." After arranging for the cremation, I started out on the return journey to Sudo-am. On the way I reflected, "Ah! When I departed there were two of us, but now I return alone." Feeling quite sad, I resolved then and there to awaken before his memorial ceremony forty-nine days hence so that I could help liberate his spirit.

Although the summer meditation retreat was over, I was still responsible for the requirements of the community and could not immediately enter retreat. By the time I had arranged all the necessary provisions for the hermitage, there were only eight days remaining before his memorial ceremony. You can imagine my urgency!

There was a small cabin, named Chŏnggak (Right Enlightenment), behind the hermitage. I arranged for food to be brought to me there twice daily and intended to start a period of nonsleeping practice. After four days of sitting, I realized that much of the meditative concentration gained through my earlier practice had dissipated during the activities of the last few weeks. Most of the time I was plagued by either drowsiness or fantasizing. With such poor practice, how could I hope to be able to help my friend at the time of his final crossing over to his next life? Consequently, I decided to fight my drowsiness by meditating in the standing posture with palms together in front of me (hapchang). After five days the other monks came to consult with me about the ceremony that was soon to take place, but I sent them away to arrange it themselves in consultation with the relatives of the deceased. Remaining alone, I decided that I wouldn't give up under any pretext, even if I were about to die—such was my determination to continue.

In standing meditation, the hardest part is to get past the first two hours without moving, after which the main difficulties are overcome. Whether sitting, reclining, or standing, it is finally all the same as the body settles into samādhi. Consequently, although seven full days had passed since I had begun this nonsleeping practice, I felt neither tiredness nor pain in my legs.

The ancient masters had good reason for advocating this nonsleeping practice. As it drew near to 9 P.M. on the last day before the ceremony, the clock on the wall made a click just before striking the hour. When I heard that click I took one step over into enlightenment. On that occasion I composed the following verse:

> One sound swallows up all the trichiliocosm.
> This solitary fellow shouts nine repeated "hahs!"
> The tick-tock of the clock is the long, wide tongue [of the teachings].
> Each piece of [the clock's] metal and wood is but the pure body [of the
>   dharmakāya Buddha].

What did it mean when the clock struck nine? My intense standing practice had removed the obstructions of torpor and restlessness. Its effect was like that of a clear sky completely devoid of clouds. It instantaneously allowed me to enter and abide at the original place. It was in this manner that I stood throughout those seven days and nights.

So if practitioners go a little way along the path and then start to lose their impetus, as if their underpants were slipping, they are worthless, whatever they try to do. Those who have their minds set on cultivation should be endowed with spirits that are willing, if necessary, to bore through rocks with their fingers in order to become enlightened.[25]

Kusan later deprecated the quality of this initial breakthrough as being nothing more than the first entrance through the door leading to enlightenment.

Wishing to be closer to his teacher, Hyobong, who by then had assumed the position of Sŏn master at Haein-sa, he stayed for the next three years in a small hermitage near that monastery. There he had what he later regarded as his first real awakening. Kusan said that he passed into a state of deep concentration that lasted for fifteen days, during which time he lost all awareness of the external world. So absorbed was he that he did not notice that birds had perched on his shoulders and pecked cotton stuffing out of his padded winter coat.

When the Korean War began in 1947, Haein-sa was soon threatened by Communist troops and Kusan and his teacher were forced to flee south toward Pusan. While in a small monastery near the city, he finally received certification (*in'ga*) of his enlightenment from Hyobong. His teaching career began with a four-year stint as abbot of Mirae-sa (Maitreya's

---

[25] Quoted, with minor adaptations, from a translation prepared by myself and two other foreign disciples of Kusan's, which appeared in Ku San, *Nine Mountains*, pp. 173–77. This same story has been retold with minor differences in Kusan Sunim, *The Way of Korean Zen*, pp. 121–26.

Advent Monastery) in Ch'ungmu, between 1954 and 1957. He subsequently was appointed to several ecclesiastical positions in the Chogye Order hierarchy.

Even after certification, however, Kusan was still dissatisfied with the quality of his meditation practice and left his administrative posts to return to solitary hermitage life. He traveled to Paegun-am (White Cloud Hermitage) in 1957, where he began a three-year period of sustained meditation that was the most severe of his monastic career. He vowed to undertake the ascetic practice of never lying down to sleep (*changjwa purwa*) and often stood in meditation for days on end. During his sitting meditation, he placed a knife attached to a long stick under his chin so that he would be stabbed in the throat if his head nodded from drowsiness. Throughout this period, his diet consisted of powdered rice and pine needles mixed with water. Finally, in 1960, at the age of fifty, he achieved great awakening (*taeo*). Kusan expressed this experience in the following verse, recited to his teacher, Hyobong:

> Penetrating deep into a pore of Samantabhadra,
> Mañjuśrī is seized and defeated: now the great earth is quiet.
> It is hot on the day of the winter equinox; pine trees are green of
> themselves.
> A stone man, riding on a crane, passes over the blue mountains.

In response, Master Hyobong said, "Until now you have been following me; now it is I who should follow you."[26] Hyobong then conferred on Kusan formal dharma-transmission (*ch'ŏnbŏp*).

Two years later, Hyobong asked Kusan to assume the abbotship of Tonghwa-sa, outside of T'aegu, and after Hyobong's death on 15 October 1966, he was recognized as that master's main successor. When Songgwang-sa returned to the control of the Chogye Order and was designated a ch'ongnim in 1969, Kusan was appointed the monastery's first pangjang, or Sŏn master,[27] and devoted himself for the next fourteen years to reestablishing the long practice tradition of the monastery. I will discuss the last years of Kusan's tenure at Songgwang-sa in the epilogue.

Let me turn now to the distinctive styles of practice undertaken in large Korean monasteries like Songgwang-sa, by looking first at the early years of a monk's monastic vocation.

[26] Quoted from Kusan Sunim, *Korean Zen*, p. 47.
[27] Adapted from a brief sketch of Kusan's life which I wrote for Kusan's privately published collection of lectures, *Nine Mountains*, pp. 215–17.

CHAPTER FOUR

A Monk's Early Career

KOREANS REFER to all Buddhist monks and nuns as *sŭnim*, a term of respect that is a contraction of *sŭng*, the Sino-Korean transliteration of *saṃgha* (the congregation of monks), combined with the honorific Korean suffix *nim*. Korean monks use the term *chung* when referring to themselves; this is a Korean word that derives from a Sino-Korean character meaning "congregation," or by synecdoche just "monk."

Although there may be no typical Korean monk, most religious follow a vocational path that passes many of the same landmarks. Each monk is required to begin his career with six months as a postulant (*haengja*), learning the basics of monastic discipline and adapting himself to the rigorous daily schedule followed in the monastery. During postulancy, the monastic vocation means long hours of physical labor around the monastery, preparing meals in the kitchen, working in the fields, and cleaning the latrines. His ordination as a novice (*sami*; Skt. *śramaṇera*) brings with it various obligations to his home monastery and vocation master, which include an informal commitment to spend a number of years serving the temple in different support positions as a "scrutinizer of phenomena" (*sap'an*) monk—in the office, library, or kitchen, for example—or acting as an attendant to his vocation master or the monastery's elderly monks. This commitment is usually presumed fulfilled after about three years of service to his home monastery and the novice may then finally be allowed to embark on his own practice career. He is then known as a "scrutinizer of principle" (*ip'an*) monk.[1] He will often begin by spending two years in a monastery seminary mastering the śramaṇera curriculum on monastic conduct, and perhaps then continue on for three more years to complete the intermediate curriculum, which covers the doctrinal underpinnings of Sŏn meditation. Once he feels he is ready to make a permanent (though always nonbinding) commitment to the Order, he will become a fully ordained monk (*pigu*; Skt. *bhikṣu*). At that point, he may feel himself ready to begin contemplative training in the meditation hall. So it would not be at all uncommon for a monk to wait several years after his initial ordi-

---

[1] For further discussion of these two kinds of monks, see U Chŏngsang and Kim Yŏngt'ae, *Han'guk Pulgyosa* (A History of Korean Buddhism) (Seoul: Sinhŭng Ch'ulp'ansa, 1968), pp. 160–61; and Kamata Shigeo, *Han'guk Pulgyo sa* (Korean Buddhist History), trans. by Sin Hyŏnsuk (Seoul: Minjoksa, 1987), pp. 219–20.

nation until he begins any kind of meditation practice (though some especially dedicated monks might simply quit all their expected duties and go straight into the meditation hall as young novices). A monk who is inspired by his contemplation may continue on for the rest of his career as a meditation monk and, if he achieves a measure of recognition for the quality of his practice, eventually become a Sŏn master at a major training monastery. Those who find meditation less to their liking might return to their home monasteries and continue on in various support positions, perhaps eventually working their way up to abbot. And some monks of course may lose their vocations and secede from the order. In this chapter, I will explore the early stages in the monk's career, including seminary training. In Chapter Five, I will treat the support division of the monastery and turn finally in Chapters Seven, Eight, and Nine to the training offered in the meditation hall.

MOTIVATION FOR ORDAINING

What prompts a man to become a monk, or "enter the mountains" (*ipsan*), as the Koreans say? What is the attraction that young men, even in the rapidly modernizing Korea of today, continue to find in the Buddhist monastic life? The reasons monks I knew gave for ordaining today are as varied as the people themselves. While the motivation is often a complex agglomeration of internal feelings and external forces that are difficult to isolate, certain themes crop up time and again in the personal testimonies of the monks. I will discuss here some of the more common of those themes gleaned from conversations with monks I knew well.

The mid-1970s, the period of my own stay in Korea, witnessed the end of the Vietnam War, in which Korean soldiers fought in support of the South Vietnamese and their American backers. This army experience was a pervasive backdrop to the responses many monks gave when we discussed why they had ordained. All young men in Korea are conscripted for three years into the armed forces. Their stay in the army exposed these men—who were often outside their home villages (*kohyang*) and away from their families for the first time in their lives—to completely new, and sometimes traumatic, events. These events opened their eyes, several monks told me, to the suffering inherent in ordinary life and prompted them to search for alternatives. The number of monks I came across who claimed to have spent a tour of duty on the front lines in Vietnam was truly astonishing to me. After their discharge, the monastery often seemed an attractive alternative to military life and a good percentage of these new ordinands ended up remaining permanently in the monastery.

After their military service was finished, these young men emerged too worldly-wise—or perhaps world-weary—to readjust to their earlier village lifestyle. Lonely from having lost contact with their military buddies and often lacking the necessary skills to work in the more mechanized jobs of the rapidly developing urban economy, many men could not decide what to do with their lives. For many such men, the monastery functioned as kind of a "halfway house" between the disciplined, stable environment of the army and the uncertainties of civilian life, or as an attractive alternative to the assembly lines of the metropolitan factories. In the monastery, they were well received and provided for, felt themselves part of an organization that was disciplined and structured (rather like the army), and developed camaraderie with other young men with similar backgrounds. The rapport that prevails among the monks, and the close filial bonds that tie all members of the monastic family to one another, can give new postulants the reassurance and sense of place that they knew before in their home villages or in the military. Rather as in a fraternity, once they are initiated into the monastery, their place in the organization is assured, bringing some permanent meaning to their lives. Indeed, the bond among master, disciples, and home monastery that prevails throughout the order ties together monks of all ages and provides incoming postulants with a sense of belonging to a timeless institution. Amid the unsettling insecurities generated by the ongoing conflict in Korea between tradition and modernization, the stable, secure lifestyle of the monastery was a welcome alternative to many young men.

Another theme mentioned by a number of monks involved a nativistic reaction to the increasing influence that Western civilization and culture was having in Asia. Quite a number of the young monks I knew were remarkably well versed in Occidental philosophy. Korean bookstores today are jam-packed with translations and secondary studies of all major trends in Western thought, and students from high school onwards study the subject. Some monks had even gone so far in their studies as to have been philosophy majors in college. The turn away from occidental thought and back toward indigenous Eastern philosophies and religions came, with several monks I knew, in their early twenties, after a year or two of university study. Paradoxically enough, however, for many of these young men their first real contact with Buddhist culture resulted from Korean translations of Western books. I was surprised to meet several monks whose first significant interest in Buddhism came about from reading the Korean translation of Herman Hesse's *Siddhartha*. Korean renderings of English translations of the *Bhagavadgītā* and the *Dhammapada* have also proven extremely popular and influential. Indeed, Western interest in Eastern philosophy seems to have done as much to stimulate among some Koreans a revival of interest in Buddhism in Korea as have the proselytizing efforts of the Chogye Order itself. Especially for monks who have been raised in Christian families—families that often display the vehement faith that characterizes the newly converted—the inadequacies of Western religion were vividly brought to light through their comparative reading in occidental sources.

I felt deep affinities with such monks, since their motivations in ordaining were so close to my own. I had begun to read Western philosophy when I was first in junior high school, trying to resolve a question that kept troubling me: how could I live without exploiting other people? Though I found many answers to this question in my readings, Western philosophers offered few practical methods of helping one live in such a manner. My first exposure to the answers Buddhism would provide to this question came about through reading Hesse's *Siddhartha* in sophomore English class. The book was a revelation, and I immediately considered myself to be a Buddhist, even if I had little idea at that point as to what that might mean. During the summer before my senior year in high school, I by chance happened across Nyanaponika Thera's *The Heart of Buddhist Meditation*. Before I had finished the first chapter, I felt I had found both the answer to my question as well as a practical technique for living out that answer. I devoured the book from cover to cover in one sitting, my heart pounding furiously throughout, with the intense fervor only a religious convert (especially an idealistic adolescent convert) can experience. I finally knew what I would be doing with my life. Once I left for college, I was determined to major in Buddhism (even if I told my parents I was doing "Asian Studies," a slightly more marketable field to my practical-minded father) and began to study both Sanskrit and Chinese so that I could translate Buddhist texts from the original.

During my first course in Buddhism, I was already inspired to travel to Asia to become a monk. One of my professors put me in touch with an English Theravāda monk he had met in Thailand who arranged for me to enter Wat Bovoranives in Bangkok. Some months later, after completing four quarters of university study, I arrived in Bangkok, a nineteen-year-old filled with idealized images of Buddhism learned from books. Of course, I was quickly disillusioned. One of the things that immediately irked me was that Thai monks kept asking me when I planned to disrobe. This question is common in Thailand, since Thais typically ordain for only a few months as part of their Buddhist religious training, much as Protestants might attend Sunday School; they have no intention of being monks permanently. But to me it seemed almost sacrilege to ordain without a strong commitment to your vocation. It took quite a while to learn to watch myself, not others.

When my visa problems in Bangkok were temporarily resolved, I was able to spend a month in the northeast of Thailand with a meditation monk named Maha Boowa, a renowned Theravāda teacher with a forest monastery near the Laotian border. I had come to Thailand expecting to learn a methodical regimen of meditation training, similar to the Burmese Vipassanā technique described in Nyanaponika's *Heart of Buddhist Meditation*. In Burmese Vipassanā practice, the meditator follows an extremely detailed system of mindfulness training: watching your steps as you walk, feeling the sensations of lifting, touching, and placing your foot; observing your postures, etc. I arrived at Maha Boowa's monastery expecting to be immediately taught his meditation method and exhorted to get started with my practice. Instead, for the first week he didn't even notice my presence and it wasn't until a couple of weeks later that he finally consented to talk with me.

When I was finally able to meet with him, the first question I asked was, "Please tell me your meditation method and what I should do in order to achieve enlightenment." His response to me was telling, and proved to be extremely influential to my own vocation; still today, some two decades, I recall it vividly. "I can't tell you how you can become enlightened," he told me. "I know what I did for myself, but I can't tell you what is going to work for you. Each of us is different and unique. Each of us has his own predilections, backgrounds, and interests, and these things can only be understood by you personally. So if you ask me my meditation method, all I can tell you is to watch yourself, to watch your own life, try different things out and see what works for you. What works, keep doing; what doesn't work, discard and go on to something else." So here I was, an immature, idealistic nineteen-year-old, expecting to be taught some method, and instead I was being told that the only method is no method.

At the end of my month there, I had to return to Bangkok for visa reasons. One day I was sitting in my room, meditating, when suddenly outside my window, two snarling packs of dogs began to fight over some leftover food. Being the good Buddhists that they are, Thais free stray animals in the monasteries rather than destroy them. But the result is roving dog packs fighting one another constantly for any food discarded by the monks. All the dogs are in a hellish state, skin ripped off, legs broken, hopping around on three legs. As strong as my interest was in Theravāda Buddhism, that dogfight was the last straw, and I decided to get out of Thailand. I ended up at a small hermitage on Landau Island in Hong Kong, where I spent a year with a Chinese monk and a French monk who also spoke Chinese. It was an idyllic site, quiet and secluded, quite the opposite of the large Thai city monasteries.

The Chinese monk I stayed with there had developed his own personal schedule of practice. He usually sat in meditation for about ten to twelve hours a day for several days or weeks at a time (contemplating the question "Who recites the Buddha's name?"). When his practice stagnated, he unpacked his woodblock edition of the sixty-fascicle-long *Flower Gar-*

land Scripture (*Avataṃsaka-sūtra*), stacked the folios up on his meditation seat, and started chanting the text through from cover to cover. After finishing about a week later, he would then go back to his meditation. I joined him in meditation for a few hours in the morning and evening, but spent most of my time studying Chinese Buddhist texts. Every morning for two or three hours, the abbot and I would sit together and read through the text I had been preparing. It was great for my scholarship, but after a year, I felt the need for a sense of community—of Saṃgha—once again. Korea beckoned.

I found monks motivated by the philosophical interests I was describing to be rather more idealistic than many monks. They seemed to me to show more interest in learning Buddhist doctrine and practicing meditation than did their associates. Indeed, as a Westerner who had embraced Buddhism for similar reasons, I was drawn to such monks. One of my companions over two seasons in meditation hall had finished law school at Seoul National University—the most prestigious university in Korea—after studying Western philosophy, English, and finally law. Immediately after graduation, he had entered Kap-sa on Kyeryong Mountain and had spent the whole of his career in the meditation hall as an itinerant practice monk. Another monk I knew had been sent by his teacher to study Western philosophy at Koryŏ University in Seoul, one of the top private universities. After two years of college he became disenchanted with the predominantly analytical approach of Western philosophy, read *Siddhartha* and *Chuang-tzu*, and decided to drop out of school and enter the meditation hall. He was one of the most respected young meditators in Korea and is destined to become a Sŏn master once his practice matures. A postulant who came to Songgwang-sa during my last year there had been enrolled in seminary school in Kwangju, studying theology, Latin, and English in preparation for his ordination as a Catholic priest. He happened to attend a university training session given at Songgwang-sa one summer, met Kusan, began meditating and studying Eastern philosophy (the first book he read was the *Bhagavadgītā*), and finally left school to join the monkhood. He was helping Kusan and his own vocation master edit manuscripts of their respective writings. This type of monk is usually considerably less provincial and more reform minded than the majority of monks. The influx of such monks into the monasteries augurs considerable changes ahead for Korean Buddhism, especially in the tradition's attempts to make itself relevant to contemporary society.

Another reason for ordaining that was common in traditional Korea and still applies today is the desire of Buddhist families to have one son enter the monastery in order to make merit for the family.[2] If one of its

[2] See Takahashi Tōru, *Richō Bukkyo* (Yi Dynasty Buddhism) (1929; reprint, Tokyo: Kokusho Kankōkai, 1973), p. 978.

younger sons shows a particular affinity with the monastic life or seems undecided about a career, the family (particularly the grandparents) might encourage him to try the monastic life for a while and see if he finds it to his liking. Because of primogeniture, it is exceedingly difficult for the eldest son to receive his parent's permission to ordain, permission that officially is required to join the monastery (though enforcement of this provision is lax). Even if it is granted, it is almost always accompanied by the clear understanding that the monk will disrobe upon the death of his father in order to support his mother and younger brothers and sisters and to assume a position of seniority among his immediate kinsmen. This expectation is so strong that only rarely do eldest sons ordain; those few I met were almost always the idealistic monks described above. Once I heard a monk mention that since he was the eldest son, he expected eventually to return to lay life and marry. He was immediately chided by our colleagues, who saw this expression of filiality more as an excuse than a reason for secession.

But most Korean families—and even even some Buddhist ones—look upon the monk's life as a decidedly inferior calling for their sons and are adamantly opposed to their children's ordination. Occasionally a father or brother will be found traveling around the monasteries looking for his son or younger sibling, hoping to persuade him to return home. In one particularly intense scene I witnessed, a father arrived one evening at Songgwang-sa to take his youngest son, a newly shaven postulant working in the kitchen, back home with him. The postulant was quite sincere in wanting to practice and was heartbroken that his father would not give his consent. Finally, he agreed to return with his father the next morning, and the proctor put his father up in a guest room for the night. The next morning after breakfast when the father went to look for him, the postulant was nowhere to be found. Unbeknownst to all, he had packed his backpack during the night and had left on the first bus, destination unknown. Since a postulant wears the gray clothes of the monks, uses the regular monk's backpack, and is free to travel to any monastery he wants to spend his six-month postulancy, the father knew it was going to be all but impossible to trace him. Furious that his son had vanished, the father vented his spleen on the entire kitchen staff before departing. Such tension between ordinand and family is quite common in Korea. Lewis Lancaster has documented in his pollings of Korean monks that some 90 percent of Korean monks defied their family's wishes in ordaining.[3] While this figure seems somewhat inflated to me, perhaps reflecting monkish bravado, it is

[3] Lewis R. Lancaster, "Buddhism and Family in East Asia," in *Religion and the Family in East Asia*, ed. by George A. Vos and Takao Sofue (1984; reprint, Berkeley and Los Angeles: University of California Press, 1986), p. 148.

nevertheless true that the religious life is not a profession most Korean parents would prefer for their children.

Another motive for ordaining sometimes found in Korean Buddhist sources—but one which I never heard of in this day and age—was as fulfillment of a vow. The example of Chinul (1158–1210) in the Koryŏ dynasty offers a quintessential example of this motive. Chinul had suffered from debilitating illnesses since his birth, which, it is said, no treatment could cure. In desperation, his parents finally went before a buddha image and vowed that if their son were healed, they would place him in the monastery to become a servant of the buddha's (that is, to ordain). He was miraculously cured and, true to their vow, they placed their young son in the care of a senior monk at a nearby monastery.[4]

In all monasteries, there can be found examples of monks who have ordained for the two reasons that the average Korean presumes most common: failure in love or laziness. Any organization as large as the Buddhist church will be certain to attract its share of seeming undesirables. But one point that monks often made to me is that regardless of the initial motivation that prompts a man to assume a religious vocation, continued involvement in the monastic life may remold that motivation into an entirely exemplary one. Indeed, there is no way of predicting from a monk's background his ultimate success in the religious life. I knew several monks from devoted Buddhist families who ordained out of strong personal faith but were unable to adjust to the difficult lifestyle of the monastery and ended up disrobing. Finally, as monks reiterate time and again, it is not why a man initially wants to become a monk that determines the quality of his vocation, but how well he leads the life once he has ordained.[5]

POSTULANTS

To help both the monastery and the prospective ordinand determine whether the person has the physical stamina and strength of character to endure the rigors of monastic life, Korean temples adhere to a system of postulancy. Postulants, known literally as "practitioners" (haengja), were traditionally expected to complete a three-year training period prior to ordination. After liberation from Japan in 1945, this period was reduced to six months in order to expand the ranks of the Chogye Order of celi-

---

[4] See the account in Robert E. Buswell, Jr., *The Korean Approach to Zen: The Collected Works of Chinul* (Honolulu: University of Hawaii Press, 1983), p. 20, citing the *Pojo kuksa pimyŏng*.

[5] Many of the motives driving the vocations of Catholic monks, as described by Walter Capps, apply also to their Buddhist counterparts; see Capps's *The Monastic Impulse* (New York: Crossroad, 1983), pp. 1–22.

bate monks. Such expansion was necessary for the inevitable confrontation that was to come with the married monks for control of the monasteries. Back when the period was three years, there were many more postulants around at any one time to perform all the myriad tasks necessary to keep a large monastery running. Indeed, after a year or so of work, a postulant would have relatively more time to pursue religious training, with a proportionally smaller portion of his time devoted to physical labor in the monastery. With the shorter postulancy, however, all postulants must now work diligently day in and day out, which quickly reveals the depth of their commitment to the monastic life.

The choice of a home monastery (*ponsa*) is the first, and in many ways the most crucial, decision the prospective monk will make in his early career. Unfortunately, that decision must be made when he is least able to evaluate monasteries impartially and when he is least aware of what his true calling will be in the monastic life—meditation, scholarship, or administration. A few monks I knew had spent months, and in one case years, as postulants, sampling the life at different monasteries before deciding where to ordain. But most commonly, a monk begins his postulancy at the temple closest to his home village or at the largest monastery in his native province. In other cases, prospective monks are drawn to a temple because of the reputation of its Sŏn master or abbot. After ordination, however, when a monk begins to travel between different monasteries, he may eventually discover a temple with which he feels deep affinities. He may end up spending many years there, his associations with that monastery growing deeper than those with his home monastery. Even so, wherever he goes he will still identify himself as a monk from his original home monastery.

Along with the monk's ŭnsa, or vocation master, it is the home monastery that will define the monk in his colleagues' eyes. The home monastery is where the monk will have spent his six months of postulancy and usually where his ŭnsa resides. While the ŭnsa may not be physically present at all times in the monastery, he will have had a long association with the temple and usually be part of its family lineage.

The home monastery will also largely determine the monk's circle of colleagues throughout his career. At the time of his novice ordination, a permanent bond is created between himself and his colleagues in the home temple, even with those who may have a different ŭnsa teacher. There is a deep affinity among monks from the same monastery. If a monk is from one of the large monasteries, even though his ŭnsa may not be well known, he will be accepted with respect everywhere he visits. This is because larger monasteries, where the training and practice schedule is most rigorous, will generally attract a more sincere and dedicated clientele of haengjas than will smaller temples, where the practice can be rather lax. Monks who hail from small temples will be greeted with a degree of suspicion when they visit a new monastery, however talented and qualified they may in fact be. It is not unlike the way professors evaluate prospective candidates for graduate study by first looking at the schools from which they graduated.

Different temples tend to produce monks who are specialists in different aspects of the monastic life, based both upon the tradition of the monastery and the interests of its Sŏn master or abbot. Monks ordaining, for example, at Songgwang-sa—the Saṃgha-jewel temple, which has a long practice tradition—tend to be devoted primarily to meditation, even if that devotion is at times mostly lip service. Monks from Haein-sa, where the Sŏn master is also an accomplished scholar, often seek to combine both meditation and learning. Monks from Pŏpchu-sa, which has one of the largest monastic seminaries in Korea, specialize in scholarship and administration. These differences can create a friendly rivalry between monasteries and their dharma lineages.

But the home monastery can place tremendous pressure on its family members, forcing them into the many administrative positions necessary to make a major practice center run smoothly. Especially if a monk's vocation master occupies a position of authority, the disciple will almost inevitably be pressed into some sort of service as long as he resides at the home monastery. The proctor (wŏnju), for example, who has one of the most onerous jobs in the entire monastery, is always a monk from the home monastery. Discouraged by these constant administrative pressures, monks who wish to practice meditation or engage in scholarly pursuits find it prudent to stay away from their home monasteries except for an occasional, and brief, visit back home during the vacation season. Several monks told me that they had no choice but to leave their home monasteries in order to pursue the vocation that truly interested them.

After the prospective ordinand has finally decided where to spend his postulancy, he first goes through a short period of probation, working in the kitchen for three to ten days while the proctor observes him and determines whether he should be admitted to the monastery. Once accepted, another postulant shaves his head, and the proctor gives him some old, secondhand monk's clothes before escorting him to the Sŏn master's room to be introduced.

Although the new postulant now looks like any other monk, he has not yet made any official vows within the religion, nor has the monastery made any formal commitment to allow him to ordain. Before either can happen, he must satisfactorily complete six straight months in residence at the monastery. Only in the most extraordinary of circumstances is a postulant ever allowed to ordain in any shorter time, though his postulancy could last longer if he has not completed all the necessary requirements. Some postulants will stay for only a few months at one temple, and then leave again to start anew elsewhere. They either do not seriously wish to ordain, are dissatisfied in some way with the training in that particular temple, or else wish to emulate the former lengthy postulancy. I even knew firsthand of one case where a monk become nostalgic for the simplicity of his haengja life and introduced himself as a postulant at Songgwang-sa, to do manual work in the kitchen there. This "new" haengja proved to be extremely adept at learning all the kitchen work, and the monks were all sure he would become the disciple of the Sŏn master—the highest honor a postulant could receive. At the end of the retreat period, however, he told the proctor, to everyone's surprise, that he had already been a monk for three years and would be returning to his home monastery the following morning!

The life of the postulant is busier than that of anyone else in the monastery. The haengjas all reside together in very close quarters in the great room in the kitchen compound. Since they are working for most of the day, they do not require much space beyond that needed for sleeping and storing their few possessions. There is a hierarchy among the postulants based upon length of time in the monastery. Their assigned jobs also follow the same seniority system: junior postulants learn to make the rice, starting with fire making and working up to assistant to the head rice cook (*kongyang-chu*), assistant to the cook in charge of preparing all the side dishes (*chaegong*), or stew (*tchigae*) cook. As his months in the monastery accumulate, he might become the *kongyang-chu* or the assistant proctor (*pyŏlchwa*) even before he ordains, two of the most stressful jobs in the entire monastery.

As with everyone else in the monastery, the postulants rise at three in the morning, the senior haengjas checking to see that everyone else is up. After washing, they practice their chanting prior to the beginning of early morning chanting. After chanting, they have half an hour of free time before starting the morning meal, time they use for learning a chant or studying their primer of monastic discipline. Before they are allowed to ordain, they are required to learn the novice precepts and the monastic rules and decorum, memorize all the chanting—including both regular morning and evening chanting, as well as the *Thousand Hands Sūtra* (*Ch'ŏnsu-kyŏng*),[6] which is used in many formal ceremonies—and study

[6] There are several alternate versions of this text in the Sinitic Buddhist canon. The Koreans use the translation attributed to Ch'ieh-fan-ta-mo, which has the full title of *Ch'ien-shou ch'ien-yen Kuan-shih-yin p'u-sa k'uang-ta yüan-man wu-ai ta-pei-hsin t'o-lo-ni ching*, T 1060.20.105–111, or *Thousand Hands Sūtra* (*Ch'ŏnsu-kyŏng*) for short. This dhāraṇī is also known as the *Great Compassion Spell* (*Taebi-chu*). The dhāraṇī is recited in the Korean pronunciation of the Chinese transcription of the Sanskrit (or, probably more accurately, Middle Indic) incantation.

thoroughly the *Admonitions to Beginners* (*Ch'obalsim chagyŏng-mun*), the basic handbook of Korean monastic regulations and lifestyle.[7] Because of the amount of physical labor they are also required to perform, it is customary for postulants to work and study at the same time, so during any scheduled work session, the postulants constantly recite their lessons quietly to themselves. This combination of constant physical work and mental concentration is considered to be an effective means of calming the mind of the prospective novice, helping him to adapt as speedily as possible to the monastic life.

Breakfast preparation is begun around 4:30 in the morning. The postulants working on the rice will start making the fire under the cauldron to boil the water. The rice has been washed the afternoon before and the barley that is mixed into the rice has been cooked previously so that preparation can proceed as quickly and effortlessly as possible. Other haengjas will begin preparing the vegetables and stew, slicing the inevitable *kimch'i*, and preparing all the dishes and serving trays. At around 5:30, they will carry all the food into the refectory and, once the monks have begun their meal, return to eat their own breakfast in the kitchen.

After cleaning up, the postulants have some free time (until around eight in the morning) to study, when they will start general monastery cleanup or field jobs until the midday dinner preparation begins at around ten. Usually, the postulant will keep his same meal job for a few weeks so that he becomes fully proficient in it before moving on to a new position. Half an hour before the dinner service, the kongyang-chu will prepare the rice offerings (*maji*), which the postulants then distribute to all the different shrines around the monastery complex. These offerings are always carried in the right hand, just over the shoulder. A piece of bright red cloth is placed over the stainless steel maji container. After the verger of the shrine has placed the offering on the altar before the buddha image, he then strikes the shrine's gong once to signal that preparations for the lunchtime service are complete. After the service, the vergers then return the majis to the kitchen, where they are dumped into a large tub together with the rest of the rice to be served to the monks for dinner.

The postulants, kitchen monks, and lay workers will all eat together at

---

[7] The usual edition studied is Kim T'anhŏ, ed. and trans., *Ch'obalsim chagyŏng-mun kangŭi* (Annotations to the *Admonitions to Beginners*) (Seoul: Pulsŏ Pogŭpsa, 1971), which includes the Sino-Korean texts of the three works included in the collection, with Korean renderings and notes. I have translated Chinul's work in this collection in Buswell, *Korean Approach*, pp. 135–39. I have translated Wŏnhyo's work in Robert E. Buswell, Jr., "Wŏnhyo's *Arouse Your Mind to Practice!*" *Ten Directions* 10, no. 2 (Fall–Winter 1989): 17–19, which will also appear in *Sources of Korean Tradition*, gen. ed. Peter H. Lee (New York: Columbia University Press, forthcoming). There is still no published English translation of the third selection.

tables with chairs located in an open-air room adjacent to the main kitchen area. Often the office monks have been busy with their duties and arrive late for the meal, so they will eat in the back also. Unlike the refectory, there is no formal four-bowl style of eating there. After serving the laypeople, the haengjas eat quickly and start picking up the used serving dishes from the refectory. After cleaning up, they again have some free time, followed by field work, before supper preparation begins at four in the afternoon.

Since evening kitchen cleanup is rarely completed before the beginning of evening chanting, only a few of the more senior postulants will attend the service. Inside the main buddha hall, the postulants wear their regular monk's clothing and the long traveling coat (*turumagi*). They are not permitted to wear the formal robe (*changsam*) or the dyed cloak (*kasa*) until they are ordained.

After kitchen cleanup is completed, all the postulants will go to the Kwanŭm (Avalokiteśvara) shrine in the monastery, where they will practice chanting the *Thousand Hands Sūtra* together with the verger of that shrine. They also are expected to complete 108 full prostrations there each day. At Songgwang-sa, the postulants walk up the hill behind the Kwanŭm shrine to the stūpa of Chinul, the founder of the monastery, and bow there before returning to the shrine to begin their regular evening chanting. Finally, the postulants have free time to study or to attend lectures by the catechist (*kyomu sŭnim*) on the novice precepts or the *Admonitions to Beginners* before lights out at nine.

ORDINATIONS

After their six-month postulancies are over and they have mastered all the chants and books of monastic regulations, the postulants are finally ready to ordain as novice monks (*sami*; Skt. *śramaṇera*). During my years in Korea, many large monasteries still held their own ordination platforms. At Songgwang-sa, a complete ordination platform was held only once a year, during the third lunar month (usually in April), during the spring vacation period. The entire ceremony lasted three days. On the first day, the śramaṇera ordination (*sami kyesik*) was held in the early morning before breakfast, followed in the late morning and afternoon by the full ordination for monks (*pigu kyesik*). Starting that evening, and lasting for the next two days, a series of lectures on the bodhisattva precepts was held, culminating on the third day of the ceremony with a bodhisattva ordination (*posal kyesik*). This final ordination primarily targeted a massive lay audience that had been bussed into the monastery for the event. I will discuss the bodhisattva ordination in Chapter Six on relations between the monastery and the laity, so for now let me focus just on ordinations for monks.

Novice Ordination

The novice, or śramaṇera, ordination is held around four in the morning after the service in the main buddha hall. If the weather is warm, the ceremony will be held in the larger Sŏlbŏp-chŏn (Speaking the Dharma Basilica), the main lecture hall; if ondol heating is necessary, the ceremony will be transferred to the great room in the kitchen compound. Songgwang-sa held two novice ordinations each year, one in conjunction with the large ordination platform in the spring, the other in the early winter, to accommodate the next matriculating group of haengjas.

All haengja of the monastery who have completed a full six months of training at the monastery are invited, though not required, to participate. Disciples of the abbots or senior monks of the monastery's branch temples will also join the ceremony. The Sŏn master may have nuns in other parts of the country who are his disciples; they too may send their own disciples to the main temple for the novice ordination, since the Vinaya requires that nuns be ordained by both the monk (bhikṣu) and nun (bhikṣuṇī) saṃghas. The Sŏn master may conduct the novice ordination himself, but during the spring ordination platform the specialist in ordination procedure may instead be in charge.

Each of the postulants will be assigned a "beneficent master" (ŭnsa), a senior monk who serves as the formal sponsor of the haengja's candidacy for ordination, rather as does the "vocation father" in Catholic monasticism.[8] No bhikṣu with less than ten years of seniority is allowed to serve as an ŭnsa. The prospective monk's relationship with the ŭnsa is one that will last for life and will be crucial for a successful vocation. The new monk's identity will be defined by his home monastery and the reputation of his ŭnsa, so it is essential that the ŭnsa be carefully chosen.

Competition is especially keen among the postulants to have the Sŏn master as their ŭnsa. The Sŏn master is quite choosy in accepting new disciples and accedes to only a limited number of requests from the haengja. Monastic "families," like their secular counterparts, maintain the earlier Chinese emphasis on the primacy of the senior line within the lin-

---

[8] I have not found any specific references to this term in Chinese Buddhist materials and believe it may be a Korean creation. This master is the equivalent of the ch'ulga asari (lit. leaving-home ācārya), the first of the five types of teachers mentioned in the Wu-fen lü, who is defined as "the master who adminsters the śramaṇera precepts and first ordains [the postulant]." Wu-fen lü (Mahīśāsaka-vinaya) 16, T 1421.22.113a10.

eage.[9] This superior status of the Sŏn master's own line accounts for why the postulants are so intent on becoming his direct disciples. Unsuccessful candidates he assigns instead to the abbot and other senior monks in the monastery family. The ŭnsa chooses a dharma name (pŏmmyŏng) for the postulant, the ŭnsa's dharma family usually being indicated by the use of the same Sino-Korean logograph in the names of all his disciples or generations of disciples. Many postulants are heartbroken when they learn they will not become the disciple of the Sŏn master and I knew of several cases where rejected candidates left the monastery without taking ordination to start their postulancy over again elsewhere.

Before the novice ordination begins, each postulant has been given a set of formal robes by his ŭnsa. If the haengjas have done their postulancy at the main monastery, robes will have been made by the monastery's own seamstress, a posal who resides permanently in the monastery.

The novice ordination is quite simple compared to its two companion ceremonies.[10] Unlike other ordinations, the novice ordination does not require the participation of official witnesses in order to validate it. Laypeople are allowed to attend if they desire, but this is uncommon; usually only senior monks from the main monastery and branch temples will be present, along with all the represented ŭnsas. Never once did I see the family of the ordinand attend the ceremony.

For the ceremony, a dais has been placed in the middle of the room, where the master presides. A small table has been placed in front of the dais, on which are placed two candlesticks and the regular sacristal instruments—the water holder and censer. Wearing their changsams, the ordinands file into the room one by one, prostrate three times before the master, and stay kneeling on their heels in what we in the West know as Japanese fashion, one of the few times Koreans adopt that style of sitting (a position they call kkurhŏ anki). As the candidates remain seated in line, the master goes into a lengthy explanation of the meaning of the ten precepts and the importance of their new vocation. This lecture can often last an hour or more, during the whole of which the ordinands force themselves not to shift positions. I have seen many cases where the can-

---

[9] Cf. Roger L. Janelli and Dawnhee Yim Janelli, "Lineage Organization and Social Differentiation in Korea," Man, n.s. 13 (1978): 272–89, cited and discussed in Laurel Kendall, Shamans, Housewives, and Other Restless Spirits: Women in Korean Ritual Life (Honolulu: University of Hawii Press, 1985), p. 25; and see Janelli and Janelli, Ancestor Worship and Korean Society (Stanford: Stanford University Press, 1982), pp. 8–11, for the social changes accompanying the emergence of agnatic lineages in Korea.

[10] There is elaborate liturgy for this ceremony outlined in Pulgyo sŏjŏk sent'ŏ, eds., Pulgyo pŏbyo kugam (Primer of the Essentials of the Buddhist Teachings) (Seoul: Hongbŏbwŏn, 1970), pp. 234–57. Very little of this liturgy was ever used in novice ordinations performed at Songgwang-sa. For Buddhist ceremonial liturgies, see also An Chinho, Sŏngmun ŭibŏm (Ceremonial Rules of the Śākyan Lineage) (Seoul: Pŏmnyunsa, 1961).

didates could not rise afterwards, their legs having gone completely numb. The master repeats for them the ten precepts: (1) not to kill; (2) not to steal; (3) not to engage in sex; (4) not to lie; (5) not to drink alcohol; (6) not to sit or sleep on high or wide beds; (7) not to wear garlands, ornaments, or perfumes; (8) not to dance or sing to oneself or intentionally attend such performances; (9) not to handle gold or silver; and (10) not to eat in the afternoon or raise domestic animals. At the end of his recitation, he asks the ordinands, "Can you keep each and every one of these precepts without transgressing them?"[11] The repetition of this simple formula three times constitutes the actual ordination. The candidates then vow to keep the precepts for as long as they remain monks. The Sŏn master's attendant then places the miniature kasa over each ordinand's head, and at that moment they have become novices.

At the conclusion of the śramaṇera ordination, a waxed wick, called the *sambae*, is placed on the inside forearm, lit with a match, and left to burn down to the skin. This ritual is called "burning of the arm" (*yŏnbi*). While the burns are usually not severe, the novices are in obvious pain as the wick burns down, pain they try to bear stoically. Later, as the scab begins to heal, the novices sometimes pick at it so the resulting scar will grow larger and larger, another mark of monkish machismo.

Ilt'a *sŭnim*, the *Vinaya* master at Haein-sa, who is one of the most popular catechists because of his genius for storytelling, explained to me that burning the arm is done to symbolize the new novices' nonattachment to the body and disentanglement from worldly affairs. According to Ilt'a, the sūtras mention three types of physical burns to which monks subject themselves: burning the arm, burning the fingers (*yŏnji*), and burning the body (*sosin*).[12] This custom is therefore validated in the basic texts of Buddhism, he claimed. The Koreans do not go so far as the Chinese Buddhists, who light a grid of multiple wicks on the top of the ordinands' heads at the time of their ordination.[13] Ilt'a denounced this Chinese practice as having no scriptural basis. He speculated that the idea of burning the top of the head came from Chinese medicine, in which applying heat

[11] *Pulgyo pŏbyo kugam*, p. 252. See also the description of the ten precepts in the Ch'an account of the śramaṇera ordination ceremony in *Pai-chang ch'ing-kuei 5, T* 2025.48.1137c–1138a; and *Pulgyo pŏbyo kugam*, pp. 247–52.

[12] All these types of sacrifice are mentioned by the Chinese Ch'an anthologist and commentator Yen-shou (904–975) in his *Wan-shan t'ung-kuei chi* (*chüan* 2, *T* 2017.48.969c3), showing that they were all current in East Asia at least by the Sung dynasty. I will discuss the latter two types of burns in Chapter Eight in a section on ascetic practices.

[13] An account of this practice, with illustrations, appears in Johannes Prip-Møller, *Chinese Buddhist Monasteries: Their Plan and Its Function as a Setting for Buddhist Monastic Life* (1937; reprint, Hong Kong: Hong Kong University Press, 1982), pp. 318–20. See also Holmes Welch, *The Practice of Chinese Buddhism*, Harvard East Asian Studies 26 (Cambridge: Harvard University Press, 1967), pp. 298–300.

to acupuncture points on the head was considered to be a powerful curative agent. But he did note that some elderly monks who came originally from north Korea had such burn marks on their heads.

The novice ordination usually ends just before breakfast at six. In the few minutes before the meal is served, the audience of monks will congratulate the ordinands, often teasing them about being unable to stand after sitting through the master's interminable talk. After the monks have finished breakfast, they stay seated in the refectory and the new novices are led into the hall to be introduced formally to the saṃgha. The novices file into the hall and prostrate themselves three times before the buddha image. Turning toward the back of the room, they then bow three times to the Sŏn master and the rest of the saṃgha. As the novices remain kneeling, the proctor introduces them individually to the assembly, informing the monks of the dharma names of the new novices, the names of their ŭnsas, and their home monasteries. This same information will be repeated for the rest of their careers each time they are introduced at a new monastery. The Sŏn master might then make a few further comments about how important and exciting it is to have new monks in the monastery. When the master indicates his remarks are finished, the novices prostrate themselves three more times and file out.

There is no formal certificate presented to the novices during the ordination. Later, however, each new novice will be given a monk's identification card and number. The card has a small picture of the monk and his identification number, dharma name, home monastery, and ŭnsa teacher. The identification numbers are issued by the national Saṃgha headquarters in Seoul, with the supreme patriarch (chongjŏng) given the number 1, and the rest of the national hierarchy following in order. Each monastery has its own series of numbers, again with either the Sŏn master or abbot being given the number 1, and the rest of the numbers given out in succession as people ordain. These numbers are not registered with the secular government, I was told, but are only on file with the Chogye Order. Wherever the monk travels, he will always carry this card with him. The back of the card is divided into spaces and the monk is supposed to have recorded in those spaces the temples where he spends his retreat periods, and in which section of the monastery he resided (for example, meditation hall, seminary, etc.). When the monk later travels to other monasteries, this information will help the guest prefect assess the quality of the monk's training and decide whether he should be admitted to the temple as a resident.

Koreans recognize a substantial difference in the degree of commitment made by the novice and the monk. The monastery would not view so negatively a novice who decides to return to lay life, whereas it would be a major embarrassment to the monastery, and especially the ŭnsa, if one of its bhikṣus should disrobe. Despite this difference in commitment, both classes nevertheless receive equal treatment in the monastery and are allowed to participate together in all temple functions. Virtually the only difference in treatment is in seating assignments, monks sitting according to seniority within each of the two groups.

Bhikṣu Ordination

The bhikṣu ordination is procedurally more complex than the novice ordination. In the 1970s there were only five monasteries in the country permitted to hold ordination platforms conferring the complete precepts (kujok-kye) of the bhikṣu and bhikṣuṇī. These occurred at various times throughout the spring and the novice had his choice of which ceremony to attend. "Family" connections and monastery ties came into play, as they always do, in making the decision. In 1981, the Chogye Order instituted new limitations on ordinations, restricting śramaṇera and bhikṣu ordinations to T'ongdo-sa, the Buddha-jewel monastery, which was the traditional center of the Vinaya school (Yul-chong) in Korea.[14] Other monasteries thereafter were allowed only to confer the bodhisattva precepts, the precepts taken by both lay and ordained Buddhists in Korea.

Three senior monks are officially in charge of a bhikṣu ordination: the preceptor (chŏn'gye asari; lit. ācārya [teacher] who transmits the precepts), usually the Sŏn master of the monastery, who serves as the spiritual mentor to the ordinands; the confessor (kalma asari; Skt. karmācārya,[15] the procedural specialist), who oversees the conduct of the ceremony and ensures that it is performed correctly; and the ordination catechist (kyosu asari; lit. ācārya who instructs), who delivers extensive sermons on the 250 bhikṣu precepts and the 348 bhikṣuṇī precepts.[16] For a valid ceremony, a number of witnesses (chŭngsa), drawn from the ranks of the most senior monks in the monastery, were also required to attend the ordination as certifiers. These witnesses may number anywhere from six to nine monks, though most of the ordinations I observed used seven. None of these witnesses has any specific role to play; they are simply to

[14] T'ongdo-sa was founded ca. 646 during the Silla dynasty by Chajang (608–686), who is regarded as the founder of the Vinaya school in Korea. For a history of the monastery, see Han'guk Pulgyo yŏn'guwŏn, ed., T'ongdo-sa, Han'guk ŭi sach'al (Korean Monasteries), no. 4 (Seoul: Ilchi-sa, 1974).

[15] Tentative reconstruction of term.

[16] The confessor is defined as "the master who performs the procedural acts [karman] at the time of full ordination." Wu-fen lü 16, T 1421.22.113a12. The ordination catechist is described as "the master who instructs in the monk's deportments at the time of full ordination." Ibid.

be present throughout the entire ceremony. The three presiding monks and the various witnesses all sit in front of the hall on a long platform raised about four feet above the ground—hence the name "ordination platform" (*kyedan*).[17] While the Koreans are not as strict as the Theravāda orders of Southeast Asia in observing to the letter the ordination procedure detailed in the *Vinaya*, they do maintain considerable propriety during the ceremony.

The bhikṣu ordinations I witnessed at Songgwang-sa were held in conjunction with the bodhisattva-precept ceremony, vastly expanding the size of the audience because of the large number of laypeople in attendance. On the first day of the ceremony, after the novice ordination is finished and breakfast eaten, all the monks and nuns who have come to receive the complete precepts sign the roster of participants. The ordinands are required to bring their changsams and bowls, though if they have forgotten their bowls the monastery supplies them with a temporary set. The monastery provides each ordinand with the large brown kasa, which can be worn only by the fully ordained bhikṣu and bhikṣuṇī. I never knew of there being any restriction on the numbers of monks and nuns allowed to participate in the ordination; since such ceremonies occurred infrequently in Korea, however, it was not unusual for Songgwang-sa to have upwards of a hundred ordinands in attendance.

At eight in the morning, after breakfast and morning work, the ordinands gather in the lecture hall for a dress rehearsal. Although I had already received full ordination in Thailand, which the Koreans accepted without reservation, after two years in Korea I chose of my own accord to reordain as a bhikṣu to mark to myself my commitment to the Korean church. At my reordination as a bhikṣu, the ordination catechist, Ilt'a sŭnim, explained in detail the steps in the ceremony and the four most important precepts. These are the *pārājika*s (expulsion offenses), transgression of which are grounds for permanent expulsion from the order: engaging in sexual intercourse, murder, grand theft, and false claims of spiritual achievement.[18] We ordinands were also told where to get information on the seemingly myriad lesser precepts of the fully ordained monk, though the pārājikas were the only precepts about which the ordination catechist showed real concern. In his discussions with us, Ilt'a spiced his lecture with commonsense advice, including his own teacher's counsel to him when he first became a monk. His teacher told him that of course he hoped he would have a successful vocation. But if the compul-

---

[17] The term is an ancient one, appearing even in Indian *Vinaya* materials. See, for example, ibid., 11c26.

[18] See Charles S. Prebish, *Buddhist Monastic Discipline: The Sanskrit Prātimokṣa Sūtras of the Mahāsāṃghikas and the Mūlasarvāstivādins* (University Park: Pennsylvania State University Press, 1975), pp. 50–53.

sion to transgress the precepts became strong, he warned, it would be better to disrobe and return to lay life (*hwansok*) than to break one of the pārājika precepts and be expelled from the order, which would shame both himself and his dharma family. He also discussed the basic etiquette and decorum of the monk's life in greater detail than was done for the novices. His purpose was to impress upon the candidates how fortunate they were to have become monks in the first place and what an opportunity they now had to further their vocations by assuming the complete precepts of the bhikṣu. He finally sought to instill in the ordinands a sensitivity for the greatness of the religious tradition we were now joining as full members. Ilt'a was one of the first contemporary Korean monks to travel widely throughout Asia, and he described for the ordinands the Buddhist traditions he had experienced in other countries. He described Korean monastic life as offering a happy medium between the austerities of the Theravāda monasteries of Southeast Asia and the laxity he had observed in Japanese monastic practice. He also stressed how fortunate we were to be ordained into a tradition where Sŏn practice still flourished.

There is no immediate pressure placed on novices to become bhikṣus or bhikṣuṇīs. Typically, a postulant remains a novice for at least three years before taking bhikṣu ordination, to ensure his contentment with the celibacy demanded in Korean monastic life; he should also be at least twenty years old. There is, however, tacit understanding within the order that once a novice decides to take full ordination, thereby acknowledging his total commitment to the tradition, he should subsequently maintain his vocation for life; but there are no formal vows stating this commitment. In traditional Korea, monks might remain novices for most of their careers, feeling themselves unworthy of assuming the responsibility to the tradition that comes with full ordination.[19]

In recent years, there have been attempts to revive the original Indian Buddhist custom that any monk over the age of twenty was eligible to take the bhikṣu ordination, even if he had not been a novice for at least three years. When this reform was first proposed at an ordination platform held at Songgwang-sa in 1976, there was much disagreement among the presiding senior monks over its wisdom. Many felt that such relaxation of the eligibility requirements would encourage monks still relatively new to the order to make virtually a permanent commitment, placing undue pressure on them. Others ascribed this reform to political motivations from some of the larger monasteries, which have the greatest num-

---

[19] See the similar remarks about Chinese monks in Kenneth Ch'en, *Buddhism in China: A Historical Survey* (Princeton: Princeton University Press, 1964), p. 247; but cf. Welch, *Practice of Chinese Buddhism*, p. 503 n.36, who found it to have been uncommon during the Republican Era for monks to remain novices for most of their careers.

ber of ordinands, to exert more control over ecclesiastical affairs by having more bhikṣus from their temples in the order. No consensus has yet emerged within the Chogye Order on this issue.

No one in Korea expects the new monks to observe all of the 250 bhikṣu precepts or 348 bhikṣuṇī precepts found in the original Indian monastic codes followed by East Asian Buddhists. Many of the precepts are considered to be anachronistic in Korea, such as the restrictions against digging the soil or entering the harem of a kṣatriya king.[20] Others are so contrary to long-observed custom in East Asia that they are ignored, such as not eating in the afternoon.[21] But the catechist encourages all the ordinands to keep all the precepts at least for that day so that they will have a sense of how monks in the Buddhist homeland of India would have lived.

The dress rehearsal for the ordination continues until about ten in the morning. After the noon dinner, the formal ceremony begins. Only monks ordaining and those supervising the ceremony are allowed to attend, a throwback to the Indian custom that the *sīmā*, or boundary lines of the ceremony, should not be transgressed by outsiders for fear of polluting the ordination. The ceremony is officially administered by the catechist and witnessed by the other senior monks on the platform. In fact, however, the succentor of the meditation hall, or another senior meditation monk, has primary responsibility for ensuring that the ceremony runs smoothly and punctually.

The actual ordination begins with the ordination catechist's giving a short explanation of the responsibilities that come with being a fully ordained monk. Monks respond in unison to all questions. When asked, for example, their names and the names of their teachers, they all answer in unison with the different information. In this regard, Korean ordinations are rather unlike those held in Theravāda countries, where each person must answer individually to ensure that he has not been coerced into ordaining. In Theravāda countries only three monks can ordain at once, but there is no such limit in Korea: virtually any number is allowed.

During the ceremony, the monks have their bowls and kasas on the floor in front of them. Toward the end of the ordination, after the ordination catechist has asked whether they have their bowls and robes ready, the ordinands will begin walking in a sinuous, snaking line, tracing a figure eight around the hall, while chanting the *Great Compassion Mantra* (*Taebi-chu*; an alternate name of the *Ch'ŏnsu-kyŏng*) three times. During

---

[20] See Prebish, *Buddhist Monastic Discipline*, p. 88, rule no. 73, and p. 90, rule no. 82, respectively, in the lists of minor *pācattika* regulations.

[21] Rule no. 36 among the *pācittika*s; see ibid., p. 80.

the walk, the ordinands place their folded kasas on top of their heads and hold their bowls in front of them. After the third repetition of the mantra, they return to their places, put the bowls back on the floor, and drape the kasas around their changsams. At that point the ordination catechist has them repeat some of the more important of the *Vinaya* rules (the pārāji-kas and perhaps a couple of the suspension offenses), and finally proclaims them bhikṣus and bhikṣunīs. In the meantime, the office monks have used the roster of participants to prepare official ordination certificates for everyone. The ordination certificate is a large document giving the date of ordination and names of the monks who officiated over the ceremony.

One of the more controversial moves made by some *Vinaya* masters in Korea was to arrange a special ordination of Korean monks by Theravāda bhikkhus from Thailand. These *Vinaya* masters were concerned about the potential aspersions that could be cast against the purity of the Korean Buddhist ordination lineage because marriage had been officially permitted during the Japanese colonial period. Organized by Ch'aun *sŭnim*, the foremost *Vinaya* master in Korea, and Ilt'a *sŭnim*, one of the most popular ordination catechists, the ordination was held at T'ongdo-sa on 22 February 1972. The abbots of Wat Benjamobopitr, Wat Sukkot, and the Thai temple in Bodhgaya presided over the ceremony, with five other Thai monks witnessing it. This ordination was conducted within the Thai Mahānikāya ordination lineage, the largest of the two main Thai Theravāda sects. In a daylong ceremony, twenty-three Korean monks received reordination in Theravāda fashion, accepting the saffron robes and large iron alms bowl that the Thai monks had brought along with them. Twenty-three other Korean monks received reordination with traditional Korean robes and bowls.

Controversy ensued immediately. Many opinion leaders within the Chogye Order viewed the ordination as a complete fiasco, because it implied that Korean Buddhism was corrupted and that the only orthodox ordination lineage remained in Thailand. Koreans also were aware that the Thai Mahānikāya tradition was in fact introduced to Thailand from Sri Lanka, which had in turn received it from Burma, so that Thailand could hardly be considered a bastion of purity in its own right. The affair grew into a full-fledged scandal when the Thais made claims, published in Korean newspapers, that they had come to Korea not to help the Korean Buddhists reestablish their *Vinaya* tradition but instead to convert them to the orthodox Thai tradition. Many of the monks who had participated in the ceremony subsequently renounced their reordinations in prominent public displays. To my knowledge, this was the last foreign ordination performed on Korean soil.

FAMILY TIES AFTER ORDINATION

One of the euphemisms Buddhists have always used for ordination is "to leave home" (*ch'ulga*; *pravrajita*). For the majority of monks, most of the functions of their secular families are effectively served by the new "dharma family." The degree to which leaving home involves cutting off contact with the natal family, however, is left up to the individual monk, some monks returning home fairly frequently for short visits, others never seeing their parents again after they have "entered the mountains" (*ipsan*).

Most of the monks I knew maintained at least some contact with their families, seeing them perhaps once or twice every two or three years. Those coming from Buddhist families often maintain much closer contact than this, perhaps seeing their parents at home each vacation period as well as being visited by their families at the monastery. One monk I knew from a good Buddhist family said that to get his mother's permission to ordain, he had promised that he would visit her at least once a year and had kept that promise over the ten years of his career.

Home ties that are too close are usually frowned upon, because they tend to drag the monk back into family affairs, which could distract the monk from his training. Such ties are not so necessary anyway in Korea, because Korea does not follow the Southeast Asian custom in which the family is one of the major sources of the monk's support. Most monks in Thailand, for example, are temporary monks, ordaining only for the three-month rain's retreat during the summer, and it is not surprising that family relationships remain important to them. In Korea, however, where ordination implies a more permanent commitment, the monk is discouraged from accepting any family support and is urged to rely on his own dharma family in times of need. For this reason, family ties tend to fade gradually in importance as the monk's associations with his monastic family deepen.

Other monks interpret leaving home literally and decide never to see their families or past associates again after their ordination. Example of this are widespread in modern Korean Buddhism, and three cases should suffice to demonstrate its extent. Hyobong *sŭnim* (1888–1966), the teacher of Kusan and one of the most renowned Sŏn masters of the last generation, was a judge in the Japanese imperial government, the first Korean ever to serve in such a distinguished position. Once, after he sentenced a man to death, he was so affected by what he had done that he immediately decided to leave his position and become an ascetic. Without telling his family or colleagues, he simply left his office and became a candy peddler in small rural villages. After three years as a traveling sales-man, he decided to become a monk and went to the Diamond Mountains to ordain under Sŏktu *sŭnim* (d. 1954). Leading the wandering life of the itinerant meditation monk, he traveled from monastery to monastery around the peninsula. After a few years of such peregrinations, a lay vis-itor happened to recognize him as an eminent judge, but Hyobong con-vinced the visitor not to expose his past identity. It was not until after assuming the position of Sŏn master that his former lay occupation was revealed.

Hyobong's main disciple, Kusan, left home in his early thirties and never visited his family again. Some forty years later, his surviving brother and sister learned of his whereabouts and came to visit him at Songgwang-sa, which turned out to be only two hours from their home village. In tears, they told Kusan of their parents' death years before, and tried to relate to him the family's history since he had dropped out of contact. Kusan soon worked the conversation around in the direction of Buddhism and ended up giving them a long lecture on the undesirability of attachments, their present suffering and grief bearing perfect witness to the truth of his statements, he told them. His relatives left greatly edi-fied, Kusan's attendant told me afterwards, and occasionally returned for more dharma talks.

As a last example, one of Kusan's main disciples, a younger monk in his late thirties, whom I knew fairly well, entered the mountains in his teens and has neither seen nor written to his parents once since that time. He is sure that they have no idea where he is or what he is doing, or, in fact, if he is even still alive. He seemed to think things better this way, because the attachment to family, he said, was one of the most difficult bonds to overcome, especially for someone raised in traditional East Asian culture, where filial ties are extremely strong. Just to cut those ties irrevocably was the easiest way to deal with them, he felt.

If a monk does decide to break off all contact with his home, it is ex-ceedingly difficult for the family to trace him, especially if they don't know his monk's name or the monastery where he was ordained. After ordination, a monk is known exclusively by his Buddhist name, and only the office at his home monastery has on record any information about his lay status or name. Even if his family should happen to hear news of their son from someone, it would still be well nigh impossible to track his movements, since monks travel so frequently during the free seasons, rarely staying more than a few days in any one place. Finally, contact between the monk and his parents is almost entirely up to the monk him-self, and the family has little choice but to acquiesce in his decision.

SECESSION FROM THE ORDER

But family pressures and the unwavering rigor of the daily monastic schedule prove to be too much for some monks, and they secede from the order, or "return to secular life" (*hwansok*), as the Koreans call it. The two monks in my dharma family who seceded during my years in Korea were both fairly new to their vocations. I heard of no cases where a monk who had persisted for more than five years in the monastery had disrobed, suggesting that monks who are successful in their initial adaptation to the cloistered lifestyle will tend to remain for life.

No formal ceremony marks a monk's secession from the order, as is the case in Thailand, where it is the custom for laymen to ordain for only a few weeks or months at a time.[22] Most typically in Korea, a monk simply vanishes and is not heard from again. Since monks travel so much, the home monastery and his vocation master may not learn of his secession until several months hence. To avoid the awkwardness of returning to his home monastery, one of the secessionists in my dharma family simply mailed back to his vocation master his formal robes, which his teacher then passed on to one of his new ordinands. In the other case, the former monk sought to treat his secession in a dignified fashion and returned in person to Songgwang-sa to inform his vocation master of his decision and to return his monk's robes. But his vocation master refused to accept the robes and tried to convince his student to stay at the monastery and continue his career. The former monk finally left his robes with the proctor before departing for good.

If a secessionist monk could be convinced to return, there would be no stigma against simply putting his robes back on and picking up right where he had left off (though he would lose whatever seniority he had accumulated). But I never heard of a disrobed Korean monk returning to the order—another contrast to the custom in Southeast Asia, where monks may reordain up to seven times. In Korea, reordination need not even be demanded unless the monk himself wished to reassert his commitment to his vocation.

My own decision to disrobe came gradually, not because of any dissatisfaction with the contemplative life I was leading at Songgwang-sa, but because of my unfulfilled aspirations to scholarship. Since I first realized my affinities with Buddhism, I had been fighting my own internal battle

---

[22] Sŏngch'ŏl *sŭnim*, the Sŏn master at Haein-sa, performs secession ceremonies at his monastery (probably influenced by these Thai models). The ceremony has the monk formally declare that he "returns his precepts" to the Buddha before he breaks his ties to the order. Personal communication from Professor Sung Bae Park, 8 June 1991.

between scholarly and contemplative interests, which continued long after my ordination. I can vividly recall sitting outside my room at Wat Bovoranives in Thailand, just a couple of months after becoming a monk, debating whether I should continue to devote myself to studying Pali or leave it all behind and just meditate. Most of my time in Thailand and Hong Kong was spent studying Pali and Chinese and trying my hand at translating Buddhist texts. But after two years as a monk, I finally felt I was mature enough to focus exclusively on meditation and thought a Zen meditation hall would be the ideal place to pursue that aim. Kórea beckoned.

But try as I might, I just could not shake the pull of scholarship. After two years in the meditation hall at Songgwang-sa, a couple of colleagues and I decided to prepare English translations of some of Kusan's dharma talks and spent the autumn free season preparing a small book—*Nine Mountains*, which I will talk more about in Chapter Seven. A couple of years later, Kusan asked me to translate the works of Chinul, the founder of Songgwang-sa and the progenitor of a uniquely Korean style of Zen practice. Feeling myself being drawn away from meditation once again, I consented only with great reticence: I would do only what I could finish in one free season. I ended up spending three free seasons on that book, which eventually was published in 1983 as *The Korean Approach to Zen: The Collected Works of Chinul*. During the research and writing of that book, I finally acquiesced to this drive toward scholarship.

The immediate catalyst for my leaving Songgwang-sa came one morning when a couple of senior monks in the monastery administration came to my compound to discuss the renovation project they hoped to begin soon there. The plan was to turn my compound into a center where Western monks could train without being burdened by learning Korean or becoming proficient in all the monastic customs—a plan I was not yet sold on. While walking around the compound with them, one of the monks pointed to a room off the meditation hall and mentioned casually that that was where I would stay when I became overseer of the compound. I knew at that moment that if I did not leave soon, I would be saddled with more and more administrative burdens; I was only twenty-five and wanted at least a few more years for my own training. I immediately decided to broach with Kusan the idea of returning to the United States—ostensibly to arrange publication of the book on Chinul, but I now know it was as much to escape from this looming administrative responsibility. Although Kusan was reluctant to have me leave, he finally relented and gave me a ticket to the United States. He said it might be good to have me explore what kind of proselytization Songgwang-sa might be able to do in the West. We talked of my returning to Korea in a few months, but no firm commitments were made. As I look back now, I know that my battle over defining my vocation was finally over: I had chosen scholarship.

Soon after returning to the United States in the spring of 1979, I arranged to return to school at Berkeley the next fall quarter to begin work again on my B.A. I spent my first two quarters in school as a monk, still wearing the gray robes. Once I knew that I wanted to stay to finish my degree and then try to go on to graduate school in Buddhist Studies, I made my decision to secede. I disrobed in an informal ceremony at a small Zen center in Berkeley, became a layman, and assumed my new identity as a junior in college and lay Buddhist practitioner.

I saw Kusan in California on trips he took to the United States in 1980 and 1982. Even though he did chide me gently about disrobing and encouraged me to return with him to Songgwang-sa, he was never adamant about it: the door was open for me to return when and if I wanted. I have come to think that Kusan's graciousness toward me reflected his belief that a scholarly career was a viable vocation for a Buddhist in the West, which does not yet have the developed monastic traditions so necessary for a celibate lifestyle.

POSTORDINATION CAREER: SERVICE AND SEMINARY STUDY

After their ordination, the new novices continue in their old jobs in the kitchen for the next few days until they are assigned new positions in the monastery. Often this means that they move up to being the attendant of their ŭnsa or taking a position in the support division of the monastery, where the new monk usually finds himself for the first few years after ordination.

The new bhikṣus have already been monks for some years and have fulfilled the first major round of filial duties to their monastic family. While their vocation master will often prefer that they continue to serve the home monastery, the monks can now legitimately request to go elsewhere to practice.

Some may choose to enter a seminary, called either a monk's academy (sŭngga hagwŏn) or lecture hall (kangwŏn), where they may study systematically several of the basic texts of the Korean Buddhist tradition. Songgwang-sa did not have an operating seminary during the years I was resident, so I was never able to witness seminary life firsthand. My account here will draw from documents concerning the seminary curricula and schedules and discussions I had with monks who went through the seminaries at other monasteries.

It is not known when monastic seminaries were first formed in Korea, though given the strong doctrinal interests of the tradition, it must have been early on in the history of the religion. The curriculum used today in Korean monasteries is traced to the Chosŏn-dynasty Sŏn master Hwan-sŏng Chian (1664–1729), who is said to have organized his seminary while trying to find a way to teach over 1,400 students at Kŭmsan-sa.[23] He split his students into two groups: the recitation track (toksŏ-p'a) and the textual study track (kan'gyŏng-p'a). The recitation track was further subdivided into two groups. The first, the Śramaṇera Course (Sami-kwa), instructed the student in the basic codes of monastic etiquette (the Admonitions to the Gray-robed Monks, or Ch'imun kyŏnghun[24]) and in edifying tracts to help the student develop faith in his religion (the Admonitions to Beginners). The second, the Fourfold Collection Course (Sajip-kwa), covered four seminal texts of the Korean approach to Sŏn practice, focusing especially on kongan (Jpn. kōan) meditation (the Letters of Ta-hui Tsung-kao and Kao-feng Yüan-miao's Essentials of Ch'an) and Sŏn soteriology (Tsung-mi's Ch'an Preface and Chinul's Excerpts from the Dharma Collection and Special Practice Record with Personal Notes).[25] Students in the recitation track received instruction in the morning on one section of the text they were studying, which probably involved teaching them the pronunciation and meaning of individual characters in each passage. Then, for the rest of the day until late into the evening, they would recite that same section over and over again until it was memorized. Through such rote memorization, the students learned to pronounce and parse phrases of literary Chinese, as well as gaining some basic knowledge about monastic discipline and, later, the foundations of Korean Sŏn practice.

The textual study track was subdivided into three courses. In the first, the Four Teachings Course (Sagyo-kwa), the students read four seminal scriptures of the Sinitic Mahāyāna doctrinal tradition: the Book of the

[23] The following account is taken from the Yi Hoemyŏng sŏnsa sillok (Veritable Record of the Sŏn Master Yi Hoemyŏng), pp. 402–07, excerpted in Han'guk kŭnse Pulgyo paengnyŏnsa, vol. 1, kwŏn 2, Kyoyuk p'yŏnnyŏn, pp. 1–4.

[24] Tzu-men ching-hsün, recompiled in ten fascicles during the Ming dynasty by Ching-shan; T 2023.48.1044c–1097c.

[25] Ta-hui's Letters (Taehye sŏjang) are excerpted from the discourse record of Ta-hui Tsung-kao (1089–1163; T 1998A.47.811a–943a) and partially translated by Christopher Cleary, Swampland Flowers: The Letters and Lectures of Zen Master Ta Hui (New York: Grove Press, 1977). The Essentials of Ch'an (Ch'an-yao; Kor. Sŏnyo) by Kao-feng Yüan-miao (1238–1295) appears in Hsü-tsang ching (HTC) 122.352b–262b; I am presently preparing an annotated translation and study of this text. Tsung-mi's (780–841) Ch'an Preface is his Ch'an-yüan chu-ch'üan chi tou-hsü (T 2015.48.399a–413c); the entire text is translated in Jeffrey Broughton, "Kuei-feng Tsung-mi: The Convergence of Chan and the Teachings" (Ph.D. diss., Columbia University, 1975), and portions are translated in Buswell, Korean Approach, passim. I have translated Chinul's Excerpts in full ibid., pp. 262–374. The best edition of the Sa chip is that by Kim T'anhŏ, ed. and trans., Sa chip (Fourfold Collection), 4 vols. (Seoul: Kyorim, 1974).

Heroic March Samādhi (*Shou-leng-yen ching*; *Śuraṃgama-sūtra*[26]), the *Awakening of Faith* (*Ta-sheng ch'i-hsin lun*), the *Perfection of Wisdom Sūtra* (viz. the *Diamond Sūtra*; *Chin-kang ching*), and the *Book of Consummate Enlightenment* (*Yüan-chüeh ching*).[27] The next, the Great Teachings Course (Taegyo-kwa), taught the *Avataṃsaka-sūtra* and Ch'eng-kuan's commentary to that sūtra. The last, the Superlative Course (Kyŏgoe-kwa), instructed the students in two large collections of Sŏn biographies, lineages, and anecdotes: *Stories about the Sŏn School's Enlightened Verses* (*Sŏnmun yŏmsong sŏrhwa*), Kugok Kagun's (ca. thirteenth century) annotated edition of Hyesim's (1178–1234) indigenous Korean kongan collection, the *Collection of the Sŏn School's Enlightened Verses* (*Sŏnmun yŏmsong chip*); and the *Record of the Transmission of the Lamp, Compiled during the Ching-teh Era* (*Ching-teh ch'uan-teng lu*), a Chinese lamp anthology of Ch'an lineages.[28] Students who completed all of the preceding curricula could still continue in the seminary, going on to the Independent Course (Suŭi-kwa). This would involve the study of such important Mahāyāna sūtras as the *Lotus*, *Nirvāṇa*, *Vimalakīrti*, and *Kṣitigarbha*.

Rather than reciting their texts out loud, as did the other track, the textual study students would instead read silently. (To avoid disturbing the textual students with the constant cacophony of sound emanating from the reciters' room, they lived and studied separately.) They listened to lectures on the section they were studying that day, and the next day one of the students was required to give his own lecture on the same or related passage. After the noon meal, the entire class would gather in the seminary for a round of meditation, followed by more silent study. After the evening meal, the succentor (*ipsŭng*) of the seminary hall would lead the students in ten rounds of recollections of the invocation *Namu Amit'a-pul* (Homage to Amitābha Buddha). In this way three "gates" (*mun*), or modes, of Buddhist practice—Sŏn meditation, doctrinal study, and recitation of the Buddha's name—would all be cultivated by the students. At the second watch of the night (9:00 P.M.), after more silent study, the monks would retire, rising again at the fourth watch of the night (3:00 A.M.). After early morning service and breakfast, they would have another lecture and the whole sequence would start again.

Two monks from among the textual students were chosen by lottery to

[26] Tentative reconstruction of title.

[27] *Shou-leng-yen ching*, T 945.19.105b–155b; *Ta-sheng ch'i-hsin lun*, T 1666.32.575b–583b; *Chin-kang ching*, T 235.8.748c–752c; *Yüan-chüeh ching*, T 842.17.913a–922a.

[28] Kugok Kagun, *Sŏnmun Yŏmsong sŏrhwa* (Stories about the Sŏn School's Enlightened Verses), 2 vols. (reprint, Seoul: Poryŏn'gak, 1978). For the textual history of Hyesim's *Sŏnmun yŏmsong chip*, see my article "Chinul's Systematization of Chinese Meditation Techniques," p. 239 n.94. The *Ching-teh ch'uan-teng lu* appears in T 2076.51.204a–467a.

serve as the lecturer's assistant (*chunggang*), rather like a professor's teaching assistant, and the commentator (*palgi*) to each day's lesson. The lecturer's assistant would outline from memory to the assembled textual study students the main ideas of the section they were learning. Next, the commentator would open his book and explain the text word by word, all the other monks silently following along in their own books. The commentator's explanations would be based upon the main commentary to whatever text it was they were studying. If any student in the class disagreed with the commentator's explanation, he could give his own interpretation. These various interpretations would then be discussed among the students until they reached a consensus, at which point that interpretation would be judged correct. If they couldn't reach a consensus, they would consult the head lecturer (*kangsa*). Subsequently, they would decide which pages of their text to cover in the next session, and then retire to individual study. The purpose of this format was not only to inculcate the students, but also to train them to serve as lecturers themselves in the future.

The head lecturer personally instructed the students only twice monthly, on full and new moon days. At that time the different tracks and courses of the seminary would have a one-day break from their ordinary schedule. In the morning after breakfast, all the monks gathered in the lecture hall for an extra service. After the head lecturer had entered the hall and sat down upon the dais, the students placed their books on the floor in front of them, stood up, and bowed once together to the head lecturer. After they had sat back down at their places, the lecturer would then run briefly through the outlines of the texts being studied in all the different classes and, after elucidating their general meanings, would give an extemporaneous account of the significance of these doctrinal teachings. If any time remained, he might explain a point about the monk's discipline. After the completion of the lecture, the students would all rise and bow once, and file out of the hall.

Today, some 250 years later, Buddhist monastic seminaries still adhere closely to this Chosŏn dynasty curriculum. The standardized curriculum adopted in Korean seminaries is divided into four levels.[29] The elementary curriculum, or Sami-kwa (Śramaṇera Course), involves two years of study and takes the student through the *Admonitions to Beginners*, the

[29] See Yi Chigwan, *Han'guk Pulgyo soŭi kyŏngjŏn* (The Fundamental Texts of Korean Buddhism) (Kyŏngsang Namdo: Haein-sa, 1969); and Chŏng Pyŏngjo, "Han'guk Pulgyo ŭi hyŏnhyang kwa munjechŏm" (The Present Condition of Korean Buddhism and Problematic Points), *Pulgyo yŏn'gu* (Buddhist Studies) 2 (1986): 202. See also the account of the similar curriculum followed at the T'ongdo-sa seminary in Han'guk Pulgyo yŏn'gu-wŏn, eds., *T'ongdo-sa*, Han'guk ŭi sach'al (Korean Monasteries), no. 4 (Seoul: Ilchi-sa, 1974), pp. 60–61.

Śramaṇera Precepts and Decorum (*Sami yurŭi*), and the *Admonitions to the Gray-Robed Monks*. The emphasis in the works at this level continues to be on monastic conduct and etiquette and edifying tracts. The intermediate curriculum, or Sajip-kwa (Fourfold Collection Course), takes three years and introduces the students to those four texts listed earlier, which provide basic grounding in the theory and practice of Sŏn meditation. The texts by Tsung-mi (780–841) and Chinul used in this curriculum also create an awareness of the symbiosis between Sŏn and Kyo that has been an essential element in Korean Buddhist ideology since the mid–Koryŏ period. The advanced curriculum, or Sagyo-kwa (Fourfold Doctrinal Course), takes four years, and covers four central doctrinal texts: the *Book of the Heroic March Samādhi*, *Awakening of Faith*, *Book of Consummate Enlightenment*, and *Five Commentaries to the Diamond Sūtra* (*Kŭmgang-kyŏng ogahae*). Interestingly enough, three of these texts (all but the *Diamond Sūtra*) are now considered to be Chinese apocryphal scriptures, showing the impact that indigenous Sinitic scriptures have had on the East Asian Buddhist tradition.[30] Finally, the graduate level, the Taegyo-kwa (Great Doctrinal Course), requires three years, and takes the student through the entire Flower Garland Sūtra (*Avataṃsaka-sūtra*). Hence, a student who completes all four of these curricula would have spent approximately twelve years in study.

As of September 1976, twenty-two monasteries (Songgwang-sa not among them) had established Buddhist seminaries. A total of 722 religious (409 monks and 313 nuns) were studying at those seminaries, taught by a total of twenty-three lecturers. The largest study center for the monks was Haein-sa, with seventy-seven students; the largest for nuns was Unmun-sa, with 116 students. As of February 1982, nine of the largest of these seminaries had 599 students; Haein-sa and Unmun-sa continued to be the main study centers, with 112 and 147 students, respectively.[31]

Education in the seminaries is based on the style followed in the traditional Confucian academy (*sŏdang*), where rote memorization was emphasized. Study primarily involves the monks' learning to read the Sino-Korean logographs used in the texts, not necessarily discussing the ideas that they convey. Little sense of the historical context of the development of Korean Buddhism is provided to the students, nor is any material offered to help them understand the antecedents of their own tradition in India and China. Secular knowledge, such as mathematics, history, or art, is completely eschewed in the monastic curriculum.

[30] For such scriptures, see Robert E. Buswell, Jr., ed., *Chinese Buddhist Apocrypha* (Honolulu: University of Hawaii Press, 1990).

[31] See Chŏng Pyŏngjo, "Han'guk Pulgyo ŭi hyŏnghyang," pp. 200–202 for charts of the data.

Because of these perceived deficiencies, proposals to upgrade the quality of instruction are periodically broached. Yi Chigwan, a Buddhist monk who was chancellor of Tongguk University, the Buddhist university in Seoul, tried to introduce the study of basic Mahāyāna sūtras to the seminary system when he was the head lecturer at Haein-sa. In his attempted reform in 1965, he combined study of Sŏn expository texts by Tsung-mi and Chinul from the *Fourfold Collection* with some important Mahāyāna sūtras.[32] But this reform was not followed at seminaries in other monasteries, probably because there were no lecturers with the knowledge to impose such a change, and it was ultimately scrapped at Haein-sa as well.

One major idiosyncrasy of the present Haein-sa seminary is that it no longer studies Chinul's magnum opus, *Excerpts*, the culminating work in the *Fourfold Collection*. This text is a detailed analysis and critique of various regimens of Sŏn soteriology, which finally comes out in favor of a "sudden awakening-gradual cultivation" (*tono chŏmsu*) schema. But the Sŏn master at Haein-sa, Sŏngch'ŏl, who is presently the supreme patriarch (*chongjŏng*) of the Chogye Order, is a fervent advocate of the rival regimen of "sudden awakening-sudden cultivation" (*tono tonsu*). In his immensely learned, but strongly polemical treatise, *The Orthodox Road of the Sŏn School* (*Sŏnmun chŏngno*), Sŏngch'ŏl methodically demolishes Chinul's doctrinal edifice in order to debunk any claim Chinul might have to being an authentic Sŏn master.[33] The crux of his criticism is the accommodation Chinul makes for a gradual component in Sŏn soteriology, which Sŏngch'ŏl decries as "a fiction . . . that is diametrically opposed to the orthodox transmission of the Sŏn school."[34] Sŏngch'ŏl makes an exhaustive study of Ch'an literature in his attempt to demonstrate that authentic Ch'an soteriology—the school's "orthodox road," as he calls it— is sudden awakening–sudden cultivation.[35] Sŏngch'ŏl's conclusion is that Chinul "was not an enlightened master in a recognized transmission lineage, as is emblematic of the Sŏn school. The main subject of his thought is Hwaŏm-Sŏn,"[36] a pejorative term Sŏngch'ŏl uses to describe a bastard-

---

[32] For his proposed reforms, and the study schedule of the Haein-sa lecture halls, see Yi Chigwan, *Sajip sagi* (Annotation to the *Fourfold Collection*) (Kyŏngsang namdo: Haein Ch'ongnim, 1969), pp. 5–6.

[33] T'oeong Sŏngch'ŏl, *Sŏnmun chŏngno* (Kyŏngsang namdo: Haein Ch'ongnim, 1981), esp. chaps. 13 and 18. A few hints of Sŏngch'ŏl's attitudes toward Chinul appear in an English anthology of his dharma talks, *Echoes from Mt. Kaya: Selections on Korean Buddhism by Ven. Song-chol, Patriarch of the Korean Chogye Buddhist Order*, ed. by Ven. Won'tek, introduction by Ven. Won-myong, trans. by Brian Barry (Seoul: Lotus Lantern International Buddhist Center, 1988); see, for example p. 153.

[34] T'oeong Sŏngch'ŏl, *Sŏnmun chŏngnok*, pp. 170, 161.

[35] Ibid., p. 164 and passim.

[36] Ibid., p. 209.

ized form of Sŏn, in which Sŏn practice is combined with Hwaŏm scholastic doctrine. So adamant is Sŏngch'ŏl about Chinul's mistakes that he has forbidden the study of Chinul's *Excerpts* in the Haein-sa seminary.[37]

Since Chinul is the founder of Songgwang-sa, the monks there have taken umbrage at what they consider to be Sŏngch'ŏl's provocations. To counter Sŏngch'ŏl's criticisms of Chinul, and to increase awareness of Chinul's role in forging a distinctively Korean form of Sŏn, Songgwang-sa has established a separate academic institute, the Institute for the Study of Chinul's Thought (Pojo Sasang Yŏn'guwŏn), to promote Chinul studies in both monastic seminaries and universities; the institute has sponsored several international conferences to raise the profile of Chinul in Korean Buddhist studies. The controversy rages unabated between the two monasteries.

Still more recently, in 1986, Chŏng Pyŏngjo, a professor at Tongguk University, proposed another set of reforms. He suggested shortening the curriculum to eight years total, and introducing a much wider curriculum than is presently offered in the monastic seminaries. During the elementary Sami-kwa, for example, he proposes that students be taught the Buddha's life and read books on both Buddhist cultural history and Religious Studies methodologies. The intermediate level would introduce the basic "Hīnayāna" *Āgama* scriptures, as well as Indian Buddhist history, English, and philosophy. The advanced level would involve readings on the history of Sŏn Buddhism, Wŏnhyo's (617–686) thought, Chinese Buddhist history, comparative philosophy, Sanskrit, and Korean Buddhist history. The graduate level would retain study of the *Flower Garland Sūtra*, but add the *Record of Lin-chi (Lin-chi lu)* and missiology, as well as comparative study of Sanskrit, Pali, and Chinese Buddhist texts, Mahāyāna thought, and issues in Korean Buddhism.[38] No seminary has yet made any moves to incorporate Chŏng's suggestions into its curriculum.

While many monks have completed the elementary Sami-kwa, only those with a strong scholarly calling will continue on to complete the two most advanced courses of study. Virtually all religious, as part of their postulancy, will have studied the *Admonitions to Beginners* and parts of the *Śramaṇera Rules and Decorum*, so these two texts constitute the basic knowledge common to most monks in the order. Even though relatively

---

[37] A detailed critique of Sŏngch'ŏl's position appears in Sung Bae Park [Pak Sŏngbae], "Sŏngch'ŏl sŭnim-ŭi tono chŏmsu-sŏl pip'an-e taehayŏ (On Sŏngch'ŏl's Critique of the Theory of Sudden Awakening/Gradual Cultivation), *Pojo sasang* (Chinul's Thought) 4 (1990): 501–28. For a brief survey of Sŏngch'ŏl's criticism of Chinul, see Robert E. Buswell, Jr., "Chinul's Alternative Vision of *Kanhwa* Sŏn and Its Implications for Sudden Awakening/Sudden Cultivation," *Pojo sasang* (Chinul's Thought) 4 (1990): 435–37.

[38] See the detailed proposal in Chŏng Pyŏngjo, "Han'guk Pulgyo ŭi hyŏnhyang," pp. 203–4.

few monks are active in the seminary, most will therefore have received at least some grounding in Buddhist discipline. Monks who are interested in eventually entering the meditation hall are encouraged to study at least the first text of the intermediate Sajip-kwa, Ta-hui's *Letters*, since that text outlines the basics of the *kanhwa* (observing the critical phrase) technique of Sŏn meditation that is practiced in Korea. I will cover this technique in chapter seven.

PILGRIMAGE

The freedom to travel during the three-month-long haeje period, and to sojourn at any monastery in the country for as long as one wants, is one of the perquisites of the monastic life and one that virtually all monks, especially the younger ones, take to heart. Travel provides one of the few real chances monks have to meet their cloistered friends and to socialize freely. In the last couple of weeks of the restricted retreat period, some monks are already sending letters out to their friends (surreptitiously, if need be), arranging to meet at a particular monastery once the retreat is finally over. Other monks may have no particular plans, but will simply go down to the village or nearest town at the end of the retreat, hook up with other monks they find there, and start out together for another monastery. For many the immediate destination is unimportant, as long as it is away from where they have spent their last three months.

Traveling monks are welcome to stay in any temple in Korea for up to three days without any obligations or responsibilities. In the kitchen area (*huwŏn*; lit. rear precinct) of all larger monasteries, several rooms are put aside as guest rooms (*kaeksil*) for visiting monks and laypeople. The number of rooms available depends on the size of the monastery. The largest monasteries may have upwards of ten separate rooms, accommodating some four monks apiece. In smaller temples, there may be only one or two rooms, which visiting monks might have to share with male lay workers or the children of the temple's female workers.

Upon arriving at a new monastery, the visiting monk (*kaek sŭnim*) asks to be directed to the kitchen area or the proctor's room (*wŏnju-sil*), both of which are usually near the guest rooms. Someone then escorts him to either the proctor or his assistant (*pyŏlchwa*), who shows him to his room and orders a postulant to prepare a fire under the ondol floor to warm the room. The first evening of his stay, the visitor signs the monastery's registration book, providing his Buddhist name, home monastery, national identification number, saṃgha identification number, date of arrival, and intended length of stay. Even a monk returning to his home monastery has to spend the first few days in the guest area until his formal introduction for readmission to the temple is accepted. But if he has a friend in the monastery, especially someone on the support staff, the monk might stay over in his friend's room instead of the guest rooms.

Guest monks aren't expected, or generally even allowed, to participate in much of the regular life of the monastery. Because traveling monks are presumed to be tired from their journey, they rarely join in the regular morning and evening services. The visitors are served meals at their own quarters for each meal, since they are also not permitted to eat together with the monastic residents. The proctor will arrange for a postulant to bring tea to the visitors after their meals and might even come himself to chat with the monks, especially if they are old friends or family members of the monastery. The visitors are also not required to participate in any of the work scheduled around the monastery.

The guest prefect (*chigaek*) comes to the kitchen area once a day to greet any new arrivals.[39] If a visiting monk plans to reside at the monastery for the next retreat season, the prefect will question him in detail about his background and vocation. If he is satisfied with the visitor's credentials, he will sponsor the guest monk's formal introduction to the monastery. If after three days the monk decides not to stay on at the monastery, the proctor offers him enough traveling money to get him to his next destination, generally not much more than a few thousand *wŏn* (five–ten dollars).

If monks are traveling in mountainous regions where there are no monasteries, they may also stay over in a hermitage (*amja*). Because small hermitages rarely have enough extra food on hand to feed guests, visiting monks might bring along some rice, pickled vegetables (*kimch'i*), or flour to the hermitage in exchange for overnight lodging. Although I traveled all over Korea during my stay in the country, one of my most memorable trips was a week I spent traveling through the Chiri Mountain region of south-central Korea, the longest mountain range in all of south Korea.[40] While larger monasteries are located around the base of the range, only hermitages are found higher up the mountain, spaced so that a pilgrim could travel on foot from one to the next in a single day's journey. Despite being a foreign monk, I was always welcomed by the residents and fed well, if somewhat spartanly, with many wild mountain greens and roots. Unlike the guest monks at large monasteries, at a hermitage the visitor always participates in the resident monk's daily schedule, joining him in services, meditation, and meals.

The traveling monk's knapsack (*kabang*) will be filled with all his req-

---

[39] For this monastic office, see *Pai-chang ch'ing-kuei* 2, T 2025.48.1131b9–17.

[40] Chiri Mountain is now preserved as a national park of over 440 square kilometers. For discussion of this important mountain range, see Yong Bum Cho, "Chiri Mountain," *Korean Culture* 10, no. 2 (Summer 1989): 15–25.

uisites. He will have at least one extra set of clothes, socks, toothbrush, towel, and perhaps a book or two. The monasteries he visits will supply razors, blades, toothpaste, soap, and laundry powder, so he can travel lightly. Any other personal possessions he might own will be left behind at his home monastery or at a hermitage he frequents. If he is traveling to a new monastery, he will also carry his formal robes and his set of four bowls and eating utensils (chopsticks and spoon).

Once a monk on pilgrimage has passed three days at the monastery, he must decide whether to move on or stay. If he chooses to leave, the proctor will give him travel funds to his next destination. If instead he wishes to enter the monastery, he must give a formal introduction (*pangbu*; lit. room request) to the temple, in a brief ceremony performed before all the resident monks.

The monk is first given a form to fill out, which asks for his family name, dharma name, home monastery, vocation master, ordination dates, military service, and educational record. After completing it, the monk returns it to the monastery's guest prefect. (There is also an additional guest prefect who is in charge of admissions just to the meditation hall.) If the guest prefect is satisfied with the information, the monk is formally introduced to the monastery residents, usually immediately following the midday dinner. Wearing his long formal robe (*changsam*) and brownish dyed cloak (*kasa*, from Skt. *kāṣāya*), the monk enters the refectory together with the guest prefect, prostrates himself three times, first to the buddha image, then to all the senior monks, and in many cases, finally to the monks sitting at the far ends of the room. After completing this series of prostrations, he remains kneeling with his palms together in prayer position (*hapchang*) before the senior monks, while the rector (*yuna*) introduces him. The standard formula is as follows:

> Assembled monks, I make a formal introduction.
> This monk's home monastery is . . . .
> His vocation master is . . . .
> His dharma name is . . . .
> He will be entering the kitchen [meditation hall, office, etc.] for the next
> 　retreat season to practice.
> May the assembled monks acknowledge this.

Then the monk bows once more, withdraws from the room, and takes his things up to the compound where he will reside, to be greeted by his new companions. The monk is still welcome to travel for the rest of the free season, if he so desires. But to reserve his spot in the monastery for the retreat, he must leave his formal robe and bowls behind as a sign that he will return.

MONKS' CLOTHING

A monk traveling around Korea cuts a distinctive figure, with his shaved head, baggy gray clothes, and gray cloth knapsack. Unlike Japanese monks, who will often be found in street clothes, over which they wear their priestly robes, Korean monks still wear the traditional outer jacket (*turumagi*) over shirts and baggy gray pants (*paji*) with leggings (*haenggŏn*; alt. *haengjŏn*). These items of clothing were common in traditional Korea, and one still finds elderly "grandfathers" (*haraböji*) in the countryside wearing them. The only thing distinctive about the monastic version of this ensemble is the gray color.

Monks' clothes used to be cut from cotton broadcloth, but most monks now wear polyester instead, which is much easier to take care of. Only meditation monks still commonly wear natural-fiber materials, and they do it not for convenience but as a mark of their asceticism. Why this is so will be clear the first time you have to wash and iron natural cotton clothing. Cotton needs to be starched and ironed, a time-consuming process since even the starch must first be prepared by squeezing leftover rice through a cheesecloth bag. A properly starched shirt is so stiff that it will stand upright on the floor by itself. The rustling of all these starched clothes is overwhelming for the first couple of days after clothes are washed.

Another of the marks of the meditation monk is to wear old clothes covered with layer upon layer of patches. While such garments are supposed to show his detachment from material possessions, they more often serve as a kind of monastic status symbol. On several occasions I even knew a monk new to the meditation hall to trade a brand-new set of polyester robes for old patchwork clothes. During their free time, the meditation monks can often be found adding still more patches to their raiments.

Postulants new to the monastery always receive secondhand clothing. When a prospective postulant first enters the monastery, he will continue to wear his ordinary street clothes until he is given permission to begin his postulancy. He then has his head shaved and is given a set of used clothes from the monastery storeroom. Most of these will be clothes donated by monks who have received a new set. After a monk has died, however, many of his robes will be passed on, to be distributed among his disciples.

During the winter, monks also wear a thick coat, quilted with layers of cotton batting (*hatturumagi*). Since such warm coats are expensive, they will often be covered with patches to make them last yet another season. In the summer, monks may exchange their polyester or cotton clothes for robes made from coarse hemp cloth. This cool, airy fabric is ideal for the sweltering summers of Korea, but requires even more care than cotton.

It is only during formal services inside the monastery that the monks wear clothes that are distinctively monastic. The first of these is the long outer robe (*changsam*), the full-length, formal robe with huge butterfly sleeves, which is worn over the regular monks' clothing. This full-length robe is especially expensive and monks usually own only one, generally a polyester and wool blend, although the traditional cotton changsams are still occasionally found. Only monks who have been ordained for quite some time, and who have independent lay supporters, would be able to afford a second summer changsam, made of a lighter polyester fabric or of hemp. Around the changsam fully ordained monks drape the kasa, or "dyed cloak" (a transcription of the Sanskrit *kāṣāya*), a stylized East Asian version of the traditional Indian Buddhist robe. Korean kasas are nowadays always dark brown in color, though colors varied in the past from bright orange to purple.[41] They are sewn together from twenty-five pieces of cloth, made following ancient Indian Buddhist custom to look like tilled fields.[42] Novice monks wear instead a miniature version of the kasa, the "five-piece *kāṣāya*" (*ojo kasa*), a square of cloth that is hung around the neck, covering the belly. Introduced into Korea by the Japanese, the ojo kasa is one of the few remaining vestiges in the modern Chogye Order of the colonial period. Because this miniature kasa is much more convenient to wear than the full-sized kasa, even bhikṣus will often be found wearing it nowadays.

After doing a bit of traveling and spending perhaps two or three years in the seminary, the monk may decide to enter a meditation hall somewhere and begin his practice career, or return to his home monastery to undertake more support duties. I will cover the contemplative vocation of the meditation monk in subsequent chapters; let me turn now to the support division of the Korean monastery, where the majority of Korean monks are based.

[41] Married monks in the T'aego Order wear red kasas; see the picture in Martine Aepli, *Korea* (Paris: Souffles, 1988), p. 103.
[42] See Sŏk Chusŏn, *Ŭi* (Clothing) (Seoul: Tan'guk University Press, 1985), p. 161.

1. Songgwang-sa during the Japanese Occupation

2. Songgwang-sa after Suffering Massive Destruction during the Korean War

3. Songgwang-sa, ca. 1989

4. Sŏn Master Kusan

5. Postulants Preparing the Evening Rice

6. Congregation Filing toward the Refectory for the Midday Dinner

7. Dinner in the Main Refectory

8. Carrying the Warning Stick in the Meditation Hall

9. The Eminent Young Meditation
Monk, Hyeguk *Sŭnim*

10. Monks Studying in the Seminary

11. Weeding the Fields

12. Monks Harvesting Rice
in the Songgwang-sa Paddies

13. Retiling a Roof

14. Songgwang-sa's New Sŏn Master, Hoegwang Sŭngch'an, Lecturing in the Main Buddha Hall

15. Hoegwang Delivering a Formal Dharma Lecture before the Assembled Community

16. Laity Meditating during a Training Session for the Puril Hoe

CHAPTER FIVE

The Support Division of the Monastery

STANDING MIDWAY between the spiritual aims of the large monastery and the economic and social realities it constantly faces is the temple's support staff, the "scrutinizers of phenomena" (*sap'an*), or sometimes the "external protectors" (*oeho*). Since most monks in any monastery will spend much of their careers in one or another of its many support positions, I will discuss that division here before moving on later to the practice division of the monastery.

In a dharma talk, Kusan once described the many monks holding support roles in the monastery as living dharma-protectors (*pŏpho*), like the heavenly kings who guard the front entrance of the temple from baleful influences. They are charged with handling all the daily pressures and tasks facing the monastery so as to free the meditators and scholars from unnecessary distractions. The success of the large monastery as a practice center is directly dependent upon the success of these monks in discharging their responsibilities in financial matters, agriculture, and edification. Indeed, I found it one of the most striking paradoxes of the monastic institution that on the shoulders of those monks least involved in the putative raison d'être of Sŏn monks—meditation—is supported the entire practice edifice of the monastery. I hope to show here that even though many of the most dedicated and active monks in Sŏn monasteries do little, if indeed any, meditation themselves, they have forged for themselves vocations that are absolutely essential to the continued viability of the Sŏn tradition.

At the beginning of each retreat season, the monastery drafts a Yong-sang-pang (Plaque of Dragons and Elephants) listing forty-seven offices that must be filled for the three-month duration.[1] While residents of the

---

[1] These offices correspond closely to those found in Chinese Ch'an monasteries of the Sung and Yüan periods; see Satō Tatsugen, *Kairitsu no kenkyū*, pp. 523–31. Monastic offices listed in the *Pai-chang ch'ing-kuei* appear in *chüan* 4, T 2025.48.1130c–1133c; for a summary of the text, see H. Hackmann, "Pai-chang Ch'ing-kuei," *T'oung-pao* 9 (1908): 651–62. My English renderings of monastic offices generally follow those proposed by Holmes Welch in *The Practice of Chinese Buddhism: 1900–1950*, Harvard East Asian Studies 26 (Cambridge: Harvard University Press, 1967). Indian Buddhist monasteries are also known to have had support officers in charge of instruction of novices and distribution of food and drink, robes, and lodgings; for a survey of these positions, see Nand Kishore Prasad, *Studies in Buddhist and Jaina Monachism* (Vaishali: Research Institute of Prakrit, Jainology and Ahimsa, 1972), pp. 203–7.

meditation hall may be appointed to some of the less taxing positions, well over half of the offices require at least one full-time appointee, and some require more than one. The support division is headed by the abbot, who works closely with the monks who oversee the office and kitchen staff, the fieldworkers, and the teaching staff and proselytists. In order to give some sense of the range of responsibilities support monks fulfill, I will first discuss briefly the most important of these positions. I will then turn to an account of the types of work all the monastic residents must undertake in order to maintain a large monastery of over a hundred residents.

THE ABBOT

Executive control over the support positions in the monastery resides with the abbot (*chuji*).[2] At most Korean monasteries, the abbot is both the spiritual and temporal head of the temple, combining teaching and administrative roles in one office. But at the largest monasteries, like Songgwang-sa, these two responsibilities are divided: the abbot is in charge of handling only the temporal affairs of the monastery; spiritual matters are the province of the Sŏn master. At monasteries where there is such a division of authority, the abbot is subordinate to the Sŏn master, with the master having final word in all major decisions concerning the monastery. So that the Sŏn master can maintain at least some freedom from mundane decision making—freedom that is essential to the effectiveness of his teaching role—the abbot is put in charge of all the support units, especially the office (*ch'ongmu-sil*, sometimes written *chongmu-sil*), while the master oversees the "practice" (*chŏngjin*) areas, specifically the meditation hall. This division of labor helps the monastery to function smoothly and limits distractions to the monks in training.

At major monasteries, the abbot must be at least thirty-five years old, with a minimum of ten years as a bhikṣu. Abbots are generally fairly young—often in their forties, when they will have more energy to discharge their many responsibilities—though monks in their late fifties or sixties are sometimes appointed. The main factors in determining suitability of appointment are demonstrated leadership and administrative abilities, with meditative prowess being of secondary importance. The abbot will previously have proved himself in other important positions in the monastery bureaucracy, such as prior, proctor, or catechist. His familiarity with the monastic administration will, of course, help considerably in discharging his supervisory duties.

---

[2] For this position, see *Pai-chang ch'ing-kuei* 2, T 2025.48.1119a–b.

While the position of abbot would seem to bring with it much prestige, the monks typically view it as an onerous one. The heavy workload and constant responsibility do not endear the position to many of the monks qualified to serve, and the monastery family may have to go through considerable machinations to cajole someone into accepting the job. To illustrate the lengths to which a monk will go to avoid appointment as abbot, I know of few cases that rival that of Ilt'a *sŭnim*, the Haein-sa catechist who participated in my reordination in Korea. Ilt'a is a noted scholar of both *Vinaya* and Sŏn materials, whom the meditation monks also respected for his practice. He is immensely popular around Korea as an inspiring and charismatic lecturer, who first emerged as an important personage in the order during the reformation congresses of the 1950s. Given his various talents, he was an obvious choice for the abbotship of the large monastery of Haein-sa. But when the appointment was offered, Ilt'a refused to consider it, pleading lack of interest and insisting that it would disrupt his practice. In the face of inexorable pressure, he finally fled from the monastery and hid out at a lay supporter's home in Seoul. But as one of the most well-known figures within the Korean Buddhist tradition, he knew he would eventually be ferreted out. To disguise himself, he went around in mufti, wearing a suit and Western-style shoes and growing his hair and beard out. Only after a new abbot was appointed did he drop his disguise and return to Haein-sa.

A few years later, when the subject was broached again, Ilt'a left the country unannounced and reordained as a monk in Thailand. But he quickly grew tired of the torrid climate and cultural difficulties and, after a whirlwind trip around the world, returned secretly to Korea, where he lived in isolation at a hermitage on Odae Mountain in Kangwŏn province. After two years there, Ilt'a finally returned to Haein-sa, where he now lives in a hermitage in the mountains above the main monastery, seemingly convinced that he has finally gotten his message across.

The abbot will generally be a member of the same family lineage as the Sŏn master, often either a dharma brother or nephew, or one of his senior disciples. If someone from the Sŏn master's own dharma family cannot be found, the monastery will look for someone from a related family, perhaps the disciple of another senior monk at the same temple. Occasionally, it might appoint the abbot of one of the main monastery's branch temples or parish churches in the city, who would almost always have some family connections to the main temple. Only as a last resort will the monastery go outside of its own dharma family to select the abbot. Even in such a case, the nominee will almost always be someone who has spent many seasons at the monastery anyway, thus ensuring his loyalty to the temple family.

Abbots of major monasteries are appointed initially to a four-year term, which is renewable. Although the national headquarters in Seoul officially accredits the selection, the individual monastery has almost full control over its choice. Monks belonging to the monastic family try to reach a consensus about the successorship in a "forest convocation" (*im-hoe*), which brings together the senior monks in the monastic lineage as well as the Sŏn master, his senior disciples and dharma brothers, the outgoing abbot, the office monks, and the proctor. If the candidate accepts, he will be formally appointed to his position during the meeting of the resident monks that precedes each retreat season. After the rest of the monastery residents accede to the choice, his name is submitted to Chogye Order headquarters for certification. Once he is approved, as is invariably the case, the candidate is then given certification papers and a formal installation ceremony is held at the monastery. If the candidate lives at a different temple, the monastery will usually send a delegation consisting of the prior and perhaps the treasurer to lobby the candidate to accept the position. Often, too, if the present abbot is determined to resign, he might bring considerable pressure to bear on some of his potential successors to accept the appointment. Such strong-arm tactics are necessary because he knows that if a successor cannot be found, he will be obligated to continue in the job indefinitely. If there are relatively few qualified candidates at a monastery, the position might alternate between two or three monks for years on end, one resigning in favor of the next, and then being called up again upon the expiration of his successor's term.

The abbot's duties are primarily managerial. Most of the authority for the day-to-day functioning of the various units in the monastery is delegated, the abbot's main responsibility being to ensure that everyone performs his appointed task efficiently. As the head of the administration, he holds a meeting with all the main officers every morning after breakfast in order to keep tabs on conditions in the monastery. He is also called upon to be the monastery's representative at any meetings of the national hierarchy and may hold a seat on the Chogye Order's advisory board. As the temporal leader of the monastery, the abbot is also in charge of relations between the temple and outside authorities in business, economics, and government. He is frequently occupied with government officials, conferring with them about laws and regulations that might have an impact on the monastery. In recent years, abbots have been particularly involved with negotiations on land use, property redistribution, development of the monasteries as tourist areas, and government subsidies for reconstruction projects.

The abbot will also initiate contacts with other monasteries, leaving the follow-through on any joint proposals that might be broached to his subordinates. As the number of monks in Korea is relatively small, the senior monks who serve as abbots are generally well acquainted with one another, greatly simplifying such matters. The abbot also plays a big part in fund-raising activities among the laity. At times these contacts might include lecturing to lay Buddhist organizations. But for the most part he is simply the monastery's representative to the governing boards of such organizations. Teaching is usually reserved for the Sŏn masters and monks with a pronounced apostolic calling; in large monasteries, the abbot rarely, if ever, lectures. As the leader of all the monastery's branch temples, the abbot also conducts occasional inspection tours to examine conditions there. Twice a year he also sponsors a general meeting at the head monastery of all the branch temple abbots to develop joint policies and coordinated actions. For all these reasons, the abbot travels constantly throughout the year and even during the retreat period, when other monks would be prohibited from leaving the temple. Business, after all, does not wait for the free season.

As with so many other positions in the monastery, the abbot works with considerable autonomy, conferring with the Sŏn master only on more important matters. But since there are familial ties binding them to each other, the Sŏn master can be fairly sure of the abbot's loyalty and thereby help to ensure that any decisions will be made with his directives and expectations in mind. Because of this arrangement, the Sŏn master maintains effective control over the entire monastery while having to involve himself only tangentially in the actual running of the temple.

The abbot's long association with the monastery and his close family ties—if not deep friendship—with his predecessor usually ensure a smooth succession into the position. Upon the installation of a new abbot, the office staff generally resigns en masse in order to free the incoming abbot to choose his own officers. The prior, treasurer, and catechist will commonly be replaced with disciples of the new abbot, again helping to guarantee through filial ties that the office monks act in accordance with the wishes of their superior.

The abbot also holds tenuous control over the kitchen area of the monastery, again through family connections. The proctor (wŏnju) is often a disciple of the abbot, and, although he too functions autonomously, his familial associations keep his decisions in line with the abbot's expectations. Although most guests are first received by the proctor and then turned over to the guest prefect, the abbot will be notified of the arrival of important guests so that he can greet and entertain them personally. It is not at all uncommon for him to invite guests up to his room and chat with them while his attendant serves tea, fruit, and sweets. Because the proctor is also in charge of scheduling ceremonies, the abbot has some say too in their conduct and timing.

During his tenure in the position, the abbot has assigned to him a number of new disciples. All postulants must have a sponsor for their ordination (the ŭnsa), but since the Sŏn master and other monks well known for their practice are usually inundated with requests, the majority of prospective ordinands will be turned over to someone else. In most cases, this person will be the abbot. As an example of this added burden, I was told by Haein-sa monks that the Sŏn master there had accepted only nine disciples in some thirteen years, while the abbot had received some ninety disciples in just a three-year period. There is another practical reason for assigning so many postulants to the abbot: the ŭnsa sponsor is expected to provide all necessary support for his disciples, ranging from robes for their ordinations to books during the monks' stay in seminary to medical and dental expenses. The majority of senior monks, who are dependent for support on their own private supporters, would be hard pressed to provide for more than a few disciples. Someone with ready access to the large financial resources of the monastery itself is clearly necessary to support large numbers of disciples. The abbot is the logical choice.

I noted among the meditation monks a muted feeling that they are above the dictates of the abbot, since he is only an administrator, not a meditator. The abbot is, as often as not, relatively inexperienced in meditation, and some of the practice monks are patently supercilious toward him. The rector, who is superior in rank to the abbot, is the director of the meditation unit, and the practice monks place their respect more in him than in the abbot. As an example of this subtle disdain, when the abbot returns from traveling outside the monastery, all the monks in residence are expected to go to his room formally to welcome him back. I recall a couple of retreat seasons, however, when the meditation monks decided unilaterally that they were not required to greet a support monk, even if he was the abbot. Needless to say, the abbot was furious, and it was only thanks to the rector's good sense of diplomacy that the conflict was resolved.

A monk who is an effective abbot at a major monastery may be invited to assume a position at the Chogye Order headquarters in Seoul or, if he happens to have meditative attainments as well, offered an appointment as Sŏn master at a major meditation center. Two examples come to mind here. The first is that of Haech'ŏng *sŭnim*. Haech'ŏng was the assistant lecturer at Popchu-sa, one of the major sūtra-study centers in Korea. After spending three years in Thailand studying the *Vinaya* and learning some Thai and English, he returned to become the head lecturer at his home monastery. Only two years later, at the age of forty, he was appointed abbot at Pŏpchu-sa and rapidly rose to national prominence by rescuing the monastery from severe financial difficulties. Less than two years later, he was called to the ecclesiastical headquarters and six months after that was tapped to be the national prior (*chongmu wŏnjang*), the temporal head of the entire Chogye Order—truly a phenomenal rise in such a short period of time.

Kusan's career illustrates an alternative career path for an effective abbot. After receiving dharma transmission from Hyobong *sŭnim*, who was at the time the Sŏn master at Haein-sa, Kusan was appointed to the abbotship of Mirae-sa, a small branch temple of Ssanggye-sa. Soon afterwards he was appointed Chief of the Inspection Bureau (*kamch'al wŏnjang*) in the Seoul national headquarters during Hyobong's tenure as Supreme Patriarch (*chongjŏng*) of the Chogye Order. Kusan subsequently became the abbot of Tonghwa-sa, a small main temple outside the city of Taegu in North Kyŏngsang Province, where he first displayed talent as a meditation teacher. Kusan finally was appointed Sŏn master of Songgwang-sa after spearheading the drive to take the monastery back from the married monks during the Buddhist reformation that followed the Korean War. Indeed, the combined teaching and administrative duties required of the abbot at a smaller temple can be ideal training for the position of Sŏn master at a larger monastery.

THE OFFICE MONKS

Directly subordinate to the abbot are the office monks, the "three duties" (*samjik*), who coordinate monastic contacts, finances, and inculcation. The leader of this phalanx is the monk who runs the office, the prior (*ch'ongmu*, sometimes called the *chongmu*). He is in charge of the day-to-day running of the office and with keeping the abbot apprised of any secular developments that may be important to the monastery. He stands in relation to the abbot in very much the same way that the succentor stands to the rector in the meditation unit—almost his right-hand man, as it were. The prior's main duties involve coordinating the official correspondence between the monastery and the national Chogye headquarters and making sure that all communications are answered punctually. He maintains contact with lower-echelon government officials who might have some impact on monastic affairs, such as the interior officials of the district and provincial governments. He also follows up on contacts made initially by the abbot and ensures that any agreements reached are implemented. The prior's network of contacts can thus extend from the government to lay donors to branch temples to other main monasteries to the national headquarters.

The prior is also in charge of keeping full dossiers on all the monks in residence and making sure that these are kept up to date each retreat season. As all monks are required to participate in one hundred hours a year of army reserve training (*yebi-kun*) until they reach the age of thirty-five,[3] the prior has also to make sure that they are aware when their training period is approaching. If possible, he will try to arrange for all the monks in residence to attend reserve training together, so as to least disrupt the monastery's routine. The prior is also in charge of informing the local government bureau when a monk joins the monastery. During the 1970s, whenever a Korean moved he was required to submit documentation to both the old and new district offices. The prior provided the necessary forms and interceded if necessary if there were any glitches in that procedure. It is also the prior's responsibility to verify the information on ordination, home monastery, and vocation master provided by a monk who wishes to enter the monastery, to protect the temple from potentially undesirable elements. Finally, the prior is expected to act as liaison between the main monastery and its branch temples, and in this capacity often accompanies the abbot, or goes himself, on inspection tours.

The prior works in close cooperation with the treasurer (*chaemu*). Although the prior ostensibly retains supervisory control over the monastery's financial affairs, as with so many other offices in Korean monasteries, the treasurer functions all but autonomously, conferring with the prior and the abbot only on major decisions. The treasurer is in charge of keeping the books and watching over the monastery's financial condition. He provides the proctor and other monastery officials with money to purchase necessary supplies and helps individual monks in certain situations with their own financial matters. He is ultimately responsible for ensuring that kitchen and office expenditures not exceed the monastery's resources, so he must maintain close check on all debits and expenditures. He is the adviser to the abbot and Sŏn master on all financial matters, such as major capital expenditures, investments, and shrine reconstructions, and is finally in charge of putting any decisions reached on those matters into effect. Any contracts made are written up and arranged through the treasurer as well. He is also the rental agent for the monastery's paddy land, a duty that was a separate office in Chinese monasteries.[4] He also hires and pays all workers, from field hands and loggers to the skilled architects and carpenters involved in temple reconstruction. The treasurer must consequently spend much of his time outside the monastery in the local villages or nearby cities, making the necessary hiring arrangements. Finally, the treasurer processes any income accruing from donations or tourism and coordinates fund-raising activities among lay Buddhists and relevant government organs. Because the treasurer has

---

[3] Even after age thirty-five, monks still must participate in civil defense (*min pangwi*) training for a few hours each year.

[4] The Chinese monastic office of village agent (*chuang-chu*) does not exist in Korea; for this office, see Welch, *Practice of Chinese Buddhism*, pp. 26–27.

ready access to all of the monastery's financial resources, the position demands a person whose loyalty to the temple and the abbot is above reproach.

The third monk included in the office staff is the catechist (*kyomu*). His is the only position that does not involve exclusively administrative duties. The catechist is in charge of instructing the postulants in basic monastic discipline and ritual in preparation for their forthcoming ordination. He reviews the *Śramaṇera Rules and Decorum* (*Sami yurŭi*) and the *Admonitions to Beginners* (*Ch'obalsim chagyŏng-mun*) with the postulants in the evening after their workday and helps them with memorizing the *Thousand Hands Sutra*, the basic ceremonial text. The catechist is in charge as well of teaching the postulants monastic etiquette and decorum. He also assists students with organizing Buddhist groups in their high schools and universities and occasionally lectures to them in their schools or at affiliated branch temples in the vicinity. He arranges for training sessions (*suryŏn taehoe*) for students, which take place in the monastery during the winter and summer school vacations, and organizes their weeklong program of group meditation, studying, and lectures. Interestingly, a number of dedicated young monks first decided to ordain after participating in these training sessions.[5] Finally, he also helps the head lecturer procure books and supplies for the postulants and student-monks in the lecture hall and ensures that the library is stocked with the essential Buddhist reference works and new secondary studies as they are published.

While there appears to be a clear division of responsibility between these three officers, these distinctions are rather more tenuous in practice. In fact, the samjik work as a team and have considerable overlapping of duties. Especially considering the extensive traveling that each of them must undertake, one or another of the office monks is often absent from the monastery, occasionally for long periods. If someone is missing, the one or two who remain will take care of the business normally reserved for their colleagues, to keep the office work flowing smoothly.

At the largest monasteries there may be a fourth officer added to the office staff, that of the provost (*togam*). The provost is usually a relatively senior monk who has held a number of office positions previously. In China, he was the main power holder on the office staff and held considerable control over the conduct of office activities.[6] In Korea, his official

---

[5] These intensive training sessions are one example of a Buddhist proselytization technique that has been enthusiastically embraced by Christian youth groups, a point made to me by Sung Bae Park. See the next chapter for examples of Christian techniques adopted by Buddhists.

[6] See the description of the provost's position in Welch, *Practice of Chinese Buddhism*, p. 29.

duty is to coordinate the different office jobs and act as a chief of staff; in actual fact, however, his is primarily a ceremonial position, which involves considerable status but little real involvement in the monastic administration.[7] During a few retreat seasons, the monk appointed provost was not even in attendance at Songgwang-sa, but held the abbotship of a branch temple. On more important decisions, the provost might be consulted and his opinion can carry real weight, but usually he is allowed to keep to himself and use his time as he wishes. The position's prestige is on a par with that of the *sŏndŏk* ("meditative virtue"), a ceremonial post given to senior monks in the meditation hall.

Immediately under the prior's direction are the scribes, or *sŏgi*. At Songgwang-sa, these are usually Buddhist laymen trained in bookkeeping and office work, who are provided with room and board and a small salary in exchange for their service to the monastery. I also knew of a couple of postulants who entered the monastery with office experience, who were excused from kitchen work to spend their six-month postulancies working as secretaries. Scribes take care of correspondence, fill out and file government forms, and act as receptionists and accountants: in other words, they combine in one position all of the various menial jobs that take place in any office. As the scribes are often professional bookkeepers and accountants, they may also perform the vital service of counseling the office monks on financial and regulatory matters. As scribes, laymen who might not be quite ready to abandon completely the worldly life, but who nevertheless want to spend time in a monastery, are able to participate in some of the monastic routine and have contact with the monks on a personal level.

Because of their heavy work load, the office monks are the only residents excused from attending the daily monastic observances, such as morning and evening services, formal meals, and group work periods. I never perceived any resentment on the part of other monks about this privilege. I passed several free seasons in the compound next to the office and sometimes knew the treasurer to stay up all night counting the bags of fifty- and hundred-wŏn coins collected as temple admission during the hectic tourist season, finally grabbing a couple of hours' sleep before beginning his regular morning duties. One could hardly begrudge the office monks the occasional missed service.

The office monks have to retain a strong pragmatic sense, which often

[7] *Han'guk Pulgyo taesajŏn* (Encyclopedia of Korean Buddhism) (Seoul: Poryŏn'gak, 1982), s.v. "*togam*," states that this officer was "in charge of the money and grains in a monastery." In my experience at Songgwang-sa, while the monk serving as provost may take part in decisions relating to such financial matters, other officers are actually in charge of these matters. For the duties of this officer in Chinese monasteries, see *Pai-chang ch'ing-kuei* 4, T 2025.48.1132a.

presents a sharp contrast with the spiritual aims of the monastic life. The realities of the ordinary world are constantly pressing in upon the monastery, and it is up to the office monks to confront them before those realities enter too far and disturb the training of the practice monks. Let me give a few examples. One autumn, a farmer leasing the monastery's paddy land became delinquent in paying his fees. Obviously, if such delinquency were tacitly condoned by inaction, it could eventually threaten the financial stability of the monastery. It was up to the treasurer to go to the village and negotiate with the lessor, trying to reach an agreement on a new payment schedule that would take into account both the farmer's financial difficulties and the monastery's own needs. Another time, when the prior made his rounds to collect the biannual payments to the main monastery required of all branch temple abbots, he came across one recalcitrant abbot. The prior returned home a few hundred thousand wŏn short of the projected income, which jeopardized the financial security of the main monastery. The prior's inability to deal firmly with the branch abbots finally resulted in his own dismissal. Another time the monastery's ox was slowing down from old age and could no longer pull the plow; obviously, the monastery needed a younger ox, but where to get the money? If the old ox were sold (and it would certainly be destined for the meat market), the monastery might be offered a younger ox and two hundred thousand wŏn, but that would condone killing—a direct transgression of the Buddhist precepts. Obviously, financial realities dictated sale, and this is finally the decision that was reached, but not without considerable qualms of conscience on the part of the treasurer, who had to make the final decision. Indeed, this delicate balancing of temporal realities and spiritual ideals makes the office positions some of the most difficult in the entire monastery.

THE KITCHEN STAFF

Perhaps the most demanding and pressure-filled job among the support group of monks is that of the wŏnju (lit. master of the campus), the monk who fulfills the combined duties of monastery proctor and cellarer. The proctor, as I will call him, oversees all aspects of meal preparation and procurement for the monastery. Starting in the early morning after services, the proctor guides the postulants, younger monks, and laywomen in preparing breakfast, a task that will consume much of his time at dinner and supper as well. Not only does he direct the different cooks—those preparing the rice, soup, and side dishes—but he can often be found himself at one of the huge woks, cooking various dishes on his own. About every other day, in between meal preparations, the proctor travels to the nearest town to buy supplies for the monastery. These range the gamut from foodstuffs to soap to tools. When the monastery is to hold a special ceremony, either in conjunction with a funeral or a temple observance, the proctor is responsible for planning the menu and purchasing all the necessary items. Because the proctor is based in the kitchen compound, where the guest quarters are also located, he also spends much of his "free" time each day entertaining visitors to the monastery, both lay and ordained alike. And finally, since the proctor works with the new postulants to the monastery all day long, it is inevitable that he plays a major role in their training. While the catechist has primary responsibility for the postulant's liturgical training, the proctor instructs them daily in correct monastic etiquette and gives them much needed advice about adapting to monastery life. Since I have discussed the daily life of the postulants in Chapter Four, I will treat in this section the other members of the kitchen staff.

The proctor could not possibly handle all his many chores alone. The successful proctor quickly learns to delegate authority among the various members of his staff, the largest of any section of the monastery. One of the most vital members of his staff is the pyŏlchwa (lit. separate seat), who serves as the proctor's right-hand man.[8] The pyŏlchwa functions much as an assistant cellarer, traveling to the local town, often together with the proctor, to purchase supplies for the temple. Whether a senior postulant or a young novice, the pyŏlchwa has displayed leadership abilities and serves as a liaison between the proctor and the other monks of the kitchen staff.

Most of the monks working in the kitchen have only recently finished their postulancy and will serve another two or three years in various minor positions. Many will serve as vergers of the small shrine halls scattered around the monastery campus, performing alone a small service there in the morning and evening and presenting the rice offering before the altar at dinner. In addition to their specific responsibilities, these young monks also serve as a reserve labor force, helping with the myriad odd jobs around the kitchen, especially during ceremonial events, when hundreds of laypeople visit the monastery. Although they are busy with their various duties, these young monks have more free time than the postulants. This gives them a chance to memorize more chants, which they will need to know in order to perform the different services that are conducted in the various shrines. They may study also some basic sūtra texts and perhaps the writings of past Sŏn masters. But they will also have

---

[8] According to *Han'guk Pulgyo taesajŏn*, s.v. "*pyŏlchwa*," this office is also termed the *chŏnjwa*, a term known in Chinese sources. See *Pai-chang ch'ing-kuei* 4, T 2025.48.1132c13–18, where the chŏnjwa is said to be in charge of the congregation's meals.

time to spend chatting with the lay visitors to the monastery, listening to stories told by the wandering monks staying over in the temple, and in this way begin to learn about monks and monasteries beyond the confines of the home monastery.

These younger monks live together in the great room of the kitchen compound, which also functions as the refectory. They have small floor desks that they can move out of the hall during meals and sleep periods. A monk who has been away from the home monastery for some time and is reestablishing his residency is usually assigned to the kitchen first, but not given any specific duties. Even though he is a member of the monastery family, he still must go through the formal introduction just like any monk first arriving at the temple. At the beginning of the upcoming retreat season, he will then be assigned a formal position. If the monk is more senior, he might be moved out of the kitchen into a position that carries more responsibility, such as working on the office staff. If he has already spent a number of years in temple service, he might even be able to negotiate entrance to one of the practice sections of the monastery, such as the meditation hall, though he is under constant pressure to accept a support position.

But perhaps the hardest workers in the kitchen compound are the laywomen who work permanently in the monastery. These women are given the title *posal*, the Sino-Korean transliteration of "bodhisattva," beings who defer their own enlightenment so as to help all other beings gain liberation first.[9] The bodhisattvas are often laywomen who have been divorced, abandoned by their husbands, or widowed, and have no other means of support for their families than working for the monastery. When I was at Songgwang-sa, the posal who directed the cooking staff, one of the most important jobs in the monastery, was given room and board in the monastery, a small salary of about twenty thousand wŏn a month (approximately forty dollars as of 1978), and tuition for her children through high school. While hardly munificent, this salary is more than a single, unskilled woman could have otherwise hoped to make on the labor market and was more than the male farmhands earn. Other bodhisattvas help in the kitchen, directing the postulants in preparing the stew, soup, and side dishes. Another posal serves as the monastery's seamstress, sewing the long formal robes that are given to the postulants upon their ordination. The postulant's vocation master provides money for the cloth, and the seamstress purchases the cloth and makes the robes. Still

---

[9] The term *posal* has wide application in Korean society. It is used to refer to female diviners who adopt Buddhist trappings, a woman following an ascetic way of life, or any older woman who worships on behalf of her children or grandchildren at Buddhist monasteries, shamanic shrines, or sacred mountains. See Laurel Kendall, *Shamans, Housewives, and Other Restless Spirits* (Honolulu: University of Hawaii Press, 1985), p. 126.

other posals wash, starch, and iron the robes of the Sŏn master and elderly monks, and wash the guest bedding. For major work projects, such as kimch'i making, laywomen from the local village are hired on a temporary basis to assist.

MEALS

The meals prepared by the kitchen staff are the highlights of a monk's spartan day. For a monk in a large training monastery, the rigid daily schedule and disciplined training regimen do not allow much opportunity to indulge in any of those little pleasures most laypersons take for granted. There is no television to watch, no newspapers to read, no time for naps. With so few outlets for sensual indulgence (precisely the intention of the tight regimen), the highlights of the day are meals, which the monks attack with great, if barely restrained, gusto. Korean monasteries serve three regular meals a day: breakfast, at around six (called *ach'im kongyang*); dinner, at around 11:30 in the morning (*chŏmsim kongyang*); and supper, at around five (called *chŏnyŏk kongyang*).

In the monasteries, meals are called "offerings" (*kongyang*), to distinguish them from the vernacular Korean "meal [of rice]" (*pap*). There are many similarities between the monastic diet and that of the rural, agricultural peasantry.[10] The major difference is that all meals served in the monasteries are vegetarian. The bodhisattva precepts of the Mahāyāna branch of Buddhism forbid monks from eating the flesh of any sentient being.[11] The Koreans follow this precept quite strictly (as do Chinese monks, but not the Japanese or Tibetans). No meat, fish, eggs, or dairy products are included with meals, though the monks may drink a cup of warm, powdered milk back at their residences after breakfast as a kind of "tea" (*uyu ch'a*). No alcohol is allowed inside the monasteries. About the only exception to this rule that I knew of was the innocent attempts monks sometimes made to ferment green plums into a weak plum wine; on the rare occasion when the wine turned out to be drinkable, there might be enough to share a couple of small shots with his friends on a

---

[10] For details on the peasant diet, with nutritional statistics, see Clark W. Sorensen, *Over the Mountains Are Mountains: Korean Peasant Households and Their Adaptation to Rapid Industrialization*, Korean Studies of the Henry M. Jackson School of International Studies (Seattle: University of Washington Press, 1988), pp. 91–126.

[11] The third of the forty-eight minor precepts of the bodhisattva; see *Fan-wang ching* (Book of Brahmā's Net), *T* 1484.24.1005b10–13. For the compilation of this important preceptory scripture and its role in Japanese monastic discipline, see Paul Groner, "The *Fan-wang ching* and Monastic Discipline in Japanese Tendai: A Study of Annen's *Futsū jubosatsukai kōshaku*," in *Chinese Buddhist Apocrypha*, ed. by Robert E. Buswell, Jr. (Honolulu: University of Hawaii Press, 1990), pp. 251–90.

warm summer's evening when it was too hot and humid to sleep. But I never knew any monk in a large practice center like Songgwang-sa to be inebriated.

The basis of virtually all meals is steamed rice (*pap*), generally regular white rice (*ipssal*, *mepssal*) that has been mixed with barley (*pori*) to make the rice go farther and to provide extra texture. Steamed rice is made anew for each meal in a huge iron cauldron (*sot*) over the firebox in the kitchen, which additionally heats the ondol floor in the refectory. After cooking the rice, water is poured into the cauldron, to make a kind of milky-colored tea (*sungnyung*), which the monks will drink at the conclusion of the meal. Any leftover rice will be saved for the lay workers to eat as a snack while they are working. Periodically our proctor received orders from the Sŏn master to cook brown rice (*hyŏnmi*) instead, though few monks liked it; they claim it is hard to digest. Only under duress will the monks tolerate rice gruel (*chuk*), most often made from brown rice, on winter mornings. The monks almost to a man hate gruel, claiming that it leaves them hungry, thereby interfering with their practice. It has been estimated that grains provide 70 to 80 percent of the caloric intake of rural Koreans, an amount that seems true for the monasteries as well.[12] On special occasions, rice will be replaced by noodles as the starch in the diet, which the monks will then consume in huge quantities.

In addition to steamed rice, meals always include some type of soup (*kuk*), made from dried brown seaweed (*miyŏk*; *Undaria pinnatifida*), vegetables (especially mung bean sprouts), or kimch'i. The soup is generally based on *toenjang*, a fermented bean paste like the Japanese miso, and flavored with soy sauce (*kanjang*) and sesame salt. Sprouted mung beans are another frequent ingredient in soups.

Bean products comprise one of the largest components of the monastic diet during all seasons. The basis of many bean products is *meju*, a fermented bean paste somewhat like the Japanese *nattō*. *Meju* is used as major ingredient in producing soy sauce, red-pepper paste, and *toenjang*. Cooked black beans, seasoned with soy sauce, sugar, and white sesame, are served at least once a day. Tofu (*tubu*), or bean curd, frequently appears on the menu, but this is always purchased from a professional maker, who delivers it to the monastery on the back of his motorcycle. When the tofu is especially fresh, it is served steamed in whole blocks, to be dipped into a sauce made of soya, sesame oil, and red-pepper sauce.

An unusual related product is *tot'ori-muk*, or acorn jelly. Dried acorns are blanched and the flesh pounded into a powder with a mortar and pestle. After soaking the acorn flour in water for one week, during which

---

[12] See research by K. Y. Lee and Yi Kiryŏl, cited in Sorensen, *Over the Mountains*, p. 95. For analysis of rural Korean diet, see ibid., p. 99, tab. 4.2.

time the water is changed at least three times, the flour is then covered with liquid and slowly simmered in a cauldron until it forms a jelly. This jelly is then molded to form cakes, which are served with soy sauce and red pepper. Because it is so time consuming to prepare, acorn jelly is served only on special occasions.

Side dishes (*ch'an*, or *panch'an*) vary according to season. Pickled vegetables, or kimch'i, are served with every meal. Kimch'i is of various types, made from Chinese cabbage (*paech'u kimch'i*), cubed daikon radish pickled in salt and red pepper (*kkaktugi*), or whole cucumbers (*oi kimch'i*) that have been pickled, sliced lengthwise, and stuffed with shredded carrot and daikon radish.

During the long winter, between late October and early April, meals are monotonous, with rice, kimch'is, whole daikon radish, potatoes, and sweet potatoes served in a seemingly endless variety of ways. By March, the pickled vegetables have gotten so ripe that they can't be eaten unless they're cooked, so there will be many kimch'i stews and fried kimch'is. Finally, in early spring, lettuce (*sangch'i*) and greens sprouted during the winter in the monastery's greenhouse will finally be available to supplement the diet. As the weather warms, wild mountain greens (*san namul*), such as *minari* (*Cardamine leucantha*), will be harvested by laywomen for the monks. During the summer, an abundance of fresh vegetables are served daily: fresh cabbage, radish, and cucumber kimch'is, and *ssam* (rice wrapped in lettuce). A common vegetable during this season is *toraji*, or bellflower root, served fried with red pepper. *Tŏdŏk* (*Codonopsis lanceolata*), another root, which the Koreans consider to be second only to ginseng (*insam*) in potency, is shredded, crushed, and then fried with sesame oil and red pepper. In autumn many fruits are added to the diet, including apples, pears, persimmons, and chestnuts. Fruits are never served with the regular meal but instead as a dessert or between-meal snack.

Monastery side dishes are seasoned with a minimal number of spices, the most basic of which is salt. Because of Mahāyāna dietary restrictions, monks don't eat the garlic or onions that are so ubiquitous in the diets of ordinary Koreans.[13] Those spices are presumed to be mild aphrodisiacs, something celibates can do without. To compensate for the blandness of the food, the kitchen staff replaces the garlic and onions with lots of red pepper (*koch'u*), along with red-pepper paste (*koch'ujang*), brown sesame (*tŭlkkae*), and white sesame (*kkae*).

On festive days, white rice is replaced by glutinous rice (*ch'apssal*) for the ceremonial dinner. In addition to the regular side dishes, the meal will

[13] The fourth of the forty-eight minor precepts in the *Fan-wang ching*, T 1484.24.1005b14–16.

include a whole range of special dishes, such as fried tofu, vermicelli with fried vegetables, and many kinds of vegetable tempura. Thin sheets of dried laver, or *kim* (*Porphyra tenera*), are served; these sheets are eaten in great quantities with a dollop of rice and kimch'i. After the meal, the monks are served glutinous rice cakes (*ch'apssal ttŏk*, or just *ttŏk*), fruit, and hard candy or peanuts. This is the standard festival meal, which is also served when a layperson offers a meal to the monastery (*taejung kongyang*), typically in conjunction with the forty-ninth-day ceremony for a deceased relative.

Once a year, on certain festival days, other foods will be prepared. On the winter solstice, for example, the monks are served a special breakfast of *p'atchuk*, gruel made from mashed and strained red beans with glutinous rice dumplings. Harvest Moon Day (*ch'usŏk*), full moon on the eighth lunar month, brings *songp'yŏn*, a special kind of rice cake steamed over pine needles to give it a delicate pine scent. On New Year's Day, the monks are offered huge quantities of sweet, hard candies made from maltose mixed with roasted black beans, soybeans, millet, or popcorn. Apart from these few extraordinary occasions, however, the food served in the monastery remains fairly much the same.

All meals are served in the great room of the kitchen compound, which does triple duty as refectory, dormitory for the kitchen monks, and study hall for the postulants. The seating arrangements are much as they were for services in the main buddha hall. The Sŏn master sits on a cushion in the back center of the room, flanked by the abbot on his right and the rector on his left—the heads, respectively, of the support and meditation divisions of the monastery. The monks in each division fan out around the perimeter of the room in order of seniority, so that the youngest novices will sit at the front of the room facing the Sŏn master. On the wall around the perimeter of the refectory is a narrow shelf, on which the monks store their sets of four bowls and eating utensils. These sets were traditionally made of lacquered wood, but nowadays are almost always molded from plastic. The bowls fit one inside the other, so that they take up little space when put away or transported.

Once the meal bell strikes at the refectory, the monks make their way down to the room, take their set of bowls off the shelf behind them, and assume their assigned places on the floor. After everyone is settled, the verger of the refectory strikes the chukpi three times, the monks bow to one another with palms together in hapchang, and the meal begins.

The monks begin by folding out placemats and spreading their bowls. The rice bowl, the largest of the four, is placed on the left, front spot on the placemat, with the next largest bowl, for soup, beside it on the right. On the row behind is a smaller bowl for the side dishes, with the smallest bowl of all used to hold clear water, which will be used at the end of the meal to wash all the bowls and utensils.

Before the meal begins, the proctor has laid out in a row facing the Sŏn master a large water pitcher, followed by a massive bowl of rice and a large soup bucket. Smaller bowls of side dishes are placed at regular intervals along the room and passed among the monks. After the monks have spread their bowls, the verger strikes the chukpi once more, and the youngest monks rise to serve the water, rice, and soup to all the monks. Monks accept about half a bowl of water in the large bowl, pour it between the next two bowls, and then store it in the smallest bowl. In the meantime, another young monk has arrived to dish out the rice. The monk hands over his rice bowl and keeps his palms together in hapchang while the rice is being served. He then accepts the bowl back from the server with both hands, holds the bowl over his head for a moment, and then returns it to its spot on his placemat. The soup server arrives next, followed by the pans of side dishes. The rice server will come around once more, and the monk may return some rice if he has received too much— or more commonly take a bit more.

The verger strikes the chukpi three more times; the monks bow and begin eating. During the meal the side dishes may be passed back up the row one last time for a second helping. At all times, silence is maintained, and extreme care is taken to use one's utensils as quietly as possible, not scraping the spoon against the side of the bowl, for example.[14]

After a few of the monks have finished eating, the verger strikes the chukpi once again, and the young monks go out of the room and bring in pitchers of rice water, which have been left on the veranda outside. They take these pitchers around to all the monks, who accept it in the rice bowls. The rice bowl is then rinsed out and the rice water passed from the soup bowl to the side-dish bowl. After rinsing all three bowls, the monk drinks all the water down. He then pours the clear water he had stored in the small water bowl into his rice bowl and cleans it by hand. He follows by cleaning his other two bowls. Another monk then comes around with a bucket into which the monks pour the wash water. This water must be perfectly clear, with no specks larger than a pinhead; otherwise the monk will have to drink it too. This waste water is later offered to the hungry ghosts; since the ghosts' mouths are so tiny, the monks say, they will be hurt by larger particles. After washing, the bowls are wiped with a cloth, placed back one inside the other, and wrapped up. Once everyone is finished, the verger strikes the chukpi again, and the monks rise and return

[14] These are Korean adaptations of ancient Indian rules against eating while making various noises; see nos. 38–40 of the śaikṣa rules, in Charles S. Prebish, trans., *Buddhist Monastic Discipline: The Sanskrit Prātimokṣa Sūtras of the Mahāsāṃghikas and the Mūlasarvāstivādins* (University Park: Pennsylvania State University Press, 1975), p. 100.

their bowls to the shelf behind them. Then, while still standing, all the monks turn back around and bow to one another as the verger strikes the chukpi three times. Everyone then files out of the refectory. The whole meal is over in half an hour, of which only about ten minutes have been spent eating, the rest occupied with setting up, serving, and cleanup.

The midday dinner is a more elaborate version of this procedure, punctuated by chanting (see Appendix), during which the monks wear their formal robes. At breakfast and supper, the meals are rather more informal, though even then a dignified atmosphere prevails throughout.

LAY WORKERS

The majority of work around the monastery, including most large renovation and construction projects, farming, and logging, is performed by lay workers, either hired from the local villages on a daily basis or employed permanently by the monastery. The permanent employees are housed in a separate building away from the main monastery grounds. Songgwang-sa, like most large training monasteries, had from five to fifteen full-time workers at various times, most young men from nearby villages. When there is more work to be done than these men can handle, the prior has the leader of the permanent staff go into the nearest village the previous evening and put out a general call for workers. The next morning, the prior or treasurer will go into the village personally to hire as many men as he needs from among those who have turned out. Almost everyone who is willing to work will be hired, since most tasks around the monastery do not require specific skills. Women are also often hired to assist the resident posals and postulants for jobs involving large amounts of kitchen or food preparation and storage work. Such work is particularly necessary on the days when huge lay assemblies gather at the temple for ceremonies, and during the autumn harvest.

Pay for these temporary workers is consistently low: five hundred wŏn a day (as of 1978) plus meals—which means three full vegetarian meals, plus a large snack of rice, noodles, or rice cakes and tea, both late morning and afternoon. A large drum of makkŏlli, a kind of beer made (at least originally) from fermented rice, is also brought up from the village for the lay workers to drink during the long workday. Permanent workers receive the same pay plus full room and board (in extremely cramped quarters) and free cigarettes, in exchange for virtually full-time work from sunrise to sundown, seven days a week.

The custom of leaving most of the work for lay workers harkens back to the system, current since Koryŏ times, of having large armies of slaves attached to monasteries, who worked the temple lands in exchange for subsistence-level returns.[15] The villages located within a three- to five-kilometer radius of a monastery were often originally the homes of such slaves, who could number in the thousands. Even today, much of the land tilled by local peasants is still owned by the monastery, and rented out to the villagers in exchange for a substantial portion of the crop (around 50 percent, according to the prior at Songgwang-sa).

GROUP WORK

Some jobs are so labor intensive that they are too much for even temporary workers to finish. The proctor then calls out the postulants and young monks working in the kitchen area to help with the tasks during their short free periods from regular duties. But when the work is truly overwhelming, as at planting and harvesting times, the entire congregation (*taejung*; lit. great assembly) of the monastery must be summoned. These group work sessions (*taejung ullyŏk*) are one of the few times when the strict division between the support and practice sections of the monastery is abrogated.

During these group work sessions, every able-bodied monk in residence is expected to attend. About the only exceptions to this general call are the office monks, who are so busy throughout the day that their presence is never required, though they too may turn out if their schedules allow. Shrine vergers, who must maintain temple offering and chanting schedules, are usually expected to appear, but are permitted to leave early to perform their ceremonial duties. The meditation hall fire maker will also return early to the hall to heat the ondol floor and prepare hot water, so that the monks can clean up before dinner and supper. The majority of help is drawn from the ranks of the seminary students and meditation monks, the students being called upon first, the meditators only as a last resort. The monastery's postulants also turn out for at least a portion of the work, but they always work separately from the monks.

The rector (*yuna*; Skt. *karmadāna*) announces the group work session at the conclusion of breakfast. The rector is in charge of assigning respon-

[15] The oldest extant Koryŏ document of such an award of slaves involves Songgwang-sa. The manuscript, written in 1281 in a problematic mixed script (using some Sino-Korean characters for phonetic value only), states that even though the national master Wŏno Ch'ŏnyŏng (1215–1286) has gone forth as a monk, he may retain all of the bequeathed properties, including slaves, of his deceased father; and those properties are not to be privately owned, but are for the public use of the monastery. The document is listed as Korean National Treasure no. 572 and is preserved in the Songgwang-sa museum. For the text and a tentative translation of the document, see Han'guk Pulgyo yŏn'guwŏn, ed., *Songgwang-sa* (Seoul: Ilchi-sa, 1975), pp. 66–68.

sibility for overseeing the work and arranging the time. After describing the work and the amount of time he expects it will take, he asks the succentor of the meditation hall whether the proposed time is suitable for the meditators' schedule. If it is, the rector then tells the verger of the main shrine hall to strike two rounds on the large mokt'ak at the arranged time, and all the monks then assemble for the work. Long work periods begin around 7:30 A.M. and continue straight through until dinner, starting again at around 1:00 P.M. and continuing until 4:00 P.M. In the meditation hall, sitting meditation will still take place as usual in early morning and evening during these group work sessions, but the daytime is set aside exclusively for work. These periods are some of the few times during the monastic calendar that Zen monks in Korea fit the usual Western stereotype of contemplatives who combine meditation practice with manual labor.

These extended work periods are also the only times that the monks will not attend the regular noon service and formal dinner. Table meals (*sang kongyang*), either in the refectory or occasionally out in the fields during summer work, are provided for the monks so that they will not have to stop early to clean up and put on their formal robes. As with lay workers, the proctor knows that the monks expect a large "snack" between regular meals, so during the mid-morning and afternoon, the postulants will bring up from the kitchen a treat of sweet potatoes, fruit, cookies, rice cakes, or noodles, with cool water, tea, or milk to drink.

Work sessions are casual and help to build camaraderie among the monks from all the various units of the monastery. The meditation monks are allowed to talk during the work, and during retreat periods; this is about the only time they will have personal contact with monks from other compounds in the monastery. These sessions also give the younger monks a chance to interact with the monastery's senior leaders, including the Sŏn master, the rector, and the healthy elderly monks, who all turn out for the work. These senior monks will often tell stories about their own personal experiences, stories that for me were often more edifying than the regular lectures. The stories are bawdier and told with more abandon than the tales related during the formal dharma talks, so the work sessions are frequently punctuated by raucous laughter.

One story in particular comes to mind, told by the rector one summer while weeding the radish patch. Ch'unsŏng *sŭnim* (1891–1978), a well-known disciple of Han Yongun (1879–1944), was one of the last masters in Korea to cultivate "unconstrained conduct" (*muae haeng*)—practice not limited by the usual constraints of monastic discipline and decorum. Refusing to conform even in his old age, Ch'unsŏng continually wandered from monastery to monastery, disdaining even to observe the retreat periods kept by all other monks. Tales of his audacious and often obscene conversations with laywomen—all of which tended to center around pointed references to their vaginas—are rife among the monks. In one of the more well-known stories, assassinated president Park Chung Hee's late wife, a devout Buddhist, is supposed to have invited Ch'unsŏng to deliver a lecture at her birthday celebration—his reputation somehow unbeknownst to her. Ascending the dharma platform before all the distinguished guests, Ch'unsŏng sat still for thirty minutes, not uttering a single word. Not wishing to make a scene before the First Lady, no one said anything, but the audience was growing visibly agitated. Finally, once he saw that everyone's patience had run out, Ch'unsŏng bellowed, "Today is the day the First Lady's mother burst her vagina!" and walked out. Needless to say, he was not invited back.[16]

Very occasionally, I heard monks complain about these work sessions. The most pointed comment was made by one monk who said that men left their families to become monks precisely to avoid just these sorts of tasks. But almost everyone, especially those in meditation hall, seems to enjoy the work. Not only does it provide a break from the rigors of the daily schedule, but the frequent meals and snacks and the lively banter make the atmosphere more entertaining than is usually found in the monastery. Korean monasteries are rarely lugubrious, but during these work sessions they can be genuinely fun.

FIELD WORK

Most group work is cyclical, centering upon seasonal field chores. In mid-spring, the major part of the planting begins. The monks first help the lay workers prepare the fields for planting by removing whatever boulders have worked their way to the surface during the winter, and by gathering up rocks and stones. Long steel rods are used to work boulders loose from the soil, a procedure that can often require several monks working together for long periods before success. After the workers have cut furrows for planting, the monks will then line up from one end of the field to the other and walk down the furrows, planting the seed. Chinese cabbage (*paech'u*), white daikon radishes (*muu*), potatoes, and red peppers are the main staples planted in mid-spring.

Late June brings rice-planting time. The rice seedlings are gathered by the workers from their starter beds in the paddies, tied together in bundles, and thrown out into the fields at well-spaced intervals. On the des-

---

[16] A selection of some of Ch'unsŏng's dharma talks appears in Kim Kilsang, ed., *Kosŭng pŏbŏ cheil chip* (First Volume of Sermons of Eminent Monks) (Seoul: Hongbŏbwŏn, 1969), pp. 290–306. The picture of Ch'unsŏng that accompanies the lectures has him sitting naked except for his *kasa*, the brown outer cloak.

ignated day, all the monks are called out into the paddy fields. Rolling their pants up above the knee and removing their outer coats, the monks line up in long rows that stretch the length of the field. Two monks will hold a long string to guide the placement of the rows, which always are kept as straight as possible. The farmer monk (*nonggam*) usually directs this relatively skilled task.

At least once during the summer, all the fields will be weeded, a tedious job that usually continues for three to four days, which will hopefully suffice for the entire growing season. Any other weeding that might later be necessary will usually be done by workers—almost always women— hired from the local villages.

Late autumn and early winter bring the most work for the congregation. During this period, the monks harvest all the vegetables, especially the staples of cabbage, radishes, and red peppers, and bury the root crops in long trenches for storage through the winter. Harvesting rice and sesame seed is usually left to the skilled hands of the lay workers.

KIMCH'I-MAKING SEASON

This season is also when kimch'i making, or *kimjang*, occurs. The preparation of winter kimch'i (spicy Korean pickles) is the most involved project of the year, involving the concerted efforts of all the monks, several laywomen hired especially for the job, and the entire kitchen staff. A resident laywoman posal, who is most experienced with pickling, is put in overall charge of the kimjang process. One of the monks, usually the proctor or the farmer monk, is appointed as the general overseer to supervise the monks and keep everyone's nose to the grindstone. Korean monasteries prepare a variety of kimch'is, very much like those eaten among the lay population: pickled Chinese cabbage (*paech'u kimch'i*), cubed radishes (*kkakttugi*), young radishes, with greens attached (*yŏlmu kimch'i*), radish leaves (*much'ŏng kimch'i*), and pickled cucumbers (*oi kimch'i*) in the summer. The only real difference is that, because of Mahāyāna dietary restrictions, the monasteries never add sardines, green onions, or garlic to their mixtures; the major spice is red pepper. Massive quantities of red pepper are included in the mixtures, but not just for taste: it is also the major source of Vitamin C during the long winter months.

For kimch'i to ferment properly, harvesting and pickling must take place under specific weather conditions. If the vegetables are harvested and pickled too early in the season, when the weather is not yet cold enough, the concoction will sour quickly and rot. But if harvesting starts too late, the weather will be too severe to allow easy harvesting and preparation. Consequently, kimch'i making usually takes place during the first or second week of the winter retreat, the fortnight-long Sinitic season called *iptong*, or "entering winter" (the twenty-first day of the ninth lunar month, usually mid-November). Always, the farmer monk will wait for signs that winter has fully set in before issuing the call to start harvesting the vegetables. This means that a few days of frost would have already occurred, during which the outer leaves of the cabbages would have been tied around the tender core to save the plant from freezing. During my five years in Korea, it seemed that invariably we began kimjang on the day of the first snowfall, when temperatures were below freezing and the river frozen over with a thin sheet of ice.

About three straight days of work are required to make the kimch'i. Teams of monks hike into the fields to carry down the harvest of cabbages and radishes on Korean A-frame backpacks (*chige*), while other monks wait at the river to wash the produce. Washing the vegetables is the worst job, as one must break through the ice in order to wash the crop in the freezing water. The radishes are dumped into large wooden troughs, hollowed out of massive logs, which are filled with water; the vegetables are then sloshed back and forth with long wooden poles to wash off the dirt. The cabbages are washed individually in the river by monks wearing thermal gloves covered by rubber gloves, but that is never enough to protect their hands from the icy cold of the water. The cabbages are then carted up to the bathhouse, where they are rolled in sea salt and stacked in a corner overnight.

The next day the salt is rinsed off and the cabbages smeared with the kimch'i seasoning of red-pepper paste, sliced carrots, pickled radish, cucumber, parsley, and sesame oil, which the laywomen had been preparing in the meantime. The prepared cabbages are then stuffed whole into large earthenware jars, called *hangari*, each several gallons in volume, and covered with brine, the pickling agent.[17] These jars are then buried up to their necks in the earth to guard against freezing in winter and to keep the pickles cool as the weather warms in spring. These pickled whole cabbages, called *t'ong kimch'i*, are one of the main staples of the monastic diet and slices are served at every meal. Radishes are prepared in much the same way, but are diced or quartered and placed in jars, the larger specimens being buried whole in large pits in the ground, to be dug up as needed during the winter. These winter kimch'is will keep for about four months, though by March they will be so ripe that they will have to be cooked in stews to be edible.[18]

---

[17] Hangari are a variety of Korean earthenware (*onggi*), for which see Robert Sayers with Ralph Rinzler, *The Korean Onggi Potter*, Smithsonian Folklife Studies, no. 5 (Washington, D.C.: Smithsonian Institution Press, 1987).

[18] For details on the traditional Korean diet, see Sorensen, *Over the Mountains*, pp. 91–126.

MEJU MAKING

At around the same time of year, the monks prepare the Korean meju, a fermented soybean paste akin to the Japanese nattō. Meju is used as a major ingredient in many Korean products, including soy sauce, red-pepper paste, and toenjang, the fermented bean stock (like the Japanese miso) that is used in stews and soups. The afternoon before the meju is to be made, all available cauldrons in every compound of the monastery are used to cook soybeans. The postulants and kitchen monks attend to the fires. After simmering throughout the night, the soft soybeans are poured into huge wooden tubs and brought to the meal room. All the monks gather there immediately after morning chanting, joined by the meditation monks, who have sat for only one hour, virtually the only time that early morning practice is interrupted for work. The soybeans are then pounded into a mash with a large wooden hammer. This mash is then placed on long wooden tables, where the monks form it into small loaves, which are pounded against the table to increase their density and make them stick together better. These loaves are temporarily stored in the cool end of the room to harden, before being hung outside from the roof rafters for a few days to dry and begin fermenting. Meanwhile the postulants have begun to cook another round of beans in the cauldrons where beans had cooked the night before. By about three in the afternoon, the new batch of beans is ready, and the monks reconvene to repeat the same procedure.

FRUIT PICKING

During the few weeks prior to the winter retreat season, all the monks in the meditation hall begin picking the fruit trees planted in the hills around the outskirts of the monastery. The meditation monks are permitted to store away much of the fruit for themselves, so no one complains about the work. Chestnuts usually ripen first and are knocked from the trees with long bamboo poles. The monks peel the spiny husks of the fruit off with their shoes, since the spines are too sharp to handle with the hands, or burn them off in the coals of the ondol fire. The chestnuts are then stored away, to be roasted or cooked through the winter.

Pine nuts (*chat*) are another staple the meditation monks harvest in the late autumn. The nuts are separated from the rest of the cone by hitting the cone with a hammer, showering the nuts in all directions, or by burning the cone in fire, which leaves the nuts scattered among the ashes. The latter method is used if the cones are still sappy. The nuts so painstakingly gathered are divided between the Sŏn master and other elderly monks and the meditation hall residents. Some monasteries rely on pine nuts as a major cash crop.

Toward the end of autumn, the frost will finally ripen the persimmons. After harvesting, persimmons are either peeled and sliced, to be dried on bamboo-slat tables, or peeled and skewered whole and dried on long wooden shafts. Persimmons can also be stored in their natural state, by placing them in lofts around the monastery on top of loose straw, so that the individual fruits do not touch each other. If stored carefully in this manner, the persimmons will usually last through most of the winter, becoming progressively sweeter as they are touched by frost. Dried persimmons will last throughout the year, the thin coating of natural sugar that forms on the outside of the fruit acting as a preservative.

SPECIAL MEALS

Special meals also occasionally call for the participation of all the monks. On the winter solstice, p'atchuk (red-bean soup with glutinous rice dumplings) is traditionally served at breakfast, and the monks will be summoned the evening before to prepare the dumplings. The kitchen staff has prepared the dough for the dumplings previously and it remains for the monks to roll them into bite-sized balls. At infrequent intervals, usually not more than two or three times a year, *mandu* (Chinese-style ravioli) are also prepared by all the monks, usually sometime during the final week of the retreat. Because of the tedium of preparing the dough, rolling it out, filling it with a bean curd mixture (not meat), shaping it, and finally cooking it, mandu are served only rarely in the monasteries.

FOREST FIRES

Most Korean monasteries are located deep in the mountains, where they are prone to forest fires. Almost every year a major fire will break out in the mountains, especially now that hiking and mountain climbing have become so popular among the tourists who visit the monastery sites. When a monk discovers a fire, he tolls the large temple bell to summon all the monks. Once the monastic officials have decided on a plan for attacking the fire, all able-bodied monks are called out for fire-fighting duty; only the elderly monks will remain behind in the monastery to assist in preparing food. The lay workers and villagers usually assume that the fire will burn itself out; they seldom came up into the mountains to help us fight the fire until they had finished their day's work.

Fire fighting is usually done with the same long-handled bamboo brooms used for sweeping the monastery, together with sickles and rakes. Most fires burn only in the underbrush, so if they cannot beat the fire down with their brooms, the monks will try instead to create a fire line to block the flames. Monks usually work in teams, with one monk clearing the brush with a sickle to make a fire line about three feet in width and his companion raking clean the fire line down to bare earth. The monks work together in a long line, stretching as far as the manpower allows. Because most fires happen deep in the mountains, water is rarely available to douse the flames.

Fires can sometimes burn for hours in the dense underbrush. The longest fire I helped to fight lasted for a day and a half, with the monks working virtually nonstop. During the fight, the proctor takes charge of preparing and delivering food to the monks off in the mountains. If the fire lasts for more than a few hours, the proctor will have the postulants carry large tubs of food up to the monks on A-frame backpacks (*chige*). The monks will then take breaks in small groups to eat at the command center and will also carry fruit back to the fire lines for snacks.

During that long fire, my Korean partner and I were at the end of the fire line, about a half a mile away from the rest of the monks, and about fifty feet below the fire. Because we had worked for several hours straight and it was such a long way back to the command center, we were afraid we would exhaust ourselves if we hiked all the way back to eat. We would have to do something else about food. While we were clearing the fire line, my partner had been digging up roots of wild tŏdŏk (*Codonopsis lanceolata*) and *toraji* (bellflower), the vines of which most rural Koreans can identify on sight. Koreans regard these two roots as being somewhat akin to ginseng in potency. As the sun was setting, the monk dug a small pit just below the fire, threw the roots in the pit, covered them with brush, and waited for the fire to burn over it. Once the fire had passed, he doubled back to the spot and dug up the roots; we feasted that night on roasted roots. I am still amazed at the stamina we gained from that meal: even after fighting the fire for eighteen straight hours and walking five kilometers back down the mountain in the dark, I still could not sleep that evening.

Fires inside the monastery compounds are fortunately rare, for the wooden buildings go up like a tinderbox if ignited. Some of the larger and richer monasteries have begun to install pressurized water mains to fight temple fires, but the vast majority of monasteries still depend on outmoded, hand-operated fire-fighting equipment, or passed buckets of water. One monk from my home monastery returned from a winter retreat one spring with serious health problems resulting from fire fighting. He had gone down a well in the middle of winter to hold a hose during a large fire at the monastery where he had been staying. Several hours in the freezing water had partially paralyzed his legs and produced serious internal problems. The ever-present danger keeps the monks vigilant about fires; apart from small altar fires ignited by burning candles or incense, fires are fortunately rare.

CONSTRUCTION

Construction is almost always done by trained professionals: lay architects, builders, carpenters, and woodworkers. A monk in some official capacity—usually prior, treasurer, or proctor—will be on hand to oversee the construction, even though he usually does not participate himself in building. If the construction is to take place over a long period of time, as is always the case for new buildings and major renovations of existing structures, the workers are housed and fed in the monastery itself. Temple construction and painting are arts now known only to a few skilled lay workers, only rarely to monks. I have never heard of a monk-builder—presumably because of the long years of apprenticeship required to learn the complicated honing and woodcutting techniques—but there are still a handful of monks around who know how to paint the decorative trim (*tanch'ŏng*) under the eaves of temple buildings.

The congregation is generally called out to assist only with unloading the heavy roof tiles or woven-grass floor mats (the Japanese *tatami*). Roof tiles are generally off-loaded from the delivery truck and stacked near the building site. Later, when they are ready to be placed on the roof, the monks will stand in a long line stretching from the stack of tiles up long boards to the roof itself, and pass along the tiles, one by one, up to the roof, where the roofers make the final placement. Sometimes monks also help with preparing the clay mortar that is used to attach the tiles to the roof and to fill in the walls. The walls of the wooden buildings are made of split bamboo strung together with reeds and then lashed to the main frame of the building. The monks smear clay mixed with chopped rice straw to the side of the wall, as if it were plaster. The remaining construction and painting is left up to the lay craftsmen.

After sketching in broad swathe the operation of the monastery, let me turn next to the ways in which the temple interacts with the world beyond its precincts.

CHAPTER SIX.

Relations with the Laity

IN Chapter One, I described the measures through which the Chosŏn dynasty, with its pronounced neo-Confucian orientation, drastically limited the Buddhist presence in the towns of Korea. Urban monasteries were disestablished and monks relegated to isolated mountain sites, where they had little contact with the laity. The monastic communities became increasingly insular, concerned more with sustaining their threatened traditions than with proselytizing among the people. Buddhism's difficulties in defining its relevance to the wider society have been exacerbated in recent times by the rapid changes wrought in Korea through industrialization cum modernization along Western lines, changes that have challenged the religion.[1] This chapter will explore one means by which the Buddhist monastic community has attempted to respond to these pressures: the creation of lay societies affiliated with the major monasteries. I will focus on one of the most successful of these societies, the Puril Hoe (Buddha Sun Society), a lay group associated with Songgwang-sa.[2] These organizations are quite different from groups organized among the laity in the cities.[3] Those groups are independent lay associations founded by the urban laity itself, which can have only minimal contacts with the main Chogye Order of Korean Buddhism. The associations that I will discuss here are closely tied to the major monasteries and have been formed to foster the Chogye tradition.

In addition to the problems remaining from the Chosŏn dynasty persecution, the social agenda of the Korean government that came to power after the end of the Japanese colonial period had a serious impact on Buddhism. A series of land reforms drastically reduced the monasteries' land

---

[1] These challenges are, of course, not faced only by Buddhism. Chungmoo Choi has documented how the conflict between cultural revivalism and modernization has created problems of commercialization among contemporary shamans in Korea; "The Competence of Korean Shamans as Performers of Folklore" (Ph.D. diss., Indiana University, 1987), esp. chap. 2.

[2] This chapter adapts material that appears in my article "Monastery Lay Associations in Contemporary Korean Buddhism: A Study of the Puril Hoe," in *Contemporary Korean Religion*, Korean Research Monograph, ed. by Lewis R. Lancaster (Berkeley: Institute for East Asian Studies, 1992).

[3] These are treated by Byung-Jo Chung (Chŏng Pyŏngjo) in his chapter in Lancaster, *Contemporary Korean Religion*.

holdings, and in turn their annual income. Though the government offered financial incentives to monasteries that developed their grounds as national parklands, these government subventions hardly made up for the economic shortfall. Many monasteries also required extensive rebuilding after the Korean War. Increased support from lay Buddhists offered the most promising solution to these financial problems.

Unfortunately, after enduring five hundred years of persecution, during which Buddhism had limited interaction with most Koreans, the religion had few models of its own for creating such contacts with the laity. The Buddhist presence in the cities remained so small that it exerted little influence on the religious life of most Koreans. Even today when Koreans think of the centers of the Buddhist religion, they think not of the new city temples, such as Chogye-sa, but of such ancient monasteries as T'ongdo-sa, Haein-sa, or Songgwang-sa, all located deep in the countryside. If the monks at such major monasteries, the elite of the Korean monastic community, were to have any influence on ordinary Koreans, they would have to find ways to create direct contacts between themselves and the laity. And if money was to be raised to support these monasteries, the increasingly well-to-do urban population would have to be tapped. Lay societies affiliated with the monasteries offered a solution to both concerns.

EARLY MODELS FOR LAY SOCIETIES

There had been Buddhist religious societies, known as kyŏlsa, during the Koryŏ dynasty, but these hardly offered a viable model for contemporary Korea. In those premodern religious societies, laity and monks practiced together in the monasteries for extended periods, following rigorous schedules of study, meditation, chanting, and work. The most prominent of these religious societies was the Chŏnghye kyŏlsa (Samādhi and Prajñā Community, later known as Susŏn-sa, or Sŏn Cultivation Community), which was established by Chinul (1158–1210), at the monastery now known as Songgwang-sa. Extant records tell of a flourishing community of several hundred people, which included both ordained monks and lay adherents from many strata of society. Along with attending daily lectures on such seminal Sŏn texts as the *Platform Sūtra* and the letters and records of the Chinese Ch'an monk Ta-hui Tsung-kao (1089–1163), the systematizer of the kōan system of Zen meditation training, the participants also meditated together and engaged in group work projects (ullyŏk).[4] While these Koryŏ period religious societies were not the imme-

---

[4] See Yi Kyubo's (1168–1241) account of this society, made one generation after Chinul,

diate model for the contemporary lay associations, it is nevertheless relevant that one of the first, and most successful, of these modern groups was established by Songgwang-sa. It is known as the Puril Hoe, the Buddha Sun Society, after Chinul's funerary name: Puril Pojo *kuksa* (the national master Buddha Sun Who Shines Universally).

THE PURIL HOE

Songgwang-sa and its residents suffered tremendously during the Korean War, as I noted in Chapter Three. In 1951 communist guerillas killed the few elderly monks who remained at Songgwang-sa as caretakers and burned much of the monastery to the ground. When Kusan arrived to take control of Songgwang-sa in 1967, he faced a monumental task in restoring the monastery to its former glory. While some reconstruction of the monastery had taken place between 1955–1961, major work remained to be done. There was no main buddha hall, meditation hall, seminary, or library. Once Songgwang-sa was designated a ch'ongnim in 1969, residential quarters were insufficient to accommodate the many monks whom Kusan hoped would now flock to the monastery. Funds for such construction projects were, however, extremely limited. Land reform had drastically reduced the amount of income Songgwang-sa received from rental of paddy fields. In addition, the monastery was all but completely isolated in one of the poorest regions of Korea, far from Seoul and Pusan, the centers of prosperity in those days of burgeoning industrialization. How to raise the profile of Songgwang-sa on the national Buddhist and religious scene? How to raise the massive amounts of funds that would be necessary to rebuild Songgwang-sa to its prewar scale?

Kusan's solution was to fashion for his monastery a lay association, called the Puril Hoe, that would have branches in all the major cities of South Korea. This move would create a network of lay followers who identified themselves not just with Buddhism, but specifically with Songgwang-sa. This was a radical move for a country where regional loy-

in Robert E. Buswell, Jr., *The Korean Approach to Zen: The Collected Works of Chinul* (Honolulu: University of Hawaii Press, 1983), p. 34. For the Koryŏ-dynasty kyŏlsa movement, see Han Kidu, "Koryŏ Pulgyo ŭi kyŏlsa undong" (The Religious Society Movement of Koryŏ Buddhism), in *Han'guk Pulgyo sasang-sa: Sungsan Pak Kilchin paksa hwagap kinyŏm* (History of Korean Buddhist Thought, Presented in Commemoration of the Sixtieth Birthday of Sung-san, Dr. Pak Kilchin), ed. by Sungsan Pak Kilchin paksa hwagap kinyŏm saŏphoe (Pak Kilchin Festschrift Committee) (Iri: Wŏn Pulgyo Sasang Yŏn'guwŏn, 1975), pp. 551–583; Ko Ikchin, "Wŏnmyo Yose ŭi Paengnyŏn kyŏlsa wa kŭ sasang-chŏk tonggi" (Wŏnmyo Yose's White Lotus Religious Society and His Philosophical Incentives), *Pulgyo hakpo* (Buddhist Studies Review) 15 (1978): 109–20. Han, ibid., p. 552, lists fourteen separate religious societies during the Koryŏ.

alties remain strong. Traditionally, Buddhists had always identified themselves with the monastery closest to their home town or village, adherents in Taegu visiting Haein-sa, those in Pusan visiting Pŏmŏ-sa or T'ongdo-sa, and so forth. Even today, the majority of monastic postulants are born within a few kilometers of the monastery; rarely does a person ordain at a monastery in a different province. This tendency was exacerbated during the Chosŏn dynasty, where the individual monastery became the main locus of religious affiliation, detracting from the sense of a national tradition of Buddhism.

The Puril Hoe was offically founded on 5 September 1969, less than five months after Songgwang-sa had been designated a ch'ongnim. I translate the compact of the association in full below, to clarify the intent behind its foundation and the services it was to perform on behalf of the monastery:

The Compact of the Puril Hoe

The Buddhadharma is the great path of loving compassion and wisdom. Wisdom is that which develops limitless competence throughout endless lives. The great loving compassion of the buddhas and bodhisattvas is that which works amid the troubles and anxieties of this Saha world solely on behalf of sentient beings.

In the past, during the golden age of Silla and Koryŏ, numberless eminent monks and virtuous religious bequeathed to us this grand illumination through manifesting such loving compassion and wisdom. They emanated brilliant sunlight that shone upon the country and the culture of our nation.

Songgwang-sa on Chogye Mountain, in particular, is unique in this country as the monastery representative of the saṃgha jewel, a place where buddhas are selected. This is because it is that great site of sanctity where the sixteen national masters, beginning with national master Puril Pojo [Buddha Sun Who Shines Universally], appeared in unbroken succession. The time is truly ripe to begin this great enterprise on behalf of Buddhism at this *bodhimaṇḍa* [site of enlightenment]—an institution that nutures people on the path—which has now been reinaugurated as an ecumenical place of cultivation [where training will be offered in all schools of Buddhism].

However, if we are to accomplish this historic, saintly enterprise, we must possess lofty religious conditions on the inside and pure conditions of external protection on the outside. Here [in this compact], as an act of active worship, we announce this decision: we will form the Buddha Sun Society as a support organization for this monastery.

All we children of the Buddha, *dānapatis* [lay donors] of pure faith, take the initiative by entering into this association so as to sustain the life of wisdom of the buddhas and patriarchs. We will support to the best of our abilities the Chogye Ch'ongnim, which nutures savants so that they may serve as paragons to humans and gods. That genuine Buddha Sun will then shine throughout the entire world, illuminating all the world systems of the ten directions as if they were the lands of the buddhas. We pray with utmost sincerity that all sentient beings may together achieve buddhahood.

Ninth month, fifth day, of the year 1969

Chogye Ch'ongnim

Songgwang-sa

The Monastery Representative of the Saṃgha jewel

The Chogye Order of Korean Buddhism

[signed]

Pangjang Kusan Suryŏn

Together with Representatives of the Founders of

The Puril Hoe of Chogye Ch'ongnim

To emphasize that the Puril Hoe was to be a broadly based lay movement, Kusan held its inaugural meeting not at Songgwang-sa, but instead in the city of Taegu, in South Kyŏngsang province, near to Haein-sa. Moving quickly to build upon his monastery's natural base of support in the Chŏlla region, in the same year he established a branch in Kwangju, the closest major city to Songgwang-sa, with branches following in 1970 at Pusan and Taejŏn. A Seoul affiliate of the Puril Hoe was founded in 1974, based at Pŏmnyŏn-sa, a converted gentry (*yangban*) house donated by a devoted lay follower of Kusan's line. Branches of the Puril Hoe were eventually established in most of the major cities of Korea and even overseas, in Los Angeles and Geneva. (See the chronology at the end of this chapter.)

As of 1988, the membership of the Puril Hoe numbered approximately ten thousand, of whom 70 percent were women. Of this membership, some one hundred were especially active, holding leadership positions in the organization. Upon acceptance into the association, new pledges pay an initiation fee of some one hundred thousand wŏn ($150) and one bag of rice (*ssal*). Annual dues are approximately thirty thousand wŏn ($45).[5]

The bylaws (*hoech'ik*) of the Puril Hoe clearly bring out the fund-raising motives underlying its creation. These explicitly state that the main purpose of the association is "to support [*huwŏn*] the Chogye Ch'ongnim and its domestic and overseas Puril International Meditation Centers."[6] The compact signed by the founders of the association also notes that "we will form the Buddha Sun Society as a support organization for this mon-

[5] Information on membership and fees has been supplied in a 14 February 1989 communication from Mr. Kim Hosŏng of the Pojo Sasang Yŏn'gu-wŏn.

[6] *Puril hoe hoech'ik*, bylaw no. 3.

astery."[7] The Puril Hoe raises some two hundred million wŏn (three hundred thousand dollars) annually, which is used both for the needs of Songgwang-sa and to pay for annual pilgrimages by the membership to the monastery.[8]

The money raised by the Puril Hoe has been absolutely vital to rebuilding the monastery. The success of the Puril Hoe in fund-raising is easily seen in a quick walk around the campus of Songgwang-sa. During Kusan's tenure as Sŏn master, a new Taeung-chŏn was constructed, followed by a new Kwanŭm-chŏn (Avalokiteśvara Shrine), and a museum, starting the process of filling in the monastery's burned-out center. On the mountain slope in back of the main shrine hall, a large meditation hall and lecture hall were built, facilities necessary for the new ch'ongnim to serve its anticipated role as a practice center for all major branches of Korean Buddhist thought and praxis. Shortly before Kusan's death in 1983, Hyŏnho *sŭnim*, one of his first disciples, was appointed abbot of the monastery. He has started the most ambitious construction project in the monastery's recent history.

The main buddha hall that Kusan built was moved beam by beam to a new location in the central campus of the monastery and replaced with a huge new hall, the second largest in Korea after Chogye-sa's, the administrative headquarters of the main Buddhist order. A new museum is nearing completion, which dwarfs its predecessor, as well as new abbot's and guest quarters, an assembly hall for lay meetings, and a modern bathhouse and toilets. The massive expansion in the monastery's infrastructure will finally allow Songgwang-sa truly to fulfill its charge as a ch'ongnim: to serve as an ecumenical center for all branches of Korean Buddhism. Fund-raising continues for a memorial reliquary for Kusan, modeled after the Buddha's own stūpa. Through these continuing projects, Songgwang-sa has more than doubled in size since 1965, with much of that construction funded by the Puril Hoe.

But the benefits created by the association are not purely one sided. In the cities, the Puril Hoe sponsors periodic lectures and Buddhist ceremonies for its lay followers. Several times each year the Sŏn master of Songgwang-sa, or another senior monk, visits the centers. His visit typically involves a Buddhist service and chanting, followed by a dharma talk and vegetarian feast. In conjunction with the regular lay association, the monastery also sponsors a youth group of college-age students. This group not only helps to inculcate students in traditional Buddhist beliefs and practices, but serves a necessary social function as well, providing an acceptable venue for young men and women to meet. Indeed, many con-

---

[7] See translation above.
[8] Information supplied by Mr. Kim Hosŏng in a 14 February 1989 communication.

temporary marriages have their genesis in the "church socials" sponsored by these Buddhist youth groups.

To cement communications even further between the monastery and its lay members, the association in 1980 began publishing a monthly newsletter, the *Newsletter of the Buddha Sun Society (Puril Hoebo)*. This newsletter, which is now into its ninth year, typically includes dharma talks by the Sŏn master at Songgwang-sa, comparative articles on Buddhism and Western thought, travel pieces about other Buddhist countries, and even a cartoon, *Zen Master Talk (Sŏnsa iyagi)*. In 1984, a Puril Publishing Company was also founded to publish and distribute religious tracts that would edify the laity and three Puril bookstores were opened to sell both those books and other Buddhist literature.

Not all of the association's activities occur in the cities. To strengthen the laity's connection to Songgwang-sa, an intensive training session is held at the main monastery each April, during an annual ceremony honoring the memory of Chinul, the national master Puril Pojo, the eponymous namesake of the association. Adherents are bussed in from all over the country. This session lasts for three days, following a rigorous schedule that includes morning and evening services, extensive lectures on Buddhist doctrine, and meditation practice. The highlight of the session is a bodhisattva-precepts ceremony (*posal kyesik*), which follows the novice and bhikṣu ordinations discussed in Chapter Four. People are free to take bodhisattva precepts as often as they like, and both monks and laypeople may retake those precepts several times during their lives, some doing it as often as once a season.

East Asian Mahāyāna countries encourage their lay adherents as well to take the bodhisattva precepts, deriving from the apocryphal *Book of Brahmā's Net* (*Pŏmmang-kyŏng*; *Brahmajāla-sūtra*[9]).[10] For the ceremony, an ordination platform is constructed inside the lecture hall at the monastery, and three senior monks are placed in charge, with some seven other senior monks witnessing the ceremony as certifiers (*chŭngsa*), as I discussed previously in treating bhikṣu and bhikṣuṇī ordinations.

The bodhisattva-precepts ceremony begins with a long opening address by one of the senior monks, usually the Sŏn master. This address is printed and distributed to the participants at the conclusion of the ordination. The following morning the regular service is held, followed by extended chanting of the name of Avalokiteśvara bodhisattva (Kwan-

[9] Tentative reconstruction of title.

[10] *Fan-wang ching* (Book of Brahmā's Net), *T* 1484.24.997a–1010a. For background on this important preceptory scripture, see Paul Groner, "The *Fan-wang ching* and Monastic Discipline in Japanese Tendai: A Study of Annen's *Futsū jubosatsukai kōshaku*," in *Chinese Buddhist Apocrypha*, ed. by Robert E. Buswell, Jr. (Honolulu: University of Hawaii Press, 1990), pp. 251–90.

seŭm *posal*), the bodhisattva of compassion. Throughout the remainder of the day, there are three-hour-long lectures in the late morning, afternoon, and evening. Those lectures are delivered by the ordination catechist and can be much more animated than those of the Sŏn master. They are intended to appeal to the laypeople, who predominate at the bodhisattva ordination. The lectures deal primarily with the forty-six bodhisattva precepts, but the catechist spices his lectures with often funny stories illustrating the precepts he is explaining, so these lectures are both entertaining and edifying. Peals of laughter emanate from the hall during these lectures. Those few catechists, such as Ilt'a *sŭnim*, who can hold an audience's attention are much in demand. Novices and monks who have ordained on the previous day also attend the lectures. But while the number of monks will rarely number over a hundred, more than a thousand laypersons might participate in the bodhisattva ordination. Sometimes the second day of the ordination will culminate in an all-night meditation period known as *yongmaeng chŏngjin* (lit. ferocious effort).

After breakfast on the third morning, the actual transmission ceremony begins. The confessor reads off the formula constituting the ceremony and the audience repeats it in unison, an exchange that takes about an hour. The preceptor then proclaims that they have received the precepts and should keep them carefully. The participants then begin chanting the *Great Compassion Mantra* many times over as monks go around administering the arm-burn (*yŏnbi*), symbolizing nonattachment to the body, in this case only a light touch to the forearm with a glowing incense stick. The burn is treated lightly, with many of the people laughing over the procedure. After everyone has received their burns, the laypeople line up in groups according to their home cities and a monk reads off their names and distributes their ordination certificates. At the conclusion of the ordination, the participants form a long line, with the new bhikṣus and bhikṣunīs in front, followed by the novices, and finally the laypeople. Placing their bodhisattva-ordination certificates on their heads, the participants place their palms together in front of them and snake through the courtyard, following a grid of the Realm of Reality Chart (*pŏpkye-to*; *dharmadhātu-maṇḍala*) that has been outlined in chalk on the dirt of the courtyard. After dinner, laypeople board busses taking them back to their home cities and the monastery rapidly returns to its normal schedule.

While these monastery sessions may have some similarities to the older kyŏlsa associations of the Koryŏ period, in which the laity trained for extended periods at the monastery, there is one major difference. In the kyŏlsa, ordained religious and lay adherents practiced together in the same compound on a semipermanent basis. But these modern lay training sessions are of limited duration and are almost totally segregated from the regular activities of the monastery.

THE MODEL FOR CONTEMPORARY LAY ASSOCIATIONS

There is no direct precedent in the indigenous Buddhist tradition for such urban lay associations affiliated with distant mountain monasteries. Before the advent of modern transportation, it would, of course, have been impractical for a monastery even to consider creating a nationwide network of adherents. But problems of access are far from the only reason. The traditional lifestyle of Korean Buddhist monasteries was hardly conducive to extensive interactions between the laity and the monks. Buddhist monks are not priests, and few have ever sought out any pastoral role. Most monks believe that only the seniormost among them have the wisdom and experience necessary to offer spiritual advice to others and are hesitant to take on such a role until they have completed at least twenty years of training.

Where then did the Buddhists derive their model for these urban lay societies? I suspect there is a non-Buddhist source: Christian church fellowships. While none of the monks whom I consulted acknowledged this source, there is much indirect evidence to support it. Contemporary Buddhists have watched with intense interest, if not acute anxiety, the rapid inroads Christianity has made in Korea, especially over the last three decades. As Donald Clark has noted, these conversions are not just a matter of "rice Christians" who have been won over to the faith thanks to the eleemosynary largesse of Western missionaries.[11] Rather, I believe that the close, often daily, contact between the Protestant pastor and his flock may have filled an emotional need in the religious life of ordinary Koreans that the typically aloof Buddhists were hard pressed to satisfy. In addition, many Koreans consider the increasingly secular character of their society to be more consonant with Prostestantism than with a cloistered tradition like Buddhism. Since Korean Buddhists have not actively proselytized since early in their history, the Christian techniques being used successfully around them may have provided the most readily available models.

[11] Donald N. Clark, *Christianity in Modern Korea*, Asian Agenda Report, no. 5 (Lantham, Md.: University Press of America, 1986), p. 51. For a survey of Christian pressures on contemporary Buddhism, see Henrik H. Sørensen, "The Conflict between Buddhism and Christianity in Korea," in *Symposium on Korea*, East Asian Institute Occasional Papers 1, ed. by Simon B. Heilesen (Copenhagen: East Asian Institute, University of Copenhagen, 1988), pp. 24–31. A valuable survey of Christianity in Korea, with an interesting case study of its indigenization, appears in Youngsook Kim Harvey, "The Korean Shaman and the Deaconess: Sisters in Different Guises," in *Religion and Ritual in Korean Society*, Korea Research Monograph, no. 12, ed. Laurel Kendall and Griffin Dix (Berkeley: Institute of East Asian Studies, 1987), pp. 149–70. For the tactics used by Christian missionaries in spreading their religion among Koreans, see L. George Paik, *The History of Protestant Missions in Korea: 1832–1910* (1929; reprint, Seoul: Yonsei University Press, 1970), pp. 198–255.

Such adaptation of Christian missionary methods would hardly be without precedent in Buddhism. Indeed, it is a quintessential example of the Buddhist doctrine of *upāya* (*pangp'yŏn*), or skill in means, in which heterodox ideas are adapted to the needs of the religion. As a missionary religion itself, Buddhism displayed tremendous flexibility in its early period by adapting its message to the needs and interests of the indigenous Korean population.[12] Its long centuries of supremacy in Korea may have fostered some complacency, which was now threatening the very existence of the religion. If Buddhism could not adapt to this new challenge offered by Christianity, its viability was threatened.

Some of these attempts at adapting Christian missionary techniques seem at times artificial and trite. One of the examples I found to be most blatant began among lay Buddhists in the cities and has spread even to monastery support organizations: the Buddhist adaptation of hymns introduced by Christian missionaries. A similar move was made in Ceylon (now Sri Lanka) during the late nineteenth century by Colonel H. S. Olcott, the American theosophist, who founded many Buddhist organizations there that drew their inspiration from Christian models. To strengthen indigenous Buddhism against the inroads Christian missionaries were making in Ceylon, Olcott drafted a Buddhist "catechism," and encouraged the Ceylonese to use songs based on Christmas carols to celebrate Wesak, the Southeast Asian holiday commemorating the Buddha's birth, enlightenment, and death.[13] The urban laity in Korea also began to sing traditional Buddhist ritual chants to the melodies of Christian hymns. These new songs have become so much a part of urban lay Buddhism that the monks from the mountain monasteries acquiesce and let the laity use their own chants in joint ceremonies. The culture shock is striking when mountain monks participate in urban services. While the laity sing their Buddhist hymns, often with piano or organ accompaniment, the monks perform in traditional *pŏmp'ae* style, with its cacophony of sound. Often neither group knows the other's chanting style, and both must stand in mute silence until their fellow adherents are finished—striking testimony to the rapid changes Buddhism is undergoing in Korea, prompted by pressures from its religious rivals. Still, one has to wonder to what extent the success of Buddhist proselytization efforts will depend on song rather than the relevance of its underlying message to contemporary Koreans.

[12] See the discussion in Robert E. Buswell, Jr., *The Formation of Ch'an Ideology in China and Korea: The Vajrasamādhi-Sūtra, A Buddhist Apocryphon*, Princeton Library of Asian Translations (Princeton: Princeton University Press, 1989), esp. chap. 4.

[13] Richard F. Gombrich, *Precept and Practice: Traditional Buddhism in the Rural Highlands of Ceylon* (Oxford: Clarendon Press, 1971), p. 53.

THE BENEFITS OF LAY ASSOCIATIONS

I have suggested that fund-raising was one of the reasons behind the creation of lay associations affiliated with Buddhist monasteries. While admitting this, it would be going much too far to imply that the monks' motives in forming such organizations were exclusively venal. Declining Buddhist influence in Korean culture and society compelled Buddhist monks to think of new ways in which Buddhism might better appeal to the laity. Concerned monks like Kusan realized that the continued viability of Buddhism in Korea demanded a strong base in the lay population. The stagnation of Buddhism during the Chosŏn dynasty may have been catalyzed by government persecutions and restrictions, but the inability of Buddhists to spread their message beyond the confines of the monastery only furthered that religious lassitude. As has been the case with Western Catholicism in recent decades, a celibate, cenobitic community will have trouble attracting a continuing flow of novices unless its message is seen as relevant by ordinary people. It is from among the laity, after all, that the next generation of monks and nuns must come. Lay societies are one solution to this estrangement of the Buddhist laity from the monks. These societies help to ensure that the laity is brought into contact on a regular basis with the leaders of the Buddhist monastic tradition, and that those senior monks will remain cognizant of the needs and interests of the laity. This knowledge then allows the monks to hone their message more sharply. Only such a process of mutual awareness, evaluation, and experimentation can widen the appeal of Buddhism and restore it to its traditional place in Korean religious life.

The interactions created through the lay societies have benefited symbiotically the laity, the monks, and the religion as a whole. Through periodic lectures and retreats, the Buddhist laity gained access to the seniormost monks in the religion, who routinely would have devoted themselves to monastic, not lay, training. The laity were also provided with a living paradigm of Buddhist rectitude, a concrete example of the spiritual benefits forthcoming from Buddhist practice. Monks were better able to target different strata of Korean society, urban elite and blue-collar worker alike. Indeed, the message of Buddhism has begun to change, and sometimes radically, through these contacts: Rather than otherworldly transcendence, the social value of the Buddhist worldview and ethical observances is often emphasized. The recent movement of *minjung* Pulgyo, or Buddhism for the masses,[14] is but one example of this new social consciousness among contemporary Buddhists. Finally, these urban organizations have helped Buddhism to defend itself, and its lay

[14] See the chapter by Sung Bae Park in Lancaster, *Contemporary Korean Religion.*

adherents, against the inroads made in contemporary Korea by Christian missions, as well as to begin to create a message that could appeal to a wider cross-section of Korean society. Only such a message will allow Buddhism to grow beyond its present base of support.

But these lay associations are only one step—and a relatively minor one at that—in what I fear will be a wrenching process of change for Korean Buddhism. Buddhism in Korea today is at a crucial crossroads in its 1,500-year history. Complacency in its own past traditions will further estrange the majority of Koreans from Buddhism. But wholesale adaptations of rival religious models or a headlong movement toward modernity will prompt charges of spiritual bankruptcy and hypocrisy. Only some happy medium between these two extremes—a quintessential application of the Buddhist ideal of the Middle Way—offers hope of a successful consummation of this process.

CHRONOLOGY OF THE PURIL HOE

1967, March	Kusan moves to Songgwang-sa
1969, April 15	Songgwang-sa raised to ch'ongnim status and Kusan promoted to pangjang
1969, June	Discussions begin toward formation of Puril Hoe
1969, September 5	Puril Hoe founded and Kusan appointed head
1969, September 5	Incorporation meeting of Puril Hoe held in Taegu
1969, September 20	Kwangju branch of Puril Hoe established
1970, January 15	Pusan branch of Puril Hoe established
1970, March 3	Taejŏn branch of Puril Hoe established
1970, October 15	Restoration of Susŏn-sa, Meditation Hall at Songgwang-sa, with funds provided by Puril Hoe members
1974, January 5	Pŏmnyŏn-sa, Seoul branch temple of Songgwang-sa, established
1974, March 25	Chinju branch of Puril Hoe established
1974, March 25	Masan branch of Puril Hoe established
1974, March 25	Sunch'ŏn branch of Puril Hoe established
1974, March 31	Seoul branch of Puril Hoe established
1977, July 7	Ch'ungmu branch of Puril Hoe established
1978, March 25	Songgwang-sa center for Puril Hoe established
1979, March 25	Hyŏnho *sŭnim* selected head of Puril Hoe
1979, December 4	Chinhae branch of Puril Hoe established
1980, May 26	Ch'ŏngju branch of Puril Hoe established
1980, September 9	*Puril hoebo* (monthly newsletter) begins publishing
1980, December 14, 21	Koryŏ-sa founded in Los Angeles as branch temple of Songgwang-sa; first overseas branch of Puril Hoe established there
1981, November 25	Onyang branch of Puril Hoe established
1982, May 27	Kwangyang branch of Puril Hoe established
1982, April	Kangnŭng branch of Puril Hoe established
1982, April	Cheju Island branch of Puril Hoe established
1982, July	Pulsŏng-sa founded in Geneva, as branch temple of Songgwang-sa; established as European branch of Puril Hoe
1982, September	Taegak-sa founded in Carmel, California, as branch temple of Songgwang-sa; Puril Hoe branch established
1982, November	Ch'angwŏn branch of Puril Hoe established

1983, March 25	Inch'ŏn branch of Puril Hoe established
1983, March 25	Hyŏnho appointed abbot of Songgwang-sa
1983, April 7	Chŏnju branch of Puril Hoe established
1983, December 16	Kusan dies
1984, March 25	Hoegwang appointed new pangjang of Songgwang-sa and new head of Puril Hoe
1984, June 20	Puril Publishing Company founded
1984, August 1	Puril Bookstores open in Seoul, Kwangju, and Songgwang-sa
1985, October 1	Puril Hoe office founded in Seoul
1986, March 25	Kimhae branch of Puril Hoe established
1986, March 25	Naju branch of Puril Hoe established
1987, February 22	Research Institute for the Study of Chinul's Thought (Pojo sasang yŏn'gu-wŏn) established; Pŏpchong *sŭnim* appointed head

CHAPTER SEVEN

The Practice of Zen Meditation in Korea

ZEN, or Sŏn, as the school is known in Korea, existed on the Korean peninsula as early as the end of the seventh century, virtually simultaneously with the incipiency of its Chinese counterpart, Ch'an.[1] But it was not until the ninth century, toward the end of the Unified Silla dynasty (668–935), that it became a palpable force within the Korean Buddhist tradition. This influence it was able to achieve through the formation of the so-called Nine Mountains school of Sŏn (Kusan Sŏnmun)—nine centers of Sŏn practice scattered throughout the Korean peninsula, which derived for the most part from lineages of Chinese Ch'an belonging to the iconoclastic Hung-chou, or proto-Lin-chi, line.[2] Early in the succeeding Koryŏ dynasty, however, these different sites fell into decline, and the Sŏn school seems to have become virtually moribund by the end of the eleventh century.

The contemporary Sŏn tradition owes its origins to the eminent Koryŏ monk Chinul (1158–1210), the founder of Songgwang-sa. Chinul was a monk who retained a strong personal commitment to Sŏn meditation, but who was equally concerned with the resonances between Sŏn and companion strands of Buddhist thought and practice. By demonstrating that the underpinnings of Sŏn's unique forms of praxis could be corroborated in the doctrinal teachings of the more scholastic schools of Buddhist thought, Chinul brought Sŏn into the mainstream of Korean Buddhism. His successors put the tradition on a road that would culminate in the domination of Korean Buddhism by Sŏn.[3] Despite the continued atten-

[1] For the early period of Korean Sŏn and its connections with the nascent Chinese Ch'an tradition, see Robert E. Buswell, Jr. *The Formation of Ch'an Ideology in China and Korea: The Vajrasamādhi-Sūtra, A Buddhist Apocryphon*, Princeton Library of Asian Translations (Princeton: Princeton University Press, 1989).

[2] The most comprehensive treatment of the Nine Mountains schools in any language appears in Henrik H. Sørensen, "The History and Doctrines of Early Korean Sŏn Buddhism" (Ph.D. diss., University of Copenhagen, 1987). See also Seo Kyung-bo's problematic "A Study of Korean Zen Buddhism Approached through the Chodangjip" (Ph.D. diss., Temple University, 1970; mimeographed reprint, Seoul: Poryŏn'gak, 1973).

[3] I have translated all of Chinul's major works in Robert E. Buswell, Jr., *The Korean Approach to Zen: The Collected Works of Chinul* (Honolulu: University of Hawaii Press, 1983), which includes also a historical introduction describing Chinul's importance in the development of the Korean Buddhist tradition. An abridged paperback version of that book, with selections from three representative works of Chinul, has appeared as *Tracing Back*

tion to intra-Buddhist ecumenism in modern Korea, Sŏn dominates all large practice centers, and its meditative techniques are virtually all that are taught today.

OBSERVING THE CRITICAL PHRASE

Chinul is also notable for being the first in Korea to promote a new form of Sŏn practice, which had been systematized in China by Ta-hui Tsung-kao, one generation before Chinul. This is the technique of kanhwa Sŏn (Ch. *k'an-hua* Ch'an), the Sŏn approach of "observing (*kan*) the critical phrase (*hwadu*; Ch. *hua-t'ou*)." We in the West usually know this technique in its Japanese incarnation as kōan meditation, the contemplation of Zen conundrums, about which D. T. Suzuki wrote so extensively from the standpoint of the Rinzai tradition. Thanks to the backing of Chinul and his successors at Songgwang-sa, hwadu meditation quickly became the most common form of practice in Korean Buddhism. Kanhwa Sŏn's preeminence was cemented in the fourteenth century by such Korean monks as T'aego Pou (1301–1382), who returned from China after mastering the hwadu technique and receiving transmission from teachers in the Chinese Lin-chi (Kor. Imje; Jpn. Rinzai) lineage. From that point on, the Lin-chi school, and the hwadu technique for which it is known, dominated Korean Buddhist praxis.[4]

The hwadu is a question, peculiar to the Sŏn school, that promotes spiritual inquiry. The hwadu is considered to be the essential theme, principal topic, or "critical phrase," of the kongan (Ch. *kung-an*; Jpn. *kōan*), or Zen case. Let me take as an example the kongan involving Chao-chou Ts'ung-shen (778–897), which remains the most popular today in Korea and in the Japanese Rinzai tradition:

> Once a monk asked Chao-chou, "Does a dog have Buddha-nature, or not?"
> Chao-chou replied, "No!" (Ch. *wu*; Kor./Jpn. *mu*).[5]

---

the Radiance: Chinul's Korean Way of Zen, Classics in East Asian Buddhism, no. 2 (Honolulu: University of Hawaii Press, a Kuroda Institute Book, 1991). See also Hee-sung Keel, *Chinul: The Founder of the Korean Sŏn Tradition*, Berkeley Buddhist Studies Series, vol. 6 (Berkeley: Center for South and Southeast Asian Studies, 1984).

[4] For Chinul's role in the eventual domination of Lin-chi Ch'an praxis in Korean Buddhism, see Robert E. Buswell, Jr., "Chinul's Ambivalent Critique of Radical Subitism in Korean Sŏn Buddhism," *Journal of the International Association of Buddhist Studies* 12, no. 2 (1989): 20–44.

[5] This famous *kung-an* appears as the first case in the *Wu-men kuan* (Gateless Checkpoint), *T* 2005.48.292c. For the history of its use in Chinese Ch'an Buddhism, see Robert E. Buswell, Jr., "The 'Short-Cut' Approach of *K'an-hua* Meditation: The Evolution of a Practical Subitism in Chinese Ch'an Buddhism," in *Sudden and Gradual: Approaches to*

Here, the entire exchange between Chao-chou and the monk would be the kongan; the most critical phrase in the exchange—the word "no" (*mu*)—would be the hwadu.

The "root paradigms" of Sŏn—which Victor Turner terms a religion's "cultural goals, means, ideas, outlooks, currents of thought, patterns of belief, and so on"[6]—have been formulated by the tradition as kongans or hwadus, which serve as contemplative themes. Kongans, it will be recalled, are interchanges between an enlightened master and his disciples, in which the master's original "creative deed becomes an ethical and religious paradigm"[7] for the subsequent tradition by being transformed into a topic of meditation. The meditator's reflection on the intent behind the master's enigmatic response creates an awareness of the significance of a past Sŏn master's action, celebrated in the kongan story, "the very essence of which is its immediacy and spontaneity. It is structure that is transmitted, by rote and repetition."[8] The meditator is instructed to concentrate on a single hwadu, continuously and without distraction. Regardless of whatever it is that the student may be doing—whether walking, eating, working, or going to the toilet—the hwadu is to be kept vividly before him at all times. Kanhwa Sŏn forces the student to begin to think as the enlightened masters of old, to enact in his own mind the mental processes that led to the past master's expression of his enlightenment.

Kongans might also be regarded as "cultural schemas," following Sherry Ortner, who defines such schemas as "preorganized schemes of action, symbolic programs for the staging and playing out of standard social interactions in a particular culture."[9] These schemas, Ortner argues, may help to mediate cultural or religious contradictions—such as the Sŏn claim that despite apparently irrefutable evidence to the contrary, we are actually enlightened. These schemas are "a statement of relations between two major cultural values, and it says that both are attainable

---

Enlightenment in Chinese Thought, Studies in East Asian Buddhism, no. 5, ed. by Peter N. Gregory (Honolulu: University of Hawaii Press, 1987), p. 369 n.95.

[6] Turner defines root paradigms as referring "not only to the current state of social relationships existing or developing between actors, but the cultural goals, means, ideas, outlooks, currents of thought, patterns of belief, and so on, which enter into those relationships." Victor Turner, *Dramas, Fields, and Metaphors: Symbolic Action in Society*, Symbol, Myth, and Ritual Series (Ithaca, N.Y.: Cornell University Press, 1974), p. 64; see also ibid., chap. 6.

[7] Ibid., p. 249.

[8] Ibid., p. 251.

[9] Sherry B. Ortner, *High Religion: A Cultural and Political History of Sherpa Buddhism*, Princeton Studies in Culture/Power/History (Princeton: Princeton University Press, 1989), p. 60.

simultaneously, and indeed that each is a condition of the other."[10] In kanhwa practice, the meditator is not trying to achieve or to create awakening. Since Sŏn doctrine considers enlightenment to be innate in the minds of all sentient beings, enlightenment is not something that needs to be achieved or created; it is now, and indeed has always been, the fundamental fact underlying everyone's existence. The individual has, however, so thoroughly convinced himself that he is not enlightened that he finds it virtually impossible to accept that fact. Now utterly estranged from his true status as an enlightened person, the person must be taken through a period of transition—which his meditation practice provides—during which his true status is revealed to him and its frightening truth made acceptable. The institution of the meditation hall, and the technique of kanhwa Sŏn, are designed to mediate this religious contradiction between the apparent reality of ignorance and the promise of enlightenment, and ultimately to transform the student from an ordinary monk into an enlightened master.[11]

Going back now to the hwadu "no," because this answer is diametrically opposed to the pan-Mahāyāna teaching that all beings—dogs, of course, included—have buddha-nature, it throws a gauntlet down before a student's conventional understanding and challenges him to examine why it is that Chao-chou would make such a seemingly nonsensical reply. The introspective focus[12] created through single-minded consideration of the meaning of this statement eventually leads the student to the source of thought—that nondual state before discrimination arises in the mind, which is considered to be identical in all beings. Through this experience, the student knows what Chao-chou's state of mind was like just prior to making his famous statement and he is thus able to grasp intuitively why it was that Chao-chou would say "no." The student becomes as if he himself were Chao-chou, for he has tapped that same source of thought from which Chao-chou's own answer arose. He can, in other words, know as Chao-chou knew. Once the student has realized this nondual state of mind, there is no need any longer to try to *explain* why Chao-chou said "no"; rather he simply *knows* it intuitively for himself. His intuition allows him to grasp effortlessly the meaning of all the other

[10] Ibid., p. 78.

[11] This interpretation follows Lévi-Strauss's analysis of social constructions having no apparent practical value that serve to mediate cultural contradictions; see Claude Lévi-Strauss, *The Raw and the Cooked*, trans. by J. Weightman and D. Weightman (New York: Harper and Row, 1969); noted and discussed in Ortner, *High Religion*, p. 76.

[12] The introspection engendered through kanhwa Sŏn seems closely akin to the Latin *meditatio*, which one Catholic monk has interpreted as "pondering in its more literal sense of letting the matter weigh quietly within." M. Basil Pennington, *Monastery: Prayer, Work, Community* (San Francisco: Harper and Row, 1983), p. 58.

thousands of hwadus used in the Sŏn school, for his mind is now able to emulate the minds of all the previous Zen masters—or, perhaps better, his mind has now become that of all the previous masters. He is then considered to have received the "mind-to-mind transmission" of the buddhas and patriarchs and is, in a word, enlightened.

CONTEMPORARY MEDITATION TRAINING

I have written extensively elsewhere about the theory behind the hwadu technique in Korea and China.[13] Rather than repeating that material, what I believe would be more useful here is to explore how a Sŏn master in the contemporary Korean tradition goes about training his students in meditation on the "critical phrase." I was often with Kusan when he instructed students in various stages of kanhwa Sŏn. I was personally on the receiving end of those instructions many times, especially during my first year at Songgwang-sa and, during retreat seasons, together with small groups of Korean monks from the meditation hall. Later, as Kusan's translator, I was with him several times as he took new foreign monks and the periodic Western visitors who visited Songgwang-sa through the initial process of learning the hwadu. After much prodding from his ordained Western students, Kusan consented in 1976 to write down these oral instructions in a short work that he first titled *The Road to the Other Shore* (*P'ian e kil*) and later *Stone Lion at the Crossroads* (*Nekŏri tol saja*).[14] I will draw liberally on that work in this account. While Kusan, like all Sŏn masters, brought his own style and personality to his instructions, the approach to Sŏn practice he outlines in that work is representative of the contemporary Korean tradition as a whole.

[13] For detailed discussions of the origins and practice of kanhwa Sŏn in both China and Korea, see my articles "*K'an-hua* Meditation," pp. 321–77; and "Chinul's Systematization of Chinese Meditative Techniques in Korean Sŏn Buddhism," in *Traditions of Meditation in Chinese Buddhism*, Studies in East Asian Buddhism, no. 4, ed. by Peter N. Gregory (Honolulu: University of Hawaii Press, 1986), pp. 199–242.

[14] This text was translated into English that same year in *Nine Mountains*, a privately published book of Kusan's sermons; see Meditation Master Ku San, *Nine Mountains* (Songgwang-sa, 1976; many reprints). That book of English translations of some of Kusan's sermons was compiled and translated by myself (Hyemyŏng) and two other Western monks then resident at Songgwang-sa: Renaud Neubauer (Hyehaeng) and Stacey Krause (Hamwŏl). I quote liberally from it here, with occasional emendations. Some of the material in *Nine Mountains* was later reworked as Kusan Sunim's *The Korean Way of Zen*, translated by Martine Fages and edited by Stephen Batchelor (New York: Weatherhill, 1985), two other foreign monks who lived at Songgwang-sa after my departure. This Korean text was later included with slight revisions in a Korean collection of Kusan's discourses entitled *Sŏk saja: Kusan Sŏnsa pŏbŏ chip* (Chogye Ch'ongnim Songgwang-sa: Puril Publishing Co., 1980), published three years before his death.

In starting both lay Buddhists and monks new to meditation hall out in hwadu practice, Kusan often began by asking them what they thought was the most precious thing in the world.[15] After receiving the expected answers—some of the notable ones Kusan singled out in his book were world peace, international friendship, status, art, wealth, freedom, peace of mind, and life—he then urged the students to consider what it was that decided that world peace, or whatever their answer had been, was most precious. By a process of deduction, Kusan led the students to the understanding that it was their own minds that decided what was precious and what was not—and therefore the mind in fact was the most precious thing of all.[16]

But what was that mind which was the most precious thing in the world, that decided what was supreme? That mind, Kusan taught, initiated all action and was therefore the master of the body (*chuin'gong*). But it also subsumed all things in existence, from one's own body, to the earth, humankind, and all the animals. The entire universe was therefore no different from one's own mind. Because of its virtual omnipresence, this mind could also be called the "great self" (*taea*; Skt. *parātman*). The term "great self" should be understood carefully, so as not to suggest that it controverts the well-known Buddhist concept of nonself, or *anātman*. Kusan's analysis of the self and its relationship to all mental and physical phenomena was intended to demonstrate to the student that all things are in a state of interrelationship, one with the other; there was no self or soul that could be conceived separately from anything else. Hence, through Sŏn practice the student was to realize a universal "ecology" of mind, in which "this world, mankind and all the animals are no different from oneself. This is precisely the 'Great Self.' . . . And as we know that it is not possible to separate any component from the rest of the world, both objects and the relative self cannot really exist. Therefore, the 'Great Self' is precisely 'no-self' [*mua*; *anātman*]."[17]

But such terms as "mind," "great self," "master," or even "buddha," were all just labels, Kusan explained.[18] What was that thing in reality?

---

[15] This line of questioning goes at least as far back as Sŏktu *sŭnim*, the teacher of Kusan's teacher, Hyobong. Another of Sŏktu's students, Hyangbong, wrote an account of his first meeting with Sŏktu, in which he was questioned in this same manner, in his memoirs; see Hyangbong, *Unsu san'go* (Scattered Manuscripts of a Wandering Monk) (Songgwang-sa: Hyangbong Mundo-hoe, 1979), pp. 1–4. I have translated this memoir; see Robert E. Buswell, Jr., "The Pilgrimages of Hyangbong: Memoirs and Poems of the Kumgang Mountains," *Korean Culture* 11, no. 4 (Winter 1990): 18–23.

[16] *Nine Mountains*, p. 12; *Sok saja*, p. 10.

[17] *Nine Mountains*, p. 20; *Sŏk saja*, p. 18.

[18] Kusan here is influenced by the great Koryŏ-period Sŏn master, T'aego Pou (1301–1382), who noted, "This one thing . . . may expediently be called 'mind,' or 'path,' or 'king of the myriad things,' or 'buddha.' " *T'aego Pou kuksa pŏbŏ chip* (Collection of the Dharma

Since that thing could not be seen or touched, some of the people whom he asked this question wondered whether it was space or voidness. But, Kusan replied, can space distinguish between right and wrong, good and bad, as humans routinely are able to do? "Finally," Kusan taught, "a doubt arises as to what this thing ultimately is. . . . Thus the question 'What is it?' is generated . . . , 'What is it?' that is neither mind, buddha, a material thing, or empty space."[19]

This question "What is it?" (*imwŏt ko*, a contraction of *igŏsi mwŏs-in'go*, the Korean translation of the Chinese phrase *shih shen-ma*) is a hwadu, a phrase intended to generate inquiry, and thus serve as a basis for meditation. Korean tradition traces this hwadu to Nan-yüeh Huai-jang's (677–744) meeting with the Sixth Patriarch, Hui-neng, which is described in the expanded Yüan dynasty recension of the *Platform Sūtra*. Huai-jang had been studying with national master Hui-an on Mount Sung before he came to pay his respects to Hui-neng. When he arrived at the Sixth Patriarch's residence, master Hui-neng asked him, "Whence have you come?" Huai-jang answered, "From Mount Sung." Hui-neng then asked, "What thing is it (*shen-ma wu*) that has come in this man-ner?" Huai-jang replied, "Whatever thing you might say it is would not hit the mark."[20] From this simple exchange, Korean Sŏn has evolved this seminal meditative question. In fact, Kusan explained, the question "What is it?" could be viewed as the basis of any existential question, from "What is the meaning of my life?" to "What is the meaning of life itself?" In this wider sense, then, Koreans consider "What is it?" to be the fundamental question raised in all the thousands of hwadus used in the Sŏn school, and thus the source of all other hwadus.

In order to maintain the contemplation on "What is it?" Kusan taught the student to produce three types of mental resolution: the mind of great anger (*taebun-sim*), the mind of great ferocity (*taeyongmaeng-sim*), and the mind of great doubt (*taeŭi-sim*).[21] These three states of mind, various listings of which are a fundamental part of modern Korean Sŏn practice, were first taught in a slightly different form during the Yüan dynasty in China by Kao-feng Yüan-miao (1238–1295) in his *Ch'an-yao* (Essentials of Ch'an), and repeated in the Korean Sŏn primer, *Sŏn'ga kwigam* (Spec-

Talks of the National Master T'aego Pou), ed. and trans. by Yi Yŏngmu (Seoul: Han'guk Pulgyo T'aego-chong Chongmuwŏn, 1974), p. 98.

[19] These passages come respectively from *Nine Mountains*, pp. 36–37, *Sŏk saja*, pp. 38–39; and *Nine Mountains*, p. 42, *Sŏk saja*, p. 45.

[20] *Liu-tsu ta-shih fa-pao t'an ching* (Platform Sūtra of the Sixth Patriarch), T 2008.48.357b; this passage does not occur in the earlier Tun-huang recension of the text. Kusan paraphrases the passage in *Nine Mountains*, p. 62; *Sŏk saja*, pp. 67–68.

[21] These are discussed in *Nine Mountains*, pp. 46–55; *Sŏk saja*, pp. 48–60. In *Sŏk saja*, Kusan relates the mind of great anger to the great faculty of faith, which is the standard description within the tradition of this first type of mental resolution.

ulum on the Sŏn School), by Sŏsan Hyujŏng (1520–1604).²² Great anger, Kusan explained, comes about because one realizes that, despite having been told repeatedly by all the buddhas and Sŏn patriarchs throughout history that we are originally enlightened ourselves, we still haven't realized that fact. We have only ourselves to blame for failing to realize our innate buddhahood and thus should be furious at the state we had gotten ourselves into. But there are so many enticing pleasures in the world to distract us, it is no wonder we have been unable to renounce desire and seek enlightenment. We must have great ferocity if we are to stand up against the many distractions facing us and to have any hope of abandoning "riches, honor, glory, high office and nobility, mother, father, children, foes, friends, benefactors and loved ones. . . ." Finally, we must wonder why it is that we haven't yet awakened, despite all the valuable teachings offered in Buddhism to help us in that task. All these words of the buddhas and patriarchs are about enlightenment, so why can't we understand their true import and awaken? Our inability to understand generates great doubt.²³

As the student continues to ask himself the question "What is it?" he eventually generates a modicum of doubt. While laypeople were generally encouraged just to continue on with the contemplation of that hwadu, Kusan usually had his ordained students transfer that sensation of doubt to one of the important hwadus taught within the Zen tradition. It really was not important which of these was used, since the purpose of all hwadus is simply to raise the doubt. But the hwadu he almost always recommended to monks, as do most Korean Sŏn masters, was the famous "no" (mu) of Chao-chou. As the student's meditation matured, Kusan explained, rather than simply asking the generic question "What is it?" the student should direct that inquiry to understanding the more specific question, "With what idea in mind (kŭ ttŭs-i muŏsin ko) did Chao-chou say that a dog has no buddha-nature?"²⁴ While the hwadu "What is it?"

²² Kao-feng Yüan-miao ch'an-shih Ch'an-yao, sec. 16, HTC 122.357c-d; I am presently completing a translation and study of this important text. The Korean edition of the text is edited with Korean punctuation by An Chinho, Hyŏnt'o chuhae: Sŏn'yo (Punctuated and Annotated Edition of the Ch'an-yao) (1938; reprint, Seoul: Pŏmnyunsa, 1956). Hyujŏng repeats the same three (again, replacing the first with the great faculty of faith) in section fourteen of his Sŏn'ga kwigam, the most important Korean Sŏn text written during the Chosŏn dynasty; see Hyujŏng, Sŏn'ga kwigam (Speculum on the Sŏn School), Chŏngŭm mun'go, no. 131, trans. by Pŏpchŏng (Seoul: Chŏngŭmsa, 1976), p. 44.

²³ Sung Bae Park has made an interesting study of the polarity Sŏn meditation creates between faith and doubt in his Buddhist Faith and Sudden Enlightenment (Albany: State University of New York Press, 1983).

²⁴ Nine Mountains, p. 52; Sŏk saja, p. 56. This same approach can be found in earlier Chinese and Korean materials; see, for example, T'aego Pou's remark, "How did the idea to say 'no' arise in Chao-chou?" (T'aego Pou kuksa pŏbŏ chip, p. 109 and passim).

is perfectly adequate for generating doubt, contemplation has more power (yŏk; Ch. *li*) when it is directed toward one of the hwadus passed down within the tradition as a test of one's understanding of Sŏn. The initial question "What is it?" is thus transformed into the more specific question, "What is Chao-chou's meaning in saying that a dog has no buddha-nature?" "This 'no,' " Kusan explained, "is not the 'no' of yes or no; it is not the 'no' of true nonexistence [*chinmu*]."[25] "Before Chao-chou expressed himself by saying 'no,' " Kusan continued, "what state of mind did he have that made him use such an expression? That idea you must carefully probe again and again."[26]

Once the doubt is generated, all hwadus became essentially identical. In fact, even the question "Why?" need no longer be framed in the mind; the mind is instead infused with a preverbal sense of wonder—the question "Why?" without the word "why." I found it rather akin to the mental quandary one experiences when trying to think of a word one knows but cannot quite call to mind, or the moment of proleptic stillness just prior to a creative insight.

As the monk's inquiry coalesces around the word "no," the doubt becomes unalloyed and unobscured during all his activities. Doubt then becomes a "sensation" (*chŏng*), as the term "sensation of doubt" (*ŭijŏng*) suggests: a true palpable presence throughout one's body, not simply an intellectual consideration or mental concern with the question. Monks absorbed by the doubt, Kusan says, "forgo sleep and forget meals. Even if we want to sleep we cannot, for it is as if we are confronted by all the enemies we have made throughout ten-thousand years. We cannot go left, we cannot go right, we cannot go forward, we cannot go backward. And finally when there is no place left to keep the body, we do not fear falling into emptiness [*nakkong; kong-e ttŏrŏjida*]."[27] "Falling into emptiness" was a term Kusan often used to describe the complete absorption in the inquiry cum doubt, which would eventually allow the student to slough off both body and mind.

People with little experience in kanhwa Sŏn often mistakenly assume that the purpose of the contemplation is to answer the actual question, "Why did Chao-chou say no?" This is not really the case. As Kusan explained time and again, the purpose of the hwadu "no" is really to get the student to explore Chao-chou's state of mind just prior to saying "no." The question "Why?" is simply an expedient to help generate the sensa-

---

[25] These two mistaken ways of understanding "no" are included among the eight (alt. ten) defects of contemplation on the "no" hwadu taught by Ta-hui and Chinul. See Ta-hui's *Ta-hui yü-lu* 26, *T* 1998.47.921c, as quoted and discussed in Chinul's *Pŏpchip pyŏrhaeng-nok chŏryo pyŏngip sagi* and translated in Buswell, *Korean Approach*, p. 338.

[26] *Nine Mountains*, p. 52, *Sŏk suju*, p. 56.

[27] *Nine Mountains*, pp. 52–53; *Sŏk saja*, p. 57.

tion of doubt; it is not seeking a specific answer. All too often, Western visitors whom Kusan was instructing responded to his question, "Why did Chao-chou say no?" by turning over their teacups or hitting their hands on the ground, apparently thinking from what they had read in Western works on Zen that these were appropriate Sŏn responses. While not rejecting such answers out of hand, Kusan always immediately challenged: "Good enough, but what was your mind like *just before* you turned your cup over or hit your hand on the floor?" Unless the student could describe that source of thought from which their responses arose, Kusan would blast them as monkeys mimicking Sŏn students, who had had no true experience of enlightenment.

Because all hwadus are therefore considered to be simply an expedient means of producing the doubt, Korean Sŏn meditators keep the same hwadu throughout their entire careers, trying continually to deepen their sensation of doubt. This approach is very much unlike that of the Japanese Rinzai school (at least in the way that school's approach is presented in Western books), which developed a complex curriculum of meditation, in which the student was required to work through and master a series of as many as 1,700 kōans.[28] In the Korean view, such extensive training in different kongans (kōan) would be unnecessary, because one such case is the same as any other. Kongans are simply expedient means of generating the sensation of doubt, and once that doubt is present, it is no longer important which specific kongan one is investigating. Teachers discourage beginning students especially from trying out various kongans and prefer that they stick with the one with which they feel the most affinity.

As the investigation of Chao-chou's "no" matures, "the *hwadu* will become heavy and we will not be able to put it down. Then, when we sit down on our seat, the day and the night will pass like a second. The body will become light as if it is floating in space; we will not know whether the earth exists or not. At that time, even if we do not strive to keep the thought of the *hwadu*, naturally the *hwadu* will be raised vividly. Even if we try to discard the *hwadu*, we cannot; instead it remains vivid all the same."[29]

Master Kusan borrowed from Chinul to describe this combination of concentration plus attention, in which the doubt cum hwadu continues on its own spontaneously, as a state of alertness and tranquillity (sŏngsŏng chŏkjŏk), a phrase first used by Yung-chia Hsüan-chüeh (665–713)

---

[28] For the Japanese kōan system, see Isshū Miura and Ruth Fuller Sasaki, *The Zen Koan* (New York: Harcourt, Brace and World, a Harvest Book, 1965), esp. pp. 17–76. Professor T. Griffith Foulk of the University of Michigan, who has done extensive fieldwork inside Japanese Buddhist monasteries, tells me that in actuality no Japanese Rinzai monk ever tries to complete all of these kōans. Professor Foulk's research on Japanese Zen promises to challenge many of our long-held Western notions about the praxis of that tradition.

[29] *Nine Mountains*, p. 43; *Sŏk saja*, p. 46.

to refer to a state in which concentration (*samādhi*) and wisdom (*prajñā*) were present simultaneously.[30] Hence, the hwadu is not intended to generate a state of samādhi (a common misconception), but a state in which *both* the calmness of samādhi *and* the perspicuity of prajñā are maintained. This, too, may account for the reason why I knew few Sŏn monks to have the ability in the deep meditative absorptions, or *dhyānas* (Pali *jhāna*), that I had encountered before among the forest monks of Thailand.[31] If one were to try to place the state of mind engendered through kanhwa practice in the stages in Buddhist meditation outlined in the Theravāda school, I believe it would be rather more akin to "access concentration" (*upacāra-samādhi*), which accompanies ten specific types of discursive contemplations. In access concentration, the meditator generates sufficient concentration to remain focused on his object of meditation, but not so much concentration that his mind becomes absorbed in full-blown meditative absorption (*dhyāna*), when all sensory awareness is temporarily allayed.[32]

The student, Kusan continued, keeps on probing into the hwadu, pushing forward continually and without interruption, "digging into how the idea arose for Chao-chou to say 'no.' . . . Suddenly one morning he shouts 'Ha!,' and heaven and earth are overturned. He enters into a place unfathomable by others; and after a laugh alone, he only smiles. When he has reached that stage he can taste for himself, without one iota of difference, the flavor of the sincere words of the buddhas and patriarchs."[33] But, even then, the student must continue on to polish his understanding

---

[30] *Nine Mountains*, pp. 43–44; *Sŏk saja*, p. 47. For Chinul's usage of these terms, see Buswell, *Korean Approach*, pp. 107–11; Buswell, "Chinul's Systematization," pp. 207–10. For Hsüan-chüeh's use of the terms, see his *Ch'an-tsung Yung-chia chi*, T 2013.48.390b.

[31] See the biography of the Thai forest monk acharn Mun Bhuridatta (1870–1949) for such abilities: Phra Acharn Maha Boowa Nyanasampanno, *The Venerable Phra Acharn Mun Bhuridatta Thera, Meditation Master*, trans. by Siri Buddhasukh (Bangkok: Mahamakut Rajavidyalaya Press, 1976); the book has been extensively summarized in Stanley Jeyaraja Tambiah, *The Buddhist Saints of the Forest and the Cult of Amulets: A Study in Charisma, Hagiography, Sectarianism, and Millennial Buddhism*, Cambridge Studies in Social Anthropology, no. 49 (Cambridge: Cambridge University Press, 1984), pp. 81–110. The Thammayut sect to which acharns Mun and Maha Boowa belonged was the tradition of Thai Buddhism into which I was first ordained and trained. I personally heard many similar stories about contemporary Thai forest monks and met several Thai monks with profound ability in *jhāna* during my year there.

[32] Access concentration is specifically catalyzed by recollection of the buddha, dharma, and saṃgha, virtue, generosity, deities, death, and peace, as well as the perception of the repulsiveness of food and the analysis of the four elements; see Bhadantācariya Buddhaghosa, *The Path of Purification (Visuddhimagga)*, trans. by Bhikkhu Ñyāṇamoli (2d ed., Colombo: A. Semage, 1964), chap. 3, sec. 106, p. 113. See also the description of this type of samādhi in Nyanaponika Thera, *The Heart of Buddhist Meditation* (New York: Samuel Weiser, 1962), pp. 103ff.

[33] The passages are respectively taken from *Nine Mountains*, pp. 53, 61; *Sŏk saja*, pp. 59, 66.

by searching out masters against whom he can test himself. Hence, even after enlightenment, the student continues on with the process of "maintaining practice" (*poim-haeng*), polishing his views and understanding until he is able to convey his experience accurately to others.[34] Finally, though his own mind is no longer affected by the world around him, the student is compelled to "give rise to a mind of great compassion and save those sentient beings who have karmic affinities with the Buddhist dispensation . . . ,"[35] by becoming a teacher in his own right.

Even this short account of contemporary meditation practice in Korea shows that the meditation hall is a place where the monks come expecting a slow, gradual unfolding of truth, not a sudden rush of enlightenment. Monks on adjacent cushions are not becoming enlightened right and left throughout the retreat period, like so many spiritual firecrackers popping off, as the stories told in some Western books about Zen practice suggest.[36] Meditation monks who were serious about their practice (meaning those who had completed more than a couple of retreat seasons in the meditation hall) routinely told me that they expected to spend upwards of twenty years in meditation before they would even presume that their practice had begun to mature, let alone consider themselves ready to teach others. I noted time and again that monks with the most experience in meditation hall were those who insisted that practice would take a long time to complete, belying the continuous Zen clarion call of sudden enlightenment.

Let me continue in the next two chapters to explore the institution and officials that buttress this meditation practice: the meditation hall and its officers.

---

[34] See *Nine Mountains*, p. 61; *Sŏk saja*, p. 67.

[35] *Nine Mountains*, p. 70; *Sŏk saja*, p. 82.

[36] Philip Kapleau's *Three Pillars of Zen* (Tokyo: John Weatherhill, 1965), which has informed and inspired a whole generation of Zen students in the West, provides detailed case histories of the spectacular enlightenments (*satori*) of several Zen adepts, including Westerners, and implies that such experiences are commonplace among Zen practitioners.

CHAPTER EIGHT

Training in the Meditation Hall

MONKS WHO ARE intent upon a contemplative vocation start their training in the meditation hall (sŏnbang; lit. meditation room), which is the focus of activity for most of the largest monasteries in Korea. The Sŏn school of Buddhism in Korea, perhaps more than any other branch of the religion, has been adamant in proclaiming itself an experientially based form of religious praxis. The meditation hall is perhaps the quintessential example in Buddhism of an institution devoted to such personal spiritual experience. Because of the difficult quest they are presumed to be undertaking, the monks resident in the hall are treated as the elite vanguard of the monastery—almost to the point of being pampered. The best and the most of everything the monastery receives, whether it be fruit, sweets, or rice cakes, are sent to the meditation hall, with monks in other compounds receiving smaller shares.

Korean monks with whom I talked have two basic attitudes toward the meditation hall. First, they view it as a training ground for junior monks whose meditation is not yet mature enough to practice effectively alone in a hermitage; indeed, the majority of monks in the meditation hall are always fairly new to the practice. But second, they also think of the hall as a laboratory in which an ideal atmosphere for practice is maintained. Several of the more advanced practitioners I knew in meditation hall had spent long periods practicing in hermitages (amja). But even such experienced monks occasionally found their meditation flagging after a time. They then returned to the meditation hall for a retreat season or two to strengthen their practice, before going back to the privacy of a hermitage. The schedule and group atmosphere of the meditation hall are meant to provide a "bottom line" to the amount of practice a monk must perform, so that he can fall back only so far at those times when his desire to practice slackens. But an upper limit on practice is never enforced, and some monks will put in extra hours of sitting beyond what the schedule demands. The hall's atmosphere is formal enough to provide a stable environment in which a monk can develop his practice, yet its schedule is flexible enough so that a monk can make minor adjustments in his style of practice to suit his particular training needs at the moment.

Meditation monks are situated betwixt and between the support monks of the monastery and those monks presumed to be spiritual adepts, such as the Sŏn master and rector. Monks who enter the meditation hall are rigidly demarcated from the rest of the monastic community. During the three-month-long retreat seasons, meditators are forbidden from fraternizing with monks living in other compounds of the monastery. They are excused from the morning and evening services incumbent on the rest of the monastic residents and are freed from most of the work required to keep the monastery running. The meditator's sense of detachment from the monastic community is enhanced through the unique daily regimen of the meditation hall, unwavering for months on end. All these measures intensify the separation that the monk feels from his earlier status as a support monk or seminary student and increases his identification with the community of meditators—and ultimately, it is hoped, with the sanctified saṃgha of enlightened monks.

THE PLACE OF THE MEDITATION HALL IN KOREAN
BUDDHIST PRACTICE

The regulations and schedule of the meditation hall in contemporary Korea remain substantially the same as those from the latter years of the Chosŏn dynasty. This style, however, has changed considerably from the middle of the Koryŏ dynasty, when the indigenous Chogye school of Sŏn was founded. The few extant records of monastic training from the mid-Koryŏ period (ca. thirteenth century) suggest that there was less formal sitting in the meditation centers of that age. Chinul's *Admonitions to Beginning Students* (*Kye ch'osim hagin mun*), for example, written in 1205, five years after the foundation of Susŏn-sa (the present-day Songgwang-sa), provides some broad hints about the decorum and practice schedule followed in his monastery, which was the center of Sŏn practice during much of the Koryŏ.[1] Chinul envisioned a monastic community in which junior and senior monks considered themselves brothers. He offered different lists of rules for novices, support monks, and Sŏn practitioners, suggesting that these three groups lived separately. Probably there were specific halls designated for meditation practice and doctrinal study, much as we would find in major monasteries today.

Novices were not doing meditation practice—and were even forbidden from entering the meditation hall—but spent most of their time training in monastic discipline, performing Buddhist ceremonies, and in ritual chanting. Support monks concentrated on their appointed positions in the monastery. If those jobs meant that they had to leave the temple on business, they were to maintain proper decorum at all times and guard

---

[1] I have translated this text in Robert E. Buswell, Jr., *The Korean Approach to Zen: The Collected Works of Chinul* (Honolulu: University of Hawaii Press, 1983), pp. 135–39.

against "unconstrained conduct" (*muae-haeng*). This term refers to the iconoclastic conduct stereotypical of Sŏn adepts, which Chinul describes—rather benignly, compared to some of the portrayals found in Western literature—as monks who would "loosen their clothing, laugh and joke, talk distractedly of trivial matters, or eat or drink at improper times."[2] Meditation monks, by contast, were to devote all their time to contemplation, cutting themselves off from all contact with novices, support monks, and especially the laity. Reading and other nonessential activities were strictly limited. Chinul gives a long account telling how practice monks should listen to the instructions of the Sŏn master, suggesting that sermons were an important component of their training. The monks should be neither awed nor jaded regarding the master or his message. Ignoring the eloquence or rhetoric of the master, they should listen to the sermon with an "empty mind," using the lecture as an occasion for catalyzing enlightenment. Once the sermon was finished, the monks should continue pondering over it day and night until its recondite meaning became clear.[3] Hence, in this major Sŏn meditation center of the Koryŏ, reflection on doctrinal teachings was a major part of the contemplative vocation.

Yi Kyu-bo (1168–1241), a renowned literary and political figure of the Koryŏ, has left one of the few extant firsthand accounts of the practice at Susŏn-sa, just one generation after Chinul's death. In his *Account of a Discourse on Sŏn at Ch'angbok Monastery (Ch'angbok-sa tam-Sŏn pang)*, in his collected works, *Literary Collection of Premier Yi Kyu-bo (Tongguk Yi sangguk chip)*, Yi tells us that

> all those who have entered the community [at Susŏn-sa] are cultivating diligently. Men of eminent practice, like Chin'gong [Ch'ŏnjin (d.u.)] and the rest, have come. They have invited elder venerables in the remaining schools [of the old Nine Mountains Sŏn schools], of whom none has not joined; they have assembled like clouds. Such flourishing of a Sŏn convocation has not been known before in past or present. Pyŏn'gong [Chinul's successor, Chin'gak Hyesim (1178–1234)] is the leader of the covenant; Chin'gong is assistant director. They lecture on the *Platform Sūtra of the Sixth Patriarch* and the *Records of Ching-shan* [Ta-hui]. Each evening they discourse on emptiness. In general, this is the standard practice.[4]

Yi's terse remarks attest to a flourishing Sŏn practice at Susŏn-sa, though he gives us no specifics about the regimen. His account suggests that med-

---

[2] *Kye ch'osim hagin mun*, translated ibid., p. 137.

[3] Translated ibid., pp. 135–38.

[4] Yi Kyu-bo, *Ch'angbok-sa tam-Sŏn pang*, in *Tongguk Yi sangguk chip* (Literary Collection of Premier Yi Kyu-bo), kwŏn 25 (Seoul: Tongguk Munhwasa, 1958), p. 268a; quoted in Buswell, *Korean Approach*, p. 34.

itation may have been practiced in the predawn hours, with some manual labor scheduled in the daytime and lectures in the evening after supper. What is again striking about this schedule is the amount of time allotted to formal lectures by the leaders of the convocation. This peculiarity may derive from the ecumenical emphasis during the mid–Koryŏ period on joint training in both doctrinal study and meditation practice. Contemporary meditation schedules leave only one afternoon free each fortnight for talks by the Sŏn master, and that is usually a succinct statement of Sŏn understanding, not a lecture on a text.[5]

We are on somewhat firmer ground in discussing the regimen of the meditation hall during the late Chosŏn dynasty and the Japanese colonial period. In June 1925, Yongsŏng (1868–1937), one of the eminent conservative reformers within the order, began a thousand-day meditation retreat at Mangwŏl-sa on Tobong Mountain. His account of the organization and regulations of his retreat provides solid indications of the schedule followed by a rigorous meditation center during the first quarter of the twentieth century. According to his *Promulgation of a Religious Society That Will Cultivate Diligently Sŏn Meditation on the Live Word of the Separately Transmitted Sŏn School* (*Chŏngsu pyŏlchŏn Sŏnjong hwalgu ch'amsŏn kyŏlsa sŏnjŏn-mun*),[6] the following qualifications were required of all who were admitted to the retreat:

> 1. Participants must be determined to observe the moral and disciplinary injunctions of the *Book of Brahmā's Net* (*Pŏmmang-kyŏng*) and the *Four-Section Discipline* (*Sabun-yul*; *Dharmaguptaka-vinaya*).
> 2. All should observe celibacy (*pŏmhaeng*; Skt. *brahmacarya*) while practicing.
> 3. Everyone must possess their monk's identification papers, family records, and their robes and bowls.
> 4. Participants must be between the ages of twenty and fifty, and in good health.

The rules of his retreat, as given in the same text, were as follows:

> 1. Every first day of the month, praise the special vehicle of the Sŏn school.
> 2. Every fortnightly Poṣadha, recite the *Vinayas* of the Hīnayāna and Mahāyāna schools (viz. the *Prātimokṣa* and the bodhisattva precepts).

---

[5] For English examples of contemporary Buddhist sermons, see Ku San, *Nine Mountains* (Songgwang-sa: International Meditation Center, 1976); Kusan Sunim, *The Way of Korean Zen*, trans. by Martine Fages, ed. by Stephen Batchelor (New York: Weatherhill, 1985), which reproduces some material from the preceding work; and Song-chol, *Echoes from Mt. Kaya: Selections on Korean Buddhism*, ed. by Ven. Won-tek and trans. by Brian Barry, with introduction by Won-myong (Seoul: Lotus Lantern International Buddhist Center, 1988).

[6] Reproduced in *Han'guk kŭnse Pulgyo paengnyŏnsa* (The Last Century of Buddhism in Korea) (Seoul: Minjoksa, n.d.), vol. 1, *kwŏn* 2, *Sŏnbang p'yŏnnyŏn*, pp. 1–4.

3. Every twentieth day of the month, discourse on the method of critical-phrase meditation; this refers to the formal dharma lecture.

4. Practice not eating in the afternoon (*ohu pulsik*). (This rule did not apply to people in support roles.)

5. Maintain silence at all times. (This rule also did not apply to support officials.)

6. Permission must be received to leave the meditation hall during the retreat period.

7. Participation is mandatory in all activities.

The rules Yongsŏng promulgates for his meditation hall were intended to combine Sŏn practice with Kyo (doctrinal) ideology. This is not only a return to the ecumenical spirit of the Koryŏ dynasty, but also parallels antisectarian trends seen during the Chinese revival of Buddhism during the Republican Era.[7] Indeed, there are many parallels between Yongsŏng's regulations and practices instituted during the contemporaneous Chinese Buddhist revival. As but one example, the practice of not eating in the afternoon, while still a fundamental part of the monk's discipline in Southeast Asia, was never common in the East Asian traditions of Buddhism. Ecumenical contacts with the Theravāda monks of South and Southeast Asia prompted the Chinese to try and reestablish that practice in their country. Yongsŏng, a strong proponent of the celibate faction within the schismatic order of his time, probably advocated this rule as a means of restoring the traditional discipline of the bhikṣus and demonstrating the moral superiority of the celibates.

Despite the new pressures placed on traditional Buddhist practice in Korea by the regulations of the Japanese colonial administration, meditation was still widespread throughout the peninsula. In a monastery census done by the Japanese government-general in 1928, monasteries in all provinces—except South Pyŏngan and North Hamgyŏng provinces in the north of the peninsula—had active meditation halls.[8] In the same report, the government-general of Korea published a list of rules that were common to meditation halls throughout the country, most of which are still followed today:

1. Winter retreat runs from the eleventh through the first lunar month and the summer retreat from the fifth through the seventh lunar month, about the same schedule followed today.

2. Monks must stay for the whole retreat.

---

[7] See discussion in Holmes Welch, *The Buddhist Revival in China* (Cambridge: Harvard University Press, 1968), pp. 199–200.

[8] See *Chosŏn sŭngnyŏ su-Sŏn cheyo* (Essentials of Cultivating Sŏn among the Monks of Korea); in *Han'guk kŭnse Pulgyo paengnyŏnsa*, vol. 1, *kwŏn* 2, *Sŏnbang p'yŏnnyŏn*, pp. 17–18.

3. No snacks are allowed in the afternoon.

4. Monks cannot leave the hall except for toilet calls.

5. Monks are forbidden from entering another room unless they are ill and entering the sickroom.

6. Talking is forbidden.

7. Monks are not to be absent from their seats during the meditation periods.

8. A monk who is sick cannot reenter the hall until he is well.

9. Monks are forbidden to meditate together with the laity.

10. Monks are not allowed to wash underwear except on a "sixth" day (sixth, sixteenth, and twenty-sixth days of the lunar month).[9]

11. Do not stretch out your legs during sitting.

12. Do not talk or laugh loudly outside the meditation hall.

13. Do not change your seating location.

14. When entering the hall, always put your palms together in hapchang (añjali) and bow from the waist.

15. Anyone not sitting in the hall when the sitting session begins is forbidden to enter until the next break period.

16. Monks in the meditation hall are not allowed to participate in discussions of monastic policy. But monks who belong to that temple lineage may participate, if absolutely necessary.[10]

According to the same report, other rules followed in specific halls of the time were as follows:

1. During retreats no one under twenty years of age is allowed to enter the hall.

2. All participants must be of average character or better and equipped with appropriate monk's requisites, such as bowls and robes.

3. If a monk breaks the hall's rules, he must be expelled.

4. No reading.

5. Monks who break the precepts cannot participate in the retreat.

6. No sleeping until midnight.

7. People who fight must repent by bowing before the monks, and if they do not repent, they must be expelled from the hall.

8. Monks are forbidden to go outside the main gate of the monastery except on special business, such as if one's parents or teacher is dying; even in such exceptional circumstances, they must receive the permission of the abbot first before departing.

---

[9] This rule follows an injunction that Chinul first instituted in Korea. Supposedly lice and other insects killed on a "sixth" day were guaranteed rebirth in the pure land; therefore, the monk would not violate the precept against killing by washing his underwear. See Chinul's *Admonitions to Beginners*, in Buswell, *Korean Approach*, pp. 136, 138 n.2.

[10] See *Chosŏn sŭngnyŏ su-Sŏn cheyo*, in *Han'guk kŭnse Pulgyo paengnyŏnsa*, vol. 1, kwŏn 2, *Sŏnbang p'yŏnnyŏn*, pp. 18–21. I have condensed these lists somewhat.

9. Monks cannot ask questions during the master's lecture on Sŏn; they should instead go to his room afterwards to ask.

10. Unless a monk is sick, he must attend all required services and meals.[11]

But the practice in some meditation halls was considerably more varied than what we would find nowadays. In April 1928, a certain Kang Yu-mun visited the meditation hall at Naejang-sa and wrote an account of the practice he encountered there in the journal *Buddhism* (*Pulgyo*). Young monks, Kang tells us, were instructed in sūtra study in the morning and worked the fields in the afternoon. Time was also allotted for training in Indian-style chanting (*pŏmp'ae*) and the monk's dance (*sŭngmu*). Only in the evenings did they sit in formal meditation.[12] This would be a most peculiar schedule in contemporary monasteries.

In modern Korea, meditation monks constitute a small, but elite group within the ecclesia. As of 1976, a monastic census counted forty-five Sŏn compounds (*sŏnwŏn*) in operation in Korean monasteries, with a total of 929 students enrolled (533 monks and 396 nuns). This was substantially the same as a subsequent census in December 1982, in which twenty-two of the largest Korean monasteries claimed to have 950 meditation students in residence (602 monks and 348 nuns). These numbers are certainly exaggerated, however, and probably include many monks resident in the monastery who were only tangentially involved with the meditation hall. Songgwang-sa, for example, is claimed to have had seventy-nine monks training in the meditation hall during the 1982 census; but even with two separate halls operating during particularly busy retreat seasons during the mid-1970s, I never knew there to be more than fifty monks in training at any one time. Even accepting the most generous figures, then, meditation students still number less than about 5 percent of the total number of monks and nuns ordained in the Chogye Order.[13]

THE SCHEDULE OF THE MODERN MEDITATION HALL

Koreans prefer consistent meditation over longer periods (at least three months in duration). Meditation halls throughout Korea today all follow the same annual schedule I described in Chapter Two, in which the three months of summer (the fourth through seventh lunar months) and winter (the tenth through first lunar months) are set aside for formal retreats (*kyŏlche*; lit. binding rule), and the three months of spring and autumn

[11] Ibid., pp. 21–26.

[12] See the journal *Pulgyo* (Buddhism), nos. 46–47 (1928), pp. 82–83.

[13] For these figures, see Chŏng Pyŏngjo, "Han'guk Pulgyo ŭi hyŏnhyang kwa munjechŏm" (The Present Condition of Korean Buddhism and Problematic Points), *Pulgyo yŏn'gu* (Buddhist Studies) 2 (1986): 204–5.

are free seasons (*haeje*; lit. slackened rule). Only during the free seasons are monks allowed to travel between monasteries or to leave the monastery for other than the most urgent of business. During the retreats, strict decorum is maintained, and a rigorous practice schedule is followed; in the winter, this will usually involve upwards of fourteen hours of sitting daily (slightly less during the hot, humid summers), with between four and six hours of sleep. Typically practice is divided into three- or four-hour blocks, such as 3:00–6:00 A.M., 8:00–11:00 A.M., 1:00–4:00 P.M., and 6:00–10:00 P.M. Each of these blocks is further subdivided into fifty minutes of sitting meditation, punctuated by ten minutes of formal walking meditation. Monks are not allowed to lie down except during the evening rest period and a short break before breakfast at six. There is little work assigned to the meditation monks. For many of the meditation monks, this might mean only sweeping the monastery for about twenty to thirty minutes each morning before the late-morning sitting period. At four, after the afternoon sitting, the monks take care of their appointed duties, such as sweeping and mopping the hall, preparing the fire that heats the ondol floor, or performing a short service in one of the small shrines around the monastery campus. The rest of their time is devoted exclusively to meditation.

The hall functions as usual during the free season, but on a reduced schedule of sitting. Those few monks who have decided not to travel are free to remain in the hall to continue with their practice. Typically during the free season, the monks follow "discretionary practice" (*chayu chŏng-jin*). The bamboo clacker (*chukpi*) is then struck only at the beginning and end of each three-hour block of practice, leaving the monks free to follow their own schedule. A monk might sit for two hours at a stretch rather than fifty minutes, and then go outside to do walking meditation in front of the hall for an hour at a time rather than do the usual ten minutes of formal walking meditation. A number of the more committed meditators I knew said that they preferred the free seasons to the retreat periods. This was because they could still take advantage of the controlled, disciplined environment that the meditation hall provided, but were free to adapt the schedule to their own needs of the moment—an arrangement quite close to the freedom found in a hermitage. For some, then, the meditation hall during the free season was an ideal combination of a disciplined, but flexible style of practice.

ENTERING THE MEDITATION HALL

During the free seasons, most monks travel, either to return to their home monastery to pay respects to their vocation master (*ŭnsa*), to travel among the major meditation centers until they decide where they will spend the upcoming retreat season, or simply to sightsee. Meditation monks are constantly on the move, rarely staying at a monastery beyond the three-month retreat period. Several monks told me that they preferred to travel south to T'ongdo-sa or Songgwang-sa for the winter retreats, where it was warmer, and north to Haein-sa or Wŏlchŏng-sa (in Odae-san) for their cooler summers. During the free seasons, the number of residents in the meditation hall drops off dramatically. At Songgwang-sa, the hall was nearly emptied on the first day of the free season, to be gradually repopulated during the remainder of the period, until it was finally filled again in the two weeks preceding the beginning of the next retreat.

A traveling monk who decides to reserve a place in the meditation hall requests formal introduction (*pangbu*, lit. room request) to the monastery, in a brief ceremony performed before all the resident monks. I described this ceremony in Chapter Four, the only difference being that rather than consulting the primary guest prefect, a meditator arranges his residency request with a guest prefect (*chigaek*) specifically in charge of processing introductions to the meditation hall. The guest prefect for the meditation hall serves the important function of meeting with all prospective meditators, reviewing their credentials, and introducing them to the Sŏn master and rector. At the best meditation halls, a candidate for residency who is not known to the guest prefect will always be asked for proof of attendance at a hall during the previous season, or if he is new to meditation, he will be evaluated on the basis of the quality and reputation of his ŭnsa and home monastery (much as any personnel officer would do in processing a résumé). All these checks help to ensure that the prospective resident will be a worthy addition to the practitioners in the meditation hall. Since there are only a few hundred meditation monks in all of Korea—only a few score of whom are long-term practitioners—most of the experienced meditators know one another quite well, and this meeting can be as much a social event as a formal interview.

After his introduction is accepted by the monastery, the new resident is escorted to the meditation hall by the guest prefect, where he is greeted informally by his fellow residents. The guest prefect gives him bedding and shows him to a locker for his things, places a cushion down on the floor at the appropriate place of seniority, where the monk will sit and sleep for the rest of the retreat, and finds him a spot for his formal robes, again in seniority order. The monk is now a full-fledged member of the hall and can remain for as long as he wishes, unless he is expelled for disciplinary reasons, something that happened only once in my five years in the meditation hall at Songgwang-sa. During the remainder of the free season, the monk is still allowed to travel, but he must leave his long formal robe (*changsam*) behind to reserve his place in the hall for the retreat season, showing thereby that he intends to return.

DESCRIPTION OF THE MEDITATION HALL

The meditation hall at Songgwang-sa, as at most Korean monasteries, is a long, narrow ondol room, with cabinets and pegs for hanging chang-sams along the shorter walls and sliding wood-and-paper doors along both longer sides of the room. There is an enclosed fire room outside at one end of the building, a wooden veranda around the entire outside perimeter of the hall, and a smaller locker room off the main hall, where the monks store their few belongings. Two bamboo poles are suspended from the ceiling in the middle of the room for hanging the dyed brown cloaks (*kasa*). One large cushion, three feet square and padded with cotton batting, is used by each monk, with a smaller and thinner spare cushion to support his seat. These cushions are arranged in two long rows, with about half a cushion's distance between them and three feet in between each row. The most senior monks sit in the middle of the rows, the junior monks fanning out towards the ends.

Such items as a warm, padded coat (*hatturumagi*) may be kept to the side of one's cushion, but must always be stacked neatly. During summer, a large mosquito net, sized to fit the entire perimeter of the room, is hung inside and the paper is stripped off the doors and replaced with plastic screening to increase ventilation. Monks are required always to enter and leave the hall via the door closest to their cushion so as not to disturb their fellow meditators, and shoes are left outside on a step set below the veranda nearest to that door. Bedding is kept in the cabinets set into the wall inside, from where it is removed at night. The monks sleep on their cushions, at the same spot where they sit. The next morning, the bedding is refolded and put back into the cabinet. Meals are taken in the refectory together with the other monks, except for the midnight meal eaten during the intensive one-week period of nonsleeping meditation called "ferocious effort" (*yongmaeng chŏngjin*), which I will describe later. After returning from the refectory after each meal, tea is served to all the monks in the meditation hall: usually powdered milk in the morning, an herbal or grain tea at noon, and green tea in the evening. Tea is served by the juniormost monks in the hall, usually young novices, who are given the title of "tea boys" (*tagak*), in individual cups in the center of the meditation hall. In the strictest halls, however, each monk will sit at his customary seat and tea will be brought by the tea servers, so that there is no opportunity—or excuse—for socializing. After the monks are finished, the tea makers will wash the cups and clean up.

The main meditation hall at Songgwang-sa, one of the largest in Korea, could accommodate only about twenty-four meditators at a time, twelve in each row. The monks sit facing away from one another, towards the nearest wall, except during the seven-day meditation intensive (see below), when they sit facing one another. Enough space is left around the inside perimeter of the hall to allow circumambulation between sitting periods. An altar is set into one of the long walls, which usually enshrines an image of Mañjuśrī, the bodhisattva of wisdom. Songgwang-sa's hall had instead simply a large round mirror for the altar, meant to symbolize the great, perfect mirror wisdom (Skt. *ādarśanajñāna*) of buddhahood.

In the early morning, after rising at 2:00 or 3:00 A.M., the monks remove their kasas from the bamboo pole, drape them around their regular clothes (not around their changsams, as is done for services and formal occasions), and prostrate themselves together to the altar three times, with the verger of the hall striking the bamboo clacker (*chukpi*) to indicate the timing. After the monks take off their kasas, regular sitting begins. So as not to interrupt their sitting schedule, monks in meditation hall do not attend the regular morning and evening services in the main buddha hall. The only ritual activity in which they are involved is the noon service before dinner.

MEDITATION HALL DECORUM

On the evening before the beginning of the three-month retreat, a meeting of all the monks in the monastery will be held in the dining room, to elect officers and assign positions to each and every monk and layperson staying for the retreat, positions they will keep for the next three months. Although it is supposed to be a democratic election, in actuality most of the positions have been assigned previously and the meeting simply serves as a formal announcement to the monastery at large. First to be elected is the Sŏn master (*pangjang*), followed by the rector (*yuna*). Once the rector is announced, two younger monks from the meditation hall come forward with a small floor table holding the monastery chukpi, prostrate themselves three times, and present the clacker to the rector. The elderly monks who hold honorary positions follow, followed by all the holders of meditation hall positions, the holders of agricultural and administrative positions, and finally the abbot (*chuji*) and his office staff.

The meditation hall positions have been painstakingly awarded in a long meeting of the meditation monks, held before the general meeting of the full congregation. The meditation monks also decide at their meeting the schedule they will follow for the next three months. Although the Sŏn master can encourage a certain number of hours of sitting meditation and sleep per day, the monks who are actually participating in the retreat have the final say in exactly what schedule they will follow. It occasionally happened in the retreats I joined that the wishes of the hall residents and the Sŏn master conflicted. But, even then, the autonomy of the meditation hall prevailed over almost all other sources of power in the monastery, and the hall residents always got their way.

Most monks sit in quarter-lotus position, one leg crossed over the other, which is the traditional Korean sitting posture. Older monks will often adopt the posture used by the Korean gentry class, *yangban chase*, in which the legs are folded squarely in front, with either the left or right leg folded completely over onto the other. Monks are supposed to wear socks at all times, but in summer they often go barefoot inside and wear their regular rubber shoes (*komu-sin*) outside. The monks sit comfortably, with their hands placed informally in their laps. There is little emphasis on correct posture, as in Japanese Zen institutions.[14] Monks are free to move or change their posture anytime during the sitting period, though excessive movement is discouraged. Since Koreans traditionally sit on the floor anyway, no one has any problems with long periods of sitting, and the hall was never disturbed by posture changes. Monks are forbidden from sitting with their feet extended in front of them or with their knees brought up to their chests. If a meditator becomes drowsy, he is allowed to stand in back of his cushion for as long as he wishes, holding his arms in front of him with hands held together at the waist. If his torpor is overwhelming, he can go outside for some fresh air for a moment, but only as a last resort, since opening the sliding door would distract his colleagues. Except for this reason, or for going to the toilet, monks are not allowed to leave the meditation hall during the sitting period.

If a junior monk is paying his respects to a senior monk, however, it is improper for him to assume the gentry posture of his elders. In such situations, the junior monk first sits on his heels with legs folded under himself in kneeling posture (*kkurhŏ anki*) and then, if invited to sit comfortably, assumes the quarter-lotus position. Since it is considered improper to expose your feet in front of superiors, even in the quarter-lotus position, the feet would be tucked between the calf and the thigh of the other leg and covered with the excess cloth of the monk's baggy trousers.

Ten minutes before the beginning of a meditation period, the verger of the hall will strike three rounds on the mokt'ak outside, indicating to the monks that they should stop whatever they are doing and return to the

---

[14] For background on the more formalized sitting postures of Chinese Ch'an and Japanese Zen, see Carl Bielefeldt, *Dōgen's Manuals of Zen Meditation* (Berkeley and Los Angeles: University of California Press, 1988), pp. 111–12.

hall, to take their places. The sequence is a loud rhythmic beat, trailing off.

Exactly on the hour all the monks should have already returned to the hall and be sitting quietly; the leader of the hall, the succentor (*ipsŭng*), then strikes the chukpi three times indicating the beginning of the period. Monks are not supposed to miss any of the scheduled hours of sitting. If a monk absolutely must miss a period, he has to request permission in advance from the succentor or his assistant and still be present for the opening and closing of the sitting period.

During the sitting period, the succentor only rarely carries the large warning stick (*changgun chukpi*, lit. general's stick) and then only if most of the monks are obviously drowsy. The large stick is made from a light wood rather like balsa, and is about four feet long. It is rounded at the end that is carried, and tapered to a thin, flat hitting end, so that it breaks easily. Its light weight also gives it a bit of snap when it is flailed. The master will have his attendant carve several of the sticks before the retreat begins and will have new sticks added to his stock as necessary during the retreat. One elderly monk told me that the stick was used much more frequently during meditation retreats before the Korean War; now it is used only rarely, except during the seven-day meditation intensive.

If the succentor does decide to carry the stick, he rises, picks it up off the floor to his side, and walks between the two rows, up once, down once, and back to his seat. The stick is carried in both hands, with the upper end supported on the right shoulder. If the succentor comes upon a monk who is nodding drowsily, he taps his shoulder lightly; if the monk wants to be struck to help rouse himself, the monk bows with his palms together in hapchang once, places his left hand on the ground with his right hand on his left elbow, and leans over slightly. The succentor then strikes his shoulder firmly from behind three times. The monks claim there is an acupuncture point on the head meridian located precisely at the point on the shoulder where the large stick hits; striking that point helps to stimulate the brain and ward off sleepiness, they say. The procedure is then repeated in reverse on the other shoulder. Finally, the monk bows again; the succentor bows in return, and then continues along his route. A monk will never be struck unless he requests it; the stick is meant to be an aid to his sitting, not a punishment.

At the end of the fifty-minute sitting period, the succentor strikes the chukpi once. After stretching their legs in front of themselves for a moment, all the monks rise to begin the ten-minute walking period. Walking is done at a normal or faster than normal pace around the inside perimeter of the hall, in a counterclockwise direction. This direction, contrary to the normal clockwise direction of most Buddhist circumambulation, is followed so that on their closest pass by the altar their right shoulders will face the image or mirror enshrined there. (Ordinarily, in circumambulation, the monks would circle counterclockwise around the buddha image, with their right shoulders always facing in toward the image.) During the walking period, monks are free to leave the line and go to the toilet. On the last round, the succentor picks up the chukpi, which he left on the altar on the first time around, and strikes it once; as the monks circumambulate around to their cushions, they sit down and begin the next round of sitting.

At the end of the three-hour block of meditation, the succentor again strikes his chukpi three times, indicating the end of that session. Often the monks will do some simple yogic postures after the three-hour block is over to stretch their muscles.

FORMAL RULES

Each monastery usually has its own set of regulations governing the operation of the meditation hall, all of which are more or less the same. Songgwang-sa's code goes back to the time when meditation was held in the Sangsa-tang, now the Sŏn master's residence. The rules have been slightly updated from traditional listings; for example, rules forbidding anyone who dreams at night from entering the hall or prohibiting monks and novices from practicing together in the same hall have been removed. But the spirit of the rules remains the same: to cut off completely all distractions that might divert the meditator from his practice and to maintain the meditation hall's sense of isolation from the rest of the monastic community. Of these rules, the most important is that once a monk has begun the formal retreat, he is not allowed to move out of the hall for the duration. He must attend all scheduled hours of meditation, unless the succentor has given him permission in advance to be absent. A monk is not supposed to open doors during the meditation period, and when leaving the hall, he must exit via the door nearest his own cushion. Shoes must be kept on the step nearest to one's door. Monks are not allowed to visit anyone or enter any other compound in the monastery, or ever to go beyond the monastery's front gate. Silence is to be maintained at all times, both inside the hall and within the meditation compound itself, as well as when walking from the hall to the main buddha hall or the refectory. Walking to any temple functions is done as a group, in a long line in order of seniority, and in silence. Monks are expected to follow the rules as written, under the threat of expulsion. The rules are posted at the meditation hall in a prominent location just outside one of the doors; they are promulgated officially by the precentor, and the list always ends with "Spoken by the Rector" (Yuna paek).

Correspondence of any kind and all reading materials are prohibited during the retreat season. Most monks carry a copy of one or another collection of the sayings of past Zen masters, which they might occasionally peruse during the break, but they rarely bring any other books along. During the retreat period, all mail for the meditation monks is taken to the Sŏn master's room, to be held by him until the end of the retreat period. Kusan's attendant told me that if a letter arrived for a monk bearing a woman's name, the master often opened the envelope and read the letter, even discarding it if he found the content salacious or otherwise unsalutary. Other monks in the monastery receive their mail directly and without censorship. Important mail for a meditation monk will either be held at the office for the monk to read before it is sent up to the master's room or the master will read it to him there. Packages are given directly to the monks, during a break period from meditation, and if the contents are any kind of food, they share it with all their fellow residents.

Inside the meditation hall, the monks never wear their formal robes. Most will wear the long traveling coat (*turumagi*) during sitting, or the long heavy padded coat if it is really cold, but even these are not required. During the summer it is quite common for monks to roll up their pants and remove their shirts while sitting, not a terribly elegant sight, but certainly a practical way of dealing with the sultry weather. Even in the middle of winter, if the ondol floor is too hot, the monks will remove their shirts, open the doors, and sit in the cold. Formal robes are simply not functional enough to be worn all day long, and the monks never wear them inside the hall. (The only time I ever knew the monks to wear their changsams inside the hall was when they were forced to have their pictures taken.) Once the monks have returned from a formal temple function, they remove their changsam and kasa and return them to their allotted spots.

SLEEP

At precisely nine in the evening, the verger of the main buddha hall strikes the gong three times (not the usual three rounds) to indicate lights out. Anyone in the support compounds of the monastery may retire at that time, though monks often stay up past the lights-out signal. The one group of monastery residents you can be sure will immediately go to bed are the postulants. Exhausted from their long and busy day, the haengjas pull their bedding from the closet in the refectory near the kitchen and collapse into a deep sleep.

The monks in meditation hall often follow a different sleeping schedule from the rest of the monastery. They might have decided at the beginning of the retreat to ignore the evening gong and continue practicing as a group until ten, eleven, or even twelve at night.[15] At the end of their evening session, the succentor strikes the chukpi three times to bring the practice day to a close. The monks stretch out their legs very briefly before going to the cabinets at the side of the hall to fetch their bedding. Each monk has one cotton-filled quilt and one wooden pillow (*mokch'im*), which he stores in a numbered spot in the cabinets. He brings his bedding back to his cushion and stretches out, using the cushion as a makeshift mattress. If it is unusually cold, however, he might instead sleep directly on the warm ondol floor. The quilt is large and thick—about seven feet long by four feet wide, and padded with two to three inches of cotton filling—so it is quite warm. The wooden pillow, a four-inch rectangular block of wood, is de rigueur among Korean monks; no one would even consider indulging in the luxury of a stuffed pillow. After a twelve-hour meditation day with perhaps four to six hours of rest each night, not even a hard block of wood keeps the monks from sleeping soundly. To make the block more comfortable, some monks will put their smaller sitting cushion over it; but the rules of the meditation hall insist that they then place their shirt over that cushion so that it will not become soiled. Monks in other compounds follow the same general procedure for retiring.

In all of the large ondol rooms where monks sleep, the light has a dimmer switch on it. In the meditation hall, the "lamplighter" (*myŏngdŭng sŭnim*), who in the days before electricity would have been in charge of lighting the lamps around the monastery, will dim the lights inside the hall as soon as most of the monks have settled in for the evening. He never completely turns the lights off, but leaves them on low throughout the night in case someone needs to go outside to the toilet. Most monks sleep on their backs, but some imitate the Buddha's "lion posture" and sleep on their right sides. No one ever sleeps on his stomach, because the floor is too hard. The monks remove their shirts, socks, and leggings (*haenggŏn*), and sleep in their pants and undershirts. They sleep in the same spot where they sit during the day, with heads facing the middle of the hall and feet facing out toward the doors, so that no one's feet will be in anyone's face. If a monk is going to stay out late (perhaps for a meeting with the rector or Sŏn master, or to do walking meditation outside, but never, so far as I knew, to carouse), he will lay his bedding out beforehand so

---

[15] At Haein-sa, the largest training center in Korea, there are three different meditation halls, following three progressively more rigorous schedules. The elementary group of some fifty monks slept seven hours (from 9:00 P.M. to 4:00 A.M.), while the intermediate group of eighteen to twenty monks slept four hours (from midnight to 4:00 A.M.). The most advanced group, which rarely numbered over four monks, did not lie down to sleep at all, and their practice continued unabated throughout the free season. Sung Bae Park, personal communication, 7 June 1991.

that he will not disturb his colleagues when he returns to the hall. He might even set up his bed in one of the side rooms of the meditation hall and sleep there instead that night. After laying out his bedding, a monk may continue sitting on his own well into the night. To avoid any appearance of pretentiousness, however, it is considered proper decorum to lie down together with all the monks for a few minutes first before quietly sitting up again. In this way, too, the monk's colleagues feel no peer pressure to do extra sitting themselves.

At precisely three in the morning, the verger of the main buddha hall strikes three rounds on his largest mokt'ak to mark the beginning of the day and loudly recites the early morning wakeup chant, accompanied by the mokt'ak, while walking among all the compounds of the monastery. If the meditation monks are following the regular monastery schedule, they will be up at the first strike of the mokt'ak. If they are rising earlier, the succentor will have struck his chukpi once to arouse the monks from their sleep, after which the lamplighter will turn the lights back up. Some monks start the day by taking a minute or so to rub their bodies, in order, they say, to start the pneuma (*ki*) circulating. Rubbing their hands rapidly together to generate some heat, they first massage their eyes, and then rub the small of their feet, stomach, and back. Putting on their socks and leggings, the monks fold their quilts, put the bedding back in the closet, and reposition their cushions. The bedding is always folded in the same manner: first in half lengthwise, and then into quarters, so that it is neat and compact. The wooden pillow is placed inside the folded bedding. The monks then go outside to wash up, which in wintertime often means breaking the thick ice that has covered the granite water reservoirs with a wooden mallet and washing in icewater. After returning to the hall, the monks put on their shirts and kasas and stand ready for the three morning prostrations, which take place precisely ten minutes after rising. The morning sitting session starts immediately and continues until 5:30 or 6:00 A.M.

SICKNESS AND HEALTH FADS

If a monk becomes so sick during a retreat that he is unable to continue, he will retire to the sick room (*kanbyŏng-sil*): a small room located within the meditation compound. The nurse monk (*kanbyŏng sŭnim*), another of the many meditation hall positions, is in charge of procuring whatever medicine or special foods the patient might require.[16] He also administers first aid to anyone else in the hall who becomes injured or sick. No other

---

[16] For the duties of this office, see *Pai-chang ch'ing-kuei* 4, T 2025.48.1133a10-13; and *Mo-ho seng-ch'i lü* (*Mahāsāṃghika-vinaya*) 28, T 1425.22.457a.

monks are officially permitted to visit the sick room, but this rule is sometimes ignored, especially during the free season, and I occasionally joined big parties in the sick room, with the patient all but forgotten. The monastery proctor usually travels to town once or twice a week, and will inform the nurse monk beforehand so that he can make a list of whatever medicines he needed. If it is a complicated Chinese herbal prescription, the nurse monk might go to town himself to procure it.

Western medicines are popular among Koreans, especially those for stomach ailments, colds, and parasites. Monks still consume large quantities of Chinese herbal medicine, especially to increase their physical stamina. Indeed, it is common for any monk suffering from the slightest bit of tiredness or lassitude to consume *poyak*, various Chinese herbal concoctions intended to increase vigor.

Diet fads, reputed to increase stamina, periodically swept through the meditation hall at Songgwang-sa, brought from all over the country by the traveling monks. Dried, powdered pine needles are a popular supplementary diet item, reputed to aid digestion by adding bulk to the diet. Often monks will have a private supply and will take one or two tablespoonfuls after each meal, with water, or with warm milk in the morning. This powder is prepared from fresh pine needles picked from the seasonally appropriate side of the pine tree (south in winter, north in summer, east in spring, and west in autumn, ostensibly the side that receives the optimal amount of solar energy). The needles are washed and dried slowly on the ondol floor so that their color is not affected; drying the needles in the sun tends to turn them brown, destroying their nutritional value. Once they have dried thoroughly, they are ground in a flour mill to a fine powder.

One of the weirdest health fads I witnessed in Korea was the iron-water cure-all for stomach ailments. Scrap iron was sanded down until smooth, and this was then broken into nugget-sized pieces and placed in a glass jar filled with fresh water. After letting the shards sit for three to six hours, the monk would shake the jar until the water turned red from the rusty residue that had formed on the iron, and then drink the water. This fad was the craze of the meditation hall in the winter retreat of 1975–1976, with fully half of the monks partaking in it. Supposedly, it was good for digestion, but many monks complained of diarrhea (not surprisingly it seemed to me). The fad soon passed, however, and I never knew anyone to take the concoction after that year.

BATH DAY

The day before the fortnightly Poṣadha observance, when the Sŏn master's formal dharma lecture is delivered, brings the only break from the regular meditation hall schedule. Morning and evening sitting proceeds as usual, but the day is given over to bathing and washing clothes.[17] This is the only day when hot water is available for bathing, and the monks take full advantage of it. Although small amounts of hot water for washing one's feet, socks, rubber shoes, and face, are prepared every day in the cauldron in the meditation hall fire room, there is never enough for even a sponge bath, so the monks look forward with great relish to bath day. The monks are also allowed to talk for that day only, and a party atmosphere prevails. The proctor sends up apples and sweets in the morning, and milk is served twice: once at regular teatime after breakfast, and once again at around ten in the morning. Throughout the morning, the monks shave one another's heads with regular double-edged safety razors and then walk down to the bathhouse.

Baths are taken in order of seniority, with the Sŏn master and elderly monks going first, usually right after breakfast, followed by senior meditators; the rest of the rank and file of the meditation hall bathe later in the morning; the office and kitchen monks, in the afternoon; postulants and layworkers, after evening service; and finally laywomen (posal), late in the evening. The bath is traditional Korean style, with a large soaking tub, ringed outside by a raised seat, where the monks sit while they soap up or scrub off. Bathing is done in the nude, not wearing a bathing cloth as Theravāda monks are required to do. The bath monk (yoktu sŭnim), usually one of the monks in the meditation hall, is in charge of making the bath, and he begins the fire under the huge cauldrons at around four in the morning so that the bath will be ready as early as possible in the day.

Bath day is intended as much for rest and relaxation as for bathing and washing clothes. A fancy meal is served at the midday dinner. Along with the ubiquitous kimch'i, it includes sticky rice, bean curd, seaweed sheets, seaweed soup, and often Chinese vermicelli—all expensive dishes that are too heavy and rich for days when the monks are meditating full time. In the afternoon, the monks may often go off in small groups for short walks around the mountains, or take three or four hours for a longer hike to one of the many hermitages located in the mountains around the main monastery. Other monks will take the time to repair clothes, sew new patches on patchwork clothes, darn socks, or just rest and chat. After supper, the meditation hall returns to its regular schedule of evening sitting.

[17] A fortnightly bath was first ordered by the Buddha in the Prātimokṣa. See pācittika no. 50 and pāyantika no. 60, in Charles S. Prebish, trans., Buddhist Monastic Discipline: The Sanskrit Prātimokṣa Sūtras of the Mahāsāṃghikas and the Mūlasarvāstivādins (University Park: Pennsylvania State University Press, 1975), pp. 84, 87.

ESCAPING FROM THE MONASTERY

As I have mentioned, it is a monastery rule that no one can leave the meditation hall during retreat periods. A monk who is frustrated with the practice and determined to leave must therefore go through considerable machinations in order to escape. The succentor during one of my early retreats told a story about how Korean monks in ages past who left during the retreat had their feet chopped off. While I doubt any punishment so severe was ever administered, there is still a lot of pressure exerted on the residents to complete the entire retreat.

The most skillful escapee I knew of was a monk who ran away during the middle of the winter retreat in 1974. His was a classic strategy.

Monks occasionally take their bowls back from the meal room to give them a good washing with soap and water, but there is no fixed time when this is to be done. To begin his escape, this monk brought his bowls back from the dining room the night before he planned to leave, washed them, and then put them into his locker. He carefully packed his clothes, bowls, and possessions into his knapsack and stashed the pack behind the stone wall ringing the monastery after the monks had retired that evening. The next morning after predawn sitting, he feigned stomach trouble and skipped breakfast, staying behind doing walking meditation inside the hall. While the other monks were eating, he wrapped up his changsam and kasa, moved the other changsams up one peg to hide the fact that his was missing, and changed the placement of the kasas on the bamboo pole as well, spacing them out a bit farther so that his would not be missed. He put his sitting cushion back into the cabinet and moved the other cushions in his row slightly farther apart so that its disappearance would also not be readily noticed. Finally, taking his robes, he picked up his pack behind the wall and headed out.

The first bus leaving from the local village didn't depart until a few hours later in the morning, and once the late-morning sitting had begun, the succentor finally noticed that the monk was missing. Wondering what had happened to him, he broke the lock the monk had placed on his locker (unusual enough in Korea to suggest that something was amiss) and found all the monk's clothes missing. Suddenly all the pieces of the puzzle fit together. It was especially embarrassing to the succentor, since the escapee was his dharma brother. The succentor sent the two strongest monks down to the village to catch the escapee and bring him back, giving them bus fare to the next station in case they missed him in the village. The monk would not have been brought back forcibly, but he would have been coerced to return and complete the retreat; the enforcers might have gone so far as to take the fleeing monk's pack off his back to entice him to return. But this monk had thought of everything. We learned later that year that he had climbed all the way over the mountain and taken the bus from a village on the far side of the mountain so that he would not be caught.

During retreat season, no major monastery would accept a newly arriving monk, so the escapee had gone to his vocation master's hermitage until the free season began. The ŭnsa was understanding, preferring to have his disciple come to him rather than going elsewhere, for both of them would have lost face if he had shown up at another monastery during the retreat season.

THE FORTNIGHTLY LECTURE

The day after bath day, on full and new moon days, is the traditional Poṣadha observance. On this day, the Sŏn master delivers his formal lecture to the congregation. At Songgwang-sa, our *Vinaya* master (*yulchu sŭnim*) had spent some time in Southeast Asian monasteries and was impressed with their custom of reciting the rules of monastic discipline on the Poṣadha day; he had started to recite on alternate fortnights the Bodhisattva precepts from the *Book of Brahmā's Net* or the monastic rules from the *Prātimokṣa* for the assembled monks in the mornings after breakfast, a custom that was uncommon in Korea. At Songgwang-sa, during the summer retreat the Sŏn master's lecture was generally held in the cooler main buddha hall; in the winter it usually took place in the refectory, which was the largest ondol room in the monastery. The rector officially announces the time and place for the lecture to the assembled monks following breakfast. No lectures are held at all during the free seasons so this is one of the rare occasions when the monks hear directly the master's personal expression of his own understanding of Sŏn.

The monks maintain the regular meditation schedule during the late morning, participate in the midday dinner ritual, and then return to the meditation hall for tea. At ten minutes to one, the verger of the main buddha hall strikes the main monastery gong four times, and then strikes the smaller gong outside the refectory ten times to hasten the monks to the event. The lecture is perhaps the most formal occasion to occur in the monastery. It is one of the few times apart from dinner when the meditation monks will wear their formal robes—both changsam and kasa. After the monastery residents have gathered in the hall, the gong inside the main buddha hall is rung three rounds to announce the beginning of the lecture.

A small dais is set up in front of the buddha image in the hall, where the Sŏn master will sit while lecturing. It is about three feet high, with a short lectern in front, on which is placed candles and incense. The monks are seated in rows in front of the dais. The meditation monks sit separately from the rest of the monastery population on the right side of the dais. On the left are the postulants, support monks, nuns, and laypeople. For both sections, the more junior members of the community sit at the front, the more senior at the back. The seniormost monks in the monastery sit aligned at the very back of the hall: the cushions of the Sŏn master (empty during the lecture, of course), flanked by those of the rector and the abbot, are aligned with the dais, directly in front of the centermost door entering into the hall.

Once the audience is settled and still, the Sŏn master enters from this center door and takes his regular seat amid the assembly. His attendant enters simultaneously from a side door at the front of the hall, as is appropriate to his status, and takes his seat next to the dais. The monk coordinating the ceremony, usually the verger or a senior monk, strikes the mokt'ak once. The audience then rises and recites in unison a short series of verses (see Appendix). The assembly resumes its seats and listens silently as the monk coordinating the ceremony and an assistant perform a ten-minute ritual.

After that ritual is finished, two monks from the audience, usually the master's attendant and one of the younger meditation monks, come forward and prostrate themselves three times before the Sŏn master as an invitation to him to deliver his lecture. The master bows with palms together once at his seat in response, rises, and walks to the dais accompanied by the two monks. This procedure is intended to show that the monks are formally requesting that the master impart his dharma to the assembly, not that he is forcing his teachings on the monks. Kusan was extremely short, so his attendant would always place a chair next to the dais beforehand so that he could get up on the high seat. After the master is seated, his attendant places on the lectern one of the master's favorite books—perhaps the Records of Lin-chi (Lin-chi lu) or the Records of Ta-hui (Ta-hui yü-lu)—and pours him a cup of green tea. At Songgwang-sa, Kusan typically had Chinul's collected works before him during his lecture. While Kusan rarely read directly from that book, he had the transcript of his lecture inside its pages. After the master is seated, the verger will lead the monks in special bowing and chanting, three times requesting formally that the master impart his wisdom to them. The rector then strikes the chukpi three times, initiating some three minutes of silent meditation in order to get the monks into the appropriate frame of mind for hearing the lecture. When the rector strikes the chukpi three times to end the period, the audience, which had been facing directly forward throughout this time, turns slightly toward the dais. The master then raises his

Sŏn staff (*chujangja*) and strikes it hard against the dais three times to mark the beginning of the lecture.

The formal part of the lecture is about as far as one could imagine from the extemporaneous talks that we in the West often associate with Zen. This section of the lecture is termed a *pŏmmun* (lit. dharma gate), a formal statement of the master's own realization. Kusan always wrote this out beforehand in punctuated literary Chinese and read it line by line to the audience in Sino-Korean pronunciation, followed by a laborious translation into vernacular Korean. His pŏmmun often opened with an enigmatic Chinese poem recited—to Western ears really more "intoned"—in traditional Buddhist *pŏmp'ae* style; the remainder of the lecture was punctuated by two other poems recited in the same manner. To offer a taste of how formulaic these lectures can be, let me translate below one such formal pŏmmun, which was the opening lecture Kusan delivered during the winter retreat of 1975–1976.

> After ascending the dharma seat and looking to all the four directions, the master [Kusan] said, "Today is the beginning of this three-month retreat. Within the assembly present here now—do each of you brave men intend to go through with this retreat? Those of you endowed with the dharma-eye, speak! What is an extraordinary man?"
>
> The assembly remained silent.
>
> After a pause the master shouted and said, "The oranges of Cheju Island and the apples of Taegu: do you know where they fall? One pill of golden cinnabar [the elixir of the Taoist Perfected] swallows all the dharma realms and exudes many marvelous manifestations. Everyone is Vairocana. Everything is the Lotus Womb World. Do you understand this? You must be as audacious as someone trying to grab the eyebrows of a living tiger or to snatch the whiskers of a flying dragon—then you will know. A gāthā [verse] says:
>
>> An extraordinary man ultimately extends in all horizontal and
>>   vertical directions,
>> Even were an iron wheel grinding his head, he wouldn't be afraid.
>> Ten thousand trees of gold and jade enrich a desolate island,
>> One of their pure, fragrant fruits slackens the feeling of thirst.
>
> Though this is the case, if in one thought we suddenly transcend [saṃsāra], we can apprehend and defeat the buddhas and patriarchs. We can sport in freedom. Why should this take much time? But if liberation has not yet been achieved, we must carefully investigate our own *kongan*. By dissolving the limits of both past and future, only the mass of doubt will remain. If, during all twenty-four hours of the day, from moment to moment, the doubt is not obscured, we will gradually enter sublime states. At that moment, we cannot

grasp or reject anything; there is no up or down. With one slash of a knife we cut the mass of doubt in two and finally the mind is revealed.

But subtle streams [of defilements] are not suddenly stopped; so at that time [when the doubt has coalesced], we must brand upon our foreheads the two characters "birth" and "death." The body then becomes like a stone that has rolled to the road side; the mind is like a sharp sword that splits a wind-blown hair. We neglect our sleep and forget about food. We are not afraid of falling into emptiness and we deepen the hue of doubt surrounding the *kongan*. We keep on working closely.

If we can continue in this manner for one to three weeks, suddenly our mind and the truth will mesh. We will understand the cause and conditions of the Great Matter [of enlightenment] and will have no further doubts about the tongue tips of men [viz. the words of enlightened persons]. How could we not be happy?

Although there be such an awakening, we still must remain as if deaf and stupid and go meet enlightened mentors. Having been tested by them on the truth or falsity, shallowness or depth [of our awakening], we will understand what was still incompletely understood. We follow the stream and reach the marvel and become the master of all places. We are Mañjuśrī amid the assembly on Vulture Peak, Samantabhadra inside the tower of Maitreya. A gāthā says:

> With one blow of our fists we knock down Sumeru's peak,
> And build the palace of Maitreya.
> Kāśyapa's offering bowl is not a difficult matter.
> We make offerings to all within the great sea of the ten
>   directions.

The master shouted and descended from the dharma seat.[18]

What is distinctively Korean about this lecture is the amount of Hwaŏm imagery Kusan uses for a formal statement about Sŏn understanding. Its presence demonstrates the ecumenical character of the Korean Buddhist tradition and the continued influence on the contemporary tradition of Chinul's vision of the symbiosis between Sŏn and Doctrine (Kyo). I should also note that all of the "choreography" in the lecture— the master looking to the four directions, pausing after his questions to the assembly, shouting, and so forth—was carefully scripted in Kusan's transcript of the talk.

When the pŏmmun is finished, the master will usually say that while the formal lecture is now over he will give some further explanations in

[18] This is my own translation, with slight alterations, made with the assistance of Renaud Neubauer (Hyehaeng *sŭnim*) and Stacey Krause (Hamwŏl *sŭnim*), and published in Ku San, *Nine Mountains*, pp. 117–19. For other material on Kusan's teachings, see Kusan Sunim, *The Way of Korean Zen.*

order to help the monks in their practice. Often he then begins on a long story, now all in colloquial Korean, perhaps about his own teacher, an exchange his teacher may have had with one of his students, or maybe a poem his teacher wrote about such an encounter, with sometimes one of his own poems in reply. He may also discuss practical techniques that can help the monks in their meditation, such as the three states of mind essential to Sŏn practice. But always this second portion of the lecture is intended more as practical advice and encouragement to the monks than as a formal expression of the master's enlightenment. Unlike the pŏmmun, this section is rarely written down. Kusan once explained to me that it was unnecessary to preserve it, since it was all "dead words" (sagu) anyway, unlike the "live words" (hwalgu) of the dharma gate. I also never knew a master in Korea to deliver what the Japanese call a teishō, an oral commentary to a kōan collection or Zen anthology, in which the Japanese Zen master would read out a Zen kōan (case) or section of a case and then comment upon it.[19] The story section of a Korean master's lecture may mention the comments of earlier teachers, but there is no systematic discussion of the written word that we typically associate with the Japanese teishō. The "dharma gate" as well is intended to be a unique composition by the master himself, not simply a comment upon someone else's expression of enlightenment.

Many times during the lecture the master will ask the monks rhetorically if they understand what he is saying. On only the rarest of occasions will anyone brave a response. The monks are old hands at these kinds of lectures and the rhetorical flourishes they demand; all listen quietly, but sometimes inattentively. The meditation monks are occasionally cynical about the quality of the pŏmmun, critiquing the master's performance or remarks in much the same way that university students critique their professors' lectures.

Only twice during my five years of attending formal lectures at Songgwang-sa did a monk ever challenge the Sŏn master. Once when this happened, the monk went before the dais, prostrated himself, and said he had a question. The master ignored him for a time, but the monk persisted and Kusan harshly asked him what he wanted to ask. The monk responded, "Is my hand and the Buddha's hand the same, or different?" The master struck the monk on the shoulder with his long, heavy Sŏn staff (not the lightweight stick used to rouse monks during meditation), asking him in turn, "Do you understand?" After this same sequence was repeated several times, the monk finally ran out the front door, the mas-

---

[19] See the description of the teishō in Daisetz Teitaro Suzuki, The Training of the Zen Buddhist Monk (1934; reprint, Berkeley: Wingbow Press, 1974), pp. 98–103; see also Miura, Isshū, and Ruth Fuller Sasaki, Zen Dust: The History of the Koan and Koan Study in Rinzai (Lin-chi) Ch'an (New York: Harcourt, Brace and World, 1966), p. 30.

ter's private entrance (a symbolic act of defiance), and went back to the meditation hall. The master then laughingly poked fun at the monk and explained what he had meant. The feeling of pain the monk felt while being struck was shared by both the Buddha and ordinary human beings. If the monk had understood this, Kusan said, his question would have been moot and he wouldn't have needed to ask it. Therefore, the monk had just been playing a game with his question; he didn't really have any understanding, Kusan said, and if he persisted in this egotistical fantasy of presuming he was ready to challenge a Sŏn master, he would not get anywhere in his practice.

Another time, at a lecture at the end of the retreat season, the master was droning on (the monks remarked later), repeating stale, and long discredited, legends about Samyŏng *taesa* (Yujŏng; 1544–1610), the famous Sŏn master who led the Korean monk's militia against the Japanese during the Hideyoshi invasion of the peninsula (1592–1598). After about fifteen minutes of these stories, one of the disgusted meditation monks finally came before the dais, bowed three times, and chastized Kusan: "On the far side of the mountain, a dog barks, '*Wang, wang, wang.*' " He then turned, kicked open in defiance the master's private entrance to the hall, and stalked out. The master yelled after him, "Stop making dog noises and come back in here!" and continued with his lecture.

The rector, who is sitting at the back of the hall, has the job of keeping the audience awake during the lecture. Since the lecture follows the biggest meal of the fortnight, and the spoken Sino-Korean is difficult to follow, even for trained ears, this can often be a daunting task. When he sees nodding heads in front of him, the rector stands and walks among the monks. He is supposed to carry the large warning stick (*changgun chukpi*), but usually only carries the small clacker, hitting the dozing monks on the back to startle them with its loud snap.

When the master has finished his stories, he hits his staff down three times on the dais to close the lecture. The verger strikes the mokt'ak three times in response and the monks rise and begin chanting "Śākyamuni Buddha" while the master returns to his regular seat in the back of the hall. After continuing with this recitation of the Buddha's name for a few minutes, the monks then recite the four great vows of the bodhisattva (*sa hongsŏwŏn*) to end this ceremony (as with so many others):

> Sentient beings without limit, I vow to save,
> Defilements without end, I vow to eradicate,
> Doctrinal instructions without measure, I vow to study,
> The path to Buddhahood, which is unsurpassed, I vow to attain.[20]

[20] Chungsaeng mubyŏn sŏwŏn to, / Ponnoe mujin sŏwŏn tan, / Pommun muryang sŏnwŏn hak, / Pulto musang sŏwŏn sŏng.

As the vows end, some monks will typically shout out "*Sŏngbul ha sipsio* (please attain buddhahood!)," the monastic equivalent of the standard Korean vernacular *kamsa hamnida* (thank you). The master leaves through his own door, and the rest of the audience files out to the various compounds. The lecture has taken about forty minutes. After a ten-minute break, the mokt'ak strikes at the meditation hall to begin the afternoon sitting session. For the next fortnight, the monastery then returns to its normal retreat routine.

INTENSIVE MEDITATION

For one week during the winter retreat season, the most rigorous event in the life of the meditator occurs: yongmaeng chŏngjin, meaning literally "ferocious effort." This special meditation session is scheduled for the week preceding the Buddha's enlightenment day (*puch'ŏnim sŏngdo-il*), which in Korea is celebrated on the eighth day of the twelfth lunar month (usually in early January). This session is intended to be a kind of ritual reenactment of the fervent practice performed by the Buddha before his enlightenment, when he vowed that he would remain sitting until he had vanquished Māra and all his minions and achieved complete, perfect realization (*samyaksaṃbodhi*).

During yongmaeng chŏngjin, the monks in meditation hall do not sleep for seven straight days, breaking from their practice only for meals. They even skip the dinner ritual in the main buddha hall in order to devote themselves completely to their meditation. To help maintain the monks' stamina, the proctor brings to the hall a special midnight snack of brown-rice gruel (*chuk*), which the tagaks, the young tea boys, serve in the center of the room. After the monks have finished this quick snack, it is back to their cushions to continue sitting. The proctor also keeps a steady supply of fruits, cakes, and sweets coming up to the hall to serve with the tea that follows the regular meals. It is important to keep the monks' spirits up for this intensive period of practice, and good food helps to alleviate at least some of the rigor of the week.

Yongmaeng chŏngjin begins at midnight, so that it will end at midnight on the last day. This scheduling allows the monks to take a short three-hour rest the first night after the week-long intensive is over, and in that way hopefully be able to sustain the meditative energy they will have gained into the remainder of the retreat. The Buddha's enlightenment day also occurs about two-thirds of the way through the winter retreat, so this period will make the rest of the retreat that much more compelling for the monks.

During yongmaeng chŏngjin, the monks face one another in two separate rows down the middle of the meditation hall, rather than facing away as they usually do. The succentor strikes the chukpi three times at the beginning of the week and three times at the end, signaling that the entire week is a single meditation block. Otherwise the meditation sessions take place pretty much as always, with fifty-minute sitting periods followed by ten minutes of walking. But if the succentor feels people are tiring, he might quicken the pace to twenty-five minutes of sitting followed by five minutes of walking, have them walk for longer periods, or try any number of other stratagems to keep his charges vibrant (or at least awake). Once in the early morning, when most of the hall was flagging, the succentor led us all into the lecture hall next door, a large room with tatami floors, and had us do tumbling exercises on the soft surface. Everyone was having so much fun doing somersaults and cartwheels that we forgot, for a time at least, how tired we were.

Other than its obvious interminableness, the major difference between yongmaeng chŏngjin and regular meditation periods is that the large warning stick is in use constantly throughout each sitting period. For most of the regular retreat, the succentor carries the stick at most only once each sitting period. During yongmaeng chŏngjin, however, the stick is passed among all the members of the hall so that someone is always kept on guard. The guard stands at the cool end of the heated ondol room—to help keep himself awake—and watches to make sure that none of the monks' heads is bobbing, a sure sign of drowsiness. If he sees a monk start to doze, he walks slowly behind the monks, around the outside perimeter of the hall. If the drowsy monk does not react to the guard's presence, the guard taps him on the shoulder with the stick and gives him one round of blows. The crucial challenge for the succentor is to make sure the guard stays awake while on duty, for if the guard dozes off, the whole hall will soon follow. It happened more than once in my experience that the succentor had to get up himself and rouse a guard who was leaning against the wall, snoring. About five minutes before the end of the sitting period, the guard brings the stick before the monk next in line for duty. They bow to each other, and then the guard leaves the stick in front of his successor's seat and returns to his own seat until the walking period begins.

As grueling as yongmaeng chŏngjin might seem to the uninitiated, its purpose is not to torture the monks. Rather it provides an incredibly intense, but still carefully controlled, environment in which to meditate. The hope is that several days of sleeplessness will apply enough pressure on the meditators that they will be able to have a genuine breakthrough into their hwadu. Just before yongmaeng chŏngjin begins, the Sŏn master tries to impress upon the meditators that the only way they will be able to survive the week is to remain concentrated at all times on their hwadu and to arouse the sensation of doubt. From my own experience, the sheer enormity of the task of remaining awake for seven straight days was enough to frighten me into focusing on the hwadu, as if I were clinging to it for dear life. The instant the mind wavers, you are bludgeoned by bone-numbing fatigue, so the only hope you have of getting through the week is to maintain your concentration.

My initial exposure to this intensive form of practice was during my first retreat period in Korea. I had been in the country only about three months and still had a weak grasp at best of the hwadu technique. But I did know that I wanted to meditate and was mixing some of the mindfulness meditation I had learned during my year as a monk in Southeast Asia with an entirely amateurish version of kanhwa Sŏn. Looking back now, I realize that I was extremely vulnerable to all the terror that yongmaeng chŏngjin can exert on the novice meditator. By sheer force of will, and an acute sense of embarrassment at the prospect of being forced to drop out of the retreat, I was managing to maintain at least some semblance of practice during the first couple of days. But after the third day, even this trace was lost. I had degenerated to the point where I could no longer tell whether I was asleep or awake. I remember several times being totally confused as to whether the guard carrying the stick was actually hitting me, or whether I was dreaming the whole thing. During walking meditation I might as well have been walking in space, so ungrounded and amorphous did I feel. I was not alone in that. During one walking session, one of the other monks fell asleep while rounding the corner of the room and walked straight through one of the wood-and-paper doors along the side of the hall. He was rudely awakened as he toppled onto the wooden veranda outside. At the end of the retreat when we were finally allowed to sleep, I collapsed at my seat, utterly exhausted. Although we were supposed to awaken at three in the morning to begin anew our regular meditation schedule, I could not be roused. The monks left me laid out on my cushion and sat and walked around me. It was not until just before the late-morning meditation period began at eight that I finally awoke. Fortunately, in subsequent retreats my practice had matured to the point where I could maintain extended periods of concentration on the hwadu. Then it really was quite remarkable how effective—even almost refreshing, in a bizarre sort of way—such intensive practice could be.

ASCETIC PRACTICES

At appropriate times in the career of a meditator, he might undertake one of the many ascetic practices recognized within the Korean Buddhist tradition. Ascetic practices (*kohaeng*) have always played an important role in Buddhist spiritual culture. Because of its "middle way" philosophy, however, Buddhism has tried to limit practices to those that will help the monk overcome his attachments and weaken his desires; it eschews those that are simply glorified forms of self-mortification, which ultimately would only strengthen the fetter of pride. There is a difference of opinion among Korean monks over the benefits and range of asceticism. Many monks, especially younger ones, look with great esteem on colleagues who have undertaken particularly tortuous practices, assuming that they thereby have shown their deep devotion to the dharma. But monks criticize the more extreme forms of asceticism as being only a hindrance to progress; they praise instead those monks who show they are intent on training their minds, not just torturing their bodies. Regardless of this controversy, which has always surrounded mortification of the flesh, the practices remain popular in Korea and almost all meditation monks have tried one or another of them at some point in their careers. So, whatever their utility in spiritual development, I will review them briefly here.

Eating Only Raw Foods

One of the most common ascetic practices is that of eating only raw foods (*saengsik*). While occasionally a monk in meditation hall will follow such a dietary regimen, it most often is undertaken by monks who live in small, isolated hermitages. Far from the marketplace, they have nowhere to purchase supplies anyway and may have little arable land on which to grow their own food. This practice harkens back to Taoist dietary stigmas against cooked cereals, which were viewed as a principal cause of physical degeneration and finally death. Whatever benefits the Taoists found the practice to have had in promoting immortality, Buddhist monks find eating raw foods useful in warding off the drowsiness that accompanies heavy meals of cooked grains. Particularly for monks who are trying never to lie down to sleep (another ascetic practice I will discuss below), the feeling of physical lightness that results from eating only raw foods is conducive to this constant sitting, and the two practices are often undertaken together.

Saengsik involves eating nothing that is steamed, boiled, or fried. Boiled water is acceptable, and most monks undertaking the practice will drink hot tea, but all boiled foods are taboo, and all vegetables are eaten either raw or pickled. Uncooked grains, such as rice or barley, are ground to a fine powder, and then mixed with cold water and drunk. Raw soybeans are also powdered and consumed the same way. Monks undertaking this practice also eschew white sugar and use honey only sparingly.

Honey was a real delicacy at the time in Korea and was inordinately expensive for a monk, so it would hardly have been available anyway. Kimch'i and other pickled vegetables are permitted, as they involve no cooking in their preparation. To supplement this basic diet, monks also gather whatever wild herbs and plants they can locate in the vicinity and will often add nuts, pine nuts, and fruit to the menu, or even powdered pine needles.

In the strictest observance of this practice, followed occasionally by monks deep in the mountains, the diet will consist of cold water, powdered pine needles, and wild plants and herbs. In the *Admonitions to Beginners*, the first text read by every incoming postulant, Buddhist practice is epitomized in terms of such rigorous self-sufficiency. The final selection in that anthology is a work by the late Koryŏ period Sŏn master Yaun (d.u.), a disciple of Naong Hyegŭn (1320–1376). His selection, entitled *Checking Oneself (Chagyŏng-mun)*, describes ten ways in which the new monk guards himself from defilement. A look at the list—which includes eating wild vegetables and tree fruits and wearing bark for clothes—shows the extent to which this attitude has infused the Korean Buddhist attitude towards practice.[21]

As might be expected, the adjustment to such a restricted diet is a slow process and may take many months before the monk is able to feel truly comfortable with it. A monk beginning this practice starts gradually, adding more and more raw food to his regular diet, then shifting slowly to eating only raw food at perhaps one or two meals a day until he can finally make a complete switch. All monks I have known who have tried this practice complain of weakness during the first few months of the diet, but say that it gradually subsides until they actually gain more energy than they had while eating cooked foods. It is difficult to sustain the practice when staying in a monastery, however, and most monks who want to continue with the practice over the long term stay in hermitages. Few monks I have talked with continued more than six months at a stretch with the diet, though I heard tales of monks who found it so beneficial that they continued on for their entire lives. The difficulty of keeping to the diet when traveling or when staying in the group environment of the monastery forces most monks to give it up when they return to the meditation hall, and few go back to it once they have dropped it.

Once a monk has committed himself to the diet, it is very dangerous to make sudden changes back to cooked food. As I mentioned in chapter three in the story of Kusan's life, one of his dharma friends died from making a sudden transition back to cooked food. After three years of

---

[21] Kim T'anhŏ, ed., *Ch'obalsim chagyŏng-mun* (Admonitions for Beginners) (Seoul: Pulsŏ Pogŭpsa, 1971), pp. 50ff.

eating mainly pine needles and wild plants, he ate some glutinous rice that a layperson offered to him and died the next day of gastroenteritis.[22] To avoid such a fate, when the person switches back to a regular diet, he sticks with fresh fruits and vegetables for a time and gradually reintroduces rice gruel and wheat porridge before finally returning to a regular rice diet.

Fasting

Another relatively popular practice in Korea, which is, however, more often talked about than actually done, is fasting (*tansik*). Fasting is much in vogue as the miracle cure for almost all chronic illnesses, from stomach trouble to arthritis. Although it is considered helpful by some monks in making the body light for meditation, most monks decide to fast primarily for health reasons. Indeed, all the masters with whom I talked did not encourage a person in good health to fast, saying that fasting weakens the body to such an extent that it interferes with meditation instead of helping it.

Korean monks generally believe that the more food you eat, the more energy you will have. This outlook pervades their life, justifying many of their idiosyncrasies. For example, the meditating monks' distaste for rice gruel at breakfast comes, I was repeatedly told, from the fact that gruel leaves them so hungry by midmorning that their stomachs cave in and they can't sit up straight any more, making them drowsy and hindering their practice. It also justifies their view that they have to eat more nutritious food and have an extra meal during the seven-day yongmaeng chŏngjin in order to sustain their energy. Finally it appears in the monks' insistence that they need large morning and afternoon snacks whenever they are involved in group work sessions. Whatever the wisdom of their view, Korean monks do believe in substantial meals and typically undertake short fasts only when their health begins to suffer—a result of overeating, I often suspected.

Fasting is typically done in intervals of from three days to two weeks. Before beginning a real fast, the monk might do a preparatory two- or three-day raw fruit or vegetable fast before cutting off all food. Usually only cool spring water is taken during the fast itself, with some monks allowing themselves hot tea. Some monks told me that boiling water removed all the energy (*ki*; Ch. *ch'i*) from it, so they preferred to take water fresh from the spring with its full dose of energy. At the end of the fast,

[22] See Ku San, *Nine Mountains*, pp. 173–74.

the monk eats raw fruit for two or three more days, turning next to rice gruel or wheat porridge, before finally returning to a regular rice diet.

One monk I met who had been staying alone at a hermitage behind Poryŏn-sa, near Muju Kuch'ŏn-tong, claimed to have fasted for three years. He explained to me that he had begun by doing short fasts, which gradually lengthened to three weeks, until he finally decided to see how long he could last without eating. He continued fasting for one year straight, taking only spring water, and then after one year he began to accept food again on an irregular basis, once a week or once a fortnight, and only when it was offered to him. Now, after three years, he said that whether he ate or not, his energy remained the same. He had sustained himself all these years by drawing in the energy from the fresh water he drank and by absorbing the sun's rays directly, in a "Taoist" practice that he demonstrated for me. Facing the noon sun with arms extended and palms open, he said, he could ingest the sun's energy directly—energy that was, he explained, the same as the calories obtained from eating plants and meat, but in its raw form. To absorb the earth's energy as well, he had also started to walk barefoot through the mountains and took a daily walk up and down the mountain, a distance of about seven kilometers. While I found the monk to look rather gaunt and gangly, he certainly was not weak from his ordeal. His story has circulated widely among the meditation monks in Korea, though many chided him for engaging in "heretical" (oedo) practices.

I have also heard of one case of a monk fasting himself to death in 1978. Ch'unsŏng sŭnim (1891–1978), the master I mentioned in Chapter Five who cultivated "unconstrained conduct," contracted rectal cancer, which became an increasing burden on both himself and his attendants. Growing tired of the trouble he was causing, he decided to stop eating and finally passed away twenty days later.

Never Lying Down to Sleep

Sleeping in a sitting position without ever lying down (changjwa purwa) is one of the twelve ascetic practices sanctioned by the Buddha,[23] which he recommended for developing vigor and for counteracting the hindrance of sloth and torpor. Most masters have tried this practice themselves and recommend it for particularly intensive periods of meditation. In Korea, most monks who cultivate it simply sit on their ordinary sitting cushion, perhaps allowing their heads to nod as they sleep. The supports

[23] See Fo-shuo shih-erh t'ou-t'o ching (The Sūtra of the Twelve Ascetic Practices), T 783.17.720b–722a.

and straps that were so common among Chinese monks who engaged in this practice were never used in Korea, so far as I know; Koreans told me that if you were going to undertake this practice, you might as well do it right or not even try it. Leaning against the wall when trying to sit up is also discouraged: touching the cold mud wall of the typical Korean building is considered to be extremely unhealthy, causing everything from colds to arthritis.

Most monks who decide not to lie down to sleep often do so for only limited periods, one month to one retreat season being the most common. Some monks claim to have done it for much longer. Sŏngch'ŏl *sŭnim*, the Sŏn master at Haein-sa, is well known not to have lain down to sleep for fourteen years during his training, not even deigning to lean against a wall to rest. One older monk I knew, who was the succentor of the meditation hall for a winter retreat at Songgwang-sa, had continued with the practice for a number of years and said that it made him feel more energetic. Sleep, he felt, was like a drug that only numbed the spirit and he always encouraged other monks to cut back as far as possible on the number of hours they slept. The only concession he made to his advancing age was to allow himself to lie down when he was traveling; otherwise, he always sat up. Occasionally, a group of two or three monks might make a vow together never to lie down in the meditation hall, as a kind of a mutual support pact.

As with so many other ascetic practices, monks who have slept sitting for long periods all say that the first month is particularly trying, but that later the difficulty gradually subsides until finally one actually feels more energetic. But many monks I have talked with questioned the efficacy of never lying down over long periods of time. They pointed out that eventually there is so much accumulated tiredness in the body that one tends to fall asleep whenever one is sitting, rather than just for a few hours each night. Then meditation suffers, as sitting degenerates into a convenient excuse for sleeping all day long. These monks advocated that it was better in the long run to keep to a regular schedule of three or four hours of deep sleep, which give one the rest one needs to meditate without indulging in recumbency. From my own observations, monks who were practicing never lying down tended to nod off during meditation, suggesting that their critics had a valid point. Sometimes they even fell forward, their heads resting on the floor in front of their cushion, snoring.

Silence

Silence is officially to be maintained always in the meditation compound—an injunction that is kept with varying degrees of success. Some monks, however, take the personal vow to maintain strict silence (*mugŏn*) for varying lengths of time. Songdam *sŭnim*, the Sŏn master at Yonghwa-sa in Inch'ŏn, kept silent for over fourteen years before succeeding his teacher—so long, in fact, that he is now better known by the nickname "Silent Monk" (Mugŏn *sŭnim*) than by his ordination name. With the large numbers of monks living in the small areas of Korean monasteries, talking is definitely one of the most distracting of activities, disturbing both one's own calmness of mind and the serenity of one's companions. Although the Buddha specifically prohibited monks from keeping total silence (enjoining them, instead, to speak words that were wise and timely), the practice of silence seems an appropriate stratagem to help maintain a solemn atmosphere in a large monastery. If nothing else, silence is certainly one of the most effective methods for avoiding the social entanglements that inevitably develop within any group of people, including the monastic community.[24]

A monk who intends to undertake silence will inform his companions beforehand so that there will be no misunderstandings when he starts to ignore their queries. Silent monks end up spending most of their time alone during the break periods, often going for walks alone in the mountains behind the meditation hall. As much as possible, they try to keep communication to the basic level of hand signals. But if more complicated exchanges are necessary, they will usually carry a fountain pen and notepad and write down their responses. Silent monks also generally maintain their practice even on bath days, when talking is customarily allowed in the meditation hall.

Older monks are usually more flexible in this practice than the newer monks. Rather than adamantly refusing to speak under any circumstances, they will talk if there is something important to say and speaking would be the most convenient way of communicating it. Such monks are usually not faulted by their associates for this apparent laxity.

Finger Burning

One of the most severe ascetic practices, which involves actual self-mortification, is finger burning. Many Korean monks have burned their fingers as an ascetic practice or as an offering to the Buddha, not in association with any ordination procedure, as the Chinese used to do.[25] The

---

[24] This form of asceticism was virtually unknown in Chinese Buddhism; see Holmes Welch, *Practice of Chinese Buddhism: 1900–1950*, Harvard East Asian Studies 26 (Cambridge: Harvard University Press, 1967), p. 323.

[25] For the Chinese analogue to this practice, see Welch, *Practice of Chinese Buddhism*, pp. 324–25.

fourth finger of the left hand is the digit most commonly sacrificed, moving then to the last finger of the left, to the fourth finger on the right, and so forth. This practice harkens back to statements appearing in many Mahāyāna sūtras, which demand that the bodhisattva, in his ardor for the dharma, not begrudge even his own body. The locus classicus for such mortification of the flesh is the Bodhisattva Sadaprarudita in the *Perfection of Wisdom in Eight Thousand Lines (Aṣṭasāhasrikāprajñāpāramitā-sūtra)*. Sadaprarudita had nothing of value with which to make offerings to Dharmodgata Bodhisattva and decided to sell his own body in the marketplace as a way of raising money. As a test, Śakra, king of the gods, conjured up a young man, who offered to buy only his heart, blood, and bone marrow. Sadhaprarudita gladly accepted his offer and enthusiastically started cutting into himself, until Śakra stopped him and restored him to his former condition.[26] Although some monks I talked with questioned the value of such physical torture, most had a profound respect for the commitment and faith involved in undertaking such an act.

Burning off a finger is usually performed in a small shrine hall, with only one or two close friends in attendance. Secrecy is necessary, because monastery officials would probably intervene to stop the ceremony if they learned of it in time. A cord is first tied tightly around the entire hand above the thumb, to cut off the blood supply and deaden the nerves of the hand. A candle is melted over a strip of hemp cloth, and that waxed material is then wrapped around the finger to be sacrificed. Some material is left extending over the top of the finger to serve as a wick. The wick is then lit with a candle and the finger goes up like a torch. As the finger burns, the monk and his friends furiously chant mantras to try to keep the mind concentrated.[27] Monks I knew who had performed this act said the actual burning was relatively painless; it was the shock and anxiety about what was happening that bothered them the most. They did complain of later having to endure a dull, gnawing pain before the stump healed completely.

There are a variety of motivations that prompt a monk to take this drastic step. One is, of course, the symbolic commitment to his vocation

[26] See Edward Conze, trans., *The Perfection of Wisdom in Eight Thousand Lines and Its Verse Summary* (1973; reprint, Bolinas, Calif.: Four Seasons Foundation, 1975), pp. 283–86. This is also a popular motif in the *Jātakas, Avadānas*, and Mahāyāna sūtras. See, as but one of many examples, the story of King Śivi in the *Avadānas*, who offers first flesh from his thigh, and then eventually his entire body, to a hawk in order to save the life of a dove; *Hsien-yü ching* 1, *T* 202.4.351c5–352b8 and at many other points throughout the canon.

[27] The Korean method is slightly different from that followed by Chinese monks, as Holmes Welch outlines in *Practice of Chinese Buddhism*, pp. 324–25. In China, just the finger designated for sacrifice was wrapped tightly with string, not the whole hand. After packing the hand in mud, the exposed finger was then covered with sandalwood and incense and lit on fire.

implied in the act. Ilt'a *sŭnim*, the Vinaya master at Haein-sa, is perhaps the best known of monks to have practiced this form of self-mortification: he has burned off all the fingers on his right hand except his thumb. He explained to me that his motivation behind this act was to ensure that he could never again entertain the thought of returning to lay life, where he would need the use of his hands to support himself. Despite his handicap, Ilt'a is a noted calligrapher, holding the brush between his thumb and palm. One of his disciples, who spent much time in the meditation hall at Songgwang-sa, had burned off the three middle fingers of his right hand. His reason, he said, was to avoid military service, since without his trigger finger he would be unable to fire a rifle. His ploy had worked, and he was one of the few monks I knew who had found a way around the draft. Ilt'a's dharma family has made almost a tradition of this practice, and a number of his disciples have followed his example.

But there are monks who take the step not because of any exemplary motivation, but simply to show off. Monks who have burned off their fingers are accorded a measure of respect, particularly from the laity, and this is a quick, if painful, way of winning esteem—certainly much easier than spending years in the meditation hall. Occasionally, monks will ostentatiously flaunt their missing finger. When the palms are placed together during chanting, for instance, the corresponding finger on the other hand will fill in the missing space, or when the monk gestures, he will wave the injured hand before his audience. The monks are always critical of such ostentation.

Self-Immolation

The ultimate sacrifice any Buddhist can make is to give his life for the dharma, as we saw above in the story of Sadaprarudita. Perhaps the way of performing this sacrifice that seems most appalling to Westerners is self-immolation (*punsin* or *sosin*; *ātmaparityāga*), a practice that became known worldwide with the martyrdom of Vietnamese Buddhist monks in the 1960s.[28] The locus classicus for this sacrifice is the story of Bhaiṣajya-guru Bodhisattva in the *Lotus Sūtra* (*Saddharmapuṇḍarīka-sūtra*). As an offering to the Buddha, he perfumed his body with various perfumes, wrapped himself in scented garments, and then set himself afire. "Among the various gifts," he claims, "it is the most honorable, the supreme. For it constitutes an offering of Dharma to the Thus Come Ones."[29]

[28] See ibid., p. 328.

[29] *Miao-fa lien-hua ching* 6, T. 262.9.53b; translation from Leon Hurvitz, *Scripture of the Lotus Blossom of the Fine Dharma* (New York: Columbia University Press, 1976), p.

Self-immolation is exceedingly rare in Korea. I learned of only one case in the last two decades, which was performed not as a political gesture, as in Vietnam, but to end a terminal illness. A senior nun in a small nunnery above Tonghwa-sa had contracted stomach cancer. In intense pain, and tired of being a burden on her disciples, she decided to end it all, and made secret preparations for her own cremation. She washed and ironed all of her clothes, cleaned her room thoroughly, and left a note to her fellow nuns apologizing for the inconvenience she was creating, accompanied by money to pay for her forty-ninth-day funeral ceremony. Late at night, after all the other nuns had retired for the evening, she built a pyre at a secluded meadow just over the hill from the hermitage, sat down on it in full-lotus position, poured gasoline over herself, and struck a match. The next morning at three, when the nuns rose, she did not appear for chanting, and her attendant went to her room to check on her. Finding the note, she summoned all the nuns, and they went out to search for the site. They discovered the pyre almost completely burned down and added more wood to finish the cremation. The monks at the monastery below were summoned at sunrise and a large service was held at the site to commemorate her deed.

Minor Practices

There are a number of other minor practices that I heard meditation monks occasionally undertook. Hermit monks living deep in the mountains let their hair and beards grow, shaving only upon their departure from the hermitage. There is no particular stigma attached to monks growing their hair out in private as long as they are shaved when they are out among the public. Even so, most monks stay clean-shaven even when they live alone.

I heard once of a monk who decided that monastery life with its assured food and lodging was too soft a life, and tried living for a time as a beggar. Discarding his monk's clothing, putting on old rags, and growing out his hair, he lived with the beggars in the street until he felt that his attachment to the comforts of monastic life had weakened.

Sometimes, too, monks will copy out sūtras by using their own blood for ink, in imitation of Chinese monks who followed perhaps an over-literal interpretation of the forty-fourth precept of the bodhisattva precepts, which encourages the adherent to use his own bone as a pen for writing the sūtras, his skin as paper, and his blood as ink.[30] The monk

---

295; discussed also in Welch, *Practice of Chinese Buddhism*, pp. 326–27. The practice is mentioned in the *Vinaya*; see *Shih-sung lü* 17, T 1435.23.123b3–4.

[30] See the discussion in Welch, *Practice of Chinese Buddhism*, p. 323.

pricks his fingertip and squeezes out as much blood as possible; the blood is then diluted with water and used as ink. I knew several laypeople, too, who had undertaken this practice; one particularly devoted lay scholar wrote out all eighty fascicles of the *Avataṃsaka-sūtra* (*Hwaŏm-kyŏng*) in his own blood.

RETREATS

Emulating the six years of solitary practice Śākyamuni Buddha spent in the Himalayas before his enlightenment, Korean monks also go into occasional periods of retreat, either alone or in small groups. "Sealed confinement" (*p'yegwan*) in a small room may be undertaken by an individual monk who wants to avoid the distraction of all outside activities and completely devote himself to meditation.[31] The vow is taken for a designated period, usually an entire retreat period, but sometimes as long as three or six years. There is a meditation center on Tobong Mountain outside of Seoul that specializes in six-year private retreats. It offers individual cells for the monks and provides all the necessary facilities and services so that the monks can be undisturbed in their practice.[32] But most often confinement takes place in a small hermitage, where the monk will be undisturbed by visitors, or in an isolated building on the outskirts of a monastery. A room is specially prepared to provide all the essentials of a lengthy retreat. It has a small window through which food can be passed to the monk and a toilet. Sometimes a monk will choose a room where he cannot stand up, to force himself to sit in meditation. An attendant agrees to stay at the monastery for the duration of the retreat to take care of the monk's needs: to make his ondol fire for him, prepare his food, wash his clothes, and ward off visitors. In Korea, the door is not bricked in or locked from the outside, as was done in China, but simply closed with no lock placed on the door at all, the monks trusting that the hermit's commitment will be strong enough to sustain him.

Another retreat similar to the sealed confinement, but involving instead a group of monks, is the three-year retreat (*samnyŏn kyŏlsa*). This retreat is simply an extended version of the usual three-month kyŏlche. The monks involved commit themselves to living together, just as in a normal meditation hall, but are allowed to go outside the meditation compound during the break periods so long as they do not leave the monastery

---

[31] See the account of Chinese sealed confinement in Welch, *Practice of Chinese Buddhism*, pp. 321–22.

[32] See discussion in Seo, Kyung-bo (Sŏ Kyŏngbo), "A Study of Korean Zen Buddhism Approached through the Chodangjip" (Ph.D. diss., Temple University, 1970; mimeographed reprint, Seoul, 1979), p. 410.

grounds. Most commonly, a small group of monks decides together to start such a retreat. But occasionally a whole monastery might switch over to a three-year retreat rather than keeping to the standard three-month schedule.

Three-year retreats were frequently scheduled at Songgwang-sa—three during my five years there—but none was ever completed. The retreats were planned to begin the following retreat season, with the details spread by word of mouth among the meditating monks as they traveled during the free season. Introductions were accepted until the hall was filled; any overflow was placed in the smaller, backup meditation hall. When there were more applicants than the halls could accommodate, seniority decided who received the limited number of places, the main hall accommodating the older monks, the backup hall the younger ones. Once the retreat began, Songgwang-sa stopped observing the ordinary schedule of three-month-long retreat and free seasons alternating throughout the year and accepted no more introductions. As monks started to escape during the middle of the retreat, a common occurrence, the monastery began to accept new senior meditation monks into the retreat to keep the hall filled. I never knew a three-year retreat undertaken at a major monastery to finish, however, and all of Songgwang-sa's broke up after a year and half, at the most. Many monks may initially be attracted by the mystique of the three-year retreat, but few have the maturity of practice needed to endure its hardships. Monks begin to leave, often during the first few months, and as the group's commitment wanes, more follow. This problem of convincing monks to stay was exacerbated by the Koreans' belief that they should practice in one place only so long as the conditions there suit their needs. Once those conditions change, they are used to going out traveling until they find an appropriate spot. Hence, Korean monks tend to stay on the road much of the time, a habit that is difficult to alter. Once the number of participants in our three-year retreats had dropped to a handful, Songgwang-sa reverted to its regular retreat schedule to bring its population back up to normal.

The fewer monks who begin a three-year retreat, the greater seem its chances of success. The only three-year retreat I knew to finish was one started by a group of "friends on the path" (toban). They found a small monastery with a great room (k'ŭnbang), whose abbot gave them permission to hold the retreat there. Permission was readily granted, since such a retreat brings much prestige to a monastery. Sources of support were easily lined up, even though the temple was not particularly well off. This small group of five close friends had better cohesion and its members were more devoted to one another and to the whole idea of the retreat than was the case at large monasteries. Also, because of their personal ties, they did not want to create distractions for one another's practice by leaving and made a greater effort to stay for the duration.

END OF THE RETREAT

The three-month retreat ends on full-moon day. After meditation in the early morning and breakfast, the *Vinaya* master conducts a public reading of the precepts, either the bodhisattva precepts or the *Prātimokṣa*. Dinner follows, and the day culminates in a final lecture by the Sŏn master. During the break between dinner and the lecture, each monk in the monastery is given an envelope containing five thousand wŏn (in the mid-1970s, this was worth about seven dollars). This money will be used to fund the first leg of a monk's travels during the free season. A bundle of these envelopes is given to the meditation hall proctor (*chikse*), who distributes them to the meditation monks after the end of the lecture.[33]

No formal practice is scheduled for the afternoon following the closing lecture of the retreat. It is time to relax, and the meditation monks who remain pass the afternoon hiking in the mountains and chatting. A good half of the monks in meditation hall will leave the monastery for parts unknown that very day, with another quarter following during the first week of the free season. The monks seem to vanish for the next two months. Many go to small hermitages to visit friends or just to get away from the rigid routine of the large monasteries. Others may make a short stop at their home monasteries to pay respects to their ŭnsa teachers. Perhaps a few will even visit their parents or home villages. For most, though, it is a time for pilgrimage to other monasteries, to travel and unwind, and to reestablish contacts with fellow meditators who passed the retreat elsewhere. While many monks travel during the free season, relatively few end up in the cities, even in the capital of Seoul, because of the dearth of monastic facilities there. Most cities and towns have only small missionary halls (*p'ogyo-tang*), which may be branch temples of a large mountain monastery, functioning almost like a parish church. Such temples rarely have large guest quarters. Because of the proscription of Buddhism during the Chosŏn dynasty, no monasteries were constructed in Seoul until the very end of that dynasty and there are still few accommodations for traveling monks. What is perhaps more surprising is that few monks will be found in any of the major monasteries. Songgwang-sa often felt deserted for several weeks after the end of the retreat; often only four or five monks attended the dinner service in the main buddha hall. The medita-

---

[33] For the duties of this officer in Chinese monasteries, see *Pai-chang ch'ing-kuei* 4, T 2025.48.1132c19–24.

tion hall continues to operate, but under the looser schedule of "discretionary practice" (*chayu chŏngjin*). It is really not until about a month
before the start of the next retreat that the big monasteries begin to be
repopulated, as monks arrive to look over the meditation hall and its residents and make their decision as to where to meditate next.

CHAPTER NINE.

The Officers of the Meditation Compound

JUST AS THE support division has a number of special officers who are responsible for running the large monastery, so, too, does the meditation precinct (*sŏnwŏn*) have its own set of officers, who are charged with the meditative training of the monks.

THE SŎN MASTER

At the forefront of these officers is the Sŏn master, the spiritual and administrative head of the largest Korean monasteries. And just as the meditation hall is the locus around which much of the activity in such monasteries revolves, so, too, is the Sŏn master at the center of much of the monastery's official business.

The Sŏn master is most commonly chosen from among those advanced meditators who have had a long association with the monastery and will generally be one of the leading disciples of the former master. While the optimal candidate should have impeccable meditative credentials, it is also valuable if he has previous administrative experience, perhaps as the abbot of a smaller branch temple of the main monastery. He resides in a separate hall located within the meditation compound, in proximity to those areas where his duties most often lie. But in addition to his official residence, the Sŏn master may also have his own hermitage, perhaps at quite a distance from the main monastery itself. Kusan *sŭnim* built a private hermitage, large enough only for himself and one attendant, at the ridge of the mountains surrounding Songgwang-sa. Sŏngch'ŏl *sŭnim*, the Sŏn master at Haein-sa, has a much more lavish hermitage—really a small monastery—over a mile up the mountain. During retreat seasons, he journeys down to the main monastery for his fortnightly lecture, but quickly returns to his hermitage. Despite the rhetoric in Sŏn literature about finding peace even amid the hustle and bustle of the world, serious meditators thrive on solitude and even supposedly enlightened masters relish what chances they can make to escape from the demands of their positions. Given how public their positions are, a private retreat is the only way for them to enjoy any solitude. The new master at Songgwang-sa, Hoegwang Sŭngch'an, has a novel solution to this need for occasional release from the burdensome duties plaguing the spiritual leader of a large monastery. He was for many years the abbot at Tonghwa-sa, outside Taegu, and still has strong affinities with that monastery. Rather than a separate hermitage, he typically spends as much time as he can manage at his old monastery, including most of each free season.

Sŏn masters of large monasteries in Korea may have received either sanction (*in'ga*) or dharma transmission (*chŏnbŏp*) from a recognized Sŏn master and thus become part of a family tradition of such teachers. While these two terms are basically synonymous, Pŏpchŏng *sŭnim*, an eminent monk well known as a scholar and essayist and now the provost at Songgwang-sa, once tried to distinguish them for me. Sanction, he explained, can mean simply the informal, private recognition by a teacher of a student's potential to finish his practice and ultimately to gain enlightenment. Dharma transmission, on the other hand, is the formal, public conferral of a master's teachings to someone who has already received in'ga and is thus the official recognition that the student now has sufficient advancement in his practice to teach others. In either case, the monk does not have to be a direct disciple of the master from whom sanction or transmission is received. While Kusan had many disciples of his own throughout his career, and guided at one time or another virtually every meditation monk in the country, he died without giving either form of recognition to anyone. This reticence to confer such public recognition of meditative achievement is common to all Sŏn masters in contemporary Korea.

As with the abbot, a candidate for Sŏn master is chosen at a "forest congregation" (*imhoe*) of senior monks in the monastery's family lineages and officially appointed by a majority vote of the monks then resident in the monastery. That appointment, which carries an initial ten-year term, finally must be approved by the Chogye Order headquarters in Seoul, though that approval invariably rubber-stamps the monastery's own decision. If the master does not perform adequately, a petition signed by fifty monks would be enough to have the Chogye Order sponsor a recall election under its auspices, though again it would be the monastery residents who finally make the choice. Even if the master were deposed, the head officers, who are almost all drawn from the same lineage, would continue to control the monastery and could still try to bring in another of their own dharma family's teachers to assume the master's office.

In Korea it would seem arrogant and pretentious for such a teacher to call himself a Zen master (*sŏnsa*). The master usually uses the term *chung* (member of the congregation) to refer to himself, as do all other monks. Others simply refer to the master respectfully in the vernacular as the great monk (*kŭn sŭnim*), or by his official title, which can be either *chosil sŭnim* (monk occupying the patriarch's room) or *pangjang sŭnim* (monk in charge of the monastic quarters, or chief of the precincts).[1] The latter title is reserved for those Sŏn masters who guide the four ch'ongnims. There are also some meditators who are considered Sŏn masters even though they do not assume such a public position. They may prefer to stay with one or two disciples at an isolated mountain hermitage, thus limiting the distractions that visitors create for their practice.

The Sŏn master's main duty is to supervise the spiritual training of the monastery residents. This duty he seeks to carry out through periodic lectures, through personal interviews with his students, both lay and ordained, and, perhaps first and foremost, by acting as an exemplar of spiritual achievement for the monks to emulate. Sitting in meditation involves a relatively minor portion of his day. Only occasionally will the master join the monks in the meditation hall, and even then just for one or two fifty-minute periods at a time. One of the few times I recall Kusan sitting through an entire session at Songgwang-sa was during yongmaeng chŏngjin, the one-week meditation intensive. But the master does sit privately in his own room when he can find the time, typically late at night or before dawn.

Despite the emphasis placed on a Sŏn master's expertise in practice, his duties in fact go far beyond meditation training. He is the ultimate authority on all important decisions affecting the monastery, whether spiritual, administrative, or financial in nature. While the abbot (chuji), the head of the support division of the monastery, supervises the monastery's daily affairs, he consults closely with the Sŏn master on all matters of policy. The master holds frequent meetings with the abbot, the head office monk, and the treasurer to discuss major issues facing the monastery. Even though the Sŏn master does not actually run the monastery, since his own disciples or nephews in dharma fill most of the important posts, these filial relationships enable him to exert strong indirect control. For this reason, the monastery's spiritual and temporal concerns converge in the person of the Sŏn master. The master also does much of the entertaining of the monastery's lay adherents, many of whom will have been longtime supporters of the Sŏn master and the monastery. Indeed, there is a constant stream of visitors coming to the master's room, often to consult on relatively mundane matters, so he needs considerable fortitude to maintain his rigorous schedule.

However eminent the Sŏn master may be, his position is ultimately akin to that of others in the monastery. He is initially appointed for a ten-year term and is reappointed by the monks at the beginning of each retreat

---

[1] For the etymology of the term *pangjang*, see Martin Collcut, *Five Mountains: The Rinzai Zen Monastic Institution in Medieval Japan*, Harvard East Asian Monographs 85 (Cambridge: Harvard University Press, 1981), pp. 197–201.

season, in a kind of vote of confidence in his performance. In theory at least, the monks may remove him at any time through a majority vote of the monastery residents, though in practice this rarely occurs. The meditation monks cast their real votes on the master's abilities by their attendance at the biannual retreat seasons. When the meditation hall is full, perhaps even to the point of having to create an overflow hall to accommodate all the practitioners who want to participate, you know that a master is well regarded by his charges. Similarly, the meditation monks' absence during a retreat will be eloquent testimony to their loss of confidence in a master.

The Sŏn master's authority can be rather precarious and depends on the goodwill of the congregation. I found this out graphically during the winter retreat of 1974–1975 at Songgwang-sa. One of the other foreign monks staying in the meditation hall had developed a gastric irritation from all the red pepper that Koreans eat in their food. He complained to Kusan that the food was too spicy and asked him to have it made milder. Kusan himself had been looking for an excuse to cut back on spices anyway and ordered the proctor to make the changes.

The Korean meditation monks were livid. Having their food rendered insipid was bad enough. But for this arrogant foreigner to have gone directly to the Sŏn master to request such a change and not gone through the appropriate channels (starting with the succentor of the meditation hall) was even worse. And to top it all off, Kusan had supported this foreigner over what he knew to be the preferences of the Korean monks.

The monks struck back. The succentor of the meditation hall ordered the proctor to place separate bowls of red pepper out for the meditation monks at every meal, which, to make their point, they enthusiastically shoveled into their food. A few days later, when Kusan left Songgwang-sa for a three-day lecture tour among the urban lay societies, the succentor demanded that the rector call a meeting of the entire congregation. There he presented the meditation monks' demands that red pepper be put back in the food and that the foreigner who had precipitated all the trouble be ejected from the monastery for insubordination. Although the rector did his best to calm the inflamed emotions, he had little choice but to relent. Red pepper was restored and the foreigner was told to leave the meditation hall. (He was secreted away in an isolated compound inside the monastery pending Kusan's return, not sent away from the monastery.)

On the day Kusan returned the proctor was in a quandary: put out separate bowls of red pepper, as he had when the master was last in the monastery, or put the spice directly into the food as the monks had demanded? Apparently deciding that discretion was the better part of valor, the proctor went back to separate bowls. During the meal, a few of the monks muttered aloud about how horrible the food was—an unheard-of breach of etiquette during the silence of formal meals—and the tension was thick throughout the refectory. When the meal was finally over, Kusan sternly lectured the monks about their own insubordination and urged them to try to be understanding of the difficulties that foreigners had in adapting to Korean customs and food. A couple of the meditation monks then and there picked up their bowls and walked out, screaming that they would never again return to Songgwang-sa. By the next morning, fully half of the meditation monks had quit the monastery, completely disrupting the meditation hall for the remainder of that retreat season. Although the succentor remained behind to maintain the integrity of the retreat, only the most junior monks (and two other foreign monks, myself included, who had nowhere else to go), remained. But by the next retreat season, all was forgotten, and the meditation hall was again filled. Even a couple of the monks who had been ringleaders in the insurrection eventually returned a few seasons later, holding no grudges.

The Sŏn master interviews the meditation monks only once or twice during a retreat period. On such occasions, the meditation monks, donning full regalia, file out of the hall in groups of five or so to the master's room. There, each is interviewed separately by the master. While the other monks wait in the alcove, the monk enters the room, prostrates himself three times, and remains kneeling while he is questioned. The master asks him what hwadu he is working on, asks how he understands it, and usually ends by encouraging the monk to generate the sensation of doubt and to be diligent in his practice. These meetings are much less formal than the Japanese *dokusan*, the extremely brief, ritualized encounters between a Rinzai Zen master and the student, which may occur several times daily during a retreat (*sesshin*). Korean Sŏn interviews can be extended discussions about practice—both technique and understanding—and will continue as long as the student has questions. When the discussion is finally over and the master tells him to leave, the monk once again prostrates himself three times and withdraws with his palms together in hapchang, always facing the master. Returning to the meditation hall, he takes off his formal robes, places them back at their appropriate spot, and resumes his seat. Once most of that group have returned, the next group of five will stand, don their robes, and head for the master's room.

Whenever a monk has something he wants to ask the master, he simply has to inform the succentor of the meditation hall and he will receive ready permission to go. Such visits are one of the few times a monk is allowed to miss a meditation period. The master's acolyte greets him at the front door, ask him his name and business, and conveys this information to the master, who then admits the monk. Many younger monks are so awed by the master that they go to talk with him only when required, and even then only with much trepidation. But more senior monks, who have been practicing for years, seldom want to go either, boasting with monkish bravado that they need to get on with their practice, not chat with the teacher. Since Korean Sŏn monks generally keep the same hwadu throughout their career, there rarely is much new to ask once their concentration coalesces. These few meetings are virtually the only individual contact a meditation monk has with the Sŏn master during the entire three months of the retreat.

At several points in this narrative, I have referred to the meditation monks as the master's "students." But this master-student relationship is not nearly as formal and restrictive as we might suspect from most Western accounts of the Zen tradition. Korean Sŏn monks travel constantly throughout the country, rarely spending two consecutive retreats in the same monastery. Few develop a deep personal rapport with a single teacher. A monk's affinities are really more with his fellow meditation monks, rather than with a specific master. In fact it is the exception when a meditation monk actually comes from the monastery where he practices. When a monk returns to his home monastery, there is such heavy pressure on him to assume a position in the support section of the monastery, which is invariably understaffed, that a monk who wants to devote himself to practice does better to stay away. Often the monks of the home monastery return only once a year for a memorial observance (as for the Sŏn master's deceased teacher), and then leave the next day, before they can be forced to accept a job. During my five years in the meditation hall, I felt I knew more Haein-sa monks, and knew them better, than my own dharma brothers from Songgwang-sa. So a master's "students" are whichever monks are then resident in the meditation hall. Over the course of many retreat seasons, a master may come to have close connections with the meditation monks who return most frequently to his monastery, but there is no formal, publicly acknowledged relationship between them. A monk is identified by his home monastery and his vocation master, not by his connection to a Sŏn master. In this way, Buddhist thought and practice is kept separate from the person of the master; a monk learns from many teachers, but does not take any one person's version of the dharma to be definitive.

The Sŏn master has at least one attendant, or acolyte (sija), who stays with him, usually in the tiny alcove at the front of the master's room.[2] The acolyte is typically one of his newly ordained disciples, and this po-

---

[2] Several different types of acolytes are described in Chinese and Japanese sources, which are no longer known in Korea. For these types, and their various duties, see *Pai-chang ch'ing-kuei* 4, T 2025.48.1131c9–1132a8; and Collcutt, *Five Mountains*, pp. 239, 243–45.

sition will often be the first a young novice will hold in the monastery. The acolyte performs a variety of chores for the master: preparing tea for the master and his guests; making the herbal tonics that many Korean monks drink daily; folding the master's formal robes after services; sweeping and mopping his room; making sleeping arrangements for the master's guests; attending the master during his travels; calling monks or officers whom the master wants to see; and perhaps even handling some of his personal correspondence. The acolyte is thus a combination butler, maid, and secretary to the Sŏn master. For a novice still relatively unaccustomed to the monastic life, it is extremely tiresome to follow the same schedule as the Sŏn master. I knew several of Kusan's acolytes to become sick a few months after accepting the position and be forced to resign the post. The acolyte has little time to himself or much chance to rest, but he has the advantage of developing a close personal relationship with the master, a relationship that helps to create a familylike rapport between the older and younger generations of a monastic lineage. For this reason, despite its hardships, the position of acolyte is the most prestigious a new monk can occupy in the monastery, and the young monks will do much to impress the master enough to convince him that they are worthy of assuming the position.

THE RECTOR

Second only to the Sŏn master in the authority and respect that he commands in the monastery is the rector (*yuna*; Skt. *karmadāna*).[3] As the nominal head of the meditation compound, the rector is always a monk well known for his meditative attainments; these, in fact, will often rival those of the Sŏn master himself. Indeed, a particularly adept rector often functions unofficially as a second Sŏn master. The main difference between the two is relatively subtle: while the master guides the monks in the development of their practice, the rector's role is primarily to bolster that development. Younger meditators, for example, can be so awed by the master that they are too inhibited to ask him about their practice. The rector can, however, deal with the monks more as a colleague than as a teacher and thus develop an easier rapport with them than might the master.

The rector's principal duty is to remain available to the monks for personal advice and counsel. Rather than confronting a monk, as would the master, to force him into generating the sensation of doubt, the rector

---

[3] For the etymology of the title *yuna*, and the duties of the rector, or precentor, see *Pai-chung ch'ing-kuei* 4, T 2025.48.1132b4–20.

instead tries to encourage him to continue with his practice without becoming discouraged. He therefore teaches simply by relating his own experiences in meditation, and those of other monks he knows, or by telling folksy tales about past meditators. These tales can help to raise the spirits of disheartened students and restore their enthusiasm for meditation.

The rector during my years at Songgwang-sa was an extremely shy and soft-spoken man, who was painfully modest about his own attainments—often, the monks felt, as a subterfuge to create rapport between himself and the meditators. Though he was renowned among the meditators for his achievements, he routinely lamented that the only hope he had left for his own practice was to hurry up and die. He had made a fervent vow to be reborn in a Buddhist family in which both of the parents meditated so that he could get an early start in his next life on his unfinished practice. He often commented on his misfortune at having been able to become a monk only in his early thirties, thereby losing the best years in life for meditation. When he was a young boy, he told us, he often sat by himself in the corner of his room and dropped effortlessly into meditative absorption, or samādhi. His uncle had taught him a simple way of meditating by staring at the slats on the paper doors, which he learned to do for hours at a stretch.

Once, this same uncle mentioned in passing that a person who could develop a perpetual motion machine would not only become rich, but would make life better for the entire world. The future rector said that he was fascinated by this notion and for days on end he could think of nothing else but the question, "What is a perpetual motion machine?" So intense was his concentration that he forgot whether he was walking or eating. After a week in this state, his family, for obvious reasons, became increasingly worried about him. He finally became so frightened that he had to force himself to stop thinking about the question and eventually his concentration dissipated. Kusan once explained that what the rector had been describing was the profound fear that confronts a student in the last stages of hwadu meditation, when he is about to let go of his attachment even to his own sense of self and fall into emptiness (*nakkong*). Few practitioners are able to take this deeply unsettling step, and at his young age, with no one to guide him, it was simply too much to expect that he would have had the courage to continue.

That experience of fear constituted the rector's real initiation into Sŏn practice, though he would not learn of its significance until some twenty years later. By that time, he explained, his concentration was so poor that he had been able to duplicate the experience only twice in his entire meditative career. Now, he said, when he sat, he just fell asleep because his body was so weak; when he read the sūtras or records of Sŏn masters, he just got a headache because his eyes were so bad.

With this seemingly pathetic tale, the rector was cautioning the youthful monks who always make up the majority in the meditation hall to take advantage of the excellent opportunity they now had, which he himself had missed, and make some real progress while they were young. His humility endeared him to the meditation monks and allowed him to function that much more easily in his edifying role.

The rector's position is a hybrid one. Unlike most other offices in the monastery, his involves no administrative duties. Since the succentor (*ipsŭng*) is in control of the day-to-day functioning of the hall and the enforcement of the hall regulations, the rector's main duty is simply to ensure that the atmosphere in the meditation hall remains conducive to practice. Often the rector is a member of the same monastic or ordination family as the Sŏn master himself, and therefore has some filial ties with the master. Such ties help to maintain a harmonious relationship between the two men and the consistency of their mutual instructions. Hence, even though the rector functions independently from the master himself, their two styles complement each other. As a permanent member of the monastic staff who is, nevertheless, a full-time meditator, the rector is ideally suited to act as a liaison between the semipermanent support staff of the monastery and the itinerant monks of the meditation hall. Hence, his position helps to alleviate the misunderstandings that can occur between these relatively isolated divisions of the monastery.

Unlike China, where the rector usually participated in the formal sitting in the meditation hall and was the major authority figure, his Korean counterpart rarely practices with the other monks. Although a younger rector might join in the group meditation practice, ours at Songgwang-sa never entered the hall except for an occasional inspection. Usually the rector maintains a private room within the meditation compound, both to give himself some of the privacy a senior monk deserves, and to provide a place where the officers of the meditation hall can confer together on policy. As talking is forbidden in the hall and its immediate environs, the succentor and his deputies go to the rector's room to discuss with him any matters concerning the running of the hall. The rector rarely gives orders to the hall officers; his is mainly an advisory role. But because he does have long experience with meditation halls, his advice is welcomed.

The rector cooperates closely with the proctor (*wŏnju*) in deciding upon the schedule for any group work (*taejung ullyŏk*) that is upcoming. When a major job approaches, the proctor visits the rector at his room and they decide together on a time for the work, the goal being to create the least distraction for the meditation monks, while ensuring that the work is completed on time. Then, immediately after breakfast or dinner, the rector announces the work to all the monks in the meal room, telling them the time, place, and any particular tools or other items that they should bring along.

The rector is also responsible for organizing and directing any group meetings that involve all the monks, as well as supervising the formal dharma lectures given by the Sŏn master during the retreat seasons. He is in charge of striking the chukpi, the split bamboo clacker that is the symbol of authority in the monastery, to mark the beginning of the formal lectures. He is also officially supposed to strike the chukpi during the formal meals as well as to give the signals for the various steps in setting up, serving, seating, and cleaning up the meal room. Usually, however, he delegates this authority to the verger of the refectory.

The rector is appointed once every six months at the meeting before the formal retreat season. Like the Sŏn master and abbot, he is usually elected by acclamation and will often continue in his position indefinitely unless he is determined to retire or move on. Upon his election, two monks rise from the assembly and, taking the chukpi, which has been placed on a small tea table, they place it before the rector and prostrate themselves three times. This symbolizes that the rector is accepting the authority for the monastery's discipline, as invested in the chukpi.

For some meditation monks, like our rector at Songgwang-sa, the position may be the culmination of their careers. Ours was a meditation monk with no scholarly bent or interest in administration. He was also not the dynamic type of person who was comfortable addressing large groups of people, regardless of how personable he may have been in one-to-one meetings. For him, the rector position seemed ideal, for it required neither the teaching competence of the Sŏn master nor the facility for administration so essential for an abbot. Nevertheless, as the second-highest position in the monastery, it did provide the status and esteem to which an accomplished senior meditator was entitled. Even so, many monks who are perfectly qualified to be rectors will simply stay on in hermitages for the remainder of their days and continue practicing in solitude, disdaining to return to the large, bustling monasteries.

THE SUCCENTOR AND THE DISCIPLINARIAN

Inside the meditation hall itself live the two main deputies of the rector, who are invested with actual control over the hall's day-to-day functioning: the succentor and his assistant, the disciplinarian. In China, the succentor was little more than the acolyte of the precentor (*yuna*), or rector, as I have called him here; his role was simply to strike, on the rector's orders, the signals that indicated the different events occurring during the meditation period.[4] His status has been much upgraded in Korea, where he is invested with more real authority in the meditation compound than anyone except the Sŏn master.

The succentor is known under two separate titles, each implying slightly different responsibilities. First, as ipsŭng, or "he who upholds the thread [of practice]," he is in charge of enforcing the schedule and regulations of the meditation hall. In that capacity, he strikes the chukpi at the beginning and end of meditation periods, checks that the duties assigned to each of the meditation monks are performed, and generally keeps the hall functioning smoothly and with the least amount of distractions. He wields the warning stick (changgun chukpi) that is used to rouse drowsy monks during sitting practice. He also acts both as the spokesman for the meditation hall at any group meetings of the monastery residents and as its representative at any meetings between the Sŏn master, rector, and abbot. At some monasteries, the succentor may also be known as the yŏlchung,[5] or "he who gladdens [that is, inspires] the assembly." Implied in this title is the supervisory authority he retains over all the other precincts of the monastery and the control he is expected to exercise over the conduct of all the monastery's residents. Often, the succentor will walk around the monastery and talk with monks outside the meditation hall to get a feeling for the general attitude prevailing among the rank and file. Hence, even though the succentor is hierarchically subordinate to the rector, he often wields much more actual power than his superior.

The importance of the succentor to the disciplined functioning of the meditation hall cannot be overemphasized. The more concerned he is with the mundane aspects of life in the meditation hall—ensuring that the monks are keeping the meditation schedule, maintaining silence, and observing proper decorum—the better is the entire atmosphere of the hall. Such efficiency benefits both himself and his fellow meditators, for the group lifestyle of the hall requires close attention to seemingly trivial details if the monks are not to disturb one another, creating obstacles for their practice. Indeed, the dignity that pervades a hall supervised by a strict succentor is an inspiration in and of itself, regardless of the practical advantages to meditation accruing thereby. An intensity of practice can also be sensed in the disciplined hall that is lacking in a poorly run one.

The succentor is chosen from among the resident meditation monks

---

[4] See discussion in Holmes Welch, Practice of Chinese Buddhism: 1900–1950, Harvard East Asian Studies 26 (Cambridge: Harvard University Press, 1967), pp. 55–56.

[5] According to the Pai-chang ch'ing-kuei (chüan 4, T 2025.48.1132b23), this title was originally the translation for the transliterated term yuna. Johannes Prip-Møller uses the wrong character yüeh for this title on p. 75 of his Chinese Buddhist Monasteries: Their Plan and Its Function as a Setting for Buddhist Monastic Life (1937; reprint, Hong Kong: Hong Kong University Press, 1982), but the correct one is on p. 361.

prior to the beginning of the retreat. He is usually one of the more adept meditators in the hall, commonly one of the old hands (*koch'am*; lit. old contemplatives), in his thirties with ten years or more of meditation practice behind him. The preference for someone of this age group is intentional: the succentor should be young enough to have good rapport with the relatively new monks, who make up the majority of the hall, but also old enough to be able to deal informally and without undue diffidence with the more senior monks. Of all the qualities necessary for the smooth running of the hall—and ultimately the success of the entire venture of group meditation—harmony between the participants is most essential. A succentor who is both young in age and yet senior in rank is best able to ensure such harmony. As might be expected, the succentor is often a monk who has been ordained since his youth and knows the ins and outs of practically every aspect of monastery life. This familiarity with monastic routine becomes all the more important when his supervisory role is taken into account.

But the position of succentor is not one that is particularly prized by the meditation monks; indeed, arms must often be twisted to get the candidate to accept. Obviously, any monk who has been meditating for so long from such an early age is serious about his own practice and typically does not want to be bothered with the drudgery inherent to the succentor's many and varied responsibilities. When a qualified monk sees that there is little chance for him to avoid the position, he will usually acquiesce, but out of a sense of duty rather than real pleasure or pride. Often, there is much jockeying among the candidates to decide who will finally have to take the position. A monk who has gained a reputation as being a good succentor will find that reputation following him wherever he goes. To keep from becoming a professional succentor, he has to threaten to run away, plead sickness, or lobby for the candidacy of one of his rivals (each of whom might be trying to make the same case themselves). But a monk who has shown a particular talent for the position has either to resign himself to holding the job until the next generation of monks matures—meaning some ten years of heavy responsibility—or else retire to a hermitage where he can practice undisturbed. Perhaps not so coincidentally, then, it is often in his early thirties that a meditation monk becomes a hermitage habitué, occasionally returning to a meditation hall for a retreat or two, but remaining primarily in solitude. Finally, in his later years, as his practice matures—or his health fails—a monk might return to a large monastery as the rector, or if he has displayed real meditative and administrative abilities, as the abbot or Sŏn master.

The succentor's second in command is the disciplinarian (*ch'ŏngjung*), literally "he who purifies the assembly." The disciplinarian is officially in charge of administering punishment to monks who have broken any of the rules of the meditation hall; nowadays, however, his duty is more ceremonial. The disciplinarian position is often filled by a monk qualified to be the succentor, who has managed to wheedle his way out of that appointment. As a ceremonial post with few actual responsibilities, the duty provides a comfortable niche for the serious meditator who wants to get on with his practice.

Punishment is handled semiformally in the meditation hall. When a monk is guilty of an infraction, the succentor calls him before all the monks at the end of the meditation period. After prostrating himself three times before the seated monks, and while remaining seated on his heels before the monks with his palms together in hapchang, the culprit is asked to explain the reasons for his misconduct. If his explanation is deemed insufficient, the succentor will suggest an appropriate punishment, which is then carried out by the disciplinarian. For minor infractions, such as arriving late for the meditation period, this punishment involves nothing more than prostrating himself three times before the monks and apologizing. For more serious infractions, such as insubordination or brawling, he might be given a beating with the warning stick by the disciplinarian. And for the heaviest of offenses, such as breaking one of the major precepts, he could be beaten or even expelled.

But I found it to be only in the most extraordinary of circumstances that a monk was ever brought before the assembly for disciplining. If a pattern of misbehavior is developing, the succentor speaks with the monk privately and encourages him to reform, rather than embarrass him in front of his peers. Obviously, too, if there were lots of punishments for minor infractions being administered, the atmosphere of the hall would become poisoned, making the punishment worse than the infraction itself. The only season I participated in meditation hall when the succentor was keeping to the letter of the law and administering frequent punishments, the group became quickly disillusioned with their leader, and most ran away. Thus, if at all possible, the succentor tries to keep his reprimands on a more personal level, going public only when private negotiation proves fruitless. Most often monks circumvent reprimands by deciding on their own to prostrate themselves in repentance before their colleagues when they have committed a transgression.

Occasionally, if the succentor and disciplinarian are planning on staying in residence for more than one retreat, they might make a pact together to trade off positions the following season in order to give each of them a break from the heavy responsibilities of the main leadership position. During one of the three-year retreats begun at Songgwang-sa, the eligible monks had agreed to switch positions every month so that there would not be a burden on any one person. Finally, however, it ended up that one monk stayed on as succentor until he finally had had enough and disappeared, at which point the job passed to the next candidate.

MINOR JOB POSITIONS IN THE HALL

Everyone in the hall, in addition to the succentor and his staff, must hold a position for the retreat period. Some positions that do not require much work are set aside for senior monks, such as being verger (*chijŏn*) of one of the many small shrines scattered around the monastic campus. This job involves performing a simple service once a day of lighting candles and incense, and prostrating oneself three times before the image, along with occasional cleaning of the shrine. Other more demanding positions, such as being a firemaker (*hwat'ae*) or doing cleanup (*ch'ŏngso*) in and around the meditation hall and grounds, are typically delegated to younger monks. Finally, the youngest novices are tapped to be the meditation hall tea boys (*tagak*).

Another important job, usually filled by one of the rare meditation monks who is in residence at his home monastery, is that of meditation hall proctor (*chikse*). The proctor is the liaison between the meditation hall monks and the kitchen staff and is in charge of procuring whatever supplies are necessary for the hall residents. He lists any supplies that are low, tea needed by the tea makers, any other daily needs, and medicines a monk might request, and either gets them himself from the storehouse in the kitchen or asks the monastery proctor to buy them on his next trip into town. All needed items are obtained through this liaison so that other monks do not need to go to the kitchen area themselves.

Toward a Reappraisal of Zen Religious Experience

IN THE PRECEDING treatment of contemporary Sŏn monasticism in Korea, I have tried to convey some sense of the living context of Korean Sŏn practice. While this description is, I believe, important in its own right, I would like to suggest here more broadly what this account may tell us about many of the shibboleths concerning the nature of the Zen religious experience found in Western writing on the school. Let me examine briefly some of these shibboleths, and then offer possible alternative interpretations based on the testimony of Sŏn monastic life in Korea.

Perhaps the most fundamental self-definition of the Zen school repeated ad infinitum in Western literature—so fundamental that it is often made to constitute a virtual root paradigm of the Zen tradition[1]—is the famous four-line aphorism attributed to Bodhidharma, the Indian monk whom the Zen tradition considers to be its founder.[2] The first two lines of this verse enunciate the Zen school's own vision of its unique pedigree within Buddhism: Zen is a "special transmission of Buddhism distinct from the teachings, which is not dependent on words and letters." Taking the statement at face value, many Western writers depict Zen Buddhism as radically bibliophobic and advocate that doctrinal understanding has no place in Zen training. But would such a reading be correct? Sŏn monastic life in modern Korea suggests not. Most Korean monks training in the meditation hall have extensive knowledge of Buddhist doctrine, ranging from basic "Hīnayāna" and Mahāyāna sūtras, to theoretical treatises on Sŏn praxis and collections of Sŏn lore. Most began their meditation training only *after* they were steeped in the basic teachings of Buddhism. Many had several years of study in the seminary behind them before they even considered starting meditation; as one monk told me, an infant must learn to crawl before it tries to walk, and so too must monks study before they begin to meditate.

[1] The term was coined by Victor Turner, *Dramas, Fields, and Metaphors: Symbolic Action in Human Society*, Symbol, Myth, and Ritual Series (Ithaca, N.Y.: Cornell University Press, 1974), p. 64, and chap. 6. See also the discussion of this term in chap. 8 of his book.

[2] Although this aphorism does not appear as a set formula until the twelfth century, its individual lines can be traced to some of the earliest works of the Zen tradition. For the textual history of this aphorism, see Isshū Miura and Ruth Fuller Sasaki, *Zen Dust: The History of the Koan and Koan Study in Rinzai (Lin-chi) Ch'an* (New York: Harcourt, Brace and World, 1966), pp. 229–30.

The putative bibliophobia of Zen is also readily belied once one realizes that virtually all Korean monks can read classical Chinese, the literary language of Korean Buddhism throughout its history. While their reading is often in the recitative style taught in monastery seminaries, they usually could parse Chinese sentences accurately and pronounce ritual phrases correctly. Their knowledge of Chinese was at least serviceable and was, in many cases, impeccable. Since this extensive knowledge of literary Chinese would have been learned not in the public schools but in the monasteries (or in the traditional Confucian academies, or sŏdangs, for the very oldest of monks), doctrinal understanding is obviously something valued highly within the Korean Zen tradition. To show how far this literary knowledge extends, some of the most popular readings among Sŏn monks today in Korea are Korean vernacular translations of the Pali scriptures of Theravāda Buddhism, about as far from Zen texts as one can go in Buddhism. One monk who served as the catechist at Songgwang-sa for several years told me that the pragmatic quality of the Pali materials was especially appealing to meditators, as they did not find many practical instructions in their own Sŏn literature for dealing with the inevitable problems that can arise during meditation—lassitude, distraction, fantasizing. The monks are also aware of the scholarly debunking that much of Zen's traditional history has suffered in the last fifty years and now seem more open to using texts from other branches of the Buddhist tradition. So while meditation monks may not read regularly during retreat periods, they are decidedly not ignorant of Buddhist doctrinal teachings.

The last two lines of "Bodhidharma's" aphorism concerning the nature of Zen state that the soteriological purpose of the tradition is "to point directly to the human mind so that one may see the nature and achieve Buddhahood." But even this seemingly obvious claim that Zen is intent on enlightenment—and that, by extension, its monasteries were formed to train people in such attainment—is not necessarily borne out when looking at its monastic institutions. While it is true that the meditation hall and the monks practicing there are the focus of much of the large monastery's activities, the majority of its residents spend no time in meditation, and many have no intention of ever undertaking such training. Zen monastic life is broad enough to accommodate people of a variety of temperaments and interests—administrators, scholars, workers—offering them many different kinds of vocations.

This view of Zen as focused purely on the goal of enlightenment may derive from an exaggerated sense some scholars of religion may have of the importance of transformative experience in religious endeavors, à la William James, a point made by Michael Carrithers in his definitive study of meditation monks in Sri Lanka.[3] The testimony of the Korean monastic community, however, suggests instead that a disciplined life, not the transformative experience of enlightenment, is actually most crucial to the religion. This need not necessarily be even an examined, or an informed, life, though those would be highly prized, but one that is so closely and carefully structured as to provide little opportunity for ethical failings or mental defilements to manifest themselves. A disciplined life offers a monk the potential for mental control, which may eventually mature into a thoroughgoing concentration on his topic of meditation, or hwadu. The Koreans (and the Chinese and Indian Buddhists before them) created such structured regimens for their monasteries because they recognized that few meditators would have much chance of progressing in their practice without them. In this endorsement of discipline over transformation, the Sŏn monks of Korea would find much in common with their Buddhist counterparts in Southeast Asia—or even with the Benedictines of France.

Related to this issue of enlightenment is the presumption pervading much of Zen literature that enlightenment is realized suddenly, not through a gradual unfolding of truth. Indeed, the self-identity of some schools of Zen, such as Chinese Lin-chi, has sometimes been framed in terms of subitism: Zen praxis is characterized as focusing exclusively on the enlightenment experience itself, the claim being that a full and complete awakening would perfect automatically all forms of religious cultivation.[4] One of the most trenchant presentations of this position is found in a verse by the Chinese Lin-chi monk Chung-feng Ming-pen (1263–1323) written during the Yüan dynasty:

> Ch'an meditation does not involve any progression,
> The absolute essence is free from all extremes and representations.
> It is difficult using the limited mind,
> To cultivate the unconditioned path.
> In one realization, all is realized.
> In one flash of cognition, all is cognized.[5]

---

[3] William James, *The Varieties of Religious Experience* (1902; reprint, London: William Collins and Sons, 1969), cited and discussed in Michael Carrithers, *The Forest Monks of Sri Lanka: An Anthropological and Historical Study* (Delhi: Oxford University Press, 1983), pp. 18–20. Carrithers argues that the way of life fostered in Theravāda monasteries is not a by-product so much of meditative experience as of moral purity. See also the spectacular enlightenment stories described in Philip Kapleau's influential *Three Pillars of Zen* (Tokyo: John Weatherhill, 1965), which suggests that such experiences are commonplace.

[4] For a discussion of various interpretations of subitism in Chinese and Korean Zen, see Robert E. Buswell, Jr., "Chinul's Ambivalent Critique of Radical Subitism in Korean Sŏn Buddhism," *Journal of the International Association of Buddhist Studies* 12, no. 2 (1989): 20–44.

[5] *T'ien-mu Chung-feng ho-shang kuang lu* (Extended Records of Monk Chung-Feng of

Even a casual perusal of Korean Sŏn literature will reveal that there is much support within the Korean tradition for subitism. The technique of kanhwa Sŏn, virtually the only type of meditation used in contemporary Korean monasteries, is even termed a "shortcut" (kyŏngjŏl; Ch. ching-chieh) to enlightenment because of its emphasis on generating an instantaneous awakening instead of developing a sequential series of practices. But when Korean meditation monks who are training in the kanhwa technique routinely admit that they expect it will take upwards of twenty years of full-time practice to make substantive progress in their practice, there seem to be valid grounds for questioning how subitist in practice the Sŏn tradition really is.

Another of the putative root paradigms of Zen, which Western scholarship often reiterates, is that Zen values manual labor.[6] The locus classicus for this view is the famous phrase of Pai-chang Huai-hai (720–814), the putative creator of the Zen monastic codes, who is claimed to have said, "A day without work is a day without food."[7] Po-chang's institution of regular labor in his monastery is commonly portrayed as being one of the principal innovations of Zen Buddhist monasticism. The paradigmatic example of the Zen monk devoted to work is the Sixth Patriarch, Hui-neng (638–713), whom Zen texts depict as an illiterate country bumpkin employed as a menial laborer in the monastery's mill before his enlightenment. But the emphasis on how unusual it was for a laborer such as Hui-neng to ascend to the patriarchy suggests, to the contrary, that it was decidedly atypical for the Zen monk to work.[8] One wonders to what extent this impression of Buddhist monasticism in Western literature has been subtly influenced by Christian models, where a life of labor was especially emblematic of the Cistercians.[9] In fact, meditation monks in Korea do little, if indeed any, work; the monastery instead seeks to keep their time free for contemplation. Although every monk in the monastery has a specific duty during the retreat periods, the meditation monks are

---

Mt. T'ien-mu), Pin-ch'ieh ed. (reprint, Kyŏngsang Namdo: Pulguk-sa Sŏnwŏn, 1977), chüan 17, p. 96b.

[6] Note, as but one of many possible examples in the scholarly literature, Martin Collcutt's representative statement: "Other features of early Ch'an monastic life were its stress on frugality and the sustenance of the community by the joint labor of all its members." Collcutt, Five Mountains: The Rinzai Zen Monastic Institution in Medieval Japan, Harvard East Asian Monographs no. 85 (Cambridge: Harvard University Press, 1981), p. 9.

[7] See his biography in Ching-teh ch'uan-teng lu 6, T 2076.51.250c–251b, and Sung Kao-seng chuan, T 2061.50.770–71.

[8] An argument made convincingly by John R. McRae in his The Northern School and the Formation of Early Ch'an Buddhism, Studies in East Asian Buddhism, no. 3 (Honolulu: University of Hawaii Press, a Kuroda Institute Book, 1986), pp. 42–43.

[9] See the discussion in Max Weber, The Sociology of Religion (1922; reprint, Boston: Beacon Press, 1963), p. 181.

invariably given all the lightest jobs—serving as the verger of a small shrine (required to perform a cursory, five-minute service each day), for instance, or sweeping the meditation hall (twenty minutes). The most time-consuming work, such as tilling, planting, and working the fields or logging the forests, is done by hired laborers (who in the past would have been serfs awarded to the monasteries). The most odious of daily tasks crucial to running the monastery, such as preparing meals or cleaning the latrines, are carried out by unordained postulants. Most other important jobs are performed by the many monks, often new to their vocations, who occupy support positions in the monastery. After a monk has finished his postulancy and perhaps a few years of service to his home monastery, he could conceivably pass the rest of his life in the meditation hall, doing virtually no manual labor at all.

Western works on the Japanese tradition of Zen often convey the impression that Zen is deeply concerned with artistic expression. Probably no book has been more influential than D. T. Suzuki's *Zen and Japanese Culture* in positing this pervasive impact of Zen on indigenous aesthetic culture.[10] Suzuki's book finds Zen in areas ranging from landscape architecture to flower arrangement, the tea ceremony, haiku and other poetry, painting, Nō drama, even swordmanship and martial arts. But the testimony of Korean Sŏn monastic life (as, I have been told, is also the case in modern Japanese Zen) offers little support for such a view. Korean Sŏn monasteries provide no institutionalized backing for such aesthetic activities and set aside no time in the daily schedule for monks to pursue them. The support staff is much too busy to have time for painting or poetry. The meditation monks are required to be totally devoted to their practice and would not even be allowed to use a brush for painting or calligraphy. While the monks are concerned with keeping the monastery neat and tidy (by sweeping the grounds daily, for example), the landscaping has more the look of benign neglect than of loving attention; throwing a handful of cosmos seeds next to the mud wall surrounding their compound was about the extent of the concern the Korean monks I knew had with beautifying the natural environment. Monks drink a lot of tea, but there is none of the close attention to the details of the process that we are led to presume should be the case from the Japanese tea ceremony. Some of the elderly monks might do calligraphies when laypeople visit, but these are intended as presents for the laity, done as a tacit exchange for their support. Even if one takes a charitable view, artistic endeavors have extremely low priority in the practice of Sŏn monks in Korea.

Finally, many Western works on Zen describe the school as attempting

[10] Daisetz T. Suzuki, *Zen and Japanese Culture*, Bollingen Series 64 (Princeton: Princeton University Press, 1970).

to develop forms of Buddhist praxis that would appeal to the special religious needs of the laity—"to bring salvation within the reach of ordinary people," as one scholar has noted.[11] To show how ubiquitous this view has become with Zen scholars—even among scholars who should know better—let me cite my own work on the historical development of Zen praxis. In an article on the evolution of the kanhwa technique, I claim that Zen sought to make "the *summum bonum* of Buddhism [viz. enlightenment] readily accessible to ordinary people living active, engaged lives in the world, and not just to religious specialists ensconced in isolated mountain monasteries."[12] I describe Ta-hui, the Chinese systematizer of kanhwa Sŏn, as "embrac[ing] ordinary life as the ideal venue for Buddhist meditation practice."[13] To be fair to myself, I did qualify these statements by suggesting that Zen did not mean "to impugn cenobitic training," but was simply "countering a persistent bias in Buddhism toward celibate monastic life."[14] But even if one accepts this caveat, the realities of modern Sŏn training in Korea testify that it is only within the specialized praxis institution of the meditation hall that anyone has much of a chance to succeed at kanhwa practice. Even monks in the support division of the Korean monastery are presumed to be so busy with their sundry duties that they are not meditating. But if the demands of meditation practice are considered to be beyond the ability of even the support monks to fulfill, what reasonable hope would there be for laypeople? The protestations of past masters to the contrary, Sŏn monastic life suggests that the technique of kanhwa Sŏn was never seriously intended for the laity, but instead targeted those few monks with the fortitude to endure many years of ascetic training in the meditation hall.

Modern Sŏn monks in Korea train within an extensive web of religious thought and practice, a web that reticulates with the historical, institutional, and cultural contexts of their centuries-old tradition. These monks know that while Zen masters teach sudden enlightenment, they follow in their daily practice a rigidly scheduled regimen of training. They know that while Zen texts claim to eschew doctrinal understanding, monks are expected first to gain a solid grounding in Buddhist texts before starting meditation practice. They know that while the iconoclastic stories of the past Zen masters glorify seemingly antinomian behavior, monks are pledged to maintain a sober, disciplined lifestyle. Much of Western scholarship, by contrast, through seeking to interpret the classical literature of Zen in the abstract, divorced from such contexts, has promulgated a na-

---

[11] William Theodore de Bary, ed., *Sources of Japanese Tradition* (New York: Columbia University Press, 1958), p. 232.

[12] Buswell, "*K'an-hua* Meditation," p. 325.

[13] Ibid., p. 353.

[14] Ibid., p. 373 n.128.

ive view of the tradition as *literally* iconoclastic, bibliophobic, and anti-nomian.[15] Zen monks are sophisticated enough in their understanding of their tradition to mediate in their daily lives these polarities—polarities of structure and transformation, discipline and iconoclasm, learning and bibliophobia, morality and antinomianism; it is time that our scholarship learn to do the same.

The vision of Zen presented in much Western scholarship distorts the quality of Zen religious experience as it is lived by its own adherents. But by permitting the monastic tradition of Zen to speak for itself, as I have tried to do in this book, we glean a rather different picture of the religion. When Zen is viewed instead through its monastic training, its putative iconoclasts are replaced by dedicated cenobites, deliberate in their conduct and training. Zen's apparent bibliophobia pales to reveal meditators who are all learned in literary Chinese and who often have extensive experience in Buddhist seminaries. The proclaimed antagonism toward systematizations of religion fades before monks who follow in their own careers methodical regimens of training. The challenge supposedly made by its adherents even to the Zen tradition itself yields in the face of men with strong faith in the way of life they have undertaken. Modern Sŏn monastic life in Korea therefore offers a valuable counterparadigm[16] to the usual Western portrayals of Zen, an alternative vision that yields quite a different picture of the day-to-day reality of Zen religious experience from that to which we in the West have become accustomed.

[15] I have benefited here from T. Griffith Foulk's comments on an earlier draft of this chapter.

[16] Victor Turner, *Dramas*, p. 15.

Songgwang-sa after Kusan

IT WAS some four years after I returned to the United States that Kusan died. His health, already unstable for several years, had begun to worsen in early October of 1983, and he suffered what appeared to be a series of mild strokes. As if aware that his days were numbered, Kusan had one of his disciples write down for him his deathbed verse:

> The autumn leaves covering the mountain are redder than flowers in
>   spring.
> Everything in the universe fully reveals the great power.
> Life is void and death is also void.
> Absorbed in the Buddha's ocean-seal samādhi, I depart with a smile.[1]

But by mid-November, Kusan's health appeared to be improving. He had recovered to the point that he felt able to deliver the opening lecture at the winter retreat that was about to begin. While preparing the draft of his sermon, however, he suffered an unexpected turn for the worst—a major stroke that left his left side partially paralyzed. Although physically unable to deliver the opening lecture, he still insisted on greeting the meditation monks at his residence, and gave them some brief words of advice and encouragement. The next day a still more severe stroke left him completely paralyzed on the left side and in a badly weakened state. He remained in about the same state for the next month, unable to speak and hardly able even to open his eyes. Although he was suffering tremendous discomfort, he managed to rest quietly, continuously turning in his right hand his rosary of large wooden beads.

A few days before his death, Kusan gathered all his remaining strength and recited the following brief verse to tell his disciples that he was departing this world:

> Saṃsāra and nirvāṇa are originally not two;
> The sun rising in the sky illuminates the trichiliocosm.

As death neared, Kusan asked his disciples to lift him into a sitting position. While sitting in the meditation posture, he entered nirvāṇa at the

---

[1] Quoted in the introduction to Kusan Sunim, *The Way of Korean Zen*, trans. by Martine Fages, ed. by Stephen Batchelor (New York: Weatherhill, 1985), p. 50. My account of Kusan's death is indebted to a personal communication from the Foreign Saṃgha of Songgwang-sa, dated 18 December 1983.

Sŏn master's residence of Samil-am. The time was 6:25 P.M., on Friday, 16 December 1983.

At his death, the great bell in the courtyard at Songgwang-sa tolled 108 times. A small altar was set up in Samil-am in front of the departed master and candles and incense were lit as offerings. The entire assembly of monks filed in to bow three times and pay their last respects. He was then moved to a larger hall, where uninterrupted meditation continued before the body for twenty-four hours a day, the monks rotating in groups of five.[2]

On 20 December, the fourth day after his demise, a funeral procession of monks, nuns, and laypeople, carrying multicolored banners and all wearing white gloves, escorted the body in a casket draped with flowers to the cremation ground at a site in the mountains above Songgwang-sa.[3] Monks at the front of the procession carried a censer, a portrait of the master, and a spirit tablet, which they used to make a temporary altar at the cremation ground. A lengthy funeral service was held and Kusan's body finally cremated. The next day, after the fire had dissipated, the monks discovered fifty-three relics (sari; Skt. śarīra) glimmering in the ashes. They carefully gathered the relics with chopsticks for later enshrinement in Kusan's reliquary. The few bits of bone remaining in the ashes were pulverized between two tiles and scattered into the wind in the mountains near his private hermitage at the top of Chogye Mountain.[4] Kusan had "entered quiescence" (ipchŏk hasyŏtta), as Korean monks say of their deceased colleagues. He was seventy-four years of age.

Soon after Kusan's death, senior monks in Songgwang-sa's monastic lineage were summoned to the monastery for a "forest meeting" (imhoe) to choose a successor. But Kusan had never conferred formal dharma transmission, nor had he designated anyone to be his immediate successor, so there was no clear candidate for the position of Sŏn master. Because of Kusan's worsening health, many meditation monks had decided

---

[2] Paraphrasing a personal communication concerning Kusan's death, dated 18 December 1983, from the Foreign Saṃgha of Songgwang-sa.

[3] The banners were inscribed with such Buddhist slogans as the Avataṃsaka-sūtra's famous line "the first arousal of the thought of enlightenment is right enlightenment" (Ta-fang-kuang Fo Hua-yen ching 8, T 278.9.449c14). See the picture of Kusan's funeral procession in Kwan-jo Lee, Search for Nirvana: Korean Monks' Life (Seoul: Seoul International Publishing House, 1984), p. 96. Banners were also carried in Chinese funeral processions prior to 1949; see Michael Loewe, Ways to Paradise: The Chinese Quest for Immortality (London: George Allen and Unwin, 1979), p. 30.

[4] More commonly after a monk's cremation, any remaining pieces of bone are pulverized in a mortar, mixed with wheat paste, and formed into small balls, to be scattered around the mountains for the animals to eat. For non-Buddhist Korean funerary rites, see C. Paul Dredge, "Korean Funerals: Ritual as Process," in Religion and Ritual in Korean Society, Korea Research Monograph, no. 12, ed. by Laurel Kendall and Griffin Dix (Berkeley: Institute of East Asian Studies, 1987), pp. 71–92.

to spend the winter retreat of 1982–1983 at Songgwang-sa in order to have one last exposure to the man and his teachings. These monks included a number of senior meditators who had spent many seasons training at Songgwang-sa under Kusan and who felt they had the best sense of whom Kusan would have preferred to take over his position. But none of the accomplished meditators whom they suggested as candidates for the Sŏn master position was a member of Songgwang-sa's dharma family, though one of them had spent much of his career at the monastery and its surrounding hermitages. The monastery administration was adamant, however, that the position should go to someone in the Songgwang-sa family. After a fractitious debate, the monastery officials finally nominated as Sŏn master one of Kusan's direct disciples, Ilgak, the abbot of Tonghwa-sa (who took the name Hoegwang Sŭngch'an upon his appointment), over the meditators' objections. When it became apparent that the administration would not relent, the meditators left Songgwang-sa en masse rather than acquiesce in the decision. While a vote was eventually taken by the remaining residents and the administration's nominee confirmed, Hoegwang has struggled to gain the confidence of the meditation monks. Although I found him to be a disarmingly modest and charming man, with a warm and compassionate demeanor (and an eerie physical resemblance to Kusan), the consensus among the monks is that his dharma talks are weak—though a couple of monks with some perspective noted that Kusan's talks, too, had been poor during his first years as a teacher.

Seemingly discouraged about the entire situation, the new Sŏn master spends much of his time away at his old monastery, including almost all of the free seasons. These frequent absences have undermined morale at Songgwang-sa. Over the last several years, only a handful of meditation monks have spent retreat seasons at Songgwang-sa. To save the face of both the Sŏn master and his monastic family, the only practical recourse the monastery now has, one monk told me, was to let the master finish his ten-year term, and then not reappoint him. In the interim, power inside the monastery has shifted away from the Sŏn master to the abbot and provost.

Whatever depredations may have occurred in the quality of its meditation training, however, Songgwang-sa has prospered economically, as is the case in much of Korea over the past two decades. When I first arrived at Songgwang-sa in 1974, there were still no paved roads into the monastery and it was a grueling two-hour ride by rickety rural bus from Kwangju, the nearest major city. Although the temple had just been wired for electricity, it still had no phone lines, and certainly no sewage system or flush toilets. Such conditions are now but a vague memory. On my last stay at Songgwang-sa, in the summer of 1988, there was a beautiful paved road to the monastery, built especially to handle the caravans of tourist buses that regularly visited the temple. Songgwang-sa owned four cars of its own and kept a driver in the village on twenty-four-hour call. The monastic officials kept in touch with each other over intercoms and walkie-talkies—no more postulants sent running with messages to the abbot or the prior. While television had still not invaded the monastery, there were radios in the rooms of some of the support staff.

The many new buildings constructed since Kusan's death are the most visible signs of the vastly increased wealth of the monastery. This construction has dramatically expanded the size of the monastic campus. In addition to a huge new main buddha hall, these new structures include a museum, a large, open-air assembly hall for lay meetings, expanded abbot's and visitors' quarters, and a modern bathhouse and bathroom facilities. Plans are afoot to renovate the kitchen area and the backup meditation compound, and there is even talk of building an entirely new meditation hall separate from the main campus.

Since the monastery has had little success recently in attracting practice monks to the meditation hall, the administration has decided instead to emphasize lay proselytization (p'ogyo), sponsoring frequent training sessions for college students and laypeople. Perhaps because of the problems at the meditation hall, the seminary has received renewed attention from the administration and seems finally to be flourishing, after several false starts during my years there. There is also a strong contingent of monastic intellectuals living in the temple, drawn in large part by the reputation of Pŏpchŏng sŭnim, a renowned essayist and translator, who is one of Songgwang-sa's most eminent family members.

But the financial benefits Songgwang-sa has received from Korea's economic progress have also placed new secular pressures on the monastery, pressures that are impinging as never before on the traditional religious life. Burgeoning economic growth has created a new market among the urban middle class for leisure activities. The government has made national parks out of many of the major Buddhist monasteries, which are located in the most scenic and pristine natural sites on the Korean peninsula. Waves of tourist buses pull into the new parking lot below the monastery, disgorging hordes of Korean tourists outfitted in lederhosen and knee socks, carrying alpine gear and climbing picks for their visit to the "deep mountains." Few things can damage irreparably the delicate solitude of the contemplative life as thoroughly as noisy tourists can. Although tourists are restricted to nonresidential sections of the monastery, it is still a major disruption to have so many visitors—few of whom have any interest in Buddhism—tramping through the monastery every day.

Facing these encroachments, some Korean monasteries, such as Pulguk-sa, near the old Silla capital of Kyŏngju, have taken the drastic step of effectively abandoning their complexes to the tourist trade and moving their practice divisions into new compounds located far from the main temple. These new compounds function more as independent hermitages than as integral parts of the monastery. While such moves may be making the best of a difficult situation, monastic Buddhism is increasingly being driven out of its own sanctuaries.

With this dramatic growth in the tourist trade, the small village below Songgwang-sa has also expanded and now boasts several multistory hotels, restaurants, and cafeterias, all catering to the thousands of visitors who come to Songgwang-sa each year. In a controversial move, the monastery administration decided to construct its own hotels and restaurants in the village as a way of raising money for the monastery. While this move has benefited the monastery financially, it has also created a potential new threat to the spiritual vocations of the support officials, who must now spend much of their time in the village among the laypeople supervising these businesses.

Buddhist institutions, which outlasted some five centuries of persecution during the Chosŏn dynasty, will survive these latest challenges. Haein-sa, which is even more burdened by the tourist trade than is Songgwang-sa, has made a renewed commitment to its practice traditions and has managed to remain a pulsating monastic center in contemporary Korea. Such success in adapting to the encroachments of modern, secular society augurs well for the Korean monastic tradition as a whole—and for Songgwang-sa.

Appendix

Principal Chants Used in Korean Monasteries

I INCLUDE in this appendix translations and/or transcriptions of the major liturgical chants used in Korean monasteries. All the chants are composed in literary Chinese and are pronounced as Sino-Korean. Long portions of many of the chants involve Sino-Korean transcriptions of original (or pseudo) Sanskrit or Middle Indic codes (dhāraṇī) and spells (mantra), which are recited purely for their esoteric value.

The morning bell and evening bell chants are recited by the chief verger alone, before the morning service and evening service, respectively. The homage to the Three Jewels is the main devotional chant at both morning and evening services. The formal meal chants are recited in unison by all the monks at each midday meal. The *Heart Sūtra* is recited in unison at most ceremonial functions and services. The *Thousand Hands Sūtra* (*Ch'ŏnsu-kyŏng*) is the principal chant used in all offering ceremonies and funeral observances; it is recited alone by one ritual specialist, with perhaps one assistant, but rarely by the congregation in unison. It is also the morning wakeup chant intoned by the chief verger as he wends his way through the monastery compounds.

Morning Bell Chant

I vow that the sound of this bell will pervade the dharma-realm,
Illuminating entirely the murky darkness of the iron perimeter [of hell],
Relieving the suffering of the three evil destinies, and destroying the
    Mountain of Swords [Hell],
So that all sentient beings will attain right enlightenment.

Homage to the Master of the Teaching, Vairocana Buddha,
The compassionate lord of the Lotus-Womb World,
Who expounded the treasured verses' golden texts,
And spread open the precious cases' jade scrolls,
Wherein one dust mote penetrates fully all other dust motes,
And one realm is completely interfused with all other realms.
These are the 10,000,000,095,048 words,
Of the one vehicle's consummate teaching:
Homage to the *Expanded Flower Garland Sūtra (Spoken by) the Buddha*:

If a person wants to know,
All the buddhas of the three time-periods,
Then he ought to observe the nature of the dharma-realm:
Everything is created by mind alone.

The Mantra of Shattering Hell

Namo attasijinam sammyaksammot-tta kuch'inam om ajanababasi chirijiri
hum (*repeated three times*)

I vow that for the rest of my life, without any extraneous thoughts,
I will follow him with the unique features, Amitābha Buddha.
Thought after thought will constantly merge with the rays of his jade-like
excrescence [*uṣṇīṣa*],
Thought-moment after thought-moment will never leave the qualities of his
golden form.
Holding meditation-beads, I contemplate the dharma-realm,
While empty space becomes a string leaving nothing unconnected.
There is nowhere that Rocana Buddha is not present equally.
Through my contemplation, I seek Amitābha of the Western Region,
Homage to the great teaching-master of the Western Region,
The Buddha, the Tathāgata, of Infinite Life.

Homage to Amitābha Buddha. (*repeated a hundred or a thousand times,
as time allows*)

The Land of Ultimate Bliss has ten kinds of adornments,
Homage to Amitābha Buddha:
It is adorned with Dharmakāra's vow, his cultivation-cause,
Homage to Amitābha Buddha, (*repeated henceforth after each line*)
It is adorned with the power of his forty-eight vows,
It is adorned with Amitābha's name and the brilliance of his life force,
It is adorned with the bejeweled images observed by the three mahāsattvas,
It is adorned with the peaceful bliss of Amitābha's land,
It is adorned with jeweled rivers, running with pure and meritorious waters,
It is adorned with bejeweled basilicas with halls of wish-fulfilling jewels,
It is adorned with lengthy days and nights,
It is adorned with the Pure Land's twenty-four kinds of pleasures,
It is adorned with the thirty kinds of beneficial merit.
That buddha, who is unparalleled in heaven or on earth,
He is also unmatched throughout the worlds of the ten directions,
He has seen the annihilation of self in everything in the world.
There is no one who is like that buddha,
He can keep track of thoughts as numerous as all the dust motes in the
universe,
He can quaff all the water in the oceans,
He can control the wind that fills space.

No one can completely describe that buddha's merits,
Amitābha Buddha is omnipresent,
Keep your thoughts on him and never forget,
As thoughts probe that place of no-thought,
The six sense-gates will constantly emanate light of purple and gold.
His face, like the full moon, is at the front of the Hall of Ultimate Bliss,
His jade excrescence and his gold form radiate through space.
If a person calls his name for only a moment,
He will instantly consummate immeasurable merit.
Along with all sentient beings of the dharma-realm, I vow,
Together to enter the sea of Amitābha's great vows,
And to ferry across sentient beings until the end of time,
So that I and others may simultaneously complete the path to Buddhahood.

The Sublime Mantra of the Original Mind of Amitābha Buddha
tanyat'a om aritara sabaha (*repeated three times*)

Evening Bell Chant

Hearing the sound of this bell,
Defilements are eradicated,
Wisdom grows,
Bodhi arises.
Leaving behind hell,
Abandoning the triple world,
I vow to achieve buddhahood,
And ferry across all sentient beings.

Shattering Hell Mantra
Om karajiya sabaha (*repeated three times*)

Homage to the Three Jewels

(Chief verger alone:)

May the fragrance of our morality, our concentration, our wisdom, our
   liberation, and our knowledge and vision of liberation—may all this form
   a bright, shining, cloud-like pavilion that fills all the dharma-realm,
   thereby doing homage to the countless buddhas, their teachings, and their
   congregations, in all the ten directions.

Mantra of the Incense Offering
Om pa-ara tobiya hum (*repeated three times*)

(Entire congregation in unison:)

We most devoutly pay homage to the guiding-master of the triple world, the
   loving father of all creatures, our original teacher, Śākyamuni Buddha.

We most devoutly pay homage to the eternally existent assembly of all the buddhas in all the ten directions, throughout the past, present and future, as countless as the lands and seas in Lord Indra's net.

We most devoutly pay homage to all the eternally existent dharmas in all the ten directions, throughout the past, present and future, as countless as the lands and seas in Lord Indra's net.

We most devoutly pay homage to all the venerable bodhisattva-mahāsattvas; and especially do we pay homage to the bodhisattva of great wisdom, Mañjuśrī; the bodhisattva of great practices, Samantabhadra; the bodhisattva of great compassion, Avalokiteśvara; and the bodhisattva of great vows, Lord Kṣitigarbha.

We most devoutly pay homage to the countless assemblies of compassionate saints; and especially do we pay homage to those who received the Buddha's injunction at Vulture Peak: the ten major disciples, the sixteen [arhat] saints, the five-hundred saints, the saints who practiced alone, and all the 1,200 great arhats.

We most devoutly pay homage to the teachers who came from the west to the east to our Korean shores, to all the great patriarchs who transmitted the lamp of dharma from generation to generation, to all the masters throughout the world, and to all the great spiritual mentors as numberless as dust motes.[1]

We most devoutly pay homage to the eternally existent congregation of all the saṃghas, in all the ten directions, throughout the past, present and future, as countless as the lands and seas in Lord Indra's net.

We most earnestly desire that these inexhaustible Three Jewels will most lovingly and compassionately receive our devotions, and that they will empower us spiritually; furthermore, we vow that, together with all sentient beings throughout the dharma-realms, we may all attain the path of buddhahood at one and the same time.

The *Heart Sūtra*

Avalokiteśvara Bodhisattva, when practicing the profound perfection of wisdom, beheld that the five aggregates were all empty and passed beyond all suffering and distress.

"Śāriputra! Form does not differ from emptiness; emptiness does not differ from form. Form is just emptiness; emptiness is just form. The same is true of sensations, perceptions, impulses, and consciousness [the five aggregates].

"Śāriputra! All dharmas are marked by emptiness: they neither arise nor

[1] Songgwang-sa, as the Saṃgha jewel monastery, replaces this verse with its own unique homage to Korean teachers, honoring specifically Chinul, the founder of the Korean tradition of Sŏn, and the national masters of the Koryŏ and early Chosŏn dynasties, all of whom resided at Songgwang-sa.

cease, are neither tainted nor pure, are neither augmented nor deficient. For this reason, in emptiness there is:

no form, no sensations, perceptions, impulses, or consciousness;

no eye, ear, nose, tongue, body, or mind [the six sense bases];

no form, sound, smell, taste, touch, or mind-object [the six sense objects];

no visual sphere . . . up to no consciousness sphere [the six sense spheres];

no ignorance and also no extinction of ignorance . . . up to no old age and death and also no extinction of old age and death [the twelvefold chain of dependent origination];

no suffering, origination, cessation, or path [the four noble truths];

no cognition and also no attainment, for there is nothing to attain.

"Since bodhisattvas rely on the perfection of wisdom, their minds are untrammeled. Because they're untrammeled, they're fearless. Leaving far behind distorted views and dream-like perceptions, finally—nirvāṇa!

"Since all the buddhas of the three time-periods rely on the perfection of wisdom, they attain complete, perfect enlightenment.

"Therefore know that the perfection of wisdom is the great spell; the spell of great knowledge; the unsurpassed spell, the unequaled spell, which can allay all suffering. This is true, not false. So recite the perfection-of-wisdom spell, recite the spell that says:

gate gate paragate parasaṃgate, bodhi svāhā [*repeated three times*]

[Gone, gone, gone beyond, gone utterly beyond. Enlightenment! Hail!]"[2]

Formal Meal Chanting

(Congregation is seated; verger strikes *chukpi* (bamboo clacker) once; monks recite in unison:)

The Buddha was born in Kapilavastu,
Achieved enlightenment in Magadha,

[2] Probably all Buddhist scholars have tried their hand at translating the famous *Heart Sūtra*. My version was first prepared as part of an ongoing debate within the Kwan Eum Zen school, a group of Western practitioners of Korean Sŏn Buddhism under the direction of the Korean teacher Seung Sahn (Haengwŏn) *sŭnim*. Some of the women in that organization were disturbed at putative sexist elements in the translation of the text the school was using (suggestions, for example, that bodhisattvas were all male), while others felt that the many Sanskrit technical terms in the translation were too daunting to people new to Buddhism. I decided to try and come up with a rendering that was philologically accurate and yet still accessible, while expunging any sexist overtones. Whatever merits there may be in my rendition, the Kwan Eum Zen school sticks to tradition and continues to use its old version. The text is translated from Hsüan-tsang's definitive Chinese version (*Mo-ho po-jo po-lo-mi-to hsin ching*, T 251.8.848c), which is used in all the East Asian Buddhist traditions.

Spoke the dharma in Benares,
And entered extinction in Kuśinagara.

(Monks unwrap bowls and set them out on their placemats:)

These bowls of the Tathāgata, which respond according to one's needs,
I now set them out,
And vow, together with the entire congregation,
That the three wheels [giver, receiver, and gift] will become equally void
 and calm.

(The meal is served; after food has been distributed:)

The pure dharma body, Vairocana Buddha,
The consummate reward body, Rocana Buddha,
The myriad transformation bodies, Śākyamuni Buddha,
He who will advent in the future, the Lord Buddha Maitreya,
All the buddhas of the ten directions and three time-periods,
All the venerable dharmas of the ten directions and three time-periods,
He of great wisdom, Mañjuśrī Bodhisattva,
He of great practice, Samantabhadra Bodhisattva,
He of great compassion, Avalokiteśvara Bodhisattva,
All of the venerable bodhisattva-mahāsattvas.

(Holding rice bowl to their foreheads:)

Receiving food,
We now vow that all sentient beings,
Will have the joy of meditation as their food,
And be sated by the bliss of dharma.

(Placing bowls back down on their placemats:)

Calculating how much effort [went into producing this food], we
 contemplate on where this [food] came from.
We reflect on whether our own virtue is worthy of this offering.
Our main task is to guard the mind and leave behind faults, such as
 craving, and so forth.
We correctly consider that the salutary medicine [of food] will save our
 bodies from withering away.
We should receive this food in order to complete the task of enlightenment.

(As the rector puts aside a spoonful of rice into a bowl of water as an offering
to the ghosts, the congregation chants:)

You host of ghosts,
To you we now make offerings.
This food pervades the ten directions,
As an offering to all the ghosts.

Om siri siri sabaha

(Verger strikes chukpi three times; monks commence eating. Once the majority of monks are finished eating, the chukpi is struck once to signal that clear water for rinsing bowls is to be distributed. After bowls are rinsed and the remaining clear rinse water collected, the monks chant:)

> We take this bowl-washing water,
> Its flavor like the ambrosia of heaven.
> And offer it to the host of hungry ghosts,
> Causing them to be satiated.

> Om mahyurase sabaha

(The monks dry their bowls and wrap them back up. Once all the monks have finished:)

> The meal is finished, our countenance and strength are restored,
> Our dignified demeanor shakes the ten directions, making us heroes in all
>   three time-periods,
> It reverses causes and turns back effects inconceivably,
> All sentient beings gain spiritual powers.

(The monks rise, place their bowls back on the shelf, and turn; as the verger strikes the chukpi three times, they bow together to all the congregation. The monks then file out of the refectory.)

Chanting at Formal Dharma Lectures

We singlemindedly prostrate ourselves before all the buddhas throughout
   the ten directions and three time-periods.
We singlemindedly prostrate ourselves before all the venerable dharmas
   throughout the ten directions and three time-periods.
We singlemindedly prostrate ourselves before all the sanctified samghas
   throughout the ten directions and three time-periods.

We disciples and our master of the three repositories of the canon,
Wish only that the three jewels will serve as our witness.

We vow that this cloud of sublime fragrance,
Will pervade all the worlds of the ten realms of existence.
Each and every one of the buddha lands,
Will be imbued with this immeasurable fragrance,
Consummating the bodhisattva path,
And perfecting the fragrance of the tathāgatas.

Homage to all the bodhisattva-mahāsattvas covered by this fragrant cloud.
   (*repeated three times*)
Homage to the original teacher, Śākyamuni Buddha. (*repeated three times*)

Verse to Begin the Sermon

That unsurpassed, profound, and sublime dharma,
Is difficult to meet even in a billion eons.
Today we hear, see, receive, and keep it,
Vowing to understand the true meaning of the tathāgatas.

(After the sermon is over, the congregation recites in unison for a while:)

Śākyamuni Buddha

Concluding Verse

The merit accruing from speaking the dharma is an extremely rare act,
We dedicate this boundless, superior merit to other beings,
We vow that all sentient beings, immersed in saṃsāra,
Will quickly reach the realm of the Buddha of Limitless Light.

(Homage to:)

All the buddhas of the ten directions and three time-periods,
All the venerable bodhisattva-mahāsattvas,
Mahāprajñāpāramitā

Thousand Hands Sūtra (Ch'ŏnsu-kyŏng)

Invocation

Today in my concentrated mind,
Appear infinite bodies,
All of which are those of the great, holy Avalokiteśvara.
Each day I bow innumerable times.

Om pa-aramil (repeated three times)

Mantra That Purifies Speech

suri suri mahasuri susuri sabaha (repeated three times)

Mantra That Consoles All the Buddhist and Non-Buddhist Spirits of the Five Directions

namu samanda mottanam om toro toro chimi sabaha (repeated three times)

Verse for Beginning the Sūtra

The unsurpassed, profound, and sublime dharma,
Is difficult to meet even in a billion eons.
Today we hear, see, receive, and keep it;
Vowing to understand the true meaning of the tathāgatas.

Mantra for Opening the Treasure-Store of the Dharma

om aranam arada (repeated three times)

The Vast, Consummate, Unimpeded, Great Compassion, Great Dhāraṇī of the Thousand-Handed, Thousand-Eyed Avalokiteśvara Bodhisattva Invocation

I bow my head before the great compassion dhāraṇī of Avalokiteśvara.

The power of his vows is extensive and mighty, his body [is adorned] with all the major and minor marks [of sanctity].

His thousand-armed visage protects everything.

The brightness of his thousand eyes shines everywhere.

In his unimpeachable speech, the esoteric teaching is communicated.

In his uncompounded thought, the thought of compassion arises.

He quickly satisfies all our hopes.

He forever extinguishes all our unskillful actions.

The gods, dragons, and all the saints together compassionately protect us.

The hundred-thousand samādhis are instantly perfected.

The body that receives and keeps [this dhāraṇī] is a pennant of light,

The mind that receives and keeps [this dhāraṇī] is a treasure trove of spiritual powers.

Cleansing myself of the adventitious passions, I vow to cross the sea [of suffering],

And leap up to bodhi's gate of expedients.

I now recite [this dhāraṇī] and sincerely take refuge in it,

In the hopes that all my vows will be satisfied in this very thought.

Homage to the greatly compassionate Avalokiteśvara,
I vow that I will quickly come to know all dharmas.
Homage to the greatly compassionate Avalokiteśvara,
I vow that I will soon gain the eye of wisdom.
Homage to the greatly compassionate Avalokiteśvara,
I vow that I will quickly ferry across all sentient beings.
Homage to the greatly compassionate Avalokiteśvara,
I vow that I will soon gain skillful expedients.
Homage to the greatly compassionate Avalokiteśvara,
I vow quickly to board the ship of prajñā.
Homage to the greatly compassionate Avalokiteśvara,
I vow soon to cross beyond the sea of suffering.
Homage to the greatly compassionate Avalokiteśvara,
I vow quickly to attain the path where precepts are perfected.
Homage to the greatly compassionate Avalokiteśvara,
I vow to climb the mountain of consummate tranquillity.
Homage to the greatly compassionate Avalokiteśvara,
I vow quickly to discover the uncompounded dwelling place.
Homage to the greatly compassionate Avalokiteśvara,
I vow soon to achieve the body of the dharma-nature.

If I should go to the Mountain of Swords Hell,
That mountain of swords would spontaneously fall into rubble.
If I should go to the Boiling Fire Hell,
That boiling fire would spontaneously be extinguished.
If I should go to [any other] hell,
That hell would spontaneously vanish.
If I should go to the [realm of] the hungry ghosts,
Those ghosts would spontaneously become satiated.
If I should go to [the realm] of the Aśuras,
Their angry thoughts would be spontaneously pacified.
If I should go to [the realm of] the animals,
They would spontaneously attain great wisdom.

Homage to Avalokiteśvara ("Contemplating the Sound of the World")
    Bodhisattva-mahāsattva.
Homage to Mahasthāma Bodhisattva-mahāsattva.
Homage to Sahaśrahasta ("Thousand-Handed") Bodhisattva-mahāsattva.
Homage to Cintāmaṇicakra ("Wish-Fulfilling Jewel Wheel") Bodhisattva-
    mahāsattva.
Homage to Mahācakra ("Great Wheel") Bodhisattva-mahāsattva.
Homage to Avalokiteśvara ("Contemplating Autonomy") Bodhisattva-
    mahāsattva.
Homage to Tranquil Bodhisattva-mahāsattva.
Homage to Full-Moon Bodhisattva-mahāsattva.
Homage to Moon in the Water Bodhisattva-mahāsattva.
Homage to Kuṇḍali ("Water Base") Bodhisattva-mahāsattva.
Homage to Ekadaśamukha ("Eleven-faced") Bodhisattva-mahāsattva.
Homage to all the great bodhisattva-mahāsattvas.
Homage to the Original Teacher Amitābha Buddha.

The Great Dhāraṇī of Spiritually Sublime Phrases (*Sinmyo changgu tae tarani*)
namo-radana tarayaya
namak Aryakbarogijesaebaraya
mojisadabaya mahasadabaya mahagaronigaya
om salba payesu taranagaraya tasamyŏng
namak k'aridaba imam Aryabarogijesaebarataba
niragant'a namak-kkarinayama palt'a-isami
salbat'a sadanam suban ayeyŏm salba podanam
pabamara misudagam tanyat'a
om aroge arogamaji rogajigaranje hehe hare mahamojisadaba
samara samara harinaya
kuro kuro kalma sadaya sadaya
toro toro miyŏnje mahamiyŏnje tara tara
tarinnaryesaebara chara chara mara mimara amara

molche yehyehye rogesaebara ra-a misaminasaya
nabesa misa minasaya mohajyara misaminasaya horo horo mara
horo harye panamanaba sara sara siri siri soro soro motchamotcha modaya
   modaya
Maedariya niragant'a kamasa nalsanam parahara nayamanak
sabaha sittaya sabaha mahasittaya sabaha
sittayuyesaebaraya sabaha
niragant'aya sabaha
paraha mokk'a
singha mokk'aya sabaha panama hattaya sabaha
chagara yoktaya sabaha
sangk'asŏbnanye modanaya sabaha
mahara kut'adaraya sabaha
pama sagant'a isasich'eda karinna inaya sabaha
myagara chalma ibasanaya sabaha
namo-radana tarayaya
namak Aryabarogijesaebaraya sabaha[3]

Praising the Four Directions

First, I cleanse the eastern direction, purifying it into a place of
   enlightenment (bodhimaṇḍa).
Second, I cleanse the southern direction and obtain coolness.
Third, I cleanse the western direction and complete the Pure Land.
Fourth, I cleanse the northern direction and become eternally healthy.

Praising the Bodhimaṇḍa

As the bodhimaṇḍa is purified, without flaw or maculation,
The three jewels and the gods and dragons will now descend to this place.
I now keep and recite this sublime mantra,
Vowing to bestow love and compassion and secretly watch over everyone.

Repentance Verses

The evil actions done previously by me,
Have all resulted from beginningless greed, hatred, and delusion.
All of those evil actions that have arisen from my body, speech, and mind,
From them, I now totally repent.

---

[3] I am parsing the Sino-Korean logographs to approximate as closely as possible the original Middle Indic words in the dhāraṇī; for this transcription see Chŏng T'aehyŏk, "Ch'ŏnsu Kwanŭm t'arani ŭi yŏn'gu" (Studies on the Dhāraṇī of the Thousand-Handed Avalokiteśvara), Pulgyo hakpo (Buddhist Studies Annual) 11 (1974): 105–8. There are slight variations in pronunciations between the various Korean editions. A rough English translation of the dhāraṇī appears in Daisetz Teitaro Suzuki, Manual of Zen Buddhism (New York: Grove Press, 1960), pp. 22–23.

[Homage to] the Twelve Venerable Buddhas through Whose Intercession Karmic Obstacles Are Recanted and Removed

The Buddha Superior Storehouse of Jewels;

The Buddha Jeweled-Light King Whose Radiance Shines Like the Glow of Fire;

The Buddha King of Autonomous Power Who Possesses All Kinds of Perfumes and Blossoms;

The Buddha Ten Billion Sands of the Ganges Decision;

The Buddha Merit Awesome Like an Earthquake;

The Buddha Adamantine Firmness That Extinguishes All Distraction;

The Buddha Universal Light Like the Moon Hall, the Venerable King with the Sublime Voice;

The Buddha Storehouse of Bliss That Collects Wish-Fulfilling Jewels;

The Buddha King of Superior Fragrances;

The Buddha Lion Moon;

The Buddha King of Happiness Adorning Pearls;

The Buddha Surpassing Light of Wish-Fulfilling Jewels as in Indra's Jeweled Pennant.

Repenting from the Ten Evil Actions

Today I repent from the serious transgressions of:

> Killing living beings;
> Stealing;
> Sexual misconduct;
> False speech;
> Flattering speech;
> Backbiting;
> Harsh speech;
> Desire and lust;
> Wrathful anger;
> Deluded ignorance.

Sins that I have accumulated over hundreds of eons,
Are in one thought instantly destroyed.
Just as fire burns dried grass,
They are destroyed completely, without remainder.

Sins have no nature of their own, they arise from thoughts,
When thoughts are extinguished, sins are also dead.
When sins are dead, thoughts extinguished, and both void,
This then is called true repentance.

Repentance Mantra

Om salba motchamoji sadaya sabaha (*repeated three times*)

The collection of merits of Caṇḍi Bodhisattva,
I constantly recollect in my tranquil mind.

All kinds of great difficulties,
Cannot invade this person.
[Whether I am reborn in] heaven or among humans,
I will receive merit like the buddhas.
Coming upon this wish-fulfilling jewel,
I am certain to receive the incomparable [perfect enlightenment].

Homage to the Mother of Seven Koṭis of Buddhas, Great Caṇḍi Bodhisattva
(*repeated three times*)

Mantra for Purifying the Dharma-Realm
Om nam (*repeated three times*)

Mantra for Protecting the Body
Om ch'irim

Avalokiteśvara Bodhisattva's King of Great Knowledge Mantra Consisting of Six Syllables That Reveal the Original Mind
Om mani panme hum (*repeated three times*)

Caṇḍi Bodhisattva's Mantra
Namu sadanam sammyaksammotta kuch'inam tanyat'a om charejure
chunje sabaha purim (*repeated three times*)

I now receive and recite this great Caṇḍi Bodhisattva [mantra],
And make the great vow to attain bodhi.
I vow that my concentration and wisdom will quickly be brought to full
intensity.
I vow that my spiritual merits will all become perfected.
I vow that my supreme merits will adorn everything.
I vow that I will attain the way to buddhahood, together with all sentient
beings.

Text of the Ten Great Vows Made by the Tathāgatas
I vow that I will forever leave behind the three evil destinies.
I vow that I will quickly eradicate greed, hatred, and delusion.
I vow that I will always listen to the buddha, dharma, and saṃgha.
I vow that I will diligently cultivate morality, concentration, and wisdom.
I vow that I will constantly follow the buddhas' training.
I vow that I will never abandon the thought of enlightenment.
I vow that I will be certain of rebirth in favorable circumstances.
I vow that I will quickly see Amitābha Buddha.
I vow that I will project transformation bodies throughout worlds as
numerous as dust motes.
I vow that I will ferry across all sentient beings.

Making the Four Expansive Vows
Sentient beings without limit, I vow to save,
Defilements without end, I vow to eradicate,

Doctrinal instructions without measure, I vow to study,
The path to Buddhahood, which is unsurpassed, I vow to attain.

The sentient beings in my own self-nature, I vow to save,
The defilements in my own self-nature, I vow to eradicate,
The approaches to dharma in my own self-nature, I vow to study,
The way to buddhahood in my own self-nature, I vow to attain.

Having Made Vows, I Now Take Refuge in the Three Jewels
Homage to the buddhas who abide eternally in the ten directions.
Homage to the dharmas that abide eternally in the ten directions.
Homage to the samghas that abide eternally in the ten directions.

ach'im kongyang　아침供養
amja 庵子

chaegong 齋供
chaemu 財務
Chagyŏng-mun 自警文
Chajang 慈藏
ch'an 饌
Ch'angbok-sa tam-Sŏn pang　昌福寺談禪牓
changgun chukpi 將軍竹篦
changjwa purwa 長坐不臥
changsam 長衫
Ch'an-yao 禪要
Chao-chou Ts'ung-shen　趙州從諗
Ch'aun 慈雲
chayu chŏngjin 自由精進
chigaek 知客
Chijang 地藏
chijŏn 持殿
chikse 直歲
Ch'ilbul-am 七佛庵
ch'ilsŏng 七星
Chin'gak Hyesim　真覺慧諶
Chin'gong 真公
Ching-shan 徑山
chinmu 真無
Chinul 知訥
Chiri-san 智異山
Ch'obalsim chagyŏng-mun　初發心自警文
Chogye 曹溪
Chogye-chong 曹溪宗
Chogye-sa 曹溪寺
Chogye-san 曹溪山
Chojo yegyŏng 早朝禮敬
Chŏlla namdo 全羅南道
chŏmsim kongyang 點心供養
ch'ŏnbŏp 傳法
chŏng 情
Ch'ŏngam-sa 青岩寺
Chŏnggak 正覺
Chonggo-ru 鐘鼓樓
chŏnghwa undong 淨化運動
Chŏnghye kyŏlsa 定慧結社
chŏngjin 精進
chongjŏng 宗正

ch'ŏngjung 清衆
ch'ongmu 總務
ch'ongmu-sil 總務室
chongmuwŏn 宗務院
ch'ongmu wŏnjang 總務院長
ch'ongnim 叢林
ch'ŏngso 清掃
Chŏngsu pyŏlchŏn Sŏnjong hwalgu ch'amsŏn kyŏlsa sonjŏn-mun 精修別傳
禪宗活句參禪結社宣傳文
chŏn'gye asari 傳戒阿闍梨
ch'ŏnil kido-hoe 千日祈禱會
Ch'ŏnjin 天真
Ch'ŏnsu-kyŏng 千手經
chŏnyŏk kongyang　저녁供養
chosil 祖室
Chosŏn 朝鮮
Chosŏn Pulgyo wŏlbo 朝鮮佛教月報
Chosŏn Pulgyo yusillon 朝鮮佛教維新論
Chosŏn sŭngnyŏ susŏn cheyo
朝鮮僧侶修禪提要
chuang-chu 莊主
ch'ugwŏn 祝願
chuin'gong 主人公
chujangja 柱杖子
chuji 住持
ckuk 粥
chukpi 竹篦
ch'ulga 出家
chung 衆
chungsaeng mubyŏn sŏwŏn to / pŏnnoe mujin sŏwŏn tan / pŏmmum muryang sŏwŏn hak / Pulto musang sŏwŏn sŏng
衆生無邊誓願度 / 煩惱無盡誓願斷 /
法門無量誓願學 / 佛道無上誓願成
chungch'u-wŏn 中樞院
Chung-feng Ming-pen 中峰明本
chunggang 中講
chŭngsa 證師
Ch'unsŏng 春城
ch'usŏk 秋夕
Ch'wibong 翠峰

dokusan 獨參

Haech'ŏng 海清
Haein-sa 海印寺
haein-to 海印圖
haeje 解制
haengja 行者
haengjŏn 行纏
hae ŏ kukka 害於國家
hae ŏ yulli 害於倫理
hae ŏ p'ogyo 害於布教
hao ŏ p'unghwa 害於風化
Han Yongun 韓龍雲
hapchang 合掌
hoech'ik 會則
Hoegwang Sŭngch'an 廻光僧讚
hua-t'ou 話頭
Hŭijong 熙宗
Hui-neng 慧能
Hung-chou 洪州
Hung-chou Shui-liao 洪州水潦
huwŏn 後援 / 後院
hwadu 話頭
hwalgu 活句
hwansok 還俗
Hwansŏng Chian 喚惺志安
Hwaŏm 華嚴
Hwaŏm-chŏn 華嚴殿
Hwaŏm-kyŏng 華嚴經
hwat'ae 火臺
Hyerin 慧璘
Hyobong 曉峰
Hyŏnho 玄虎
hyŏnmi 玄米

ilchu-mun 一柱門
Ilt'a 一陀
imhoe 林會
Imje 臨濟
in'ga 印可
Injong 仁宗
ip'an 理判
insam 人蔘
ipchŏk hasyŏtta 入寂하셨다
ipsan 入山
ipsŭng 立繩
iptong 入冬

Jōdo Shinshū 淨土真宗

kaeksil 各室
kaek sŭnim 各스님
Kaesŏng 開城

Kaeun-sa 開雲寺
kalma asari 羯磨阿闍梨
kamch'al wŏniang 監察院長
kan 間
kanbyŏng 看病
kanbyŏng-sil 看病室
k'ang 炕
Kangnam 江南
kangsa 講師
kangwŏn 講院
Kangwŏn-to 江源道
kan'gyŏng-p'a 看經派
Kang Yumun 姜裕文
kanhwa Sŏn 看話禪
kanjang 간醬
Kao-an Ta-yü 高安大愚
Kao-feng Yüan-miao 高峰原妙
Kap-sa 甲寺
kasa 袈裟
ki 氣
Kibong 奇峰
Kilsang-sa 吉祥寺
kōan 公案
Kobong Pŏpchang 高峰法藏
koch'am 古參
koch'ujang 고추醬
kohaeng 苦行
kohyang 故鄉
Kojong 高宗
Kŏjo-sa 居祖寺
kongan 公案
Kongmin 恭愍
kongyang 供養
kongyang-chu 供養主
Koryŏ 高麗
Kuei-tsung Chih-ch'ang 歸宗智常
kujok-kye 具足戒
kuksa 國師
Kuksa-chŏn 國師殿
Kŭmdang 錦堂
Kŭmsan-sa 金山寺
K'ŭnbang 큰房
Kusan 九山
Kusan Sŏnmun 九山禪門
Kwakcho 廓照
Kwangju 光州
Kwanseŭm *posal* 觀世音菩薩
Kwanŭm 觀音
Kwanŭm-chŏn 觀音殿
Kye ch'osim hagin mun 誡初心學人文
kyedan 戒壇

Kyeryong-san 鷄龍山
Kyo 教
Kyŏgoe-kwa 格外科
kyogu ponsa 教區本寺
kyŏlche 結制
kyŏlsa 結社
kyomu 教務
kyŏngjŏl 徑截
Kyŏngju 慶州
Kyŏngsang namdo 慶尙南道
kyosu asari 教授阿闍梨

Liang Ch'i-ch'ao 梁啓超
Lin-chi 臨濟
Lin-chi I-hsüan 臨濟義玄
Lin-chi lu 臨濟錄
Liu-tsu t'an ching 六祖壇經

maji 摩旨
mandu 饅頭
Mangwŏl-sa 望月寺
Manhae 萬海
Ma-tsu Tao-i 馬祖道一
Meiji 明治
minjung Pulgyo 民衆佛教
min pangwi 民防衛
Mirae-sa 彌來寺
Mirŭk-sa 彌勒寺
miso 味噌
mokch'im 木枕
mokt'ak 木鐸
mu 無
mua 無我
muae-haeng 無礙行
mugŏn 默言
mu-yü 木魚
Myŏngbu-chŏn 冥府殿
myŏngdŭng 明燈

Naejang-sa 內藏寺
Nakha-tang 洛露堂
nakkong 落空
Namu Amit'a-pul 南無阿彌陀佛
Namwŏn 南原
Nan-ch'üan P'u-yüan 南泉普願
Nan-yüeh Huai-jang 南嶽懷讓
Naong Hyegŭn 懶翁惠勤
nattō 納豆
Nichiren 日蓮
Nim ŭi chimmuk 님의 沈默

nojŏn 爐殿
nonggam 農監

Odae-san 五臺山
oedo 外道
oeho 外護
ohu pulsik 午後不食
ojo kasa 五條袈裟

Paegun-am 白雲庵
Pai-chang ch'ing-kuei 百丈淸規
Pai-chang Huai-hai 百丈懷海
palgi 發起
panch'an 飯饌
pangbu 方房
pangjang 方丈
pangp'yŏn 方便
p'atchuk 팥粥
P'ian e kil 彼岸에 길
pigu 比丘
pigu-kye 比丘戒
pigu kyesik 比丘戒式
pigusŭng 比丘僧
p'ogyo 布教
p'ogyo-tang 布教堂
poim-haeng 保任行
Pojo sasang yŏn'guwŏn 普照思想研究院
pŏmhaeng 梵行
Pŏmmang- kyŏng 梵網經
pŏmmun 法門
pŏmmyŏng 法名
Pŏmnyŏn-sa 法蓮寺
Pŏmŏ-sa 梵魚寺
pŏmp'ae 梵唄
Pongŭn-sa 奉恩寺
ponsa 本寺
ponsan 本山
Pŏpchŏng 法頂
Pŏpchu-sa 法住寺
pŏpho 法護
pŏpkye-to 法界圖
pŏptang 法堂
Poryŏn-sa 寶蓮寺
posal 菩薩
posal kyesik 菩薩戒式
poyak 補藥
Puch'ŏnim sŏngdo-il 부처님成道日
Puhyu Sŏnsu 浮休善修
pulgong 佛供
Pulguk-sa 佛國寺
p'ungsu 風水

punsin 焚身
Puril Hoe 佛日會
Puril hoebo 佛日會報
Puril Pojo kuksa 佛日普照國師
P'u-yen 普眼
p'yegwan 閉關
pyŏlchwa 別座
p'yŏng 坪
Pyŏn'gong 弁公

Sabun-yul 四分律
sach'ŏn-wang 四天王
saengsik 生食
sagu 死句
sa hongsŏwŏn 四弘誓願
sambo 三寶
sambo chongch'al 三寶宗利
sami 沙彌
sami-kye 沙彌戒
sami kyesik 沙彌戒式
Samil-am 三日庵
Samil Undong 三一運動
Sami yurŭi 沙彌律儀
samjik 三職
samnyŏn kyŏlsa 三年結社
Samyŏng taesa 泗(四)溟大師
sang kongyang 床供養
Sangsa-dang 上舍堂
sansin 山神
sap'an 事判
sari 舍利
sasa muae 事事無礙
satori 悟
sesshin 攝心
shen-ma wu 甚麼物
shih shen-ma 是甚麼
sigyuk 食肉
sija 侍者
Silla 新羅
sŏdang 書堂
sŏgi 書記
Sŏkcho 釋照
Sŏkkamoni-pul 釋迦牟尼佛
Sŏktu 石頭
Sŏlbŏp-chŏn 說法殿
Sŏn 禪
Sŏnbang 禪房
sŏndŏk 禪德
Sŏn'ga kwīgam 禪家龜鑑
Sŏngbul-to 成佛圖

Songdam 松潭
Songgwang-sa 松廣寺
songp'yŏn 松편
sŏngsŏng chŏkjŏk 惺惺寂寂
sŏnsa 禪師
sŏnsa-che 先師祭
Sŏnwŏn 禪院
Sŏsan Hyujŏng 西山休靜
sosin 燒身
Sōtō 曹洞
Ssanggye-sa 雙溪寺
Sudo-am 修道庵
Sudŏk-sa 修德寺
sŭng 僧
sŭngbo sach'al 僧寶寺利
sŭngga hagwŏn 僧伽學院
sŭngmu 僧舞
Suryŏn 秀蓮
suryŏn taehoe 修練大會
Susŏn-sa 修禪社
Suu 守愚
Suŭi-kwa 隨意科

taea 大我
Taebi-chu 大悲呪
taebun-sim 大憤心
taech'ŏ 帶妻
taech'ŏsŭng 帶妻僧
taegak 大覺
T'aego-chong 太古宗
T'aego Pou 太古普愚
Taegu 大邱
Tae-Han Pulgyo 大韓佛教
T'aejong 太宗
taejung 大衆
taejung kongyang 大衆供養
taejung ullyŏk 大衆運力
t'aenghwa 幀畫
taeo 大悟
taeŭi-sim 大疑心
Taeung-chŏn 大雄殿
taeyongmaeng-sim 大勇猛心
tagak 茶角
Ta-hui Tsung-kao 大慧宗杲
Ta-hui yü-lu 大慧語錄
tanch'ŏng 丹青
tansik 斷食
t'ap 塔
tap'o 多包
teishō 提唱

teng-lu 燈録
toban 道伴
Tobong-san 道峰山
toenjang 된醬
togam 都監
toksŏ-p'a 讀書派
T'ongdo-sa 通度寺
t'onggam-pu 統監府
Tongguk taehakkyo 東國大學校
Tongguk Yi sangguk chip 東國李相國集
Tonghak 東學
Tonghwa-sa 桐華寺
Tongsan 東山
tono-chŏmsu 頓語漸修
tono tonsu 頓語頓修
Tosŏng-tang 道成堂
Toyotomi Hideyoshi 豊臣秀吉
Ts'ao-ch'i 曹溪
tubu 豆腐

ŭijŏng 疑情
ullyŏk 運力
Ŭngsŏn 應禪
Unmun-sa 雲門寺
ŭnsa 恩師

Waesaek sŭngnyŏ 倭色僧侶
Wŏlchŏng-sa 月精寺
Wit'a 韋陀
Wŏn'gam Ch'ungji 圓鑑沖止
Wŏnhyo 元曉
Wŏnjong 圓宗

wŏnju 院主
wŏnju-sil 院主室
Wŏno Ch'ŏnyŏng 圓悟天英

yangban chase 兩班姿勢
Yaun 野雲
yebi-kun 豫備軍
Yi Hoegwang 李晦光
Yi Hoemyŏng sŏnsa sillok 李晦明禪師實録
Yi Kyubo 李奎報
yŏk 力
yokpul-sik 浴佛式
yoktu 浴頭
yŏlchung 悅衆
yŏnbi 燃臂
yŏndŭng 蓮燈
Yŏndŭng-hoe 燃燈會
Yonghwa-sa 龍華寺
yongmaeng chŏngjin 勇猛精進
Yongsang-pang 龍象榜
Yongsŏng 龍城
Yongun 龍雲
yŏnji 燃指
Yüan-chüeh ching 圓覺經
Yujŏng 惟政
Yul-chong 律宗
yulchu 律主
yulsa 律師
yuna 惟那
Yuna paek 惟那白
Yung-chia Hsüan-chüeh 永嘉玄覺
Yuram 栗庵

Works Cited

UNLESS otherwise noted, all references to Buddhist canonical works are from the *Taishō shinshū daizōkyō* (*T*) edition. Citations to the *Hsü-tsang-ching* (*HTC*) are to the Hong Kong reprint edition of the *Dai-Nihon zokuzōkyō* (Hsiang-kang ying-yin Hsü-tsang-ching wei-yüan-hui, ed.). All references to Pali texts are to the Pali Text Society editions. Texts cited from these standard collections will not be listed separately in this bibliography.

Aepli, Martine. *Korea*. Paris: Souffles, 1988.

An Chinho. *Hyŏnt'o chuhae: Sŏn'yo* (Punctuated and Annotated Edition of the *Ch'an-yao*). 1938; reprint, Seoul: Pŏmnyunsa, 1956.

————. *Sŏngmun ŭibŏm* (Ceremonial Rules of the Śākyan Lineage). Seoul: Pŏmnyunsa, 1961.

An Kyehyŏn. *Han'guk Pulgyo-sa yŏn'gu* (Researches on Korean Buddhist History). Seoul: Tonghwa Ch'ulp'ansa, 1986.

An Pyong-jik. "Han Yong-un's Liberalism: An Analysis of the 'Reformation of Korean Buddhism.' " *Korea Journal* 19, no. 12 (December 1979): 13–18.

Batchelor, Martine. "Buddhist Nuns in Korea." *Karuna* (Winter 1990–1991): 16–18.

Bielefeldt, Carl. *Dōgen's Manuals of Zen Meditation*. Berkeley and Los Angeles: University of California Press, 1988.

Broughton, Jeffrey. "Kuei-feng Tsung-mi: The Convergence of Ch'an and the Teachings." Ph.D. diss., Columbia University, 1975.

Buddhaghosa, Bhadantācariya. *The Path of Purification (Visuddhimagga)*. Translated by Bhikkhu Ñāṇamoli. 2d ed. Colombo: A. Semage, 1964.

Buswell, Robert E., Jr. "Ch'an Hermeneutics: A Korean View." In *Buddhist Hermeneutics*, Studies in East Asian Buddhism, no. 6, edited by Donald S. Lopez, Jr., pp. 231–56. Honolulu: University of Hawaii Press, 1988.

————. "Chinul's Alternative Vision of *Kanhwa* Sŏn and Its Implications for Sudden Awakening/Sudden Cultivation." *Pojo sasang* (Chinul's Thought) 4 (1990): 423–63.

————. "Chinul's Ambivalent Critique of Radical Subitism in Korean Sŏn Buddhism." *Journal of the International Association of Buddhist Studies* 12, no. 2 (1989): 20–44.

————. "Chinul's Systematization of Chinese Meditative Techniques in Korean Sŏn Buddhism." In *Traditions of Meditation in Chinese Buddhism*, Studies in East Asian Buddhism, no. 4, edited by Peter N. Gregory, pp. 199–232. Honolulu: University of Hawaii Press, a Kuroda Institute Book, 1986.

————. *The Formation of Ch'an Ideology in China and Korea: The Vajrasamādhi-Sūtra, A Buddhist Apocryphon*. Princeton Library of Asian Translations. Princeton: Princeton University Press, 1989.

Buswell, Robert E., Jr. "Haein-sa: The Monastery of the Dharma Jewel." *Korean Culture* 10, no. 1 (Spring 1989): 12–21.

———. *The Korean Approach to Zen: The Collected Works of Chinul*. Honolulu: University of Hawaii Press, 1983.

———. "Monastery Lay Associations in Contemporary Korean Buddhism: A Study of the Puril Hoe." In *Contemporary Korean Religion*, Korean Research Monograph, edited by Lewis R. Lancaster. Berkeley: Institute for East Asian Studies, 1992.

———. "The Pilgrimages of Hyangbong: Memoirs and Poems of the Kumgang Mountains." *Korean Culture* 11, no. 4 (Winter 1990): 18–23.

———. "The 'Short-cut' Approach of *K'an-hua* Meditation: The Evolution of a Practical Subitism in Chinese Ch'an Buddhism." In *Sudden and Gradual: Approaches to Enlightenment in Chinese Thought*, Studies in East Asian Buddhism, no. 5, edited by Peter N. Gregory, pp. 321–77. Honolulu: University of Hawaii Press, a Kuroda Institute Book, 1987.

———. "Songgwang-sa: The Monastery of the Sangha Jewel." *Korean Culture* 10, no. 3 (Autumn 1989): 14–22.

———. *Tracing Back the Radiance: Chinul's Korean Way of Zen*. Classics in East Asian Buddhism, no. 2. Honolulu: University of Hawaii Press, a Kuroda Institute Book, 1991.

———. "Wŏnhyo's *Arouse Your Mind to Practice!*" *Ten Directions* 10, no. 2 (Fall–Winter 1989): 17–19.

———, ed. *Chinese Buddhist Apocrypha*. Honolulu: University of Hawaii Press, 1990.

———, trans. "The Reception of Buddhism in Korea and Its Impact on Indigenous Culture." Translation of Inoue Hideo's "Chōsen ni okeru Bukkyō juyō to shinkan'nen." In *Introduction of Buddhism to Korea: New Cultural Patterns*, Studies in Korean Religion and Culture, vol. 3, edited by Lewis Lancaster and Chai-shin Yu, pp. 29–78. Berkeley: Asian Humanities Press, 1989.

Buswell, Robert E., Jr., and Robert M. Gimello, eds. *Paths to Liberation: The Mārga and Its Tranformations of Buddhist Thought*. Studies in East Asian Buddhism, no. 7. Honolulu: University of Hawaii Press, a Kuroda Institute Book, 1992.

Capps, Walter. *The Monastic Impulse*. New York: Crossroad, 1983.

Carrithers, Michael. *The Forest Monks of Sri Lanka: An Anthropological and Historical Study*. Delhi: Oxford University Press, 1983.

Chang, Chung-yuan. *Original Teachings of Ch'an Buddhism: Selected from* The Transmission of the Lamp. New York: Pantheon Books, 1969.

Chang, Yun-shik. "Heavenly Beings, Men and the Shaman: Interplay between High and Low Culture in Korean History." In *Che-irhoe Han'guk-hak Kukche haksul hoeŭi nonmunjip/Papers of the First International Conference on Korean Studies*, pp. 1060–74. Sŏngnam: Academy of Korean Studies, 1979.

Ch'en, Kenneth. *Buddhism in China: A Historical Survey*. Princeton: Princeton University Press, 1964.

Cho, Yong Bum. "Chiri Mountain." *Korean Culture* 10, no. 2 (Summer 1989): 15–25.

Ch'oe, Sangsu. *Han'guk minsok nori ŭi yŏn'gu* (Studies in Korean Folk Games). Seoul: Sŏngmun'gak, 1985.

Choi, Chungmoo. "The Competence of Korean Shamans as Performers of Folklore." Ph.D. diss., Indiana University, 1987.

Chŏng Pyŏngjo. See Chung, Byung-Jo.

Chŏng, T'aehyŏk. "Ch'ŏnsu Kwanŭm t'arani ŭi yŏn'gu" (Studies on the Dhāraṇī of the Thousand-Handed Avalokiteśvara). *Pulgyo hakpo* (Buddhist Studies Annual) 11 (1974): 103–22.

Chung, Byung-Jo [Chŏng Pyŏngjo]. "Buddhist Lay Associations." In *Contemporary Korean Religion*, Korea Research Monograph, edited by Lewis R. Lancaster. Berkeley: Institute of East Asia Studies, 1992.

———. "Han'guk Pulgyo ŭi hyŏnhyang kwa munjejŏm" (The Present Condition of Korean Buddhism and Problematic Points). *Pulgyo yŏn'gu* (Buddhist Studies) 2 (1986): 195–214.

Chung-feng Ming-pen (1263–1323). *T'ien-mu Chung-feng ho-shang kuang lu* (The Extended Records of Master Chung-feng of T'ien-mu Mountain). Pinch'ieh edition. Reprint, Kyŏngsang namdo: Pulguk-sa Sŏnwŏn, 1977.

Clark, Donald N. *Christianity in Modern Korea*. Asian Agenda Report, no. 5. Lantham, Md.: University Press of America, 1986.

Cleary, Christopher. *Swampland Flowers: The Letters and Lectures of Zen Master Ta Hui*. New York: Grove Press, 1977.

Clifford, James. "On Ethnographic Authority." *Representations* 1, no. 2 (1983): 118–46.

———. *The Predicament of Culture: Twentieth-Century Ethnography, Literature, and Art*. Cambridge: Harvard University Press, 1988.

Clifford, James, and George E. Marcus, eds. *Writing Culture: The Poetics and Politics of Ethnography*. Berkeley and Los Angeles: University of California Press, 1986.

Collcutt, Martin. *Five Mountains: The Rinzai Zen Monastic Institution in Medieval Japan*. Harvard East Asian Monographs, no. 85. Cambridge: Harvard University Press, 1981.

Conze, Edward, trans. *The Perfection of Wisdom in Eight Thousand Lines and Its Verse Summary*. 1973; reprint, Bolinas, Calif.: Four Seasons Foundation, 1975.

Cox, Harvey, ed. *The Encyclopedia of Eastern Philosophy and Religion: Buddhism, Hinduism, Taoism, and Zen*. Boulder, Colo.: Shambhala, 1988.

Dai-Nihon zokuzōkyō. See *Hsü-tsang-ching*.

de Bary, William Theodore, ed. *Sources of Japanese Tradition*. New York: Columbia University Press, 1958.

Dix, Griffin. "The New Year's Ritual and Village Social Structure." In *Religion and Ritual in Korean Society*, Korea Research Monograph, no. 12, edited by Laurel Kendall and Griffin Dix, pp. 93–117. Berkeley: Institute of East Asian Studies, 1987.

Dredge, C. Paul. "Korean Funerals: Ritual as Process." In *Religion and Ritual in Korean Society*, Korea Research Monograph, no. 12, edited by Laurel Kendall and Griffin Dix, pp. 71–92. Berkeley: Institute of East Asian Studies, 1987.

Dutt, Sukumar. *Buddhist Monks and Monasteries of India: Their History and Their Contribution to Indian Culture.* 1962; reprint, Delhi: Motilal Banarsidass, 1988.

———. *Early Buddhist Monachism: 600 B.C.–100 B.C.* London: Kegan Paul, Trench, Trubner and Co., 1924.

Eliade, Mircea, et al., eds. *The Encyclopedia of Religion.* New York: Macmillan, 1987.

Fermor, Patrick Leigh. *A Time to Keep Silence.* London: John Murray, 1957.

Foulk, T. Griffith. "The Zen Institution in Modern Japan." In *Zen: Tradition and Transition*, edited by Kenneth Kraft, pp. 157–77. New York: Grove Press, 1988.

Gallen, Joseph F. *Canon Law for Religious: An Explanation.* New York: Alba House, 1983.

Gombrich, Richard F. *Precept and Practice: Traditional Buddhism in the Rural Highlands of Ceylon.* Oxford: Clarendon Press, 1971.

Groner, Paul. "The *Fan-wang ching* and Monastic Discipline in Japanese Tendai: A Study of Annen's *Futsū jubosatsukai kōshaku.*" In *Chinese Buddhist Apocrypha*, edited by Robert E. Buswell, Jr., pp. 251–90. Honolulu: University of Hawaii Press, 1990.

Hackmann, H. "Pai-chang Ch'ing-kuei." *T'oung-pao* 9 (1908): 651–62.

Han Chongman. "Pulgyo yusin sasang" (Revitalization in Buddhism). In *Han'guk pulgyo sasangsa*, Sungsan Pak Kilchin paksa hwagap kinyŏm (History of Korean Buddhist Thought, Pak Kilchin Festschrift), edited by Sungsan Pak Kilchin paksa hwagap kinyŏm saŏphoe (Pak Kilchin Festschrift Committee), pp. 1121–58. Iri, Chŏlla Pukto, Korea: Wŏn'gwang University Press, 1975.

Han'guk kŭnse Pulgyo paengnyŏnsa (The Last Century of Buddhism in Korea). 2 vols. Seoul: Minjoksa, n.d.

Han'guk minsok taegwan: Susi p'ungsok, chŏnsŭng nori (A Survey of Korean Folk Customs). Seoul: Koryŏ Taehakkyo Minsok Munhwa Yŏn'guso, 1982.

Han'guk Pulgyo taesajŏn (Encyclopedia of Korean Buddhism). 10 vols. Seoul: Poryŏn'gak, 1982.

Han'guk Pulgyo yŏn'gu-wŏn, ed. *Songgwang-sa*, Han'guk ŭi sach'al (Korean Monasteries), no. 9. Yi Kiyŏng and Hwang Suyŏng, gen. eds. Seoul: Ilchi-sa, 1975.

———. *T'ongdo-sa.* Han'guk ŭi sach'al, no. 4. Seoul: Ilchi-sa, 1974.

Han Kidu. "Koryŏ Pulgyo ŭi kyŏlsa undong" (The Religious Society Movement of Koryŏ Buddhism). In *Han'guk Pulgyo sasangsa*, Sungsan Pak Kilchin paksa hwagap kinyŏm (History of Korean Buddhist Thought, Pak Kilchin Festschrift), edited by Sungsan Pak Kilchin paksa hwagap kinyŏm saŏphoe (Pak Kilchin Festschrift Committee), pp. 551–83. Iri, Chŏlla Pukto, Korea: Wŏn'gwang University Press, 1975.

Han Yongun. *Chosŏn Pulgyo yusillon* (Treatise on the Reformation of Korean Buddhism). Edited and translated by Yi Wŏnsŏp. Seoul: Manhae Sasang Yŏn'guhoe, 1983.

Harvey, Youngsook Kim. "The Korean Shaman and the Deaconess: Sisters in Different Guises." In *Religion and Ritual in Korean Society*, Korea Research

Monograph, no. 12, edited by Laurel Kendall and Griffin Dix, pp. 149–70. Berkeley: Institute of East Asian Studies, 1987.

Havell, E[rnest] B[infield]. *The Ancient and Medieval Architecture of India*. 1915; reprint, New Delhi: S. Chaud, 1972.

Henry, Patrick G., and Donald K. Swearer. *For the Sake of the World: The Spirit of Buddhist and Christian Monasticism*. Minneapolis: Fortress Press, 1989.

Hsü-tsang-ching. Edited by Hsiang-kang ying-yin Hsü-tsang-ching wei-yüan-hui. Hong Kong: Hong Kong Buddhist Association, 1967.

Howe, Russell Warren. *Flight of the Cormorants*. San Diego: Harcourt Brace Jovanovich, 1989.

Hurvitz, Leon, trans. *Scripture of the Lotus Blossom of the Fine Dharma*. New York: Columbia University Press, 1976.

Hyangbong. *Unsu san'go* (Scattered Manuscripts of a Wandering Monk). Songgwang-sa: Hyangbong Mundo-hoe, 1979.

Hyobong. *Hyobong ŏrok* (The Discourse Records of Hyobong). Edited by Hyobong mundo-hoe. Seoul: Puril Ch'ulp'ansa, 1975.

Hyujŏng (1520–1604). *Sŏn'ga kwigam* (Speculum on the Sŏn School). Chŏngŭm mun'go, no. 131. Translated by Pŏpchŏng. Seoul: Chŏngŭmsa, 1976.

Im, Sŏkchin. *Chogye-san Songgwang-sa sago* (Repository of the History of Songgwang-sa on Chogye Mountain), Han'guk saji ch'ongsŏ (Anthology of Korean Monastic Records), no. 2. Seoul: Asea Munhwa-sa, 1977.

———. *Taesŭng Sŏnjong Chogye-san Songgwang-sa chi* (The Story of Songgwang-sa, of the Mahāyāna school of Sŏn, on Chogye Mountain). Chŏlla Namdo: Songgwang-sa, 1965.

James, William. *The Varieties of Religious Experience*. 1902; reprint, London: William Collins and Sons, 1969.

Janelli, Roger L., and Dawnhee Yim Janelli. *Ancestor Worship and Korean Society*. Stanford: Stanford University Press, 1982.

———. "Lineage Organization and Social Differentiation in Korea," *Man*, n.s. 13 (1978): 272–89.

Kamata, Shigeo. *Chosen Bukkyoshi* (History of Korean Buddhism). Tokyo: Tokyo University Press, 1987.

———. *Han'guk Pulgyo sa* (Korean Buddhist History). Korean translation of *Chōsen Bukkyōshi*, by Sin Hyŏnsuk. Seoul: Minjoksa, 1987.

Kang Sŏkchu and Pak Kyŏnggŭn. *Pulgyo kŭnse paengnyŏn* (The Most Recent Hundred Years of Buddhism). Seoul: Chungang Ilbo, 1980.

Kang, Wi Jo. *Religion and Politics in Korea under the Japanese Rule*. Studies in Asian Thought and Religion, vol. 5. Lewiston, N.Y., and Queenston, Ontario: Edwin Mellen Press, 1987.

Kapleau, Philip. *The Three Pillars of Zen*. Tokyo: John Weatherhill, 1965.

Keel, Hee-Sung. *Chinul: The Founder of Korean Sŏn Buddhism*, Berkeley Buddhist Studies Series, vol. 6. Berkeley: Institute of South and Southeast Asian Studies, 1984.

Kendall, Laurel. *Shamans, Housewives, and Other Restless Spirits: Women in Korean Ritual Life*. Honolulu: University of Hawaii Press, 1985.

Kendall, Laurel, and Griffin Dix, eds. *Religion and Ritual in Korean Society*. Korea Research Monograph, no. 12. Berkeley: Institute of East Asian Studies, 1987.

Ketelaar, James Edward. *Of Heretics and Martyrs in Meiji Japan: Buddhism and Its Persecution*. Princeton: Princeton University Press, 1990.

Kim Kilsang, ed. *Kosŭng pŏbŏ che-il chip* (First Volume of Sermons of Eminent Monks). Seoul: Hongbŏbwŏn, 1969.

Kim T'anhŏ, ed. and trans. *Chobalsim chagyŏng-mun kangŭi* (Annotations to *Admonitions for Beginners*). Seoul: Pulsŏ Pogŭpsa, 1971.

————. *Sa chip* (Fourfold Collection). 4 vols. Seoul: Kyorim, 1974.

Ko Ikchin. "Wŏnmyo Yose ŭi Paengnyŏn kyŏlsa wa kŭ sasang-chŏk tonggi" (Wŏnmyo Yose's White Lotus Religious Society and His Philosophical Incentives). *Pulgyo hakpo* (Buddhist Studies Annual) 15 (1978): 109–20.

Korean Buddhism. Seoul: Chogye Order, 1986.

Kugok Kagun (fl. thirteenth century). *Sŏnmun Yŏmsong sŏrhwa* (Stories about the Sŏn School's Enlightened Verses). 2 vols. Reprint, Seoul: Poryŏn'gak, 1978.

Ku San. *Nine Mountains*. Songgwang-sa: International Meditation Center, 1976.

Kusan. *Sŏk saja: Kusan Sŏnsa pŏbŏ chip* (Stone Lion: The Dharma Talks of Sŏn Master Kusan). Cholla Namdo: Chogye Ch'ongnim Songgwang-sa, 1982.

Kusan Sunim. *The Way of Korean Zen*. Translated by Martine Fages. Edited by Stephen Batchelor. New York: Weatherhill, 1985.

Lancaster, Lewis R. "Buddhism and Family in East Asia." In *Religion and The Family in East Asia*, edited by George A. De Vos and Takao Sofue, pp. 139–51. 1984; reprint, Berkeley and Los Angeles: University of California Press, 1986.

————, ed. *Contemporary Korean Religion*. Korean Research Monograph. Berkeley: Institute for East Asian Studies, 1992.

Leclercq, Jean. *The Love of Learning and the Desire for God: A Study of Monastic Culture*. Translated by Catharine Misrahi. 1957; trans., New York: Fordham University Press, 1982.

Lee, Kwan-jo. *Search for Nirvana: Korean Monks' Life*. Seoul: Seoul International Publishing House, 1984.

Lee, Peter H., gen. ed. *Sources of Korean Tradition*. New York: Columbia University Press, forthcoming.

Levi, Peter. *The Frontiers of Paradise: A Study of Monks and Monasteries*. New York: Paragon House, 1987.

Lévi-Strauss, Claude. *The Raw and the Cooked*. Translated by J. Weightman and D. Weightman. New York: Harper and Row, 1969.

Lewis, I. M. *Religion in Context: Cults and Charisma*. Cambridge: Cambridge University Press, 1986.

Loewe, Michael. *Ways to Paradise: The Chinese Quest for Immortality*. London: George Allen and Unwin, 1979.

Maha Boowa Nyanasampanno, Phra Acharn. *The Venerable Phra Acharn Mun Bhuridatta Thera, Meditation Master*. Translated by Siri Buddhasukh. Bangkok: Mahāmakut Rajavidyalaya Press, 1976.

Maquet, Jacques. "Objectivity in Anthropology." *Current Anthropology* 5 (1964): 47–55.

Marcus, George E. "Ethnographic Writing and Anthropological Careers." In *Writing Culture: The Poetics and Politics of Ethnography*, edited by James Clifford and George E. Marcus, pp. 262–66. Berkeley and Los Angeles: University of California Press, 1986.

McRae, John R. *The Northern School and the Formation of Early Ch'an Buddhism*. Studies in East Asian Buddhism, no. 3. Honolulu: University of Hawaii Press, a Kuroda Institute Book, 1986.

Merton, Thomas. *The Seven Storey Mountain*. New York: Harcourt, Brace and World, 1948.

Miura, Isshū, and Ruth Fuller Sasaki. *Zen Dust: The History of the Koan and Koan Study in Rinzai (Lin-chi) Ch'an*. New York: Harcourt, Brace and World, 1966.

———. *The Zen Koan*. New York: Harcourt Brace and World, a Harvest Book, 1965.

Mok Chong-bae. "Han Yong-un and Buddhism." *Korea Journal* 19, no. 12 (December 1979): 19–27.

Nishimura, Eshin. *Zenrin shugyōron* (Praxis in Zen Monasteries). Kyoto: Hōzōkan, 1987.

Nyanaponika, Thera. *The Heart of Buddhist Meditation*. New York: Samuel Weiser, 1962.

Odin, Steve. *Process Metaphysics and Hua-yen Buddhism: A Critical Study of Cumulative Penetration vs. Interpenetration*. Albany: State University of New York Press, 1982.

Ortner, Sherry B. *High Religion: A Cultural and Political History of Sherpa Buddhism*. Princeton Studies in Culture/Power/History. Princeton: Princeton University Press, 1989.

Paik, L. George. *The History of Protestant Missions in Korea: 1832–1910*. 1929; reprint, Seoul: Yonsei University Press, 1970.

Park, Sung Bae (Pak Sŏngbae). *Buddhist Faith and Sudden Enlightenment*. Albany: State University of New York Press, 1983.

———. "Minjung Buddhism." In *Contemporary Korean Religion*, Korean Research Monograph, edited by Lewis R. Lancaster. Berkeley: Institute for East Asian Studies, 1992.

———. "Sŏngch'ŏl sŭnim-ŭi tono chŏmsu-sŏl pip'an-e taehayŏ" (On Sŏngch'ŏl's Critique of the Theory of Sudden Awakening/Gradual Cultivation), *Pojo sasang* (Chinul's Thought) 4 (1990): 501–28.

Pennington, M. Basil. *Monastery: Prayer, Work, Community*. San Francisco: Harper and Row, 1983.

Prasad, Nand Kishore. *Studies in Buddhist and Jaina Monachism*, Prakrit Jaina Institute Research Publication Series, vol. 9. Vaishali: Research Institute of Prakrit, Jainology and Ahimsa, 1972.

Pratt, Mary Louise. "Fieldwork in Common Places." In *Writing Culture: The Poetics and Politics of Ethnography*, edited by James Clifford and George E. Marcus, pp. 27–50. Berkeley and Los Angeles: University of California Press, 1986.

Prebish, Charles S., trans. *Buddhist Monastic Discipline: The Sanskrit Prāti-*

mokṣa Sūtras of the Mahāsāṃghikas and the Mūlasarvāstivādins. University Park: Pennsylvania State University Press, 1975.

Preston, David L. *The Social Organization of Zen Practice: Constructing Transcultural Reality.* Cambridge: Cambridge University Press, 1988.

Prip-Møller, Johannes. *Chinese Buddhist Monasteries: Their Plan and Its Function as a Setting for Buddhist Monastic Life.* 1937; reprint, Hong Kong: Hong Kong University Press, 1982.

Pulgyo sŏjŏk sent'ŏ, eds. *Pulgyo pŏbyo kugam* (Primer of the Essentials of the Buddhist Teachings). Seoul: Hongbŏbwŏn, 1970.

Pulgyo sŏngjŏn (Buddhist Bible). Edited by Tae-Han Pulgyo Chogye-chong Pulgyo sŏngjŏn p'yŏnch'anhoe (Buddhist Bible Compilation Committee of the Chogye Order). Seoul: Tae-Han Pulgyo Chogye-chong Pulgyo Sŏngjŏn P'yŏnch'anhoe, 1972.

P'yŏn jippu (Compilation Committee), ed. *Sŏngbul hapsida: Sŏngbul-to-rŭl t'onghan Pulgyo immun* (Let's Achieve Buddhahood: A Primer of Buddhism through the Game of *Sŏngbul-to*). Seoul: Puril Ch'ulp'ansa, 1984.

Rabinow, Paul. "Representations Are Social Facts: Modernity and Post-Modernity in Anthropology." In *Writing Culture: The Poetics and Politics of Ethnography,* edited by James Clifford and George E. Marcus, pp. 234–61. Berkeley and Los Angeles: University of California Press, 1986.

Robinson, Michael Edson. *Cultural Nationalism in Colonial Korea, 1920–1925,* Korean Studies of the Henry M. Jackson School of International Studies. Seattle: University of Washington Press, 1988.

Róheim, Géza. *Psychoanalysis and Anthropology: Culture, Personality and the Unconscious.* New York: International Universities Press, 1950.

Rosaldo, Renato. *Culture and Truth: The Remaking of Social Analysis.* Boston: Beacon Press, 1989.

———. "From the Door of his Tent: The Fieldworker and the Inquisitor." In *Writing Culture: The Poetics and Politics of Ethnography,* edited by James Clifford and George E. Marcus, pp. 77–97. Berkeley and Los Angeles: University of California Press, 1986.

Said, Edward W. *Orientalism.* New York: Random House, Vintage Books, 1978.

Samu Sunim. "Eunyeong Sunim and the Founding of Pomun-jong, the First Independent Bhikshuni Order," *Spring Wind—Buddhist Cultural Forum* (special issue on Women and Buddhism) 6–1,2,3 (1986): 129–62.

———. "Manseong Sunim, A Woman Zen Master of Modern Korea." *Spring Wind—Buddhist Cultural Forum* (special issue) 6 (1986): 188–93.

Satō, Giei. *Unsui: A Diary of Zen Monastic Life.* Text by Eshin Nishimura, edited by Bardwell L. Smith. Honolulu: University Press of Hawaii, an East-West Center Book, 1973.

Sato, Koji. *The Zen Life.* With photographs by Sosei Kuzunishi, translated by Ryojun Victoria. New York: Weatherhill, 1972.

Satō, Tatsugen. *Chūgoku Bukkyō ni okeru kairitsu no kenkyū* (Studies on the Precepts of Chinese Buddhism). Tokyo: Mokujisha, 1986.

Sayers, Robert, with Ralph Rinzler. *The Korean Onggi Potter.* Smithsonian Folklife Studies, no. 5. Washington, D.C.: Smithsonian Institution Press, 1987.

Schopen, Gregory. "Filial Piety and the Monk in the Practice of Indian Buddhism: A Question of 'Sinicization' Viewed from the Other Side." *T'oung Pao* 70 (1984): 110–26.

Seo, Kyung-bo (Sŏ Kyŏngbo). "A Study of Korean Zen Buddhism Approached through the Chodangjip." Ph.D. diss., Temple University, 1970; mimeographed reprint, Seoul: Poryŏn'gak, 1979.

Shibayama, Zenkei. *Zen Comments on the Mumonkan*. Translated by Sumiko Kudo. New York: Harper and Row, 1974.

Smart, Ninian. *Reasons and Faiths: An Investigation of Religious Discourse, Christian and Non-Christian*. London: Routledge and Kegan Paul, 1958.

Sŏ, Kyŏngju, "Han'guk Pulgyo paengnyŏnsa" (A Hundred-Year History of Korean Buddhism). *Sŏnggok nonch'ong* 4 (August 1973): 37–78.

Sŏk, Chusŏn. *Ŭi* (Clothing). Seoul: Tan'guk University Press, 1985.

Sŏngbul-to (The Game of Achieving Buddhahood). Seoul: Puril Ch'ulp'ansa, 1986.

Song-chol. See T'oeong Sŏngch'ŏl.

Sorensen, Clark W. *Over the Mountains Are Mountains: Korean Peasant Households and Their Adaptation to Rapid Industrialization*. Korean Studies of the Henry M. Jackson School of International Studies. Seattle: University of Washington Press, 1988.

Sørensen, Henrik H[jort]. "The Conflict between Buddhism and Christianity in Korea." In *Symposium on Korea*, East Asian Institute Occasional Papers 1, edited by Simon B. Heilesen, pp. 24–31. Copenhagen: East Asian Institute, University of Copenhagen, 1988.

———. "The History and Doctrines of Early Korean Sŏn Buddhism." Ph.D. diss., University of Copenhagen, 1987.

———. "Korean Buddhist Journals during Early Japanese Colonial Rule." *Korea Journal* 30, no. 1 (January 1990): 17–27.

———. "The Life and Thought of the Korean Sŏn Master Kyŏnghŏ." *Korean Studies* 7 (1983): 7–33.

———. "The *T'aenghwa* Tradition in Korean Buddhism." *Korean Culture* 8, no. 4 (Winter 1987): 13–25.

Spiro, Melford E. *Buddhism and Society: A Great Tradition and Its Burmese Vicissitudes*. 2d expanded ed. Berkeley and Los Angeles: University of California Press, 1982.

Strickmann, Michel. "The *Consecration Sūtra*: A Buddhist Book of Spells." In *Chinese Buddhist Apocrypha*, edited by Robert E. Buswell, Jr., pp. 75–118. Honolulu: University of Hawaii Press, 1990.

Sungsan Pak Kilchin paksa hwagap kinyŏm wiwŏnhoe, ed. *Han'guk Pulgyo sasangsa*, Sungsan Pak Kilchin paksa hwagap kinyŏm (History of Korean Buddhist Thought, Presented in Commemoration of the Sixtieth Birthday of Sungsan, Dr. Pak Kilchin), edited by Sungsan Pak Kilchin paksa hwagap kinyŏm saŏphoe (Pak Kilchin Festschrift Committee). Iri, Chŏlla Pukto, Korea: Wŏn Pulgyo Sasang Yŏn'guwŏn, 1975.

Suzuki, Daisetz Teitaro *Essays in Zen Buddhism*, vol. 1. 1927; reprint, London: Rider and Co., 1958.

Suzuki, Daisetz. *Manual of Zen Buddhism*. New York: Grove Press, 1960.

———. *The Training of the Zen Buddhist Monk*. 1934; reprint, Berkeley: Wingbow Press, 1974.

———. *Zen and Japanese Culture*. Bollingen Series, no. 64. Princeton: Princeton University Press, 1970.

T'aego Pou (1301–1382). *T'aego Pou kuksa pŏbŏ chip* (Collection of the Dharma Talks of the National Master T'aego Pou). Edited and translated by Yi Yŏngmu. Seoul: Han'guk Pulgyo T'aego-chong Chongmuwŏn, 1974.

Taishō shinshu daizōkyō (Revised Tripiṭaka Compiled during the Taishō Reign-Period). Edited by Takakusu Junjirō and Watanabe Kaikyoku. Tokyo: Daizōkyōkai, 1924–1935.

Takahashi Tōru. *Richō Bukkyo* (Yi Dynasty Buddhism). 1929; reprint, Tokyo: Kokusho Kankōkai, 1973.

Tambiah, Stanley Jeyaraja. *Buddhism and the Spirit Cults in North-East Thailand*. Cambridge Studies in Social Anthropology, no. 2. Cambridge: Cambridge University Press, 1970.

———. *The Buddhist Saints of the Forest and the Cult of Amulets: A Study in Charisma, Hagiography, Sectarianism, and Millennial Buddhism*. Cambridge Studies in Social Anthropology, no. 49. Cambridge: Cambridge University Press, 1984.

Tatia, Nathmal. *Studies in Buddhist and Jaina Monachism*. Bihar: Research Institute of Prakrit, Jainology and Ahimsa, 1972.

T'oeong Sŏngch'ŏl. *Echoes from Mt. Kaya: Selections on Korean Buddhism by Ven. Song-chol, Patriarch of the Korean Chogye Buddhist Order*. Edited by Ven. Won-tek and translated by Brian Barry, with introduction by Won-myong. Seoul: Lotus Lantern International Buddhist Center, 1988.

———. *Sŏnmun chŏngno* (The Orthodox Road of the Sŏn School). Kyŏngsang Namdo: Haein Ch'ongnim, 1981.

Turner, Victor. *Dramas, Fields, and Metaphors: Symbolic Action in Human Society*. Symbol, Myth, and Ritual Series. Ithaca, N.Y.: Cornell University Press, 1974.

———. *The Ritual Process: Structure and Anti-structure*. Chicago: Aldine, 1969.

U Chŏngsang and Kim Yŏngt'ae. *Han'guk Pulgyo-sa* (A History of Korean Buddhism). Seoul: Sinhŭng Ch'ulp'ansa, 1968.

Weber, Max. *The Religion of India*. Translated by Hans H. Gerth and Don Martindale. Trans. New York: Free Press, 1958.

———. *The Sociology of Religion*. 1922; reprint, Boston: Beacon Press, 1963.

Welch, Holmes. *The Buddhist Revival in China*. Cambridge: Harvard University Press, 1968.

———. *The Practice of Chinese Buddhism: 1900–1950*. Harvard East Asian Studies 26. Cambridge: Harvard University Press, 1967.

———. *Taoism: The Parting of the Way*. 1957; revised ed., Beacon Press, 1966.

Wetering, Janwillem van de. *The Empty Mirror: Experiences in a Japanese Zen Monastery*. Boston: Houghton Mifflin, 1974.

———. *A Glimpse of Nothingness: Experiences in an American Zen Community*. Boston: Houghton Mifflin, 1975.

White, Hayden. *Metahistory: The Historical Imagination in Nineteenth-Century Europe*. Baltimore: Johns Hopkins University Press, 1973.

Wijayaratna, Mohan. *Buddhist Monastic Life: According to the Texts of the Theravāda Tradition*. Translated by Claude Grangier and Steven Collins. Cambridge: Cambridge University Press, 1990.

Yampolsky, Philip, trans. *The Platform Sutra of the Sixth Patriarch*. New York: Columbia University Press, 1967.

Yi, Chigwan. *Han'guk Pulgyo soŭi kyŏngjŏn* (The Fundamental Texts of Korean Buddhism). Kyŏngsang Namdo: Haein-sa, 1969.

———. *Sajip sagi* (Annotation to the *Fourfold Collection*). Kyŏngsang Namdo: Haein Ch'ongnim, 1969.

Yi, Hŭisu. *T'och'akhwa kwajŏng-esŏ pon Han'guk Pulgyo* (Korean Buddhism as a Process of Indigenization). Seoul: Pulsŏ Pogŭpsa, 1971.

Yi, Kiyŏng. *Han'guk ŭi Pulgyo* (Korean Buddhism). Seoul: Sejong Taewang Kinyŏm Saŏphoe, 1974.

———. "Pulgyo sasang" (Korean Thought). In *Han'guk hyŏndae munhwasa taegye* (Outline of Contemporary Cultural History in Korea), vol. 2, pp. 749–50. Seoul: Koryŏ University, Minjok Munhwa Yŏn'guso, 1985.

Yi, Kyu-bo (1168–1241). *Tongguk Yi sangguk chip* (Literary Collection of Premier Yi Kyu-bo). Facsimile reprint of xylographic edition in the Seoul National University archives. Seoul: Tongguk Munhwasa, 1958.

Yi Nŭnghwa. *Chosŏn Pulgyo t'ongsa* (A Comprehensive History of Korean Buddhism). 1918; reprint, Seoul: Poryŏn'gak, 1979.

Yi, Pyŏngdo and Kim Chaewŏn. *Han'guksa: kodae p'yŏn* (A History of Korean Buddhism: Ancient Period). Seoul: Ŭryu Munhwasa, 1959.

Yoon, Hong-key. *Geomantic Relationship between Culture and Nature in Korea*, Asian Folklore and Social Life Monographs, vol. 88. Taipei: Chinese Association for Folklore, 1976.

Yu, Pyŏngdŏk. "Ilche sidae ŭi Pulgyo" (Buddhism during the Japanese Colonial Period). In *Han'guk Pulgyo sasangsa*, Sungsan Pak Kilchin paksa hwagap kinyŏm nonch'ong, edited by Sungsan Pak Kilchin paksa hwagap kinyŏm saŏphoe (Pak Kilchin Festschrift Committee), pp. 1159–87. Iri, Chŏlla Pukto, Korea: Wŏn Pulgyo Sasang Yŏn'guwŏn, 1975.

Index

abbot (*chuji*), 38, 54, 70, 108–13, 171, 205, 212; duties of, 110–12; and laity, 111
Admonitions to Beginners (*Ch'obalsim chagyŏng-mun*), 80, 81, 98, 101, 115, 162, 166n, 191
Āgama scriptures, 101
amja. See hermitage
apocrypha, 99, 141
Avataṃsaka-sūtra. See Hwaŏm

bath monk (*yoktu sŭnim*), 179
Bhagavadgītā, 71, 74
bhikṣu (monk), 18, 19, 69, 86–90
Bodhidharma, 217, 218
Book of Brahmā's Net, 181. *See also* precepts
Buddha Sun Society. *See* Puril Hoe
Buddhism, approaches to the study of, 11; and Christianity, 33–34; Hua-yen school of, 50; influence of, on shamanism, 57; Japanese practice of, 24–25; Korean Chogye school of, 22; persecution of, 136; practice of, and foreigners, 19–20; proselytization, 144, 145, 146, 227; Pure Land school of, 54; repression of, in Korea, 23, 135–36, 145. *See also* Chogye Order; Christianity; Hwaŏm; shamanism

catechist (*kyomu*), 81, 118; duties of, 115
celibacy. *See* married clergy; monastic practice
ch'ongmu. See prior
ch'ongnim (ecumenical center), 36, 51, 54, 58, 63, 68, 137, 138, 139, 140, 205
Ch'ŏnsu-kyŏng. See Thousand Hands Sūtra; Great Compassion Mantra
Ch'unsŏng (1891–1978), 127–28. *See also* "unconstrained conduct"
chaemu. See treasurer
changgun chukpi. See warning stick
Chao-chou (778–897), 3, 4n, 150–52, 156–59

chart, ocean-seal, 51; dharma-realm, 51–52, 52n; realm of reality, 142
chayu chŏngjin (discretionary practice). *See* haeje
chijŏn. See verger
chikse. See proctor
Ching-teh ch'uan-teng lu, 3, 4n. *See also* lamp anthologies
Chinul (Puril Pojo) (1158–1210), 42, 54, 61, 64, 76, 81, 94, 99, 100, 101, 136, 137, 148, 149, 150, 163, 182, 184; as originator of Korean Sŏn practice, 59–60
Chogye Order (Chogye-chong), 22, 32, 34–36, 58, 63, 68, 71, 76, 85–90, 100, 106, 110, 112, 113, 135, 139, 167, 204; educational institutions administered by, 35
Chosŏn dynasty (1392–1910), 23–26, 24n, 34, 41, 57, 60, 62, 96, 98, 135, 138, 145, 162, 201, 228
Chosŏn Pulgyo wŏlbo (Korean Buddhism Monthly), 25, 30n, 167
Chosŏn Pulgyo yusillon (On the Reformation of Korean Buddhism), 26, 28
chŏn'gye asari. See preceptor
chŏnbŏp. See enlightenment
chŏnghwa undong. See purification movement
Christianity, 17, 33–34, 58, 143–44, 146; and youth groups, 115n
Chuang-tzu, 74
Chung-feng Ming-pen (1263–1323), 219
Communism, 62–63, 67, 137
confessor (*kalma asari*), 86
Confucianism, 7, 23, 64, 99; academies (*sŏdang*) of, 218. *See also* Neo-Confucianism
critical phrase. See *hwadu*

detachment (*upekkhā*), 13, 162. *See also* non-attachment
Dhammapada, 71
dharma family, 109, 111, 166, 197, 204, 211, 226
dharma talks, 127, 140, 212, 226